Driven by a Dream

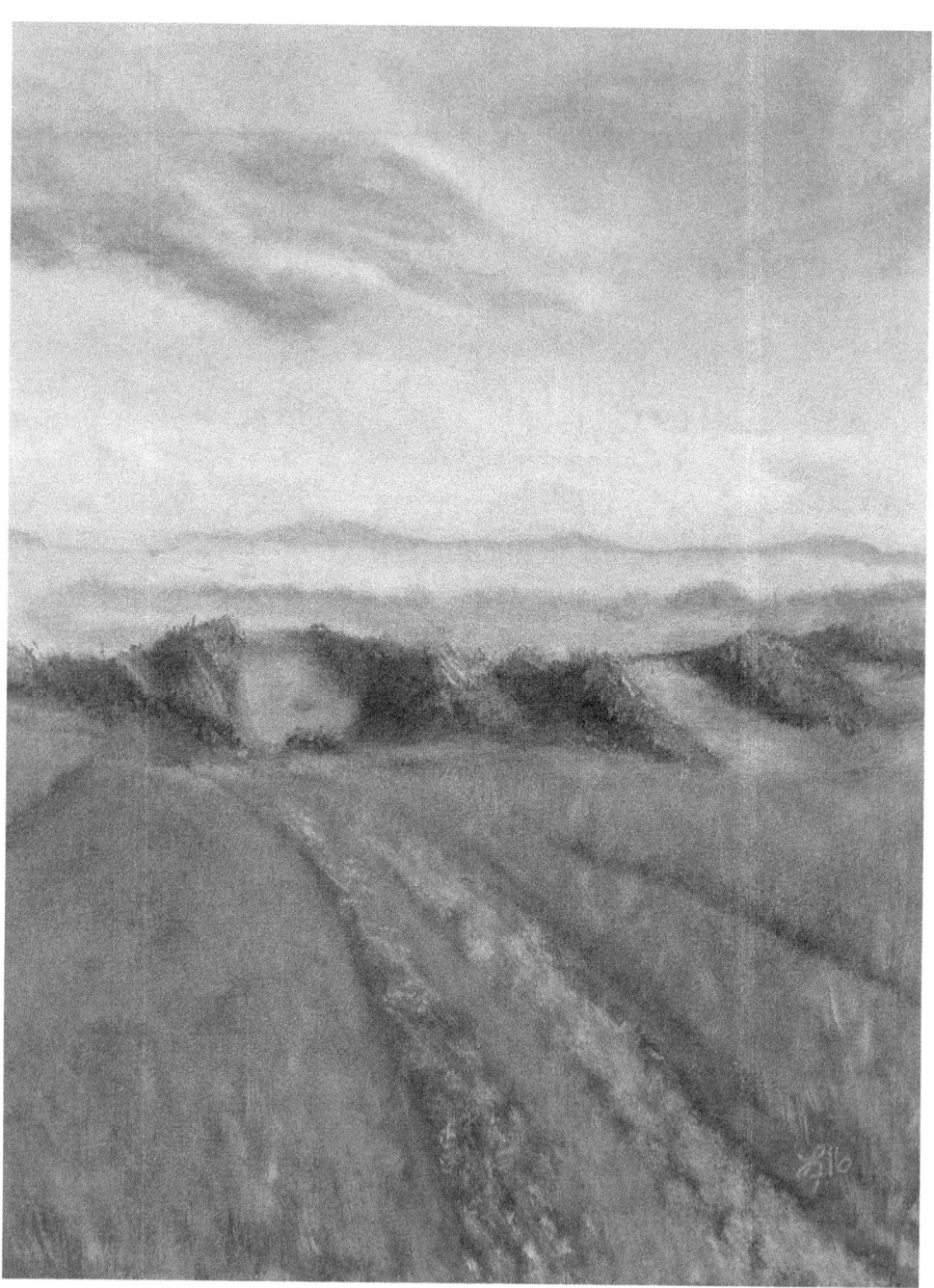

Driven by a Dream

An artist's journey

By Lacey Finchum

Editor: Kristin E Mantta
Publisher: Lace Finch Art, LLC

ISBN: 9781712862896

The events and conversations in this book have been set down to the best of the author's ability, although some names and details have been changed to protect the privacy of individuals. A few images, though the photos were taken by the author, may be copyrighted by the original artists. If your art was displayed here please let me know so that I might cite your work.

For the dreamers:
May you always have the courage to jump.
~L

On the surface, this book is about a girl searching for herself and her dreams on a solo road trip but, really it's more about the journey: healing from a tough breakup, losing her dream home, coming up with a new plan, learning to listen to her intuition, and the unexpected return at the end of it all.

It's about turning dreams into reality.

Forward

Watching paint dry was my favorite pastime in winter 2017. It's a tediously slow process and an almost invisible activity, and no one would know otherwise what you were doing just from simple observation. In fact it looks rather lackadaisical and mundane, but when stretched out daydreaming under the brush strokes of illustrated imagination amongst the melodic discussion of the most important topics like magic, faith, trust and freedom, I could literally see the hues drying into their true self as the pigment shades darkened and lightened midair.

Lacey came to paint the Northern Lights in my library when I knew I was preparing for lots of time solo and laying down post-op, so we collaborated on a glow-in-the-dark mural that created a tranquil recovery space and unique conversation piece. I've always painted on my walls, (sometimes with lipstick and nail polish, sometimes with glitter), and since my library was evolving to encompass the heart of my home, something spectacular like the Aurora Borealis seemed a fitting scene, complete with glitter!

Our first collab was a mix of true imagineering, random catching-up chatter, and talking over each other in the best ways possible-all of it, magic. So, we made a plan and shook hands and embarked on the journey of a lifetime right there in my library! I didn't truly understand then that we were making magic, but when you see the creative genius masterpiece that evolved just from me explaining all the crazy ideas in my pretty little head and her revealing scenes I never knew I dreamed but recognized as mine, magic is the only definition for what we did together in those days.

We talked and laughed and dreamed and cried and hugged and painted and poof! Magic! We could both feel it palpable in our hands and words, spilling into the space of our existence that finally helped us both take charge and realize we had the power to mold our lives. We found the magic together that made us both sparkle! "The Sparkly comes in the magic shit that happens when you learn the answers!" she told me in one of our philosophical afternoons. And every answer helped unlock my life.

Truthfully, I feel like those conversations saved my life, though I never wanted to die: I just wanted to really live. We both craved the freedom and independence and creative space of something more. I was grappling with my career path and health changes; she was just settling post road-trip back at her parents in our hometown. I had never left. She begrudgingly came back. Crazy how our small-town setting launched both our hearts into wanting big things.

And, the magic of this big thing began small in the way of breaking down every fear, worry, concern, or hesitation to do some big thing. Most of the time we didn't even know what big thing we wanted to do, just that the big thing was bubbling down in our bellies where the best ideas and inspiration swirls around until you are finally ready to act on the impulse of those big things. Our energy became lighter and lighter until The Light that danced between us electrified the moments of a-ha and Ohemgeeeee that made us feel tingly all over, "That's what it feels like! That's the sparkly magic shit!" Our imaginations fired our biggest dreams into real manifestations as it only happens in magic moments between magic makers. And so we found out how to do our big things.

She quit her job at the bar.
I quit my job teaching.
She moved away.
I stayed home.
She painted more murals.
I painted my first.
She became an author.
I became an editor.
She blessed me.
I blessed her.

All of it-magic.

So, before you begin to read Lacey's journey, take a moment and choose to believe in Magic because you, too, are a Magic Maker. It's how this book ended up in your hands. It's how the Northern Lights ended up in my library! It's how Lacey ended up.... well, you will have to read and see where she is now!

It's nothing short of magic when dreams come true, and I know Lacey and I both wish this big dream come true thing of hers to be a source of magic for you because maybe a little bit of her magic will help you believe in your magic and believe it's how you will go do your big thing! It's how she did hers and I am doing mine and you will do yours. Big things spread like wildfire when our hearts are open and ready for more- it's simply just how magic works.

It's my absolute pleasure and honor to welcome you to Driven by A Dream and introduce you to Lacey's journey. I have loved every moment of this work she so graciously included me in because to settle into an amazingly good book is magic in and of itself.

So, now, I invite you to Believe in your magic and dive right in!!

If you are a dreamer, come in,
If you are a dreamer, a wisher, a liar,
A hope-er, a pray-er, a magic bean buyer...
If you're a pretender come sit by my fire
For we have some flax-golden tales to spin.
Come in!
Come in!
Shel Silverstein, Where the Sidewalk Ends

Kristin

Preface: 5/28/19

'I could tell you my adventures - beginning from this morning,' said Alice a little timidly: 'but it's no use going back to yesterday, because I was a different person then.' ~Alice's Adventures in Wonderland by Lewis Carol

A little background... This journal opens in January 2017, three months after leaving a 12 year relationship, 4 months before my solo road trip, 2 years after picking up a paint brush, seriously, for the first time in my adult life and, 3 years after my intro into the Law of Attraction and attracting my dream home.

LOA, and my first experiment with it, produced my dream home; a cabin on 20 acres in the woods where a creek flows into a lake. I went from dreaming to signing the dotted line and moving in less than 2 months.

From that moment began my journey into self-awareness and growth, into mindset training, into meditation. Little did I know, LOA kickstarted my artistic journey and not only discovering my passion but discovering that I was fully capable of really achieving any goals I really wanted to in life.

The year after moving into my dream home, I tried painting for the first time and realized I wasn't too bad, and that I really could become an artist. That I really could be and have what I always wanted.

After that realization, I knew there was nothing that could stop me except me. I vowed then to do whatever it took to build myself, my skills, and my surroundings into exactly what they needed to be so that I could become exactly who and what I wanted. Who I was meant to be.

In January 2016 I opened my art business. Soon after decided I would be leaving my relationship and, by proxy, leaving my dream home and pursuing me, my art, and my dreams including a solo road trip that next spring (2017).

This book is that journey, internal and external. It contains entries from my personal journal as well as afterthoughts and inserts to explain or elaborate. There are even a few pro-tips that might help you on your own

10

journey, whatever it may be. May my telling this story help you as much as doing it helped me. ~L

Acknowledgements

Special thanks, in no particular order, goes to KM, RW, Mom and Dad, Grandma Joy, LL, Sunshine, Bones, MM, and RJ for your various contributions. Also, to Grandma Honey and Uncle Bob for introducing me to art. Without any of you, this book and my present life might not have been possible ~L

Driven by A Dream

Introduction

1/1/17

A new year, a new book... Do Me (Do you!) Authenticity
A new way of life
Love, Live, Laugh
"Always gotta be different, Lacey"
NO!
I just AM different
(You are different too!)
And That's OK!
Be me! (Be You)
Be the best you that you can be!
Set actionable and measurable goals!
SMASH   THEM!
Reach far, Dig Deep
Meditate
Motivate
See it thru!

1/10/17
Distractions can come from many angles.
Disregard!   Stay   focused.

This or something better!
Stay focused. Invest in yourself. Learn. Dream. Action. Learn.

"I don't fail. I collect data." Damon Johns

1/11/17 (full moon)

Who am I?

The alpha she wolf. (I read the following excerpt somewhere but not sure where... some meme? If I ever see it again, I'll cite reference but also some of the following thought is mine as well.)

She calls to her pack - her tribe- to stand together for support and food and growth. The winter winds carry her call and her pack answers.

I call out at this time for clarity, for comfort, for peace & contentment, for creative expression for love, for joy, for fulfillment. For health, wellbeing, & success. For my mate, my match, my partner. For my domain. For my tribe. "This or something better!"

1/28/19

Distractions and X's but, I'm getting stronger every day

"I have already left. I will be just fine on my own. I am enough. I want a high level of love, respect, and care."   "This or something better"

Bear Bottom or something better.
Home + Studio or something better
Art sales, self-sustained... sustainable, self-reliant, self-supported
This   or   something   better!

2/16/17

My love is kind and funny and enchanting.   My love is positive and cheerful and hardworking and spontaneous. My love is intelligent and can be intimate and romantic. My love is honest and passionate. My love is responsible and treats people with respect. My love loves me as much as   I   them.

Sunday is my last day in Northwest Indiana and I'll be headed to Arkansas for 6 weeks to prepare for my road trip. To Arkansas, to my Bear Bottom, to M... Am I on the right path?

While in Arkansas I'll plan my trip route, prepare my car, and pack. I'll also conquer some mindset issues and learn to let go of some things and people who are not for my highest good.

4/11/17 T-6 days

I leave Bear Bottom on Monday. My brain has been messy since being here. I haven't done near what I'd planned. "Hey You! Remember this when you're lonely and nostalgic. When you two are together, your brain doesn't work. You have trouble thinking and doing for yourself. All brain functions get sucked into the vortex and you can only focus on him. He doesn't love you. He doesn't know how. Love yourself!"

Set your goals. Focus. Smash them.
-see 7 national parks
-visit 10 artist communities
-figure out who you are
-figure out where you are going next
-take lots of pictures
-journal
-implement
-

What do I stand for? What's my message? How can I be of service? Who am I? Where am I going? What am I doing? Who are you?

Total Budget: $3500 (including tires and pre-trip inspection)

4/16/17 Packing

How do you pack and plan for the unknown?

Figure out what you know.

What do I know?

I know I'll be sleeping in my car, a lot. But I'll also want to sleep in a tent sometimes.
I know I have this conference at the beginning of my trip, so I'll need some nice clothes.
I want to sell some art and make some art, so I'll need my art and at least some supplies.
I plan to do quite a bit of my own cooking, so I'll need a camp stove, cookware, and dishes.
Coffee.
I should also probably have some emergency food staples…

What if I break down or run out of money and am really living out of my car for a while? I'll need tools and fishing gear.

5-7 changes of clothes.
Shower stuff
Boots, comfy shoes, flip flops, dress shoes (1-2 pair)
Cooler
Art (my best pieces, i.e. Waterbodies, Adam-Eve,
Art supplies (small canvases, paints, brushes)
Camera
Go-pro
Fishing gear
Camp box
      Tent
      Cookware
      Stove + propane
      Utensils
      Hatchet
      Filet knife
      Matches
    17

Rope

Firestarter   and   matches

First Aid Kit

Tools/Toolbox (screwdrivers (flat/Phillips), socket/ratchet set, hammer)

Sleeping pad

Pillows

Blankets

A few books including field guides and branding course

Journals

Pens

Bugspray

_____

My car: Gertie, my car, is a little grey Nissan hatchback with over 300,000 miles on her. She's in surprisingly good shape considering that. The owner's manual has a record of all the oil changes and maintenance. I chose her with this trip in mind because she was affordable, in good working order, and was a hatchback. Before I leave, I'll get new tires and an oil change.

Looking back now, I suppose I manifested her. We were looking for a Nissan Versa because we had a wrecked one with low miles and my X was insistent on getting another one for parts or something. The wrecked car was a sedan, but I knew I wanted a hatchback.

I wanted a hatchback because I needed her to hold as much gear as possible and be big enough to sleep comfortably in. I don't really know how long I'll be living out of her. Space is limited so I need to be able to use every inch of space as efficiently as possible. Everything must be essential, well organized and easily accessible.

Gertie's back seat folds down flat and the hatch/trunk is deep. I decided to build a platform out of an old door and frame that I had. We cut down the door and frame to fit snugly in the whole back half of the car then cut it in half so that the back half of the platform could be lifted to access my trunk/storage space.

Keeping the frame on the door gave a few inches of protected and flat space to be able to store my paintings under the bed and not have to bother much with them unless I needed them. This setup also allowed me to use the back-seat floor space for storage and more storage along the sides of the door/bed. I also had the whole passenger seat area for storage as well. After building the platform, it was time to install and then pack the car.

I placed a piece of plywood under the paintings and over the storage area so that I could lift it instead of having to lift the paintings.

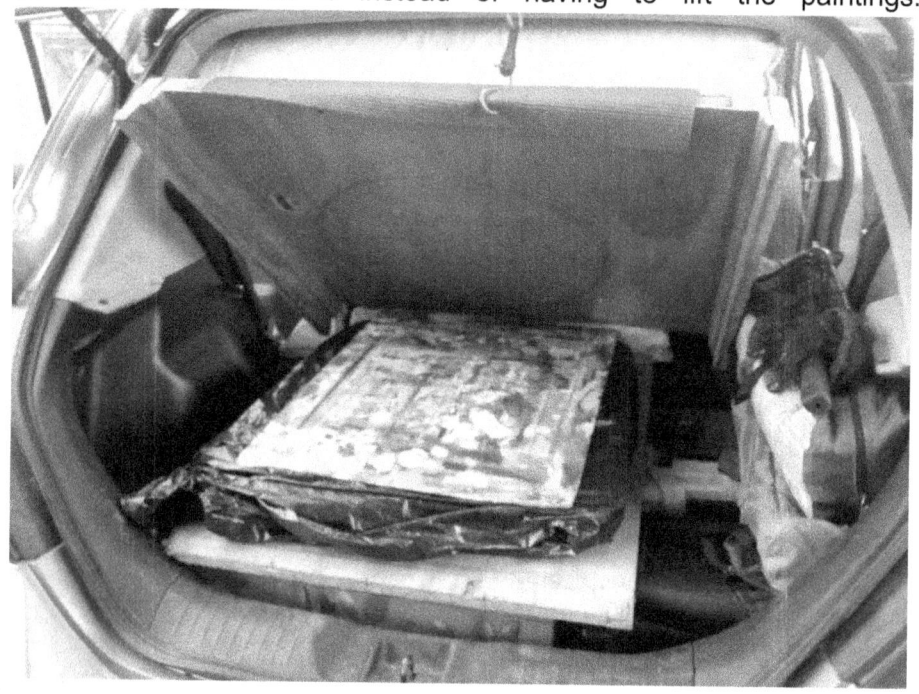

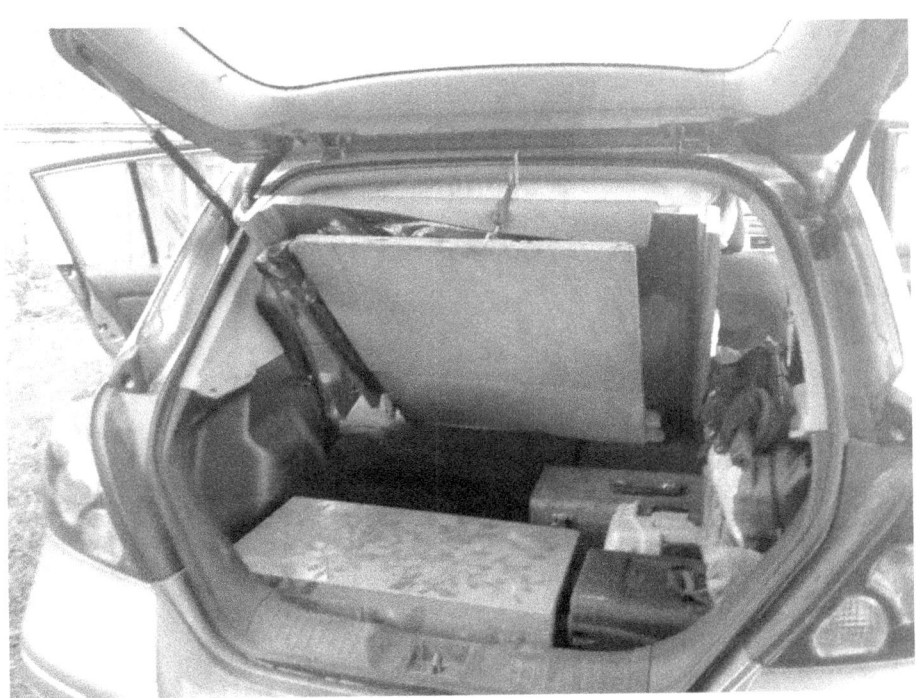

The grey camo box is my camp box. It contains my cook stove, cookware, dishes, and utensils as well as things like matches, a hatchet, filet knife, cutting board, some rope, spices, etc. to the right is a lantern that, in hindsight, I should have not taken because I don't like them and never use them. I used my headlamp OFTEN. I also should not have brought an air mattress because it was way easier to pull the mattress pad out of the car and put it into the tent than it was to air up an air mattress. I also packed a little tackle box and a toolbox. I put some loose items like a beach towel and extra food supplies in the space behind the camp box.

Along the sides of the bed were my tent, a folding chair, and some books.

On top of the platform I put a yoga mat and a 2inch foam mattress. The mattress was a little long, but I folded the overhang and it made a nice bit of extra pillow and kept the platform and mattress from sliding anywhere.

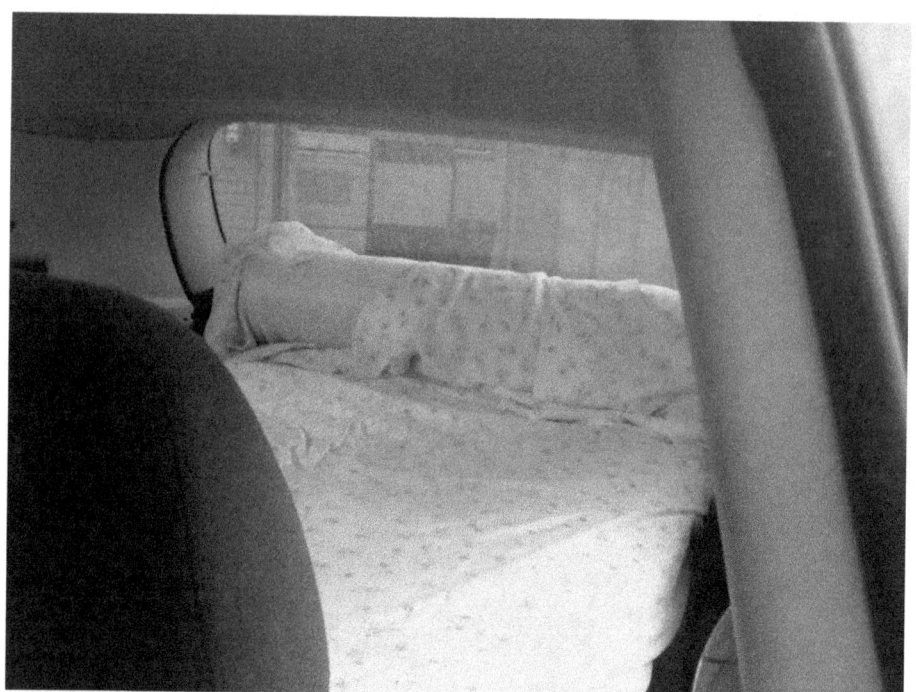

I stored some art supplies, dirty laundry, laundry soap, and bathroom supplies on the floor in the back seat. In the front seat I had a small cooler, some more art, and a jump bag with my essentials.

**** follow-up**** This set up worked great! Next time, I'd leave the lantern and air mattress at home. I'd invest in a few sunblock windshield visors for better privacy. Also, the door I used was an interior door, so it was hollow. Next time, I'd reinforce the cut edge and the hinges. This time, the hinges pulled out and the door started to sag on the cut edges. Also, the original mattress pad wasn't thick enough or firm enough and I still felt the hinges and the hardness. I added another egg crate mattress pad and a foam sleeping pad made for backpacking that finally made the set up extremely comfortable. In fact, the next bed I buy I may create a similarly styled set up for the combo of firmness and softness. I digress....

I'm all packed and I leave tomorrow. Am I nervous? Of course, but I won't allow myself to focus on that.

Right now is doing.

Action counteracts Fear.

Am I forgetting anything?

No, not forgetting… I'm leaving a bunch here though...

4/17/17 Day 1

"I take to the open road, healthy, free. The world before me."~Walt Whitman

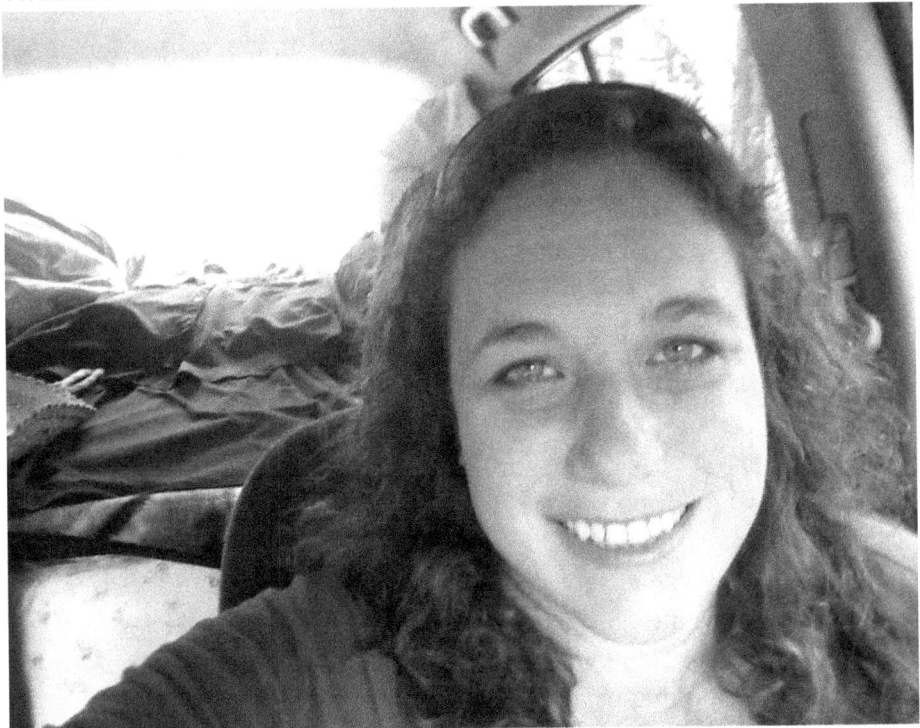

I allowed myself to sleep in as long as I needed this morning, then did a final sweep before leaving. By the time I left it was after 10am. No need to rush today. I want to take my time and see what I see.

It was a grey day when I left Bear Bottom. It made for a moody departure. I was happy to go on my trip but leaving Bear Bottom was still difficult and sad. Though, I guess, maybe less difficult and sad than the last time I left. Regardless, I still spent a good part of the day reminding myself that the only things I needed to be thinking about were me, this present moment, and where I was going to sleep tonight. I drove 250 miles stopping for lunch and to take pictures on the Buffalo River.

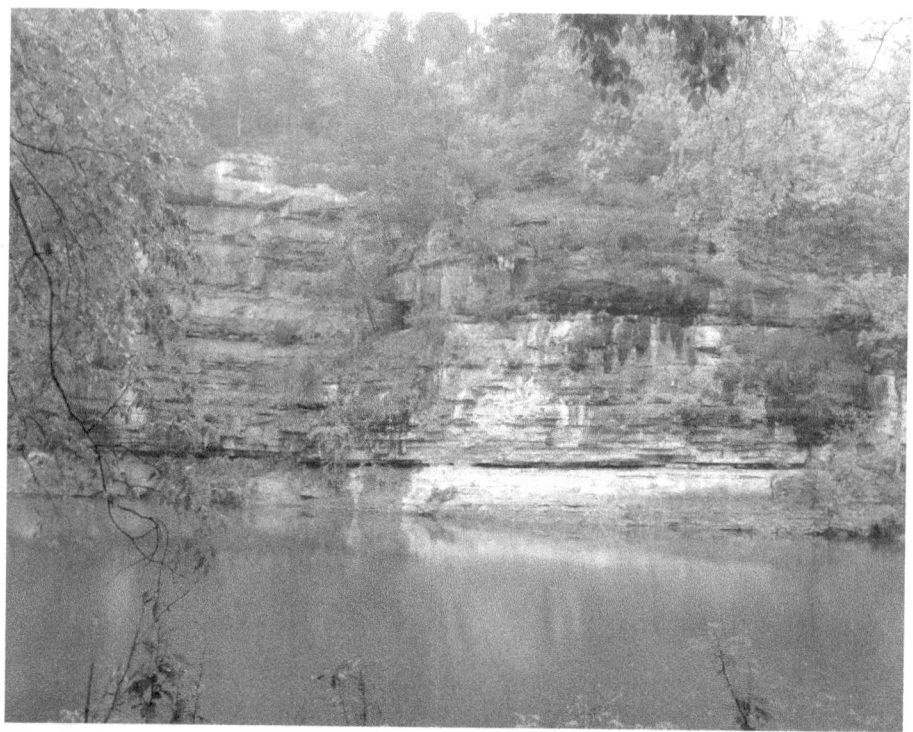

The Buffalo National River is an amazing clear water river thru north central Arkansas. It is one of the things that sold me on living there. I don't believe I have seen anything clearer. It's not just the Buffalo that's clear either. All the water is clear in north Arkansas Oh, the Natural State! The Ozark Mountains are gorgeous and perfect. They aren't near as high as the 3 major ranges, but high enough to have beautiful vistas, amazing rock bluffs, and rolling and winding roads. If you ever visit Arkansas, be sure to float the Buffalo. You can hook up with any of the amazing boat rental and guide companies to rent boats and arrange for pick-ups and drop offs. You can also do multiple day floats and camp along the river. If you do, remember to pack out your trash.

A couple hours later I stopped in Hot Springs, AR and bought a National Park pass. I only had to see like 3 or 4 parks for it to pay off. I plan on seeing at least 7.

23

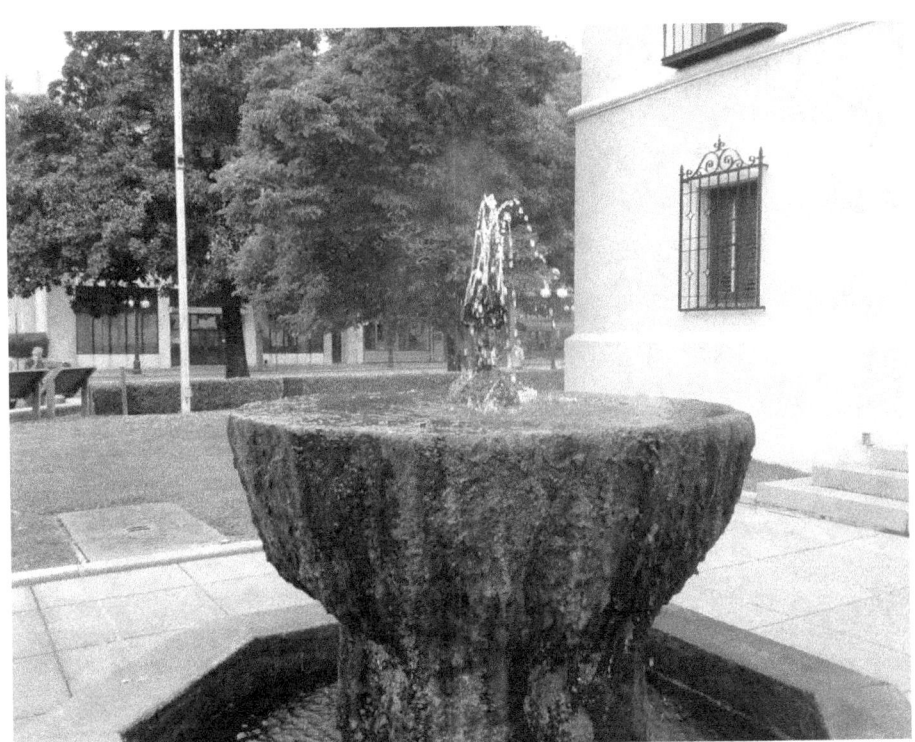

Hot Springs is one of the places I'm considering going after my trip. It has the downtown and tourist traffic to support an art gallery. But it's not quite Eureka Springs, in my book. There are several bath houses and hot, sweaty, bathed folks walking the streets lol :) It doesn't feel like me though. It doesn't seem to have the pleasant, sunshiny vibe I'm looking for.

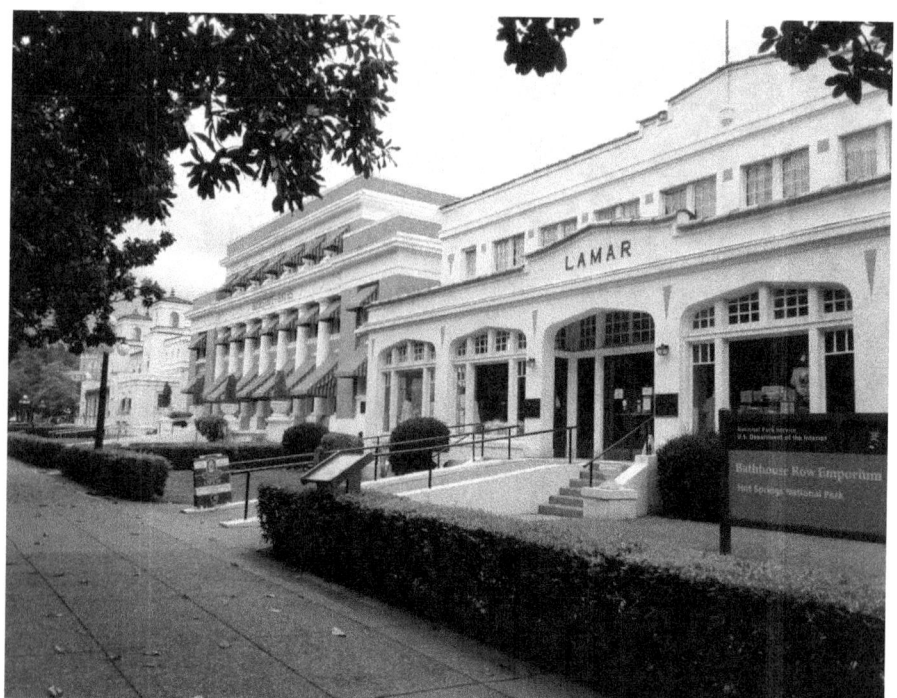

Or, maybe it's just a rainy day…

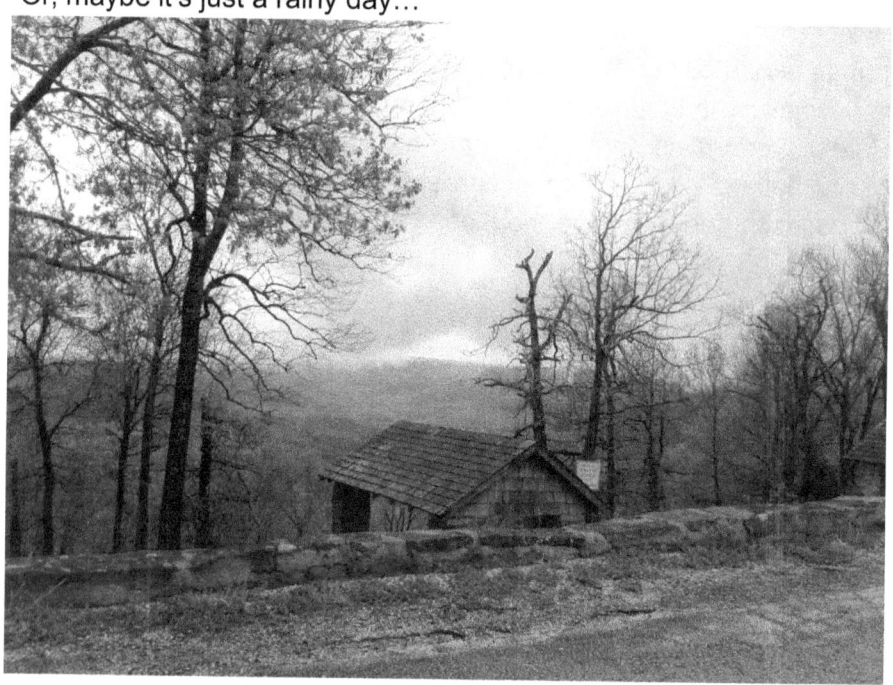

This will be the first night I sleep in Gertie. I'm kinda excited but also a little nervous. I recently read, biochemically those are the same emotions, it just depends on how we label them. We'll say I'm excited. I'm   totally   freaking   excited!

I've never slept in my car in a random parking lot before though. Also, it's hot and there are mosquitos. I've sprayed down with bugspray but, if it gets too bad, I might turn on the a/c…

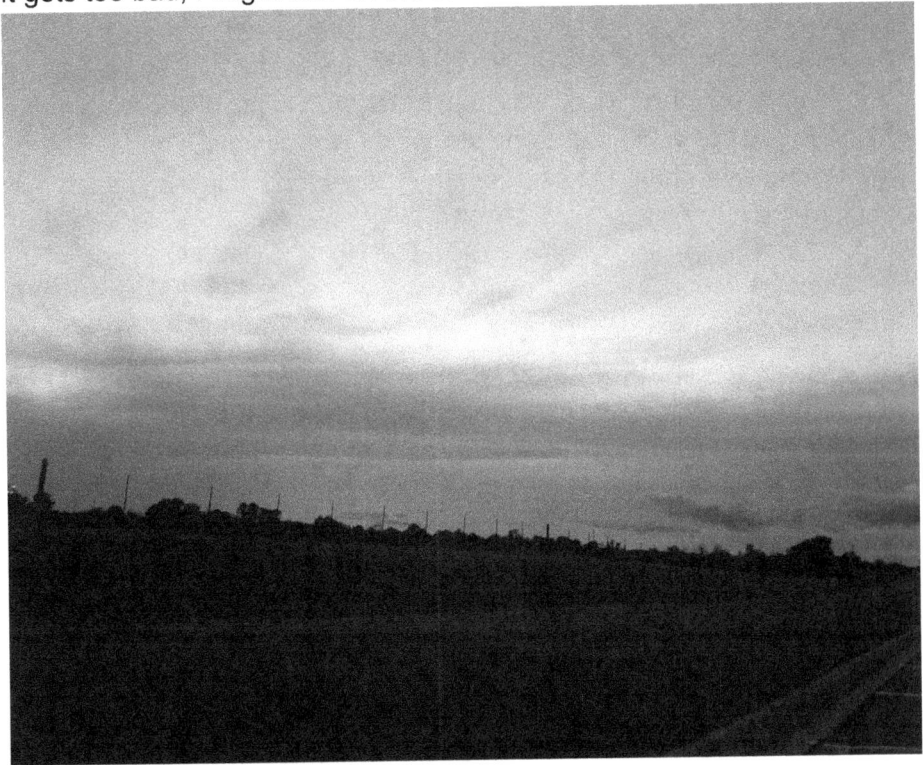

Tomorrow, I'll dig for diamonds :)

4/18/17 Day 2

Another 250 miles, another parking lot.

Gertie wasn't awful but I bought another mattress pad to make it more comfortable. I had fun digging diamonds but didn't find any. If you go, go after the rain, bring a shovel and a couple buckets. Also, sunscreen and mud boots. You can rent some screens and stuff there to help with

The park is really just a couple of farm fields with a pond and some wash stations. My advice? Look for where the water runs. Dig a couple holes and put the dirt in some buckets. Then go to a wash station. At the wash station. Listen and chat while you wash your dirt.

I met several interesting people, heard several stories, and got some tips from some who come often. It was fun for a bit. Some of the people around me found some fun rocks and stones as well as fossils and such. I dug and wandered around to see some of the various displays. I spent about half of the day there.

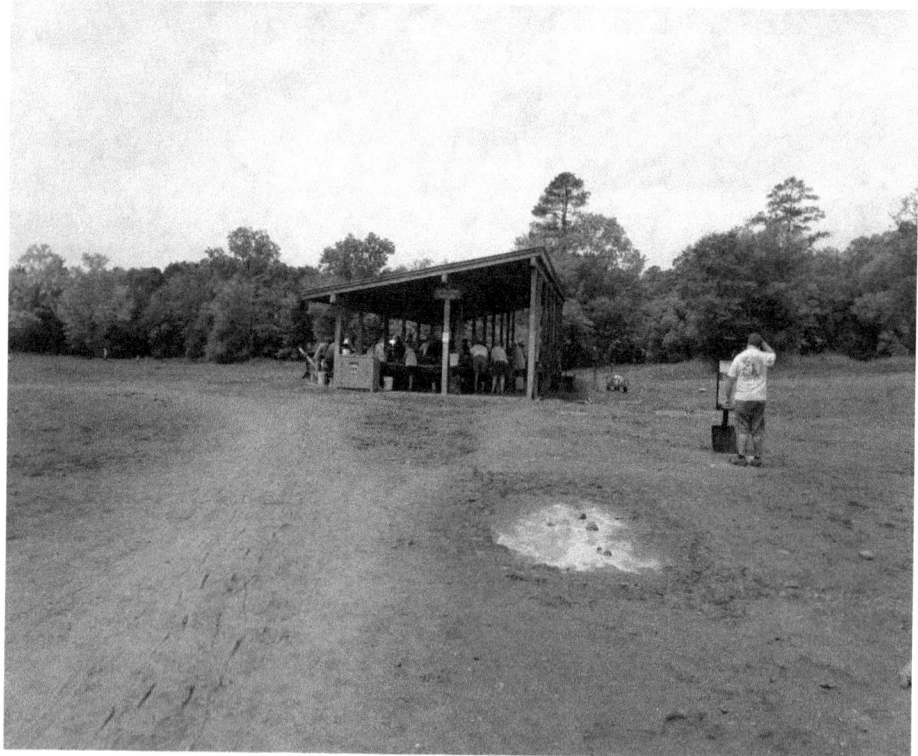

I had intended to stay in the nearby campgrounds, but they were full. That's ok because I know I need to pinch pennies where I can. Also, if I keep allowing fast food, I'll never even make California.

I'm one of those who believe everything happens for a reason. Yeah, we can argue that if we want. I don't want... I can usually find a reason if I

27

look. Sometimes it's a future reason and sometimes it's a past (you did dumb shit) reason but a reason, none the less.

Today, because I rolled on, I got to see the most beautiful sunset over a little drainage pond in Louisiana.

Tomorrow I'll need a shower.

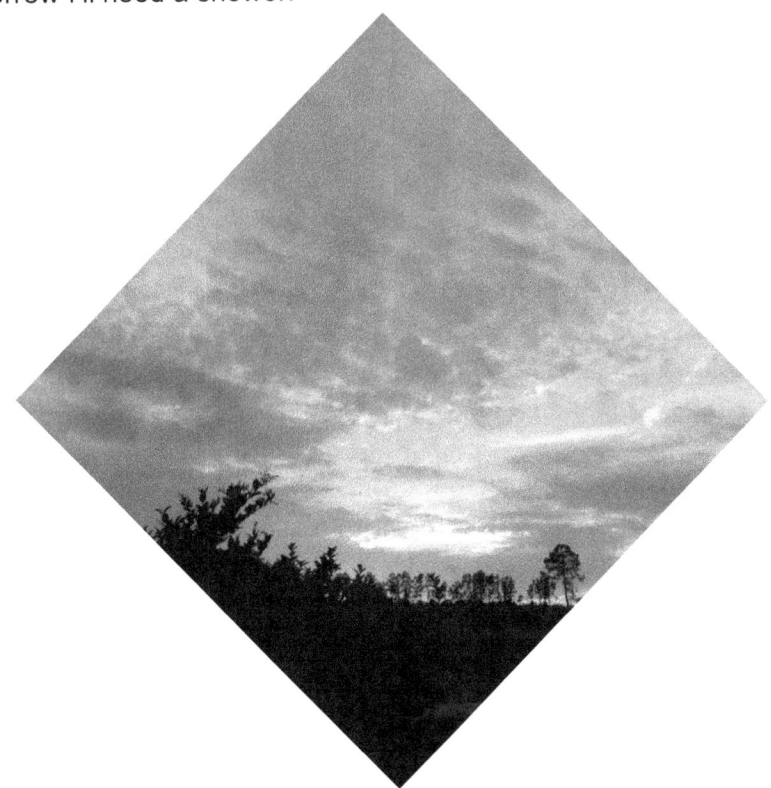

Follow your intuition. It always knows what to do.

Don't   know   how?

Close your eyes and take a couple deep breaths. And listen to your heart and your gut, not your head. Pay close attention too, she speaks softly and quickly.

4/19/17 Day 3

OMG! I just had the best dirtiest shower ever! It wasn't really that dirty, just a wrapper and hairball from the only other person in the park lol

(aside: haha, how funny, last month, in 2019, while out of town, I stayed at a place with another dirty shower. It also wasn't really dirty, just a wrapper and a hairball, lmao! The Universe or God or Source or Consciousness, whatever you like to call IT, is freaking hilarious sometimes lmao! Things will return until you clear them. If you don't do something different, nothing will change.)

I started off early this morning and only had 60 miles to drive. However, the GPS took me to the park headquarters and not the park campground which was about 20 miles away. On the way, the GPS kept taking me through these dark little neighborhoods in the woods that mildly made me nervous. Eventually I made it to the campground.

Pro tip: GPS and phone signal goes out a lot, all over this country, especially in rural or mountainous regions. Learn how to use a paper map and keep a decent map in your car for each state you drive in. Emergency supplies are a good idea too.

Tonight's campground is Boles Field. It's a small campground with showers and electric in the Sabine National Forest in Texas and, at the time, it was only $6 a night! I almost didn't believe that price was possible these days. It's true though! and, it was perfect!

The park straddles the highway and there are camping spots on both sides. One side has the National Fox Hound Cemetery and the other has an amphitheater built by the Civilian Conservation Corps in the 1930's.

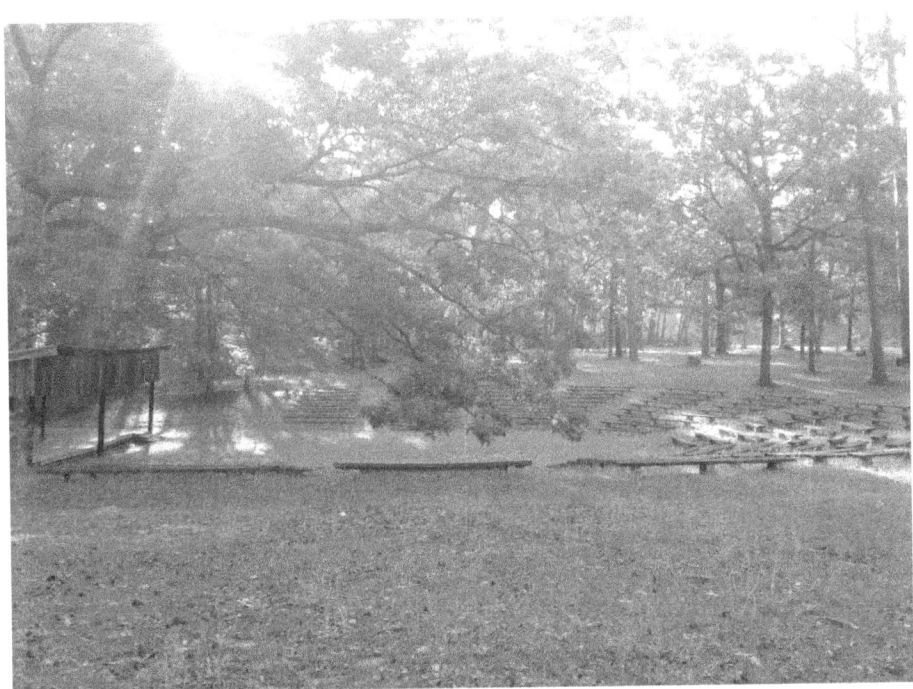

After a shower I sat down one the edge of my camp to relax, contemplate and meditate.

I thought I might journal and paint. I sat down in my chair on the edge of camp and kept getting distracted. Mostly my mind was just wandering.

— 3:03pm

Found myself sitting amongst the "venus looking glass" w/ only one flower

made the sketch — contemplating meditating + started to paint

moved 3 times to get out of sun

So, -God trip? Karma trip Bucket list, now or never —

I moved three times to get out of the sun and found myself among some Venus Looking Glass. Each had only one flower and I quickly sketched them in my journal, which was a great little exercise. It allowed me to focus for a minute and get my mind right. After journaling, I began to paint the pines reaching toward the blue skies above me.

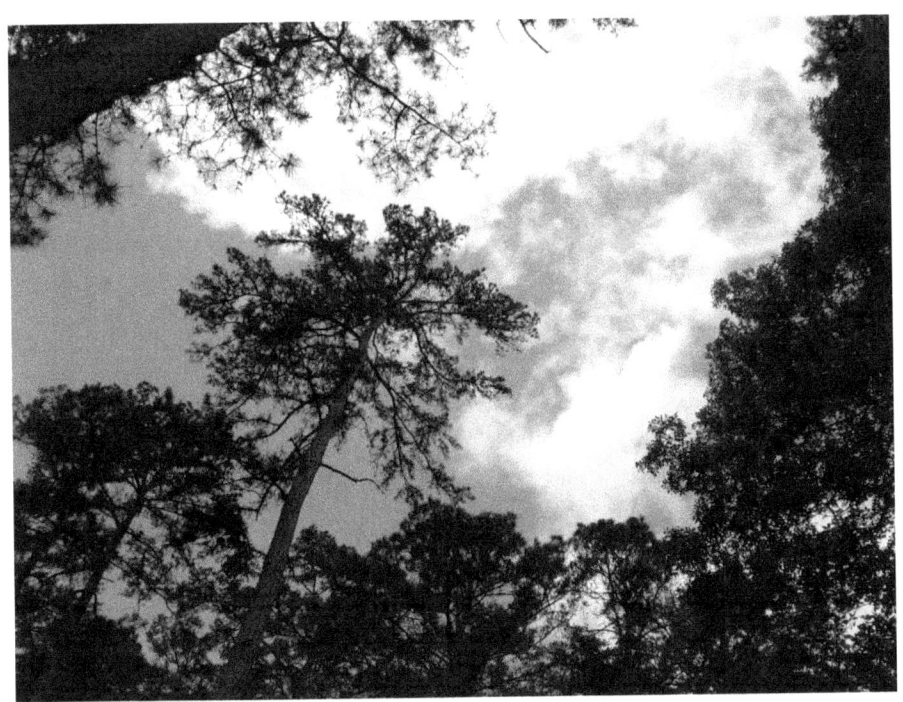

What is this trip I'm on? A God trip? A Karma trip? Bucket list? Now or never? Am I running? To or from?

I say it's all the above... It's part of my personal hero's journey... I used to always look outside of myself for a hero, for my hero. This trip is me being and learning to be my own hero. We are each our own hero. Or, we can be and probably, we must be. No one can save you but you. No one can live your life but you. No one can write your story but you.

I'd just gotten my blue sky painted when 2 older men in a fancy white pick-up truck pull in and drive really slowly around the campground. They stop to talk to me...

Amazing   how   things   often   just   work   out!

Just so happens that today I got to meet Toby and Albert who are the leader and originator of this fabulous little campground. (A great big thanks to Toby and Albert and all the other people whose help and approval it took to make this little campground exist and to keep it up.)

They are here giving a presentation to a special group today. Had I stayed near the diamond park last night, I wouldn't be here to catch this whole thing.

Remember, your heart and your gut know the way.

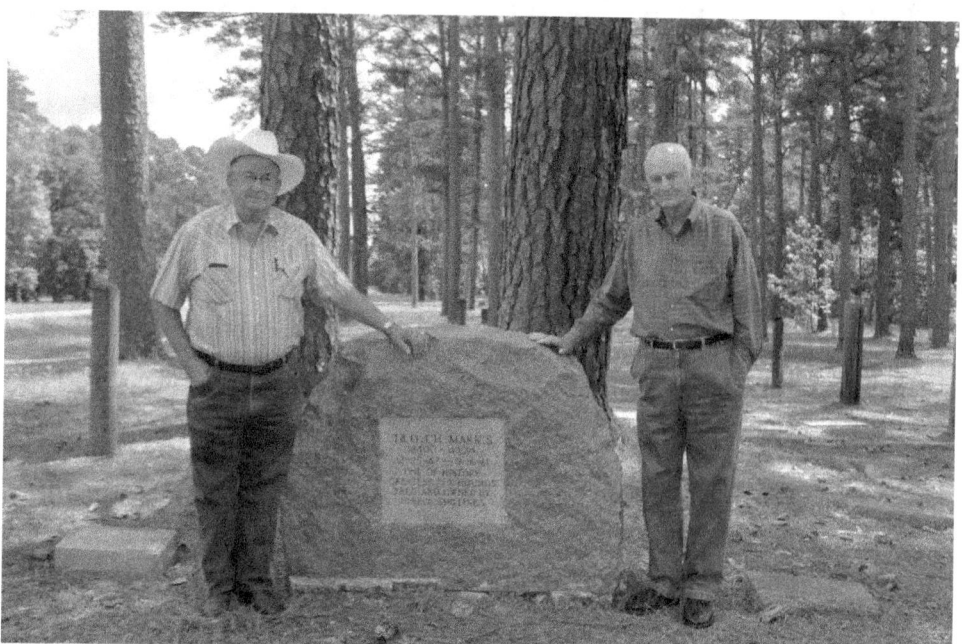

Anyway, they had been around long enough to know the Mr. Hinkle who started the Fox Hound Cemetery. This spot has been the location of a particular foxhound hunt since the early 1900s.

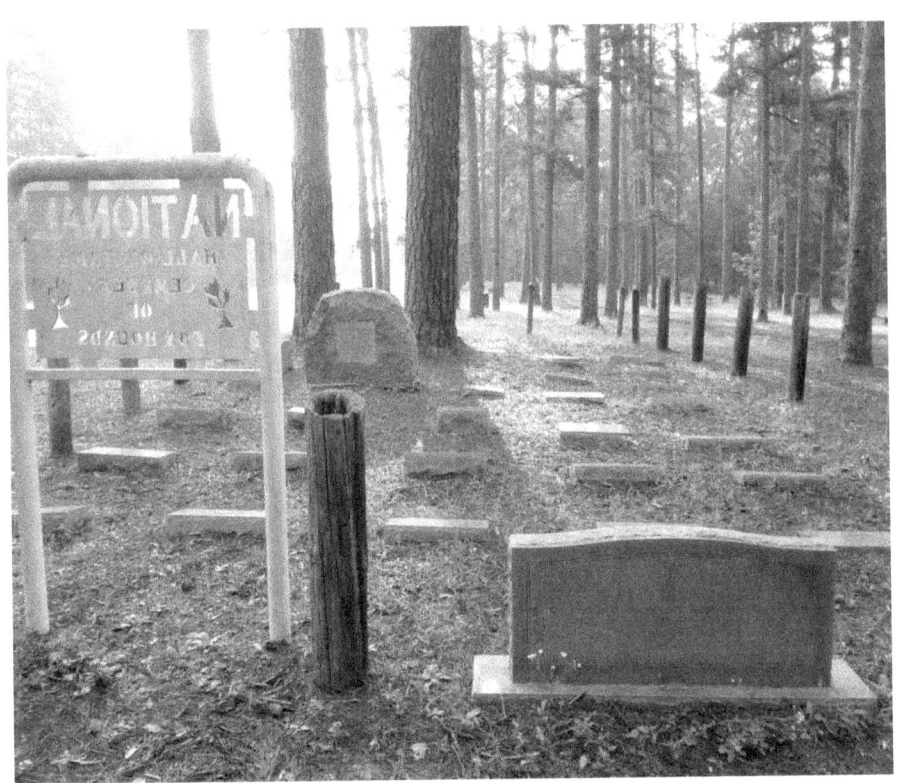

They told stories about various individuals and hunts and one in particular, the hunt that got canceled on December 8, 1941.

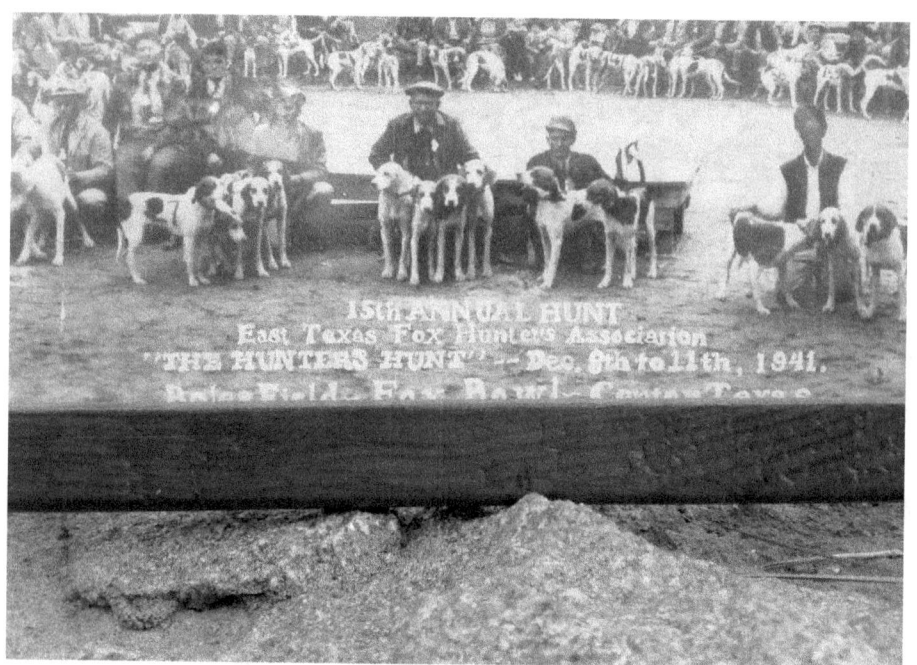

15th ANNUAL HUNT
East Texas Fox Hunter's Association
"THE HUNTERS HUNT" – Dec. 8th to 11th, 1941.

At the end of the presentation Albert blew 3 blows of the rams' horn which is used to signify the end of a hunt. The horn calls the dogs home. What a pleasure it was to be able to be there for this and to hear the stories that Toby told. Stories of some of the men and dogs who'd passed through there, and stories from his life. Stories about life.

Stories... Maybe I'm here to hear people's stories? Maybe it's to tell people's stories? Maybe we're all here for the stories...

Later that evening I sat around the fire and heard the stories of the couple who were staying there. They were from Alaska and were also on a road trip across the country. It was a pleasure to meet them and chat around the fire. They told me stories about Alaska and bears and some from their recent travels.

How fantastic this day turned out to be.

Tomorrow, Austin.

35

4/20/17 Day 4

5 or 6 hrs to Austin thru East Texas. As they say, everything is bigger in Texas…   I   say,   BUGS!

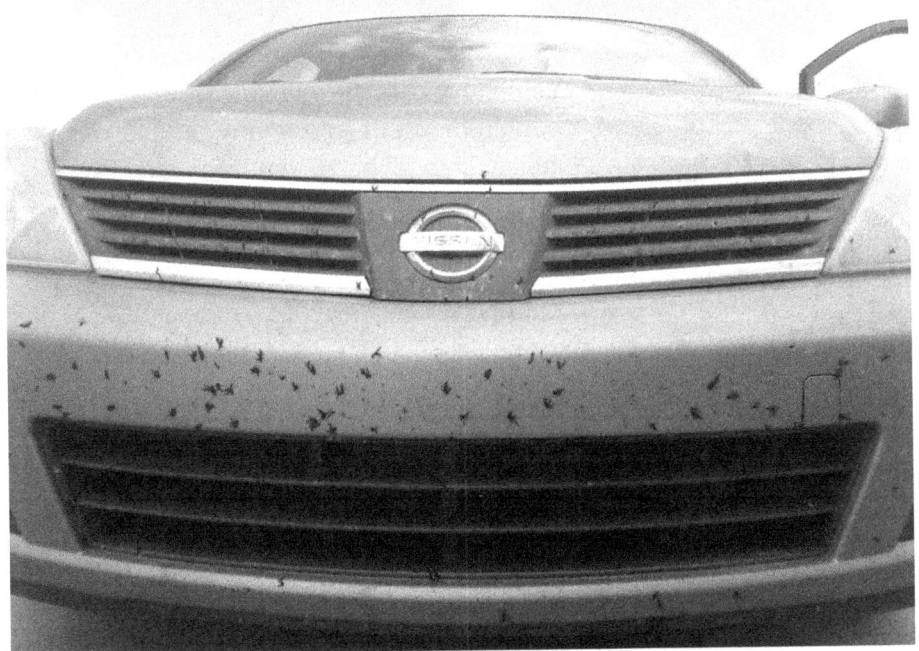

These freaky looking black flies were like none I've ever seen. They were just black, wings and all, and were so thick that the swarms looked like black smoke clouds.

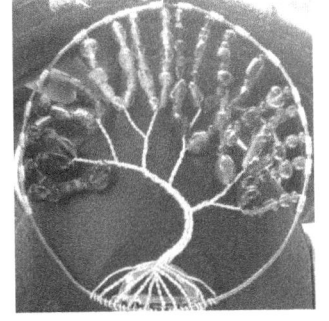

I stopped twice, once for lunch and once at a tiny post office in the middle of nowhere to mail off a couple tree sun catchers.

When you are a northerner in the south, as soon as you open your mouth and speak, you stand out like a sore thumb. "Ya ain't from 'round here, are ya?" The mail clerk (and nearly every other southerner) immediately asked. Turns out he was also from Northwest Indiana or had lived there before and had moved down here when   his   son   took   a   job   down   here   after   college.

It really is such a tiny little world we live in. It's so funny how everything connects.

———

Austin

The first thing I noticed about Austin, TX was the number of homeless. After the floods in Louisiana a couple of years ago, many people were relocated to Austin. Also, panhandling is legal here, I heard.

When I got to Austin, I went straight to my Airbnb. (my first Airbnb) It was an adorable house in a tight little neighborhood near downtown. Street parking and gardens up to the front door. It looked tiny, like a cottage. There were supposed to be several rooms. I wasn't sure if I was at the right house...

A roommate or other tenant answered the door but didn't seem to be expecting me. I got nervous. Eventually it seemed to click though, and she let me in. I was relieved...   I was in the right place.

The inside was huge! Beautiful old wood floors and fixtures, tall ceilings, and art everywhere. There was an addition in the back that added a kitchen and whole back half with a second story. I was in awe!

Later I met the host, her boyfriend, and some other short- and long-term guests. I didn't realize so many people were staying here.

Pro tip: Ask more questions. Ask better questions. Ask better questions more.

As amazing as the inside of the house was, the back garden was even better. If you know me, you already know that I spent a lot of my free time out there :) It was like a little sunken oasis. You would have no idea from the front that the back looked like this.

After a shower, I headed out for some dinner and to find where I would be spending the next three days, downtown.

I'm here for a business convention with a business mentor. I'm a little nervous. (no, flip that, I'm excited!) Lots' of people and new places can make me nervous. I'm so glad I'm here though. Before my trip, before I left Bear Bottom, I invested in a marketing and branding course which included calls with a mentor and this conference in Austin. It was a complete package kind of deal and I felt like it was a good move for me. What is an artist? She is a business, a brand.

I know me... I needed to set myself up while I was feeling it so that I couldn't or would be less likely to back out later when fear kicked in and my brain started making excuses. I know that will happen because I've wanted to cross-country road trip my whole life but have always found a reason not to, i.e., money, no one to go with, job, school, time, etc.

I knew/know this trip would be, is, was, important for me. It was something I had to do; I'd always wanted to do. I was gonna make it happen. I needed it to help me believe in myself and trust in myself again. I knew I had to do it, but I also knew that if I didn't create some insurances, I might chicken out.

I wandered around Austin for a little while and found downtown and the Congress Bridge.

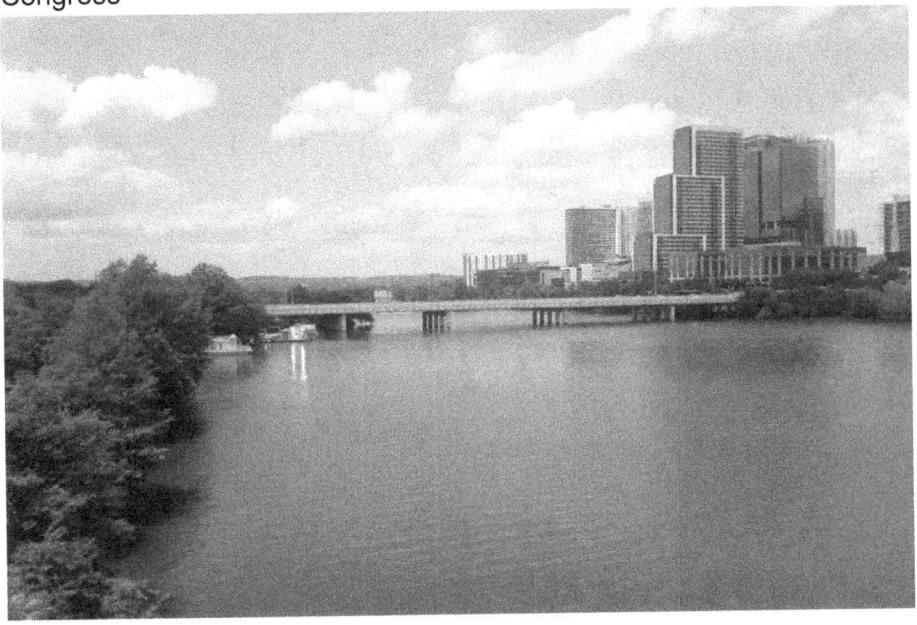

There were over 200 people gathered on the bridge around sunset to watch the bats come out to feed. It was pretty cool.

In fact, Austin is pretty cool. There are a lot of people who walk everywhere and lots of public transit, cabs, and bicycles. I love that so many cities are adopting bicycle and scooter rental programs. It's bound to make traffic better and less pollution. I also saw a native plants garden that was neat. They seem to love nature here which is awesome. It gives me some hope.

Austin could definitely be an option for me to land next. The city is quite cool. But the weather is HOT! Also, it might be a little big for me. I'm not a big city girl, too many people and too much traffic makes me anxious... But I do like its vibe and its colors. There is a river walk and kayak rentals right downtown. There are murals and there's an arts district and there's 6th street.

Must visit 6th street. All the weird and wonderful that is Austin can be seen on 6th street.

"Keep   Austin   Weird".

What am I gonna do after this trip!? Mom and dads? I'll probably be broke. I'll need some time to work. If I don't figure out how to sell art, I'm gonna need a job. What about a residency? Am I good enough to get into a residency? Is there one that pays? How do artists make money?

I saw an artist residency in Key West that sounded interesting. That could be an option. I could show my Adam-Eve paintings there. I'll look into it; there's all these requirements. And portfolio stuff, do I even have a portfolio? And do I wanna show Adam-Eve? Art must be seen. Do I want to do more? Would they even let me?

I   don't   know...   too   much...   focus...

My conference starts in the morning. I'm super excited and nervous. There is a private group for those who signed up for the same course as me, so I know some names. I wonder who will be there?

4/21/17 Day 5

The shortest notes mean I had the most fun.

I met several interesting and amazing people today! There are a lot of coaches here.... How'd I get in that circle? There are also some writers and some artists, and some dancers. Really, there are all sorts of different people here! Mostly women, but some really awesome men too!

This copywriter with crazy space pants! And a writer with pink hair!

There was one woman that I seemed to hit it off with, R. She's also from the Midwest (most here are from other places, cities. Texas, California, Hawaii, New York) She and I went for burgers and wandered 6th street discussing mindset and encouraging each other to put ourselves out there more.

That was the main message today too. Nobody is gonna know you're there if you don't let them see you. We've been challenged to go live to our audiences this weekend. Who's my audience? Who's gonna buy my paintings? Who's gonna read this? Who are you? Who am I?

Mindset. Mindset is 99%. Who said, "if you believe you can or if you believe you can't, you're right?" was that Henry Ford? I think so...

6th street was fabulous! All the weird and wonderful! Murals and art and food and music and! I traded cigarettes for a magic trick and met a human statue from SOUTH BEND, Indiana! I couldn't believe it! It's such a small world!!

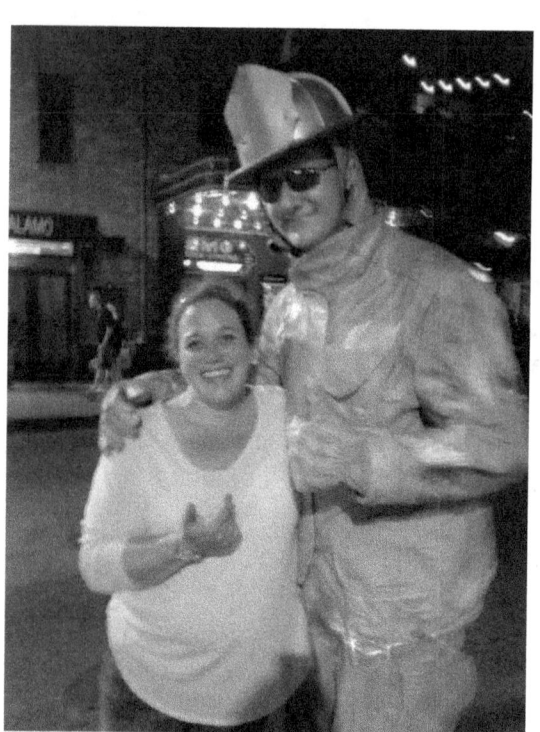

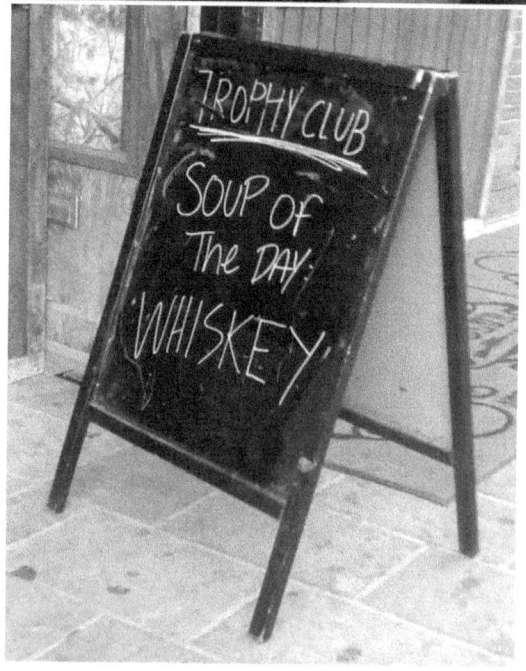

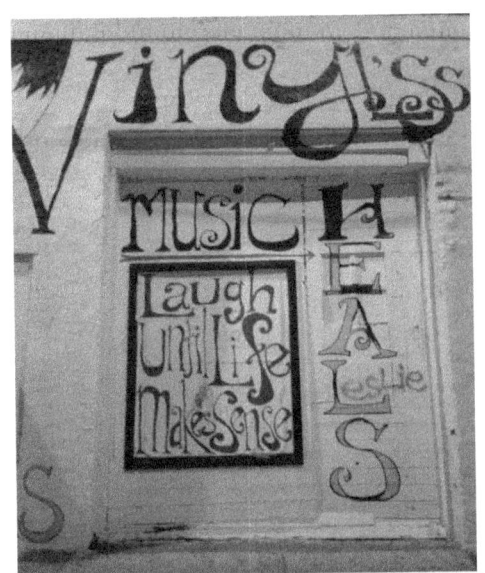

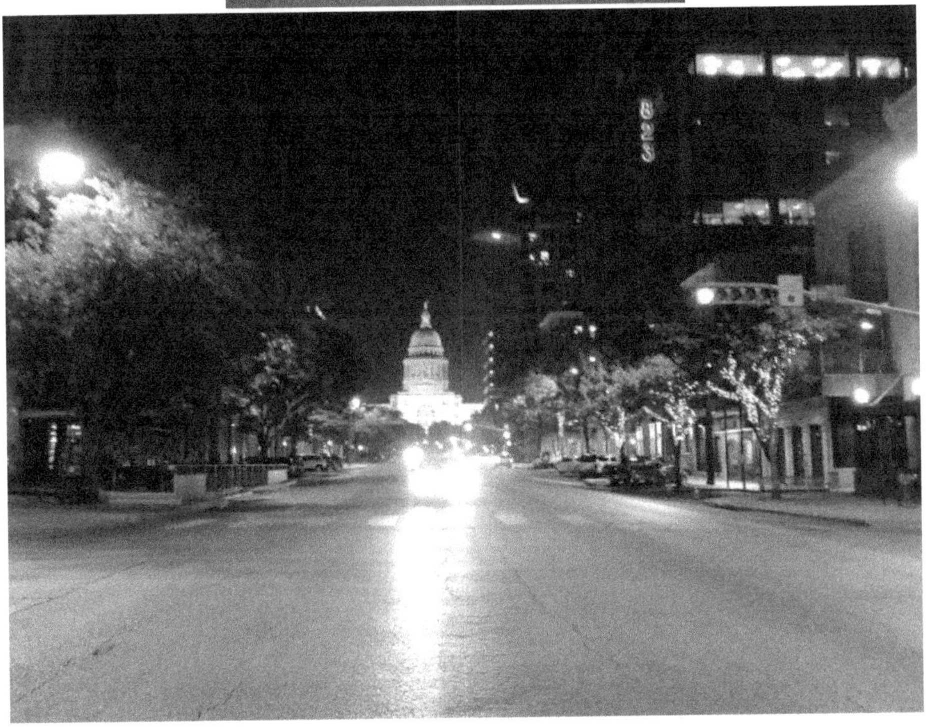

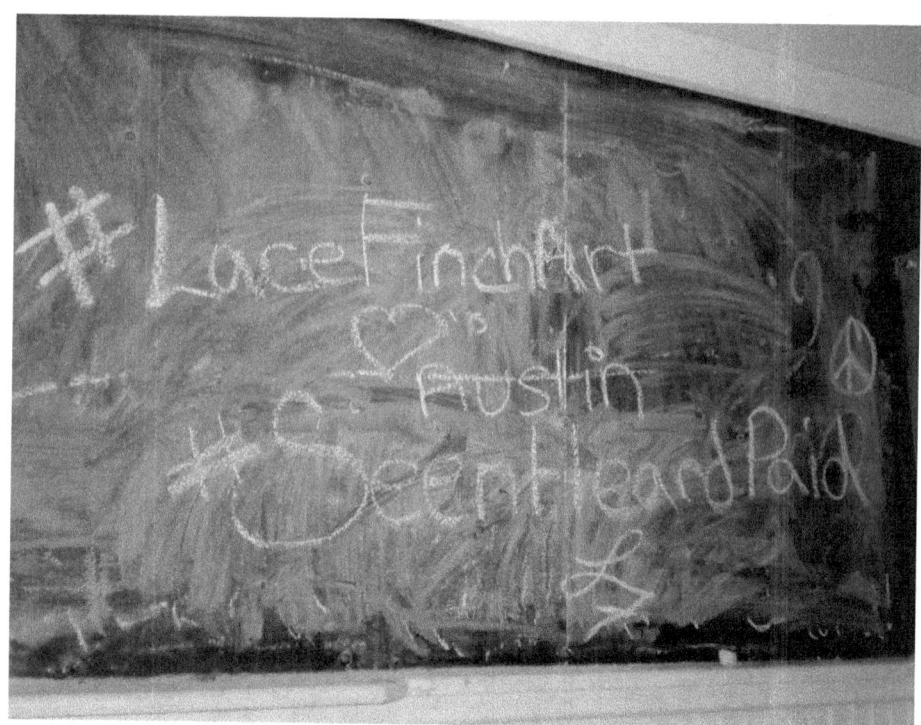

In the spirit of this conference I decided to write on this chalkboard in the bathroom at the restaurant we ate at. It's silly, I know, but it's also meaningful. I'm thankful R was here to cheer me on. As I wrote it, I could distinctly hear the mean girls laughing and pointing in my head… "look at her, that's so dumb, she's so uncool. Looser!"

Note to self: Ignore the mean girls. Do it anyway.

4/22/17 Day 6

Wow. What a very long day. A lot came up for me today during the conference sessions. I am doing a lot right! I'm doing a lot of good stuff from the start!

"Laugh till life makes sense" Then laugh some more because that's when you'll know just how funny this life really is.

We talked about copywriting and corporate sponsors and social media and serving your audience.

Today I was told that I have a magnetic personality.

It's time to come clean and be real. Let shit go! Let the fear go! Let the past go! Let the expectation go!

Nissan and Coke for sponsors? Old Navy? Pandora? Paint companies?

I am Lacey Finchum
I am Lace Finch
I am an Artist & Storyteller

I jump in headfirst and then must rein in a bit from there.

I'm an outlier. A disruptor.

Oh my gosh, this challenge... FB LIVE... UUuuugggghhh!

Nothing to it but to do it.

Gotta do it!

My tools:
Instagram: @lacefinch_art
Facebook: @lacefinchart
You Tube: LaceFinch
Website www.lacefinchart.com
Blog
Painting
Writing

What the hell am I doing?

4/23/17 Day 7 - Conference day 3

I cried all day today!

FEAR! RESISTANCE!

Afraid to fail. Afraid to succeed.

If I really want to paint naked people, I need to find people to paint!

If I were really gonna do this, I'd do it here, now.
If I were really gonna, I'd find someone here to paint…

Today I met a lawyer who gave me her card, and a launch person. She does launches? A business strategist? She told me to come stay with her when I get to San Antonio. She gave me an organization tool.

My new friend, R, offered to coach me! Oh, my goodness! I can't believe it! 2 months of coaching for a painting of equal value.

****Follow-up**** This is the painting I ended up doing for her.

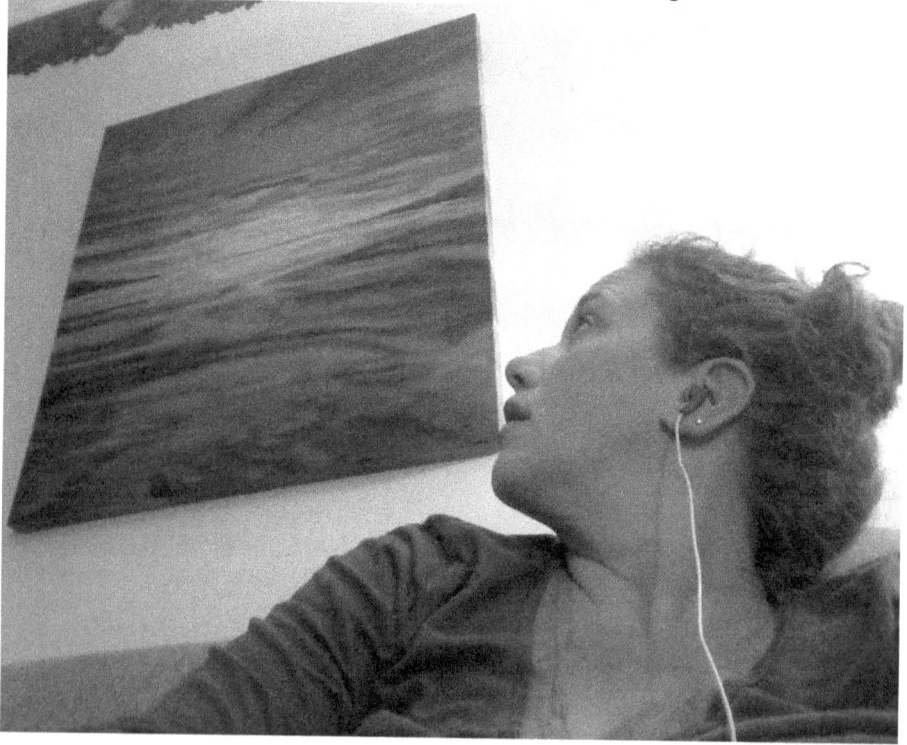

Then she says, "Ok, coaching starts now! Bring your paintings in and set them up in the lobby of this hotel"

OMG! No way! But I did it :) I didn't put out Adam-Eve, but I had them there.

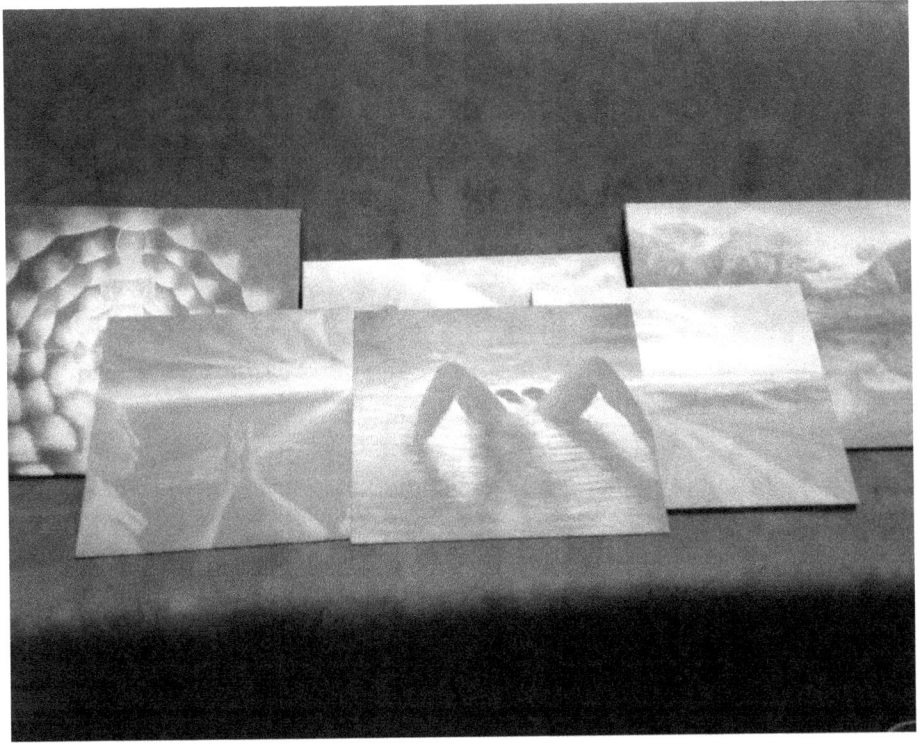

Several people stopped and chatted about them. One wanted to see Adam-Eve!

And she liked them! I should ask to paint her. Yes. I need to. I will.

4/24/17 Day 8 - Bonus Day

She's gonna let me paint her! OMG! Tomorrow! OMG! I can't believe it. Is she really!? Like Adam-Eve? Wow! Omg, I'm so excited. And so nervous! I hope I do it well!

Relax. Your fine. You'll do fine. It's easy, remember. You know what you're doing.

I can't hire R to coach me yet... I'm a mess, I need time. 90 days. Then I'll do it... is that fear talking? What's this resistance?

I Must finish this marketing course first then I'll hire R. Shit, I must pay for this course first. And this trip! Lions and tigers and bears, Oh MY!

Tonight, I'll sleep nearby and go paint tomorrow. I'm so nervous and giddy! Lol

I'm so excited! I hope I sleep.

I couldn't find a campground nearby. Walmart it is... This one's kinda scary though. There are lots of loiterers... homeless? Drugs? Etc? Some girl hollering at some guy, him squealing tires.

I'm in the light though and closer to the building this time.

Pro-Tip: Walmart and some other big box stores allow overnight parking, it's really for truckers and RVers probably but still, if you're sleeping in your vehicle, it's good to know. ALSO! Be sure to always be safe. Pay attention to your surroundings. Know who is around you etc. Lock your doors. You are in charge of you. Be smart and pay attention.

I hope I sleep...

4/25/17 Day 9

I made it :)

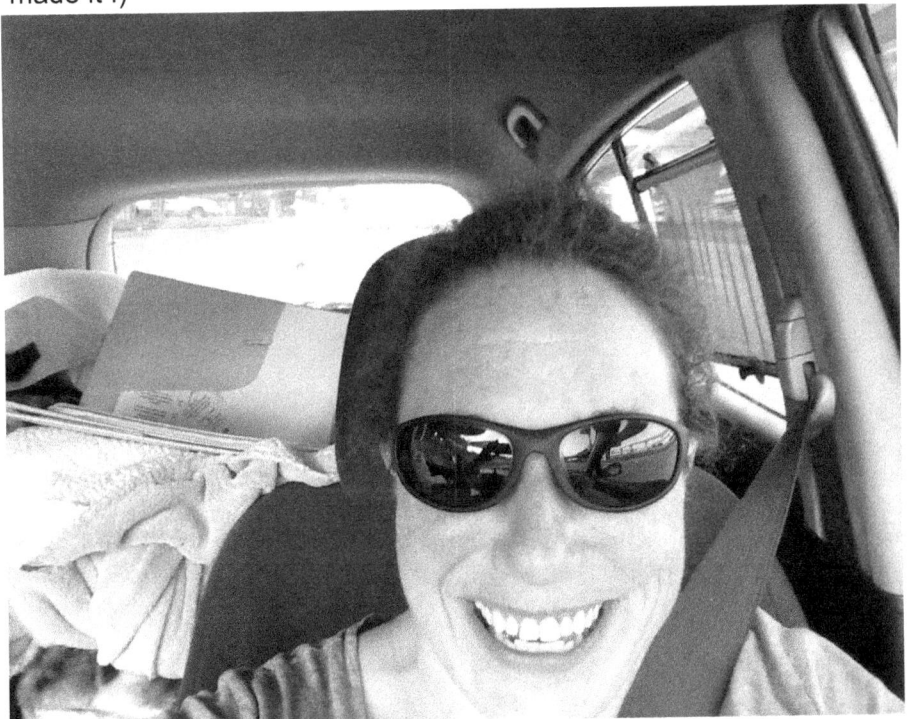

I woke up fairly early and wandered around this end of town for a bit. I went to meet my model around noon. We were both so nervous. We chatted for a couple hours before getting started. I let her lead. She turned on a record and took off her clothes while I prepared my paints and canvas. She and I were both still nervous.

I decided to let her sit comfortably and we continued to chat. I chose to paint her breasts. She thinks boobs is a funny word.

She's beautiful.

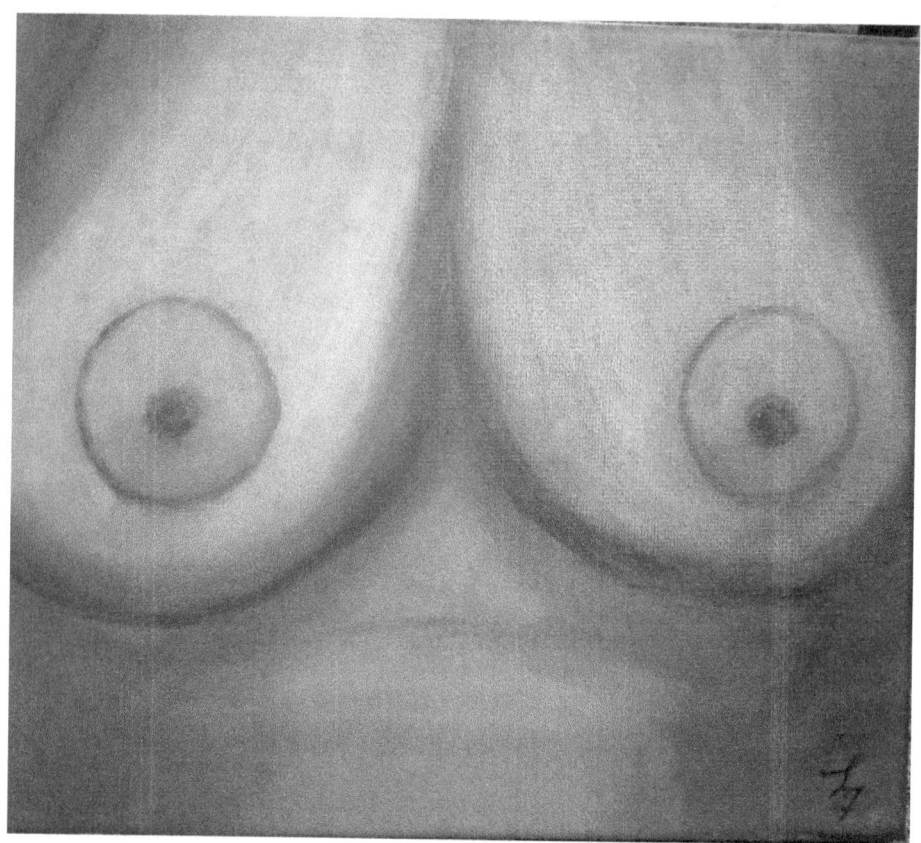

She wants to do hair and makeup for the homeless to give them confidence and help them get jobs and housing.

She's beautiful.

Tonight, I'll sleep in San Marcos.

Tomorrow I'll go to Palmetto State Park in Gonzales, TX then San Antonio. I've requested an Airbnb for San Antonio, but I haven't gotten confirmation yet.

San Marcos was uneventful...

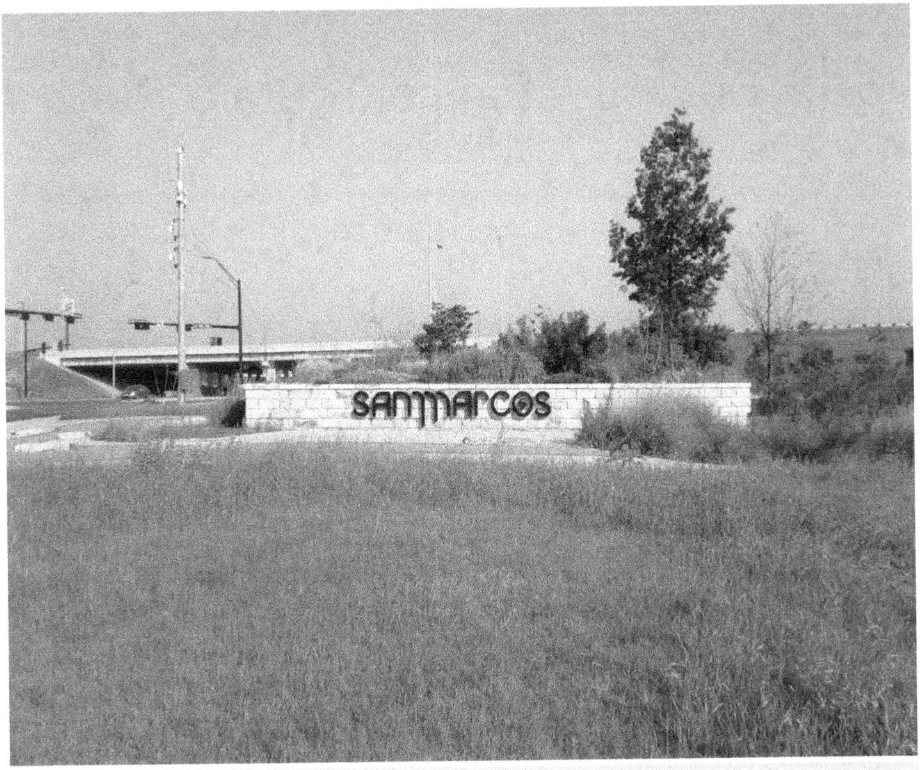

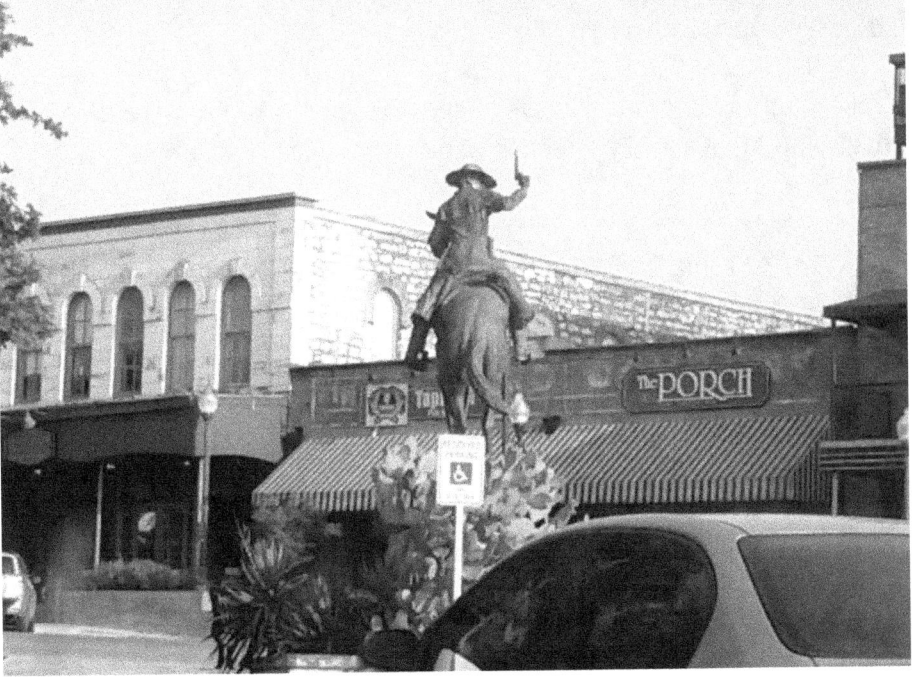

4/26/19 Day 10 - Palmetto State Park, Gonzalez, TX

Rest Day

The drive to Palmetto was lovely. It's nearly tropical looking.

I got here around 10am and I'm supposed to check out tomorrow at 2pm. There's a lake and a river. I think I'll swim later and clear my head. For now, though, I think I'll read a little and take a nap.

I finally started the book my friend Sunshine gave me. It's called "Prayer and the Art of Volkswagen Maintenance." It's about one guys road trip experience with his buddy, Paul, in a VW Bus.

I could easily love Paul.

I could easily learn to love road life.

I can take "home" with me wherever I go…You can take home with you wherever you go. It's really a feeling, a sense of being, not a place.

—————

I took a walk over the river and a swim in the little lake then had a little smoke. I feel much better now.

It's hot out but breezy. It's lovely in the woods; quiet and peaceful.

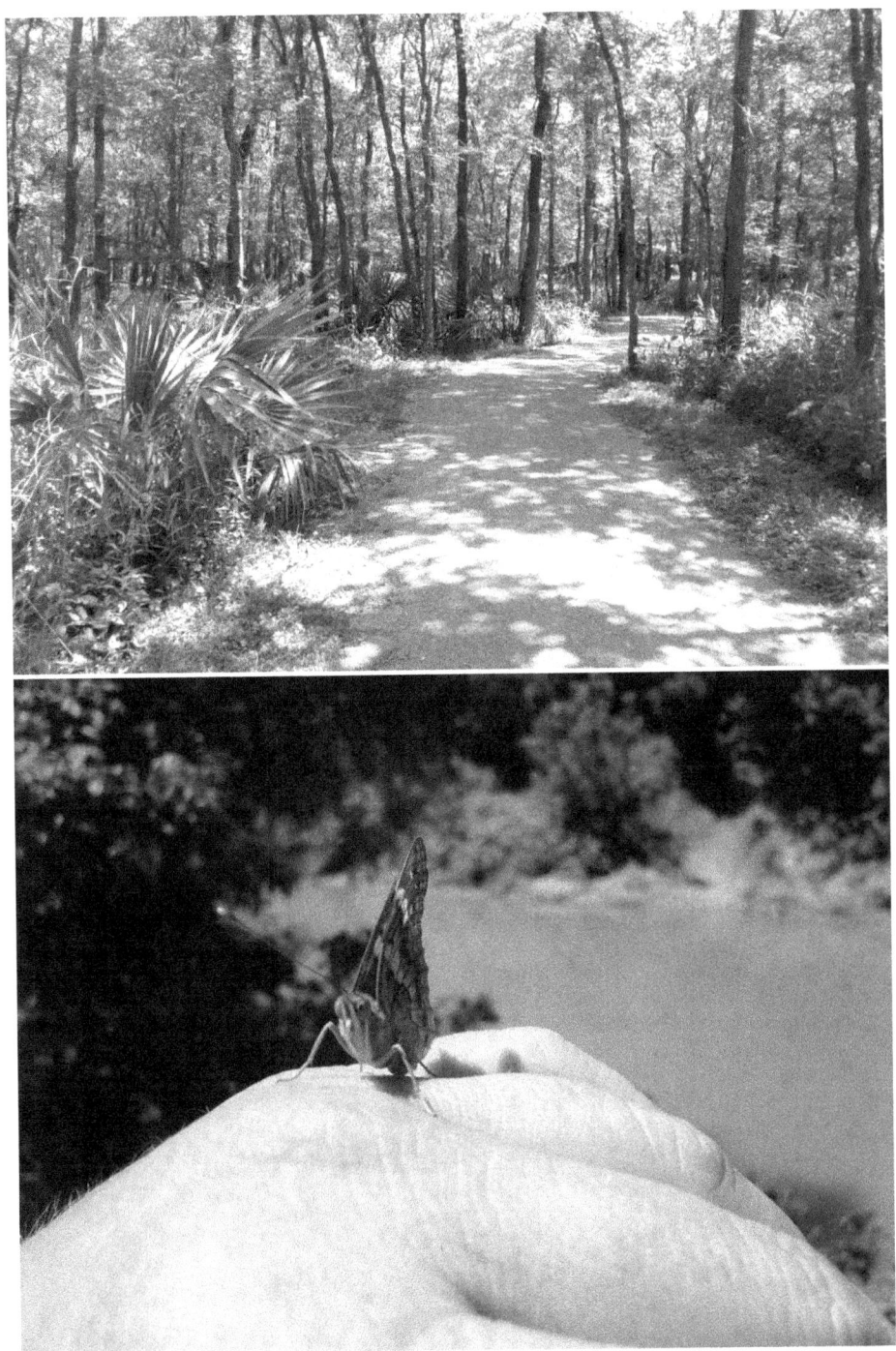

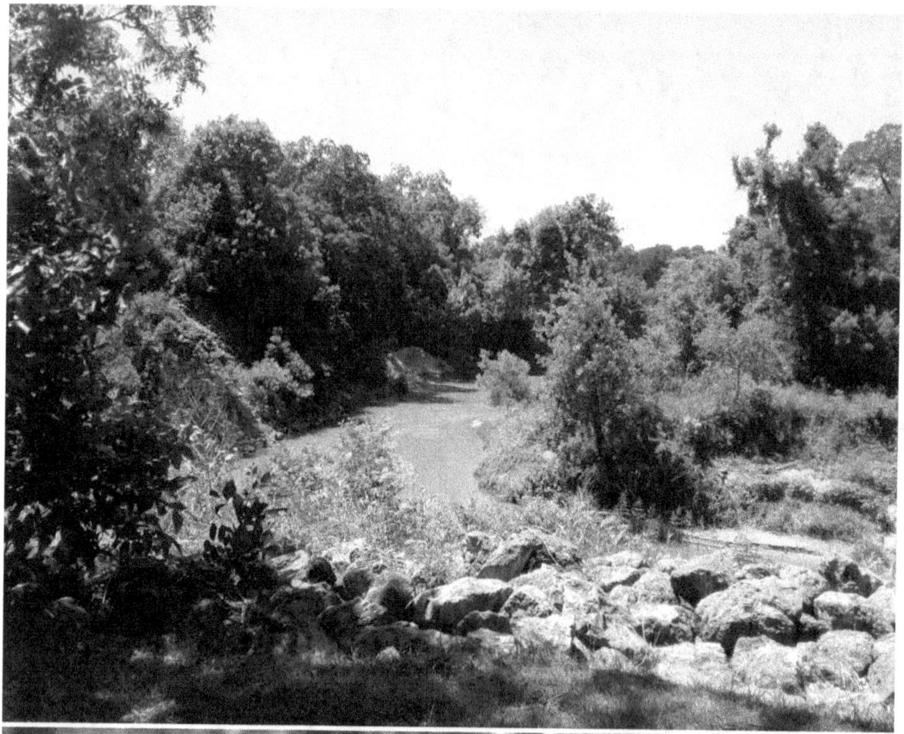

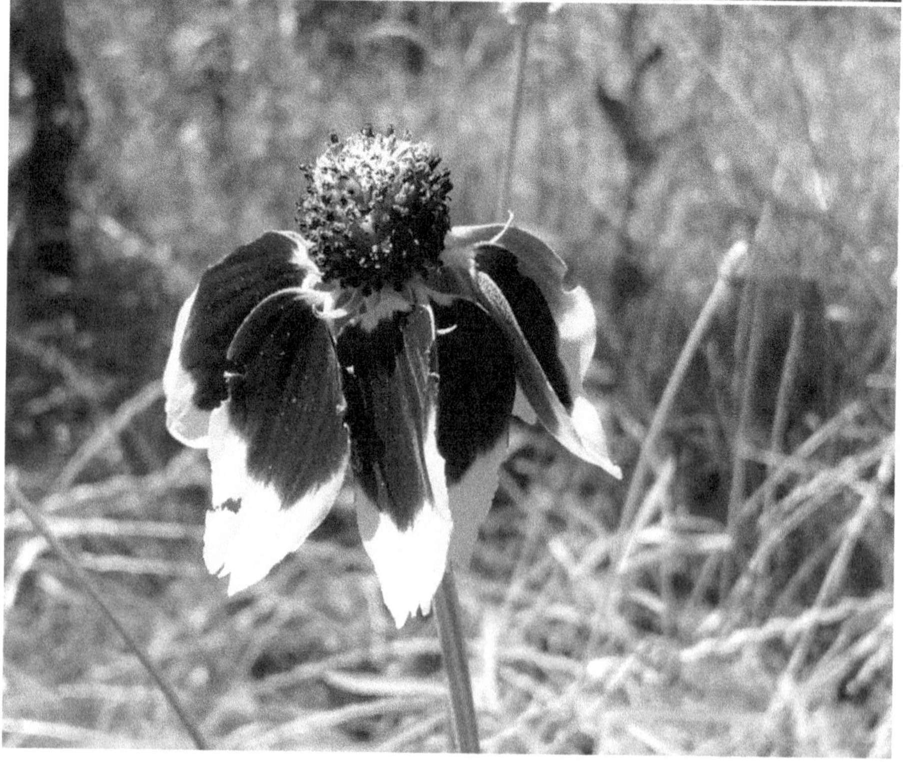

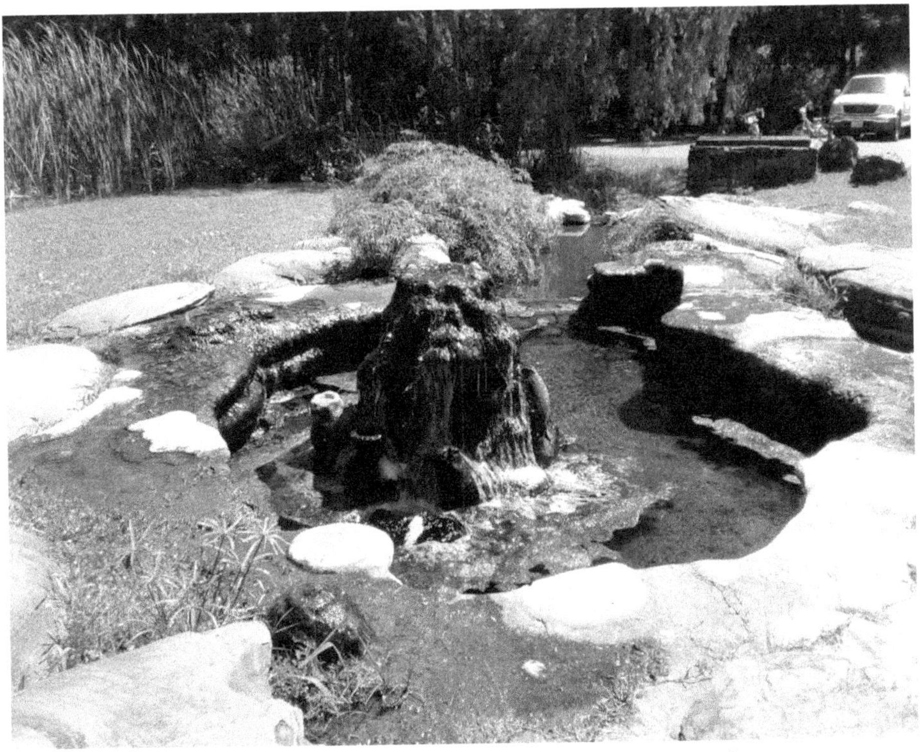

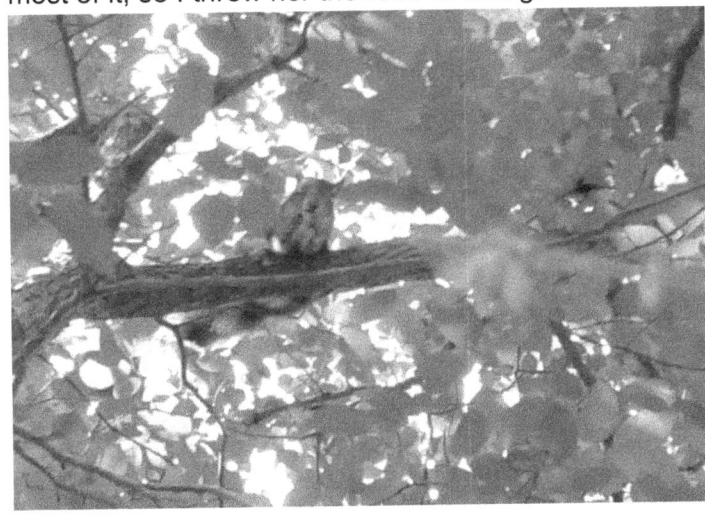

I saw some ducks and turtles at the beautiful CCC fountain.

Oh, and a squirrel ate my bread… my fault. I left the camp box open and went to take a shower. I caught her eating it when I got back. She ate most of it, so I threw her the rest. It was good bread too…

It's time to start putting my magic to work again. It's time to manifest and work some LOA. Now is time to dream and build for the future.

The inner journey holds the key…

Solfeggio 852 Hz

———

I AM BEAUTIFUL
I AM POWERFUL
I AM WISE
I AM TALENTED
I AM ABUNDANT.

I HAVE ABUNDANT MONEY
I HAVE ABUNDANT RESOURCES
I HAVE ABUNDANT FOLLOWERS
I HAVE ABUNDANT CLIENTS AND COLLECTORS

I ~~HAVE~~ AM ABUNDANT WEALTH
I ~~HAVE~~ AM ABUNDANT PEACE
I ~~HAVE~~ AM ABUNDANT LOVE

I have an in-town gallery and studio with an apartment and
a remote retreat center for art, nature, and relaxation/reflection.

There are trees and gardens and pools and tree houses

Classes for art
Paint, wire, clay, glass, sculpture, metal, wood.
Meditation/yoga studio
Residency
Gallery of past residents
Hiking
Fountains
Partnerships
Employees

55

It's time to manifest
+ work the Secret
(Inner journey holds
the key ....)
Solfegio 852 Hz

_____

• I AM Beautiful   I AM Abundant
I AM Powerful
I AM Wise
I AM Talented

            Abundant
I Have ~~poor of~~ money
I Have ~~stent~~ Abundant ~~COB~~
        Followers
I Have Abundant Client/Customer
   Collectors

~~I HAVE~~ Abundant
~~I AM~~ Wealth
~~I HAVE~~ Abund Peace
       AM
~~I Have~~ Abundant Love
   AM

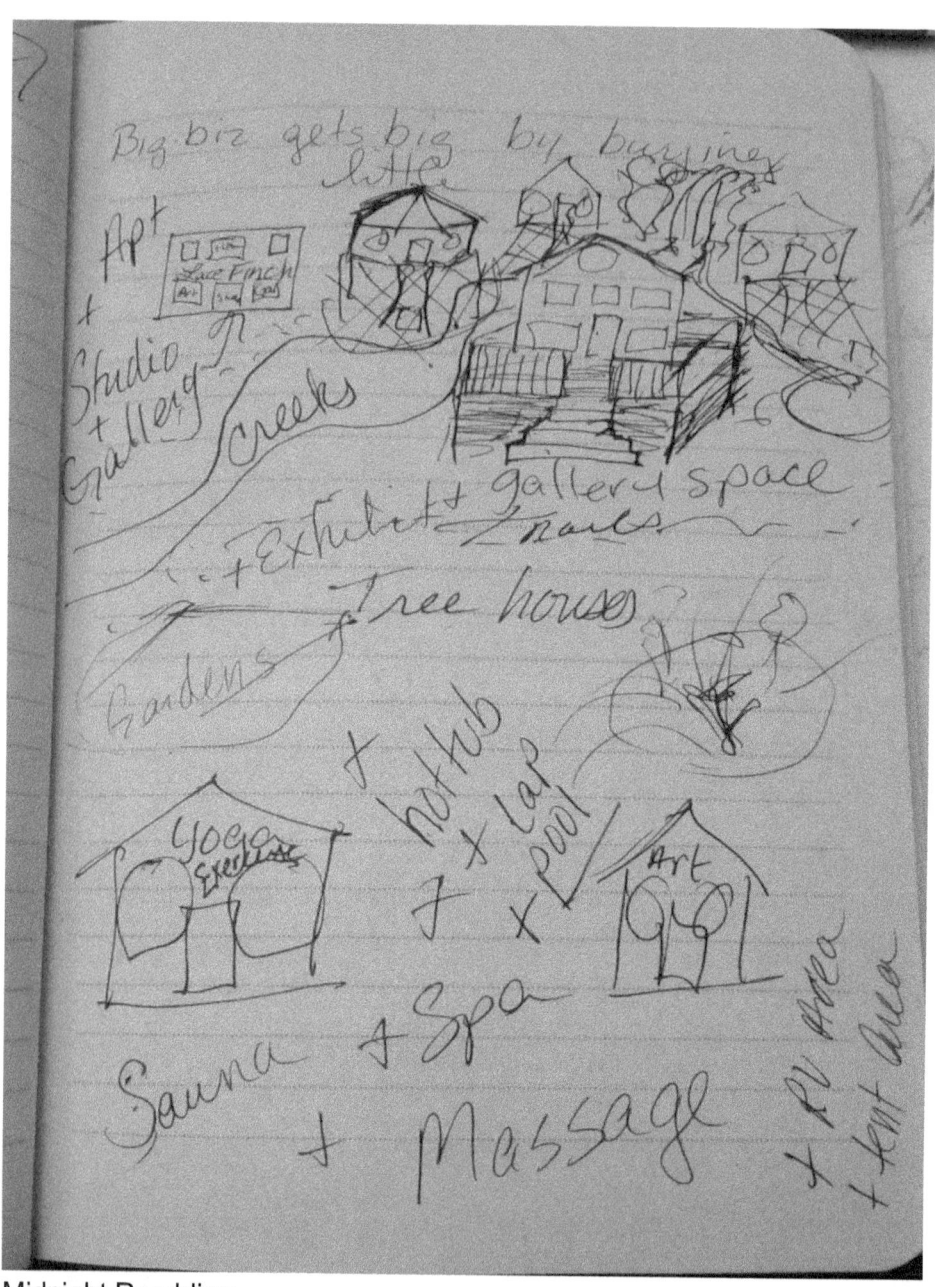

Midnight Rambling

Midnight rambling in the dark in Texas…

To share myself or not…

I come from small players. Great people but small players. Average players.

I want big!

Or alone…
Or love…
Or small…

Big is scary.

I want it.

I want different.

Thoughts…
    I could do a midnight ramblings podcast. Voice and candle flicker in the dark. My views and interviews.

Well, what's your low hanging fruit, Lace? Pick it and Eat it!
Friday auctions…. Sunday?

Experiment and test
Brand new Lace Finch.

Not personal, business…

I need a lot of people to help me

I HAVE A LOT OF PEOPLE TO HELP ME

I HAVE PLENTY OF PEOPLE TO HELP ME AND KEEP ME ON TRACK.

I'll need a coach. I'm glad I said yes to R. Always say yes to opportunity, to growth.

4/27/17 Day 11

It's Thursday and I'm in Palmetto State Park in Gonzales TX.

I want to stay another night. I need a full day to work.

I woke up to a racoon having gotten into my camp box. He ate all my good chips.
My fault... I know better... always lock up your food at camp. I threw the rest of the crumbs to the critters and got to watch some squirrels and cardinals clean up the mess.

PRO_TIP: don't leave food where wildlife can get it. Put it in your car or make sure your coolers are locked and secure. If you're in bear country, go through the effort to tie up a bear bag or use the bear box if it's provided. If you don't, you might really wish you did.

Today's contemplations.
90-day goals
1. Get my head right
2. Find a place to land
3. Sell my old pieces
4. Paint 8 new paintings
5. Paint 8 nudes

8/25/17 insert: I got my head right! It takes ongoing maintenance to maintain.
Feel good. Do good.

4/28/17 Day 12

I didn't write last night. I was exhausted! I painted at the fountain all day. 6 hours or so, in the sun. I also announced it as an auction for Sunday from 10am to 10pm. Gotta hit the reserve which is half of the regular price.

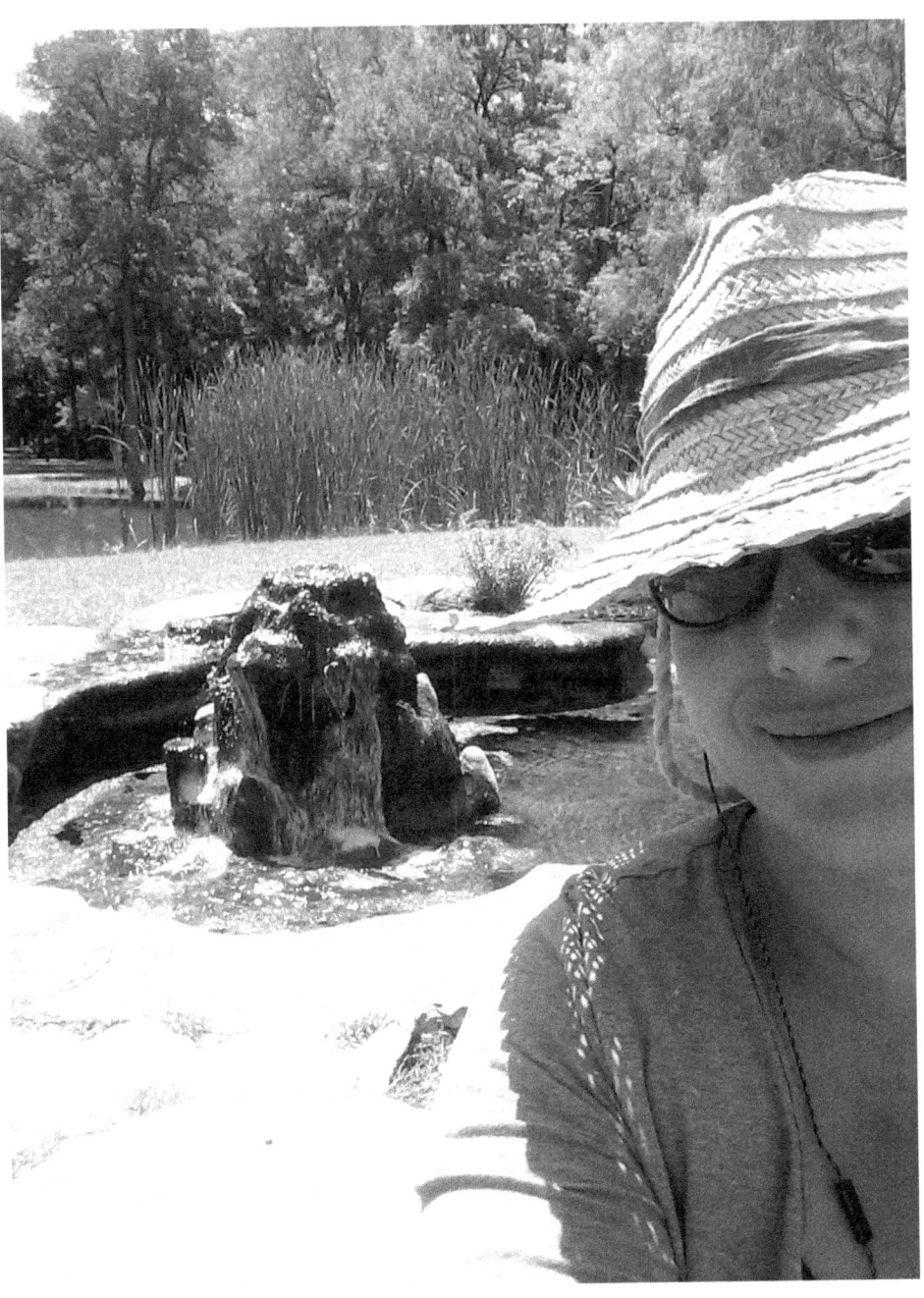

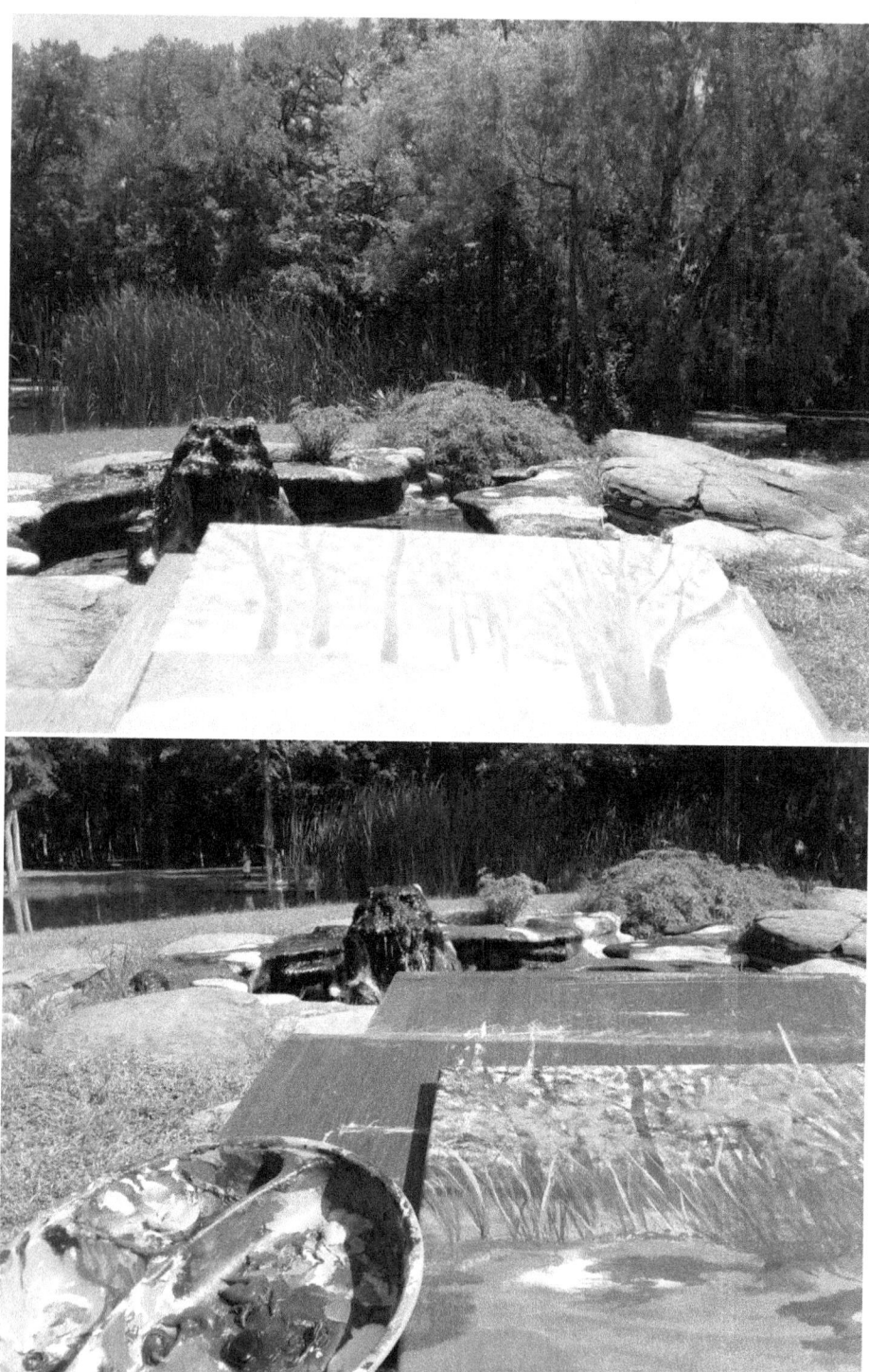

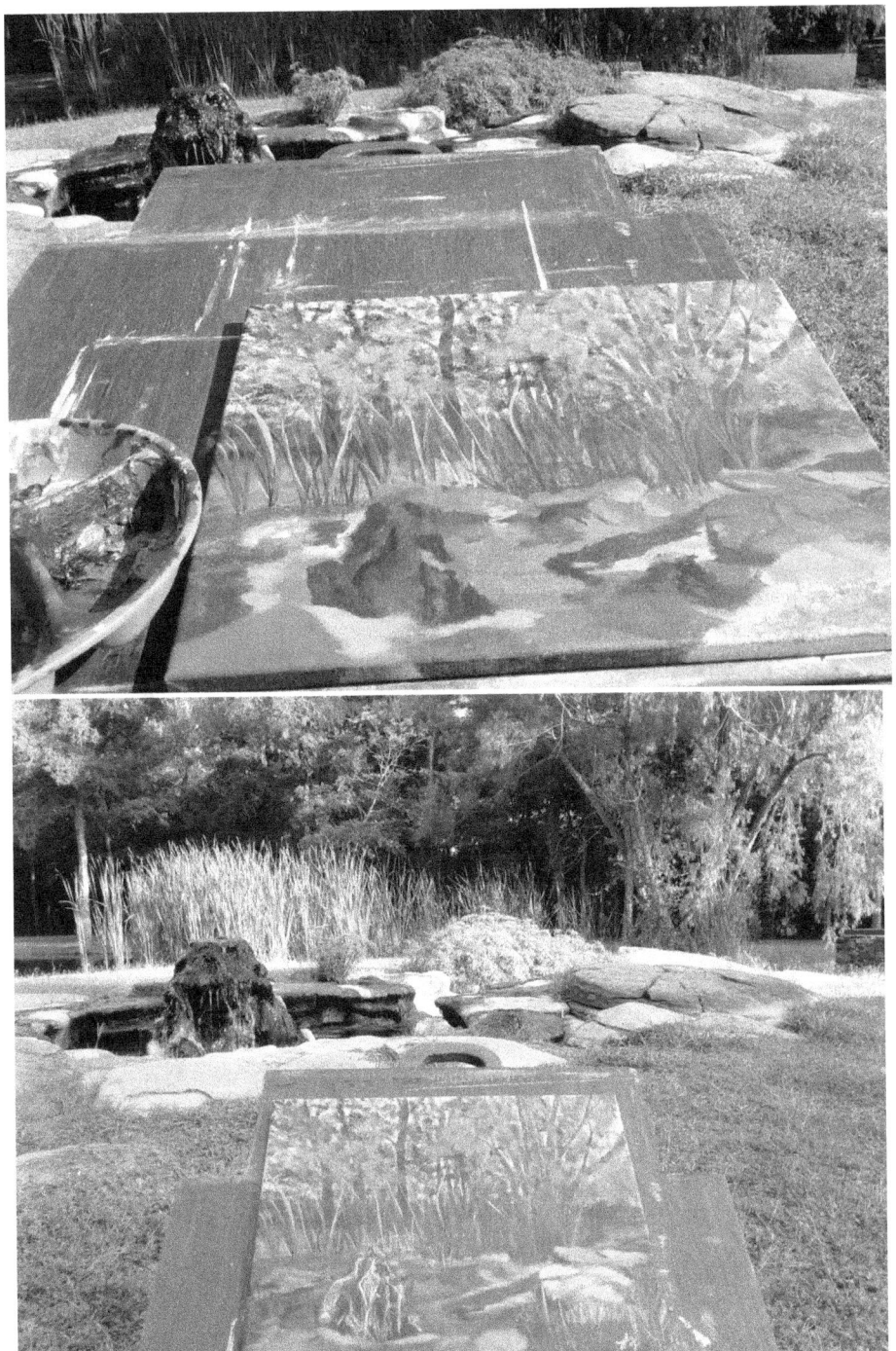

After painting I went back to camp to relax. I made a few phone calls to check in, then I broke down and called M. I told myself not to. I knew I shouldn't, but I did it anyway. It was superficial but he sounded good. It wasn't actually satisfying. I knew it wouldn't be. I've got to break this habit. I've got to break the tie in my mind!

Ask more questions! Ask better questions!

"I do not bring back from a journey quite the same self that I took." ~W. Somerset Maugham

4/29/17 Day 13 - San Antonio

Observe *Ask More Questions*

I left Palmetto yesterday morning and went to San Antonio.

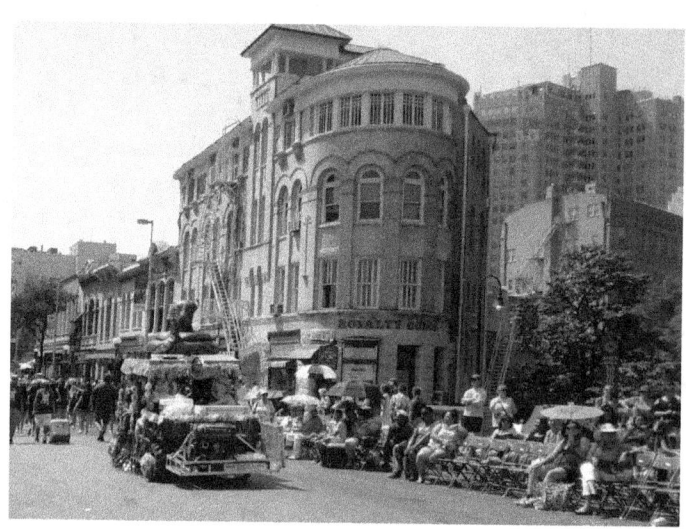

It was 94 degrees and humid.

I made it to San Antonio in time for the Fiesta Parade And $25 parking! OMG!

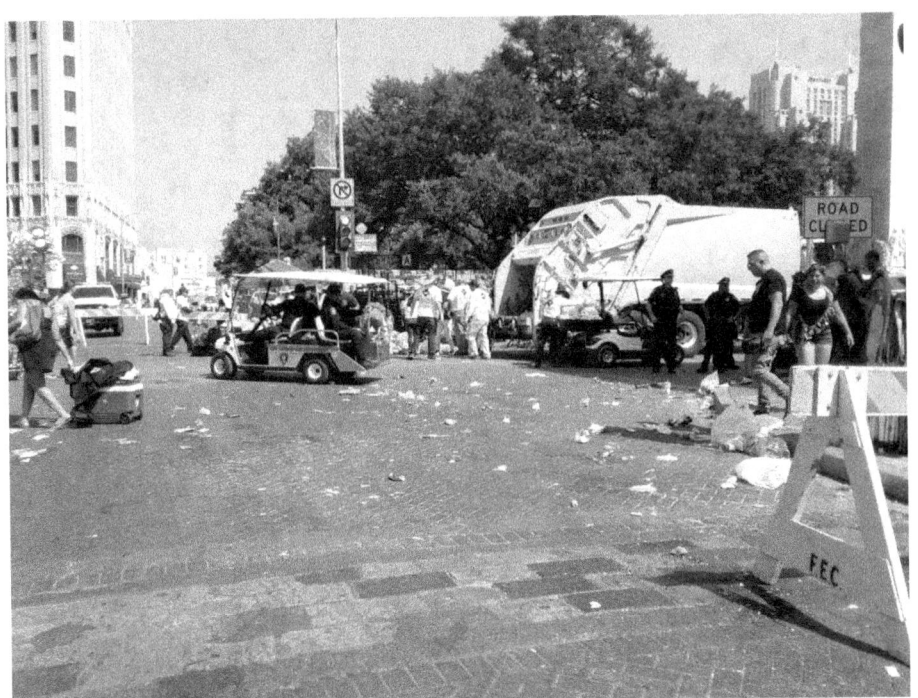

Look at all that trash! Anytime you find lots of people, you will always find lots of trash. Trash is starting to become a big topic. I'm noticing it more and more and more. A few years ago, I helped start a nonprofit in my hometown and one of our big things was picking up trash. Everyone complained about the trash and our community. They all claimed to want better but very few showed up for the work. The work is what makes the difference.

I've been to San Antonio before but even the river seemed dirtier this time. Maybe it's just Fiesta. I like San Antonio. It's kinda classic hip. There are tourists and it seems the arts are supported here. Today, there were artists set up along the canal.

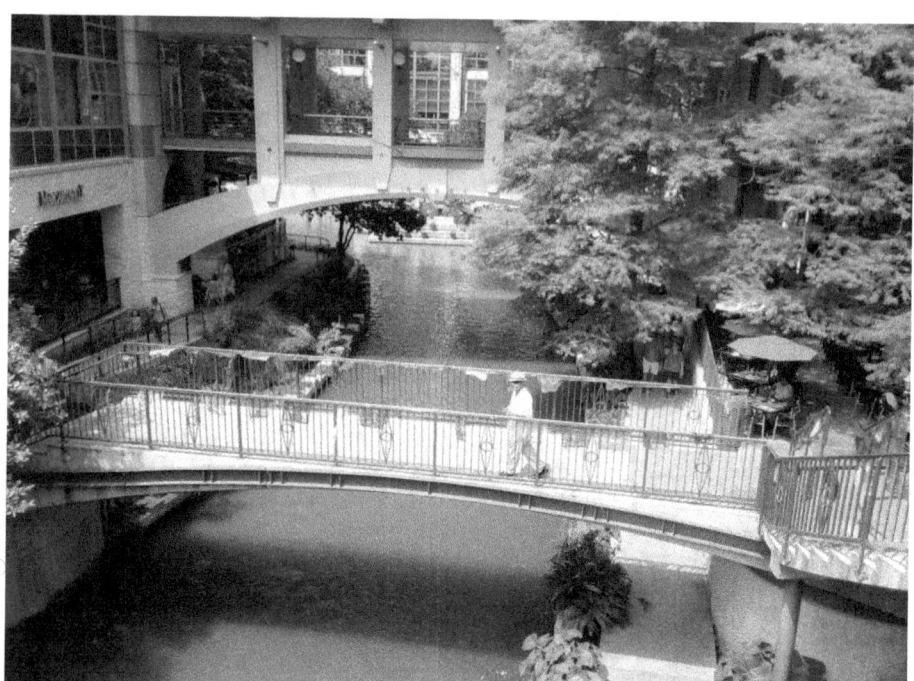

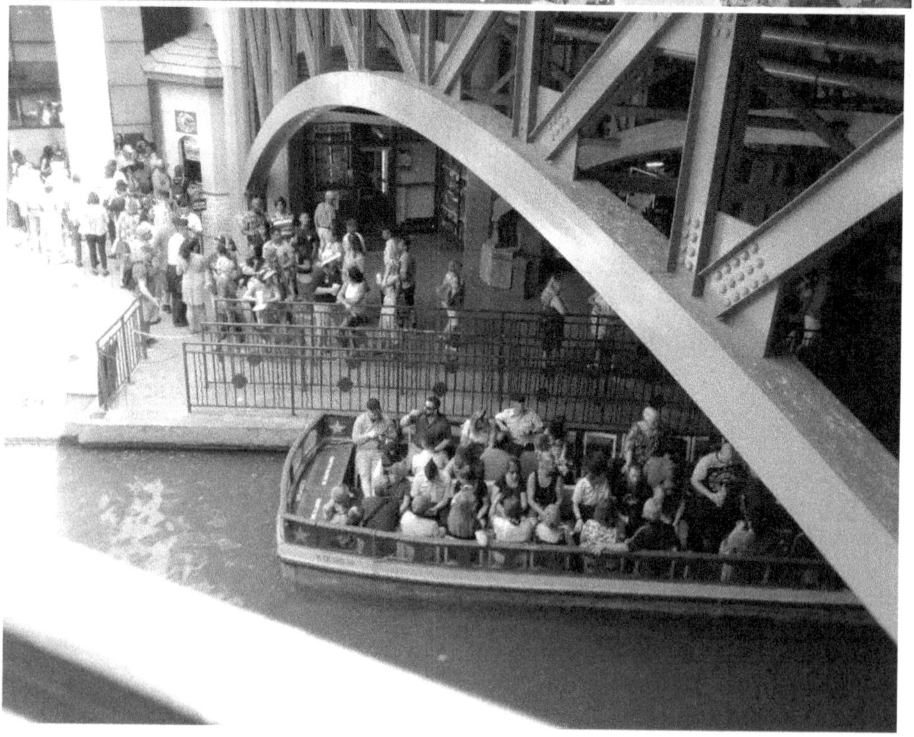

I also stopped at The Alamo and took some pictures. I didn't go in this time though. It was somehow inspiring however to see the flags lined up out front. Also, the big statue out front is pretty inspiring. I look for and see inspiration everywhere. Anything from trash to treasures, natural to manmade, can inspire the next great thought. Ideas inspire actions. Action puts the dream in motion.

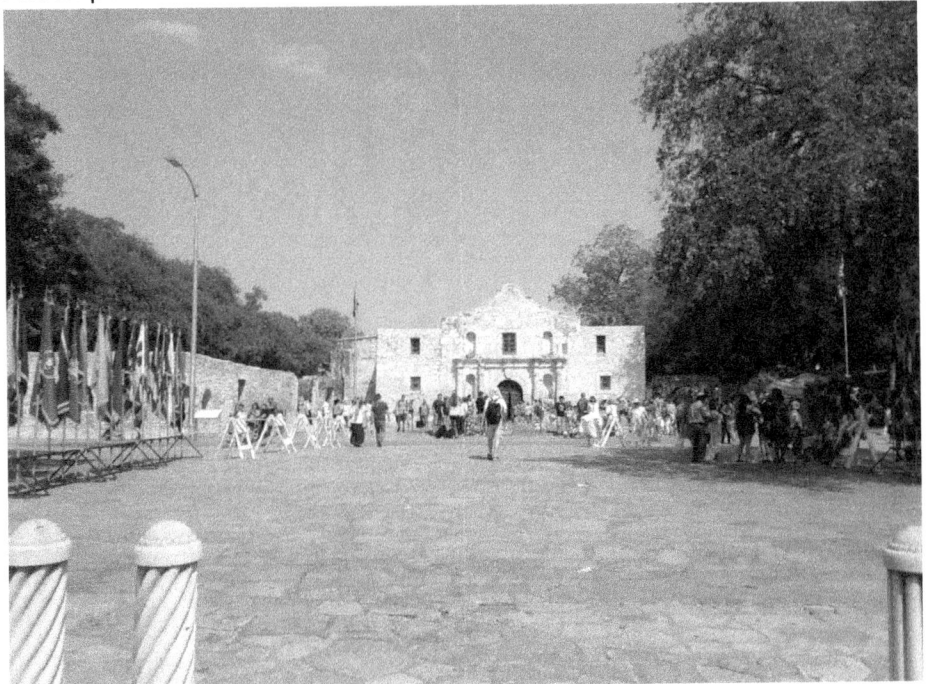

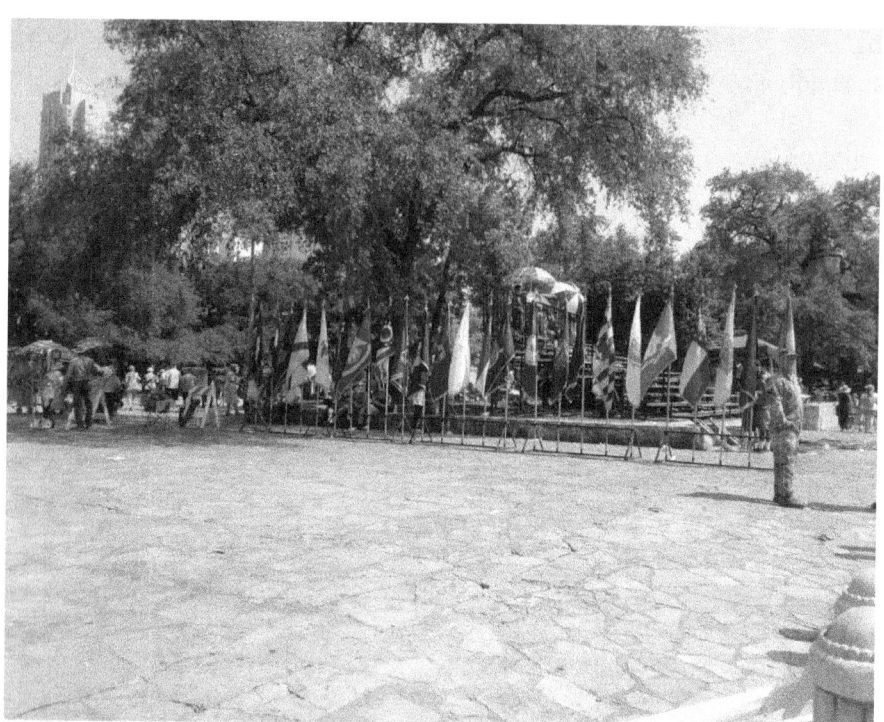

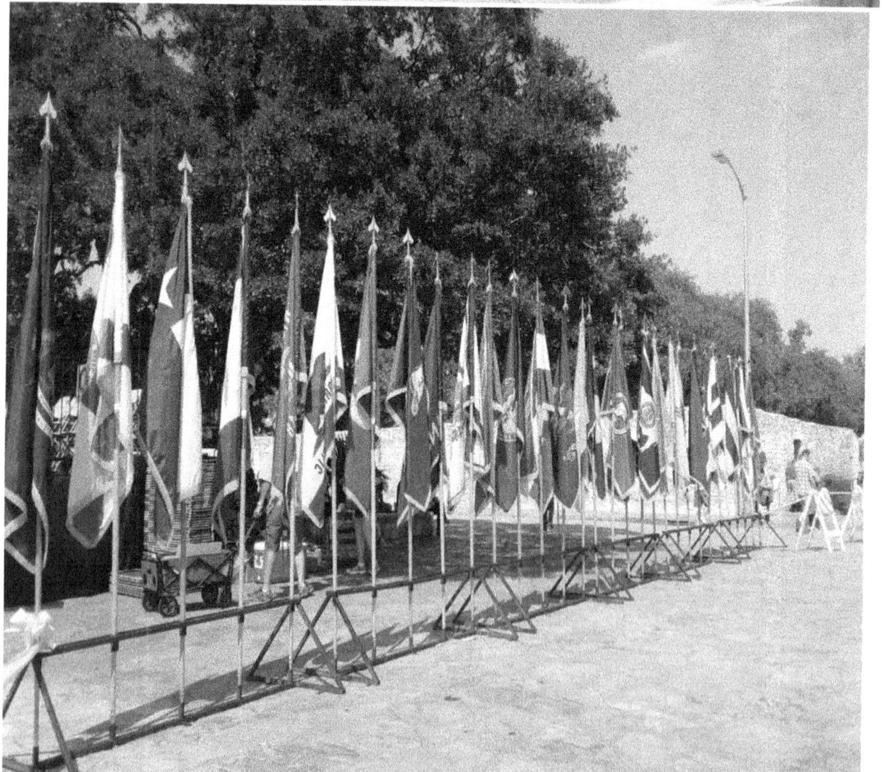

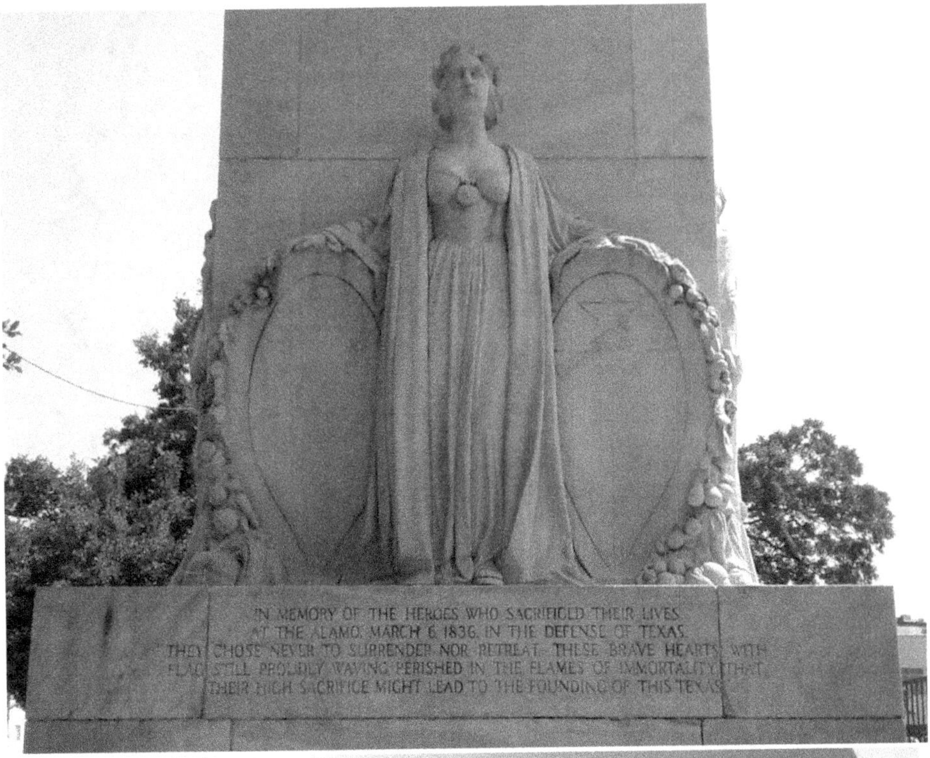

IN MEMORY OF THE HEROES WHO SACRIFICED THEIR LIVES
AT THE ALAMO, MARCH 6, 1836, IN THE DEFENSE OF TEXAS.
THEY CHOSE NEVER TO SURRENDER NOR RETREAT. THESE BRAVE HEARTS, WITH
FLAG STILL PROUDLY WAVING, PERISHED IN THE FLAMES OF IMMORTALITY THAT
THEIR HIGH SACRIFICE MIGHT LEAD TO THE FOUNDING OF THIS TEXAS.

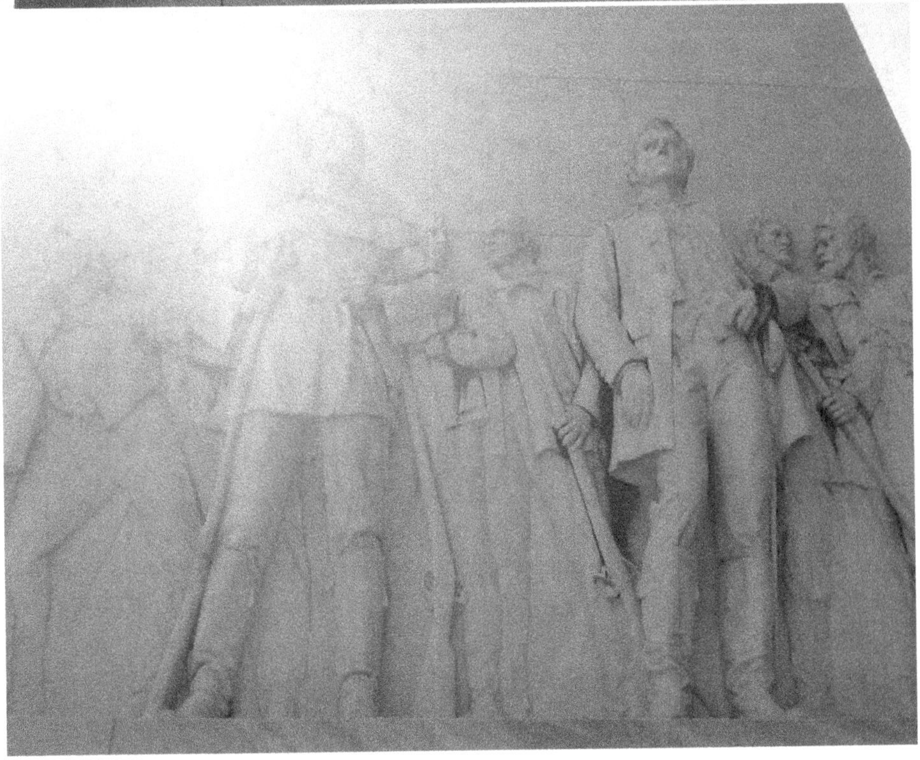

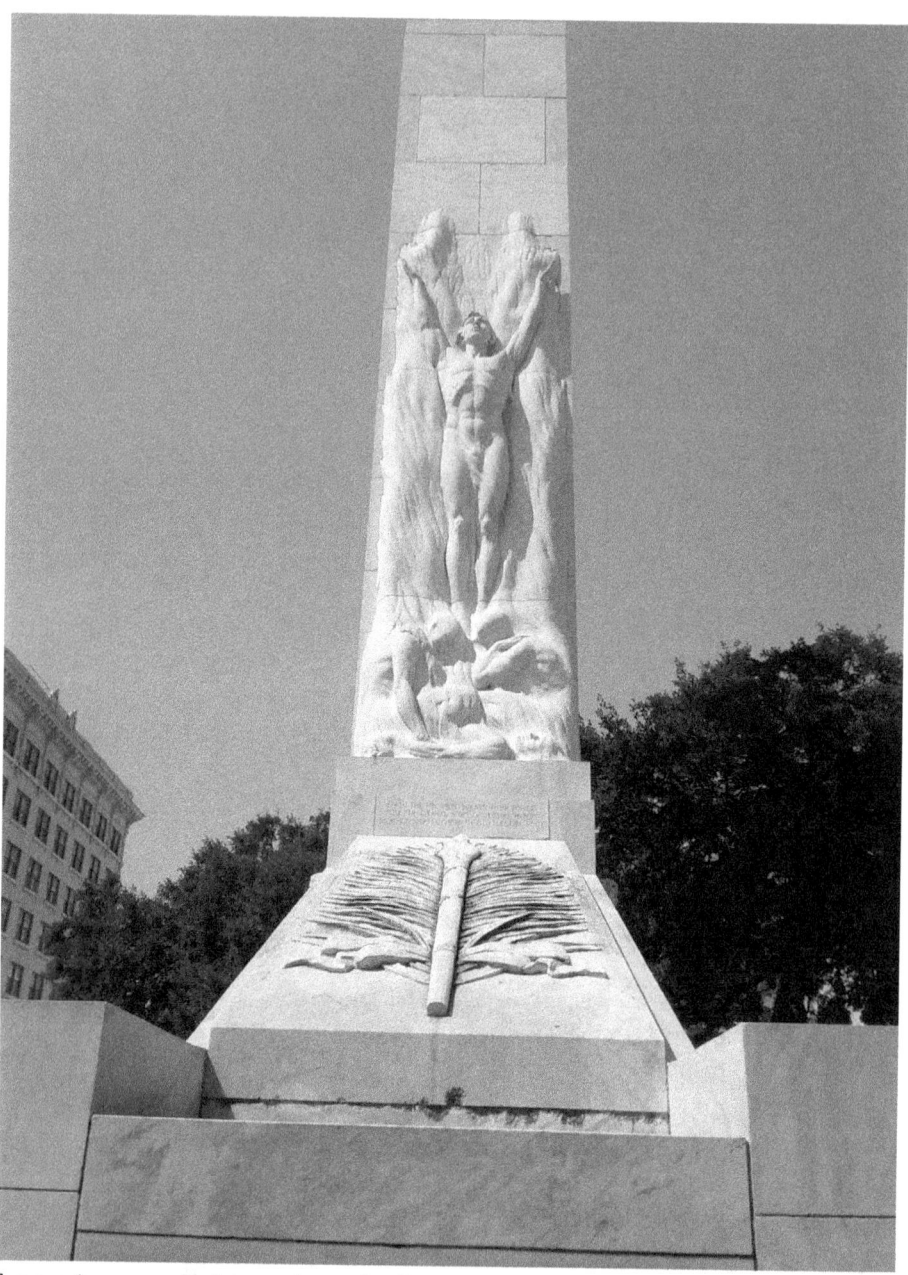

I spent a couple hours here in San Antonio. I watched the parade and wandered around the Riverwalk for a little while. I left around 4pm and drove toward Marfa, TX. It was HOT out and the city only made it hotter. Traffic was a bit dense too. It took a little while to get out of town.

Around sunset I stopped at a road-side park somewhere between San Antonio and Marfa. I'm not sure where.

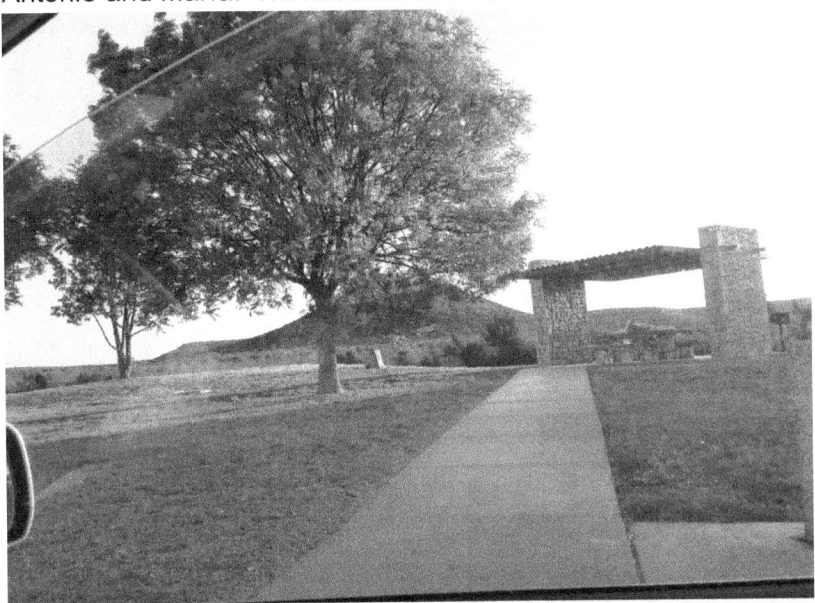

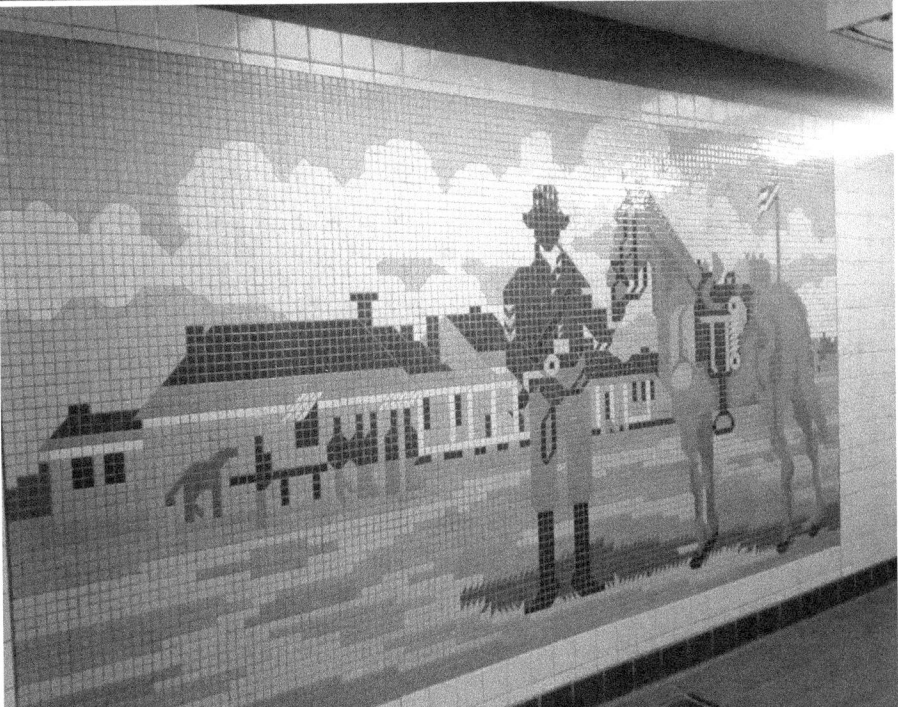

The bathroom at the rest area had this mosaic on the wall. That'd be fun to do one of these days. One of these days...

I got to Marfa this morning. It's only 55 degrees today as opposed to 94 yesterday.

As soon as I got to town, I looked for a campground. I found El Cosmico and set up camp. El Cosmico is a really cool campground with old trailers and RVS redone for cabins. There are also tent areas as well as hammocks. And outdoor showers. It's kinda wild and really neat.

After setting up camp I wandered around town and checked out a couple galleries. Marfa is an art town. An artist, Donald Judd established it. Judd is everywhere.

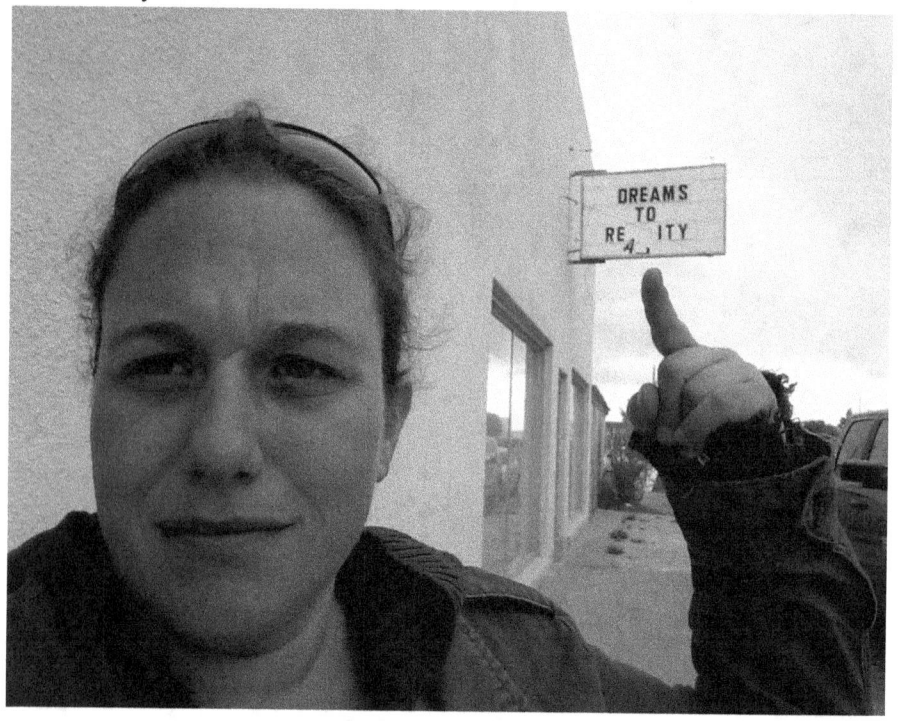

I went to the Ballroom gallery and a contemporary one. I forget the name of the second one. It was terrible in my opinion...

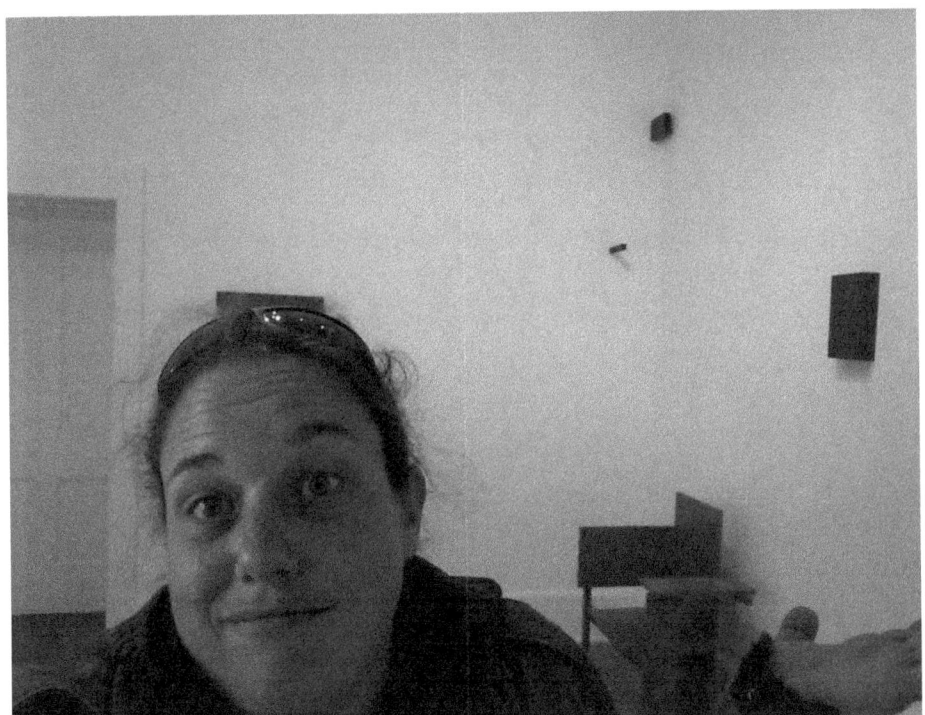

Square boxes and hexagons. I don't get it. The crystal structure drawings were interesting though.

Ballroom, on the other hand, was good. Weird. But good.
Strange Attractors was the show at Ballroom.

There was a film playing called "F for Fibonacci" that was interesting. Like a fly on the wall of someone else's life interesting… it would cut from talking about the Fibonacci sequence to watching a kid create a Minecraft world and a character named Mr. Money. I don't know… It made very little sense, but I couldn't stop watching.

The boatman from the River Styx was also there. He was a sculpture made of fungus; mycelium; mushrooms. Mushrooms grow on dead things.

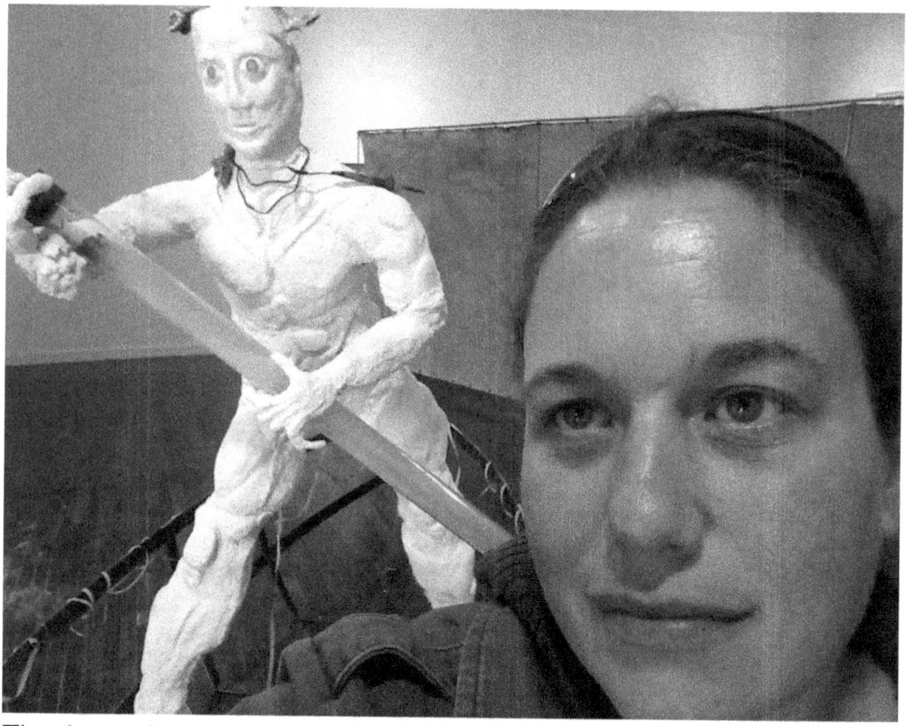

The desert floor tapestry was also interesting.

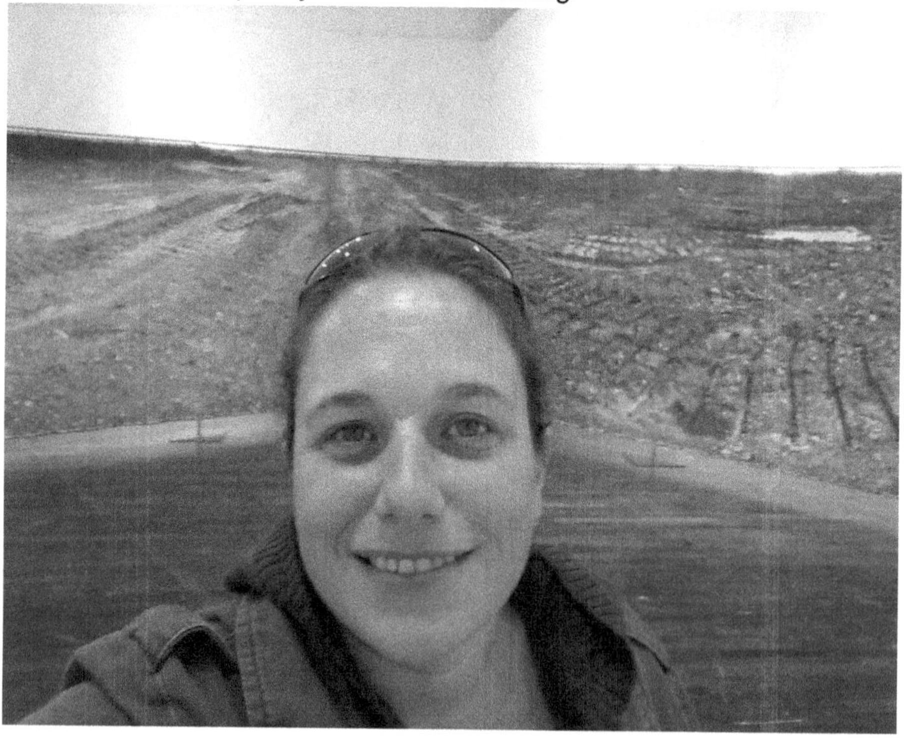

I couldn't take any more after the contemporary place though. Squares and hexagons made of wood and metal... it does nothing for me but makes my eyes roll.

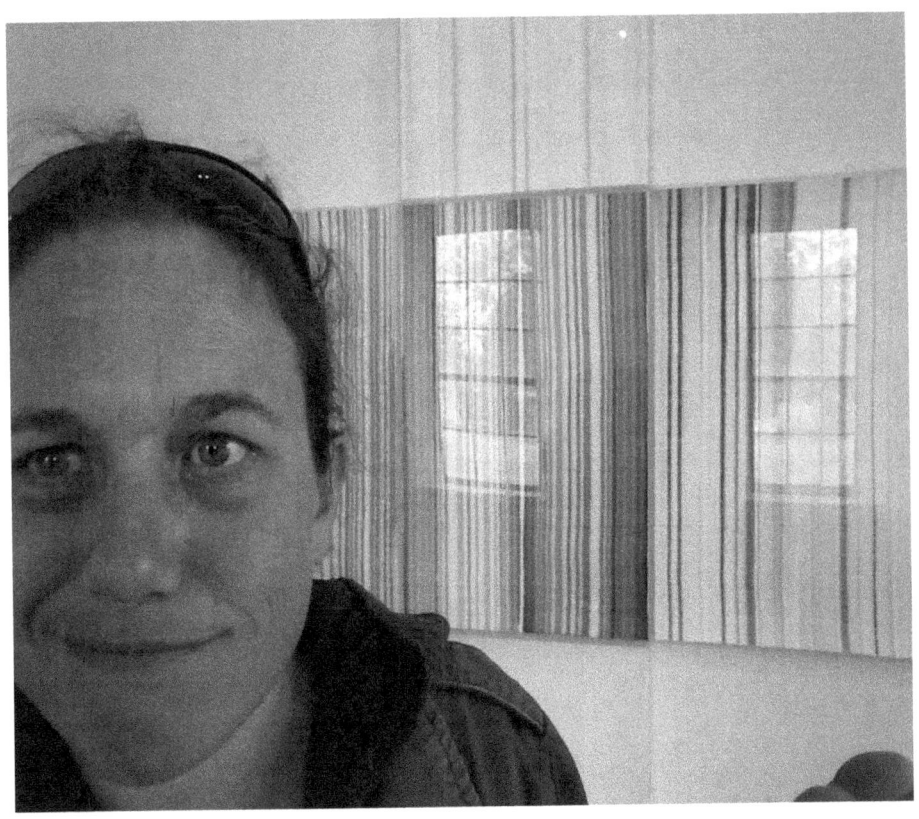

What is art? What is modern art? What is contemporary art? What is real art? Is it art just because it's created? Is there some qualification? Is art from the artist or the ether? Is it contrived or inspired? What is inspiration? Where does inspiration come from? Are these things inspired like my paintings are inspired? Like some are inspired? Does it depend on the outcome or the intention?

I don't get it...

Like the Prada store... What is that? Total absurdity? Absurdly amusing? Amusing in its ridiculousness? We'll see... I think I'll pass it on my way out of town tomorrow.

After the museums, I had lunch at a little Tex-Mex place in town then went to take a nap. In my tent. At the campground with outdoor showers that are nowhere near the tent area…

Suddenly, I woke up. My stomach was gurgling. I sleep naked. I'm in a tent. It's cold.

I hurried and got dressed and walk-ran the hundred yards or more to the bathrooms as fast as I could.

I didn't make it.

Now I have to take a shower. Outside. It's 50 degrees.

And now my clothes are wet.

And I'm wet.

It's cold.

Oy…

I went back to my tent and put on long johns, fleece pajamas, and all my blankets. It's still cold. It's shivering cold.

Tomorrow I'll have to do laundry.

Screw this cold! It's nearing dark. It's only going to get colder. I think I'll drive out to see the Marfa Lights and turn on the heat. Then at least I'll go to bed warm.

———————

There's a lookout/rest stop along Hwy 10 near Marfa where you can view the lights. It's said or questioned what these lights are. Is it paranormal? Extraterrestrial? Manmade?
I don't know…

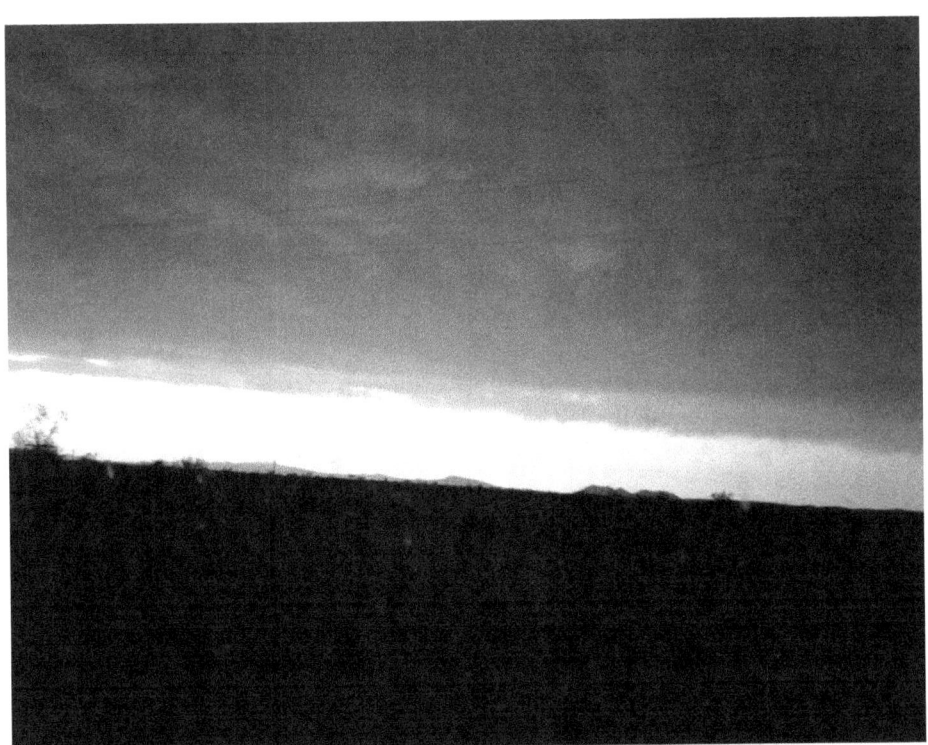

It was cloudy when I got there but eventually the cloudiness cleared and you could see the lights. I sat and did a live video (I can't find it now) and talked about being an observer and deciding what you see for yourself, not letting others tell you what you should see or how you should feel.

On that note, I won't tell you what I think the Marfa Lights are. Go have the experience for yourself. You tell me. Part of the fun is the journey; part is in the anticipation.

4/30/17 Day 14

And I thought it was cold yesterday… it's 25 degrees Fahrenheit this morning. Thankfully I had enough blankets. I stayed warm. Only my nose was cold.

The ground was hard and lumpy though, even with a found sleeping pad under my mattress pile. I kinda wish I'd slept in the car. But cleaning up after my accident would have been even more difficult.

To do:
>
>   Laundry
>   Auction
>   Head toward Carlsbad Caverns

After laundry, I packed up and headed toward the caverns.

Just outside of Marfa is the Prada Store. The absurdity of a high dollar frivolous store that no one can enter that sits in the desert alone, is pretty much the concept. That is what the artists intended to build.

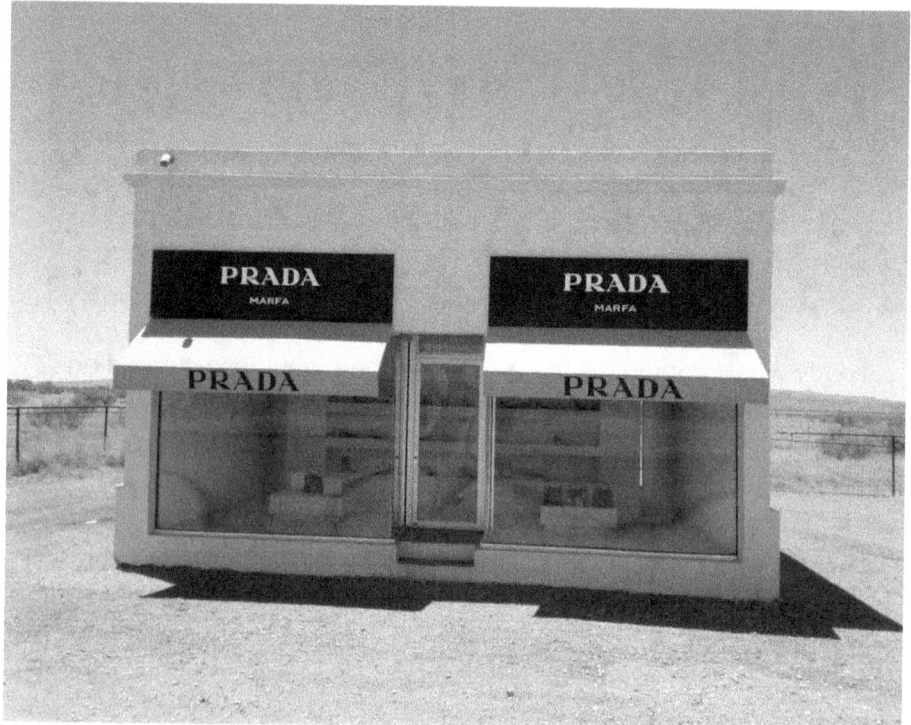

But, that's not all that the Prada Store is, as it turns out.

"If you build it, they will come." ~ Field of Dreams

There is a fence surrounding the back side of the property and the people who've stopped there leave something for the next people to find. There are all sorts of neat little trinkets and such from the travelers' journeys. A small sense of community on this solo trip. A community of travelers.

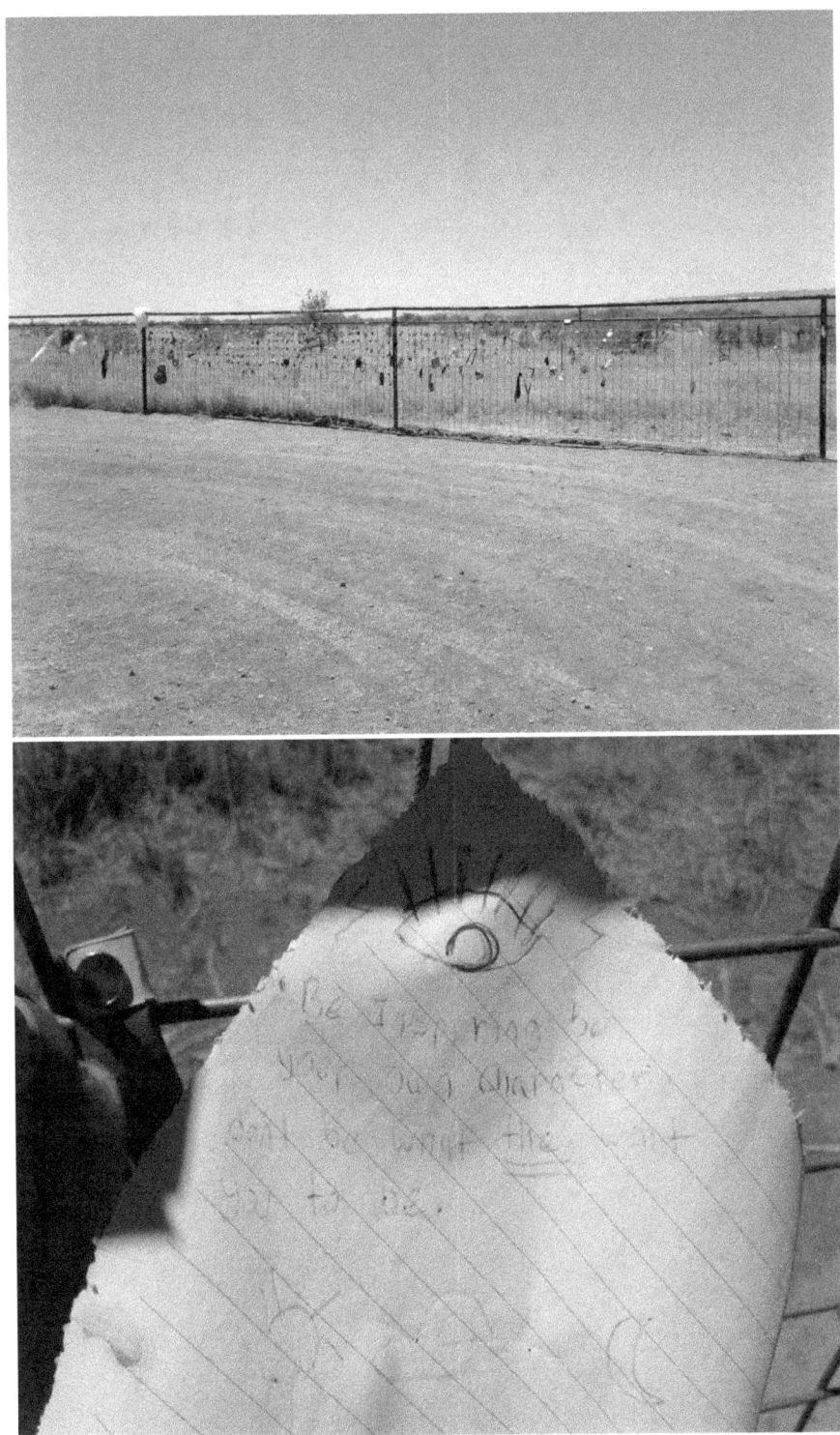

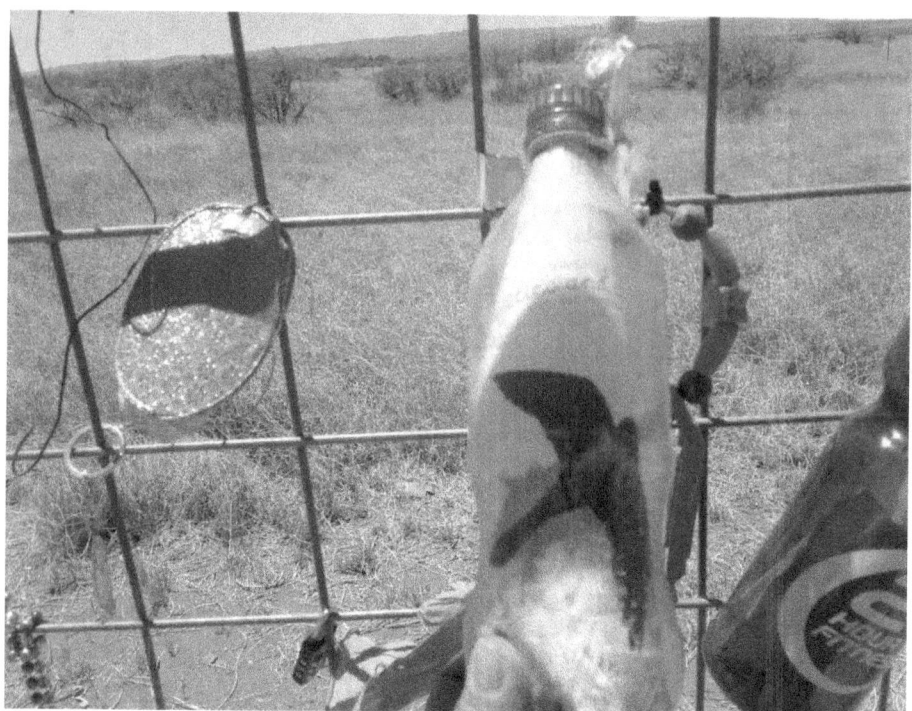

I tied an empty pop bottle to the fence and stuck a note from my journal in it. The quote on the journal page said: "I have traveled through cities and countries wide, and everywhere I went, the world was on my side". I wrote: "Don't let fear stop you from seeking your dreams." ~LF

What is art? It is connection.

_____

The rest of the drive to Carlsbad was pretty with views of the desert and Guadalupe Mountains.

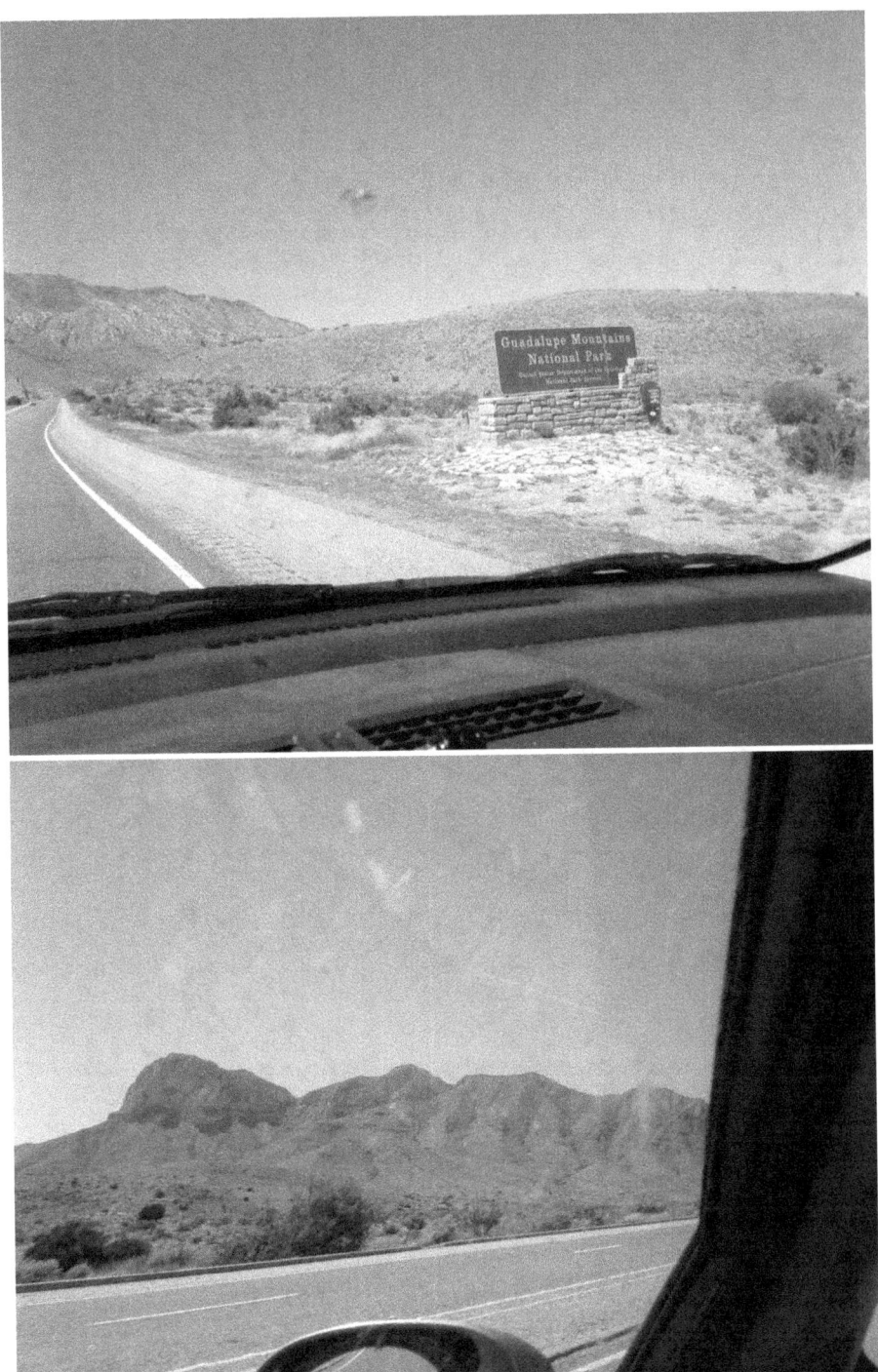

Pro-Tip: Stop at the grocery at the first place you see one after Marfa or even in Marfa. There's not much at the base of Carlsbad; a gas station/tourist trap, campground, hotel, and a diner. The diner was ok… but there weren't many options. If I'd bought hot dogs, I would have had a fire that night

Aliens… tomorrow I'm headed to Roswell…

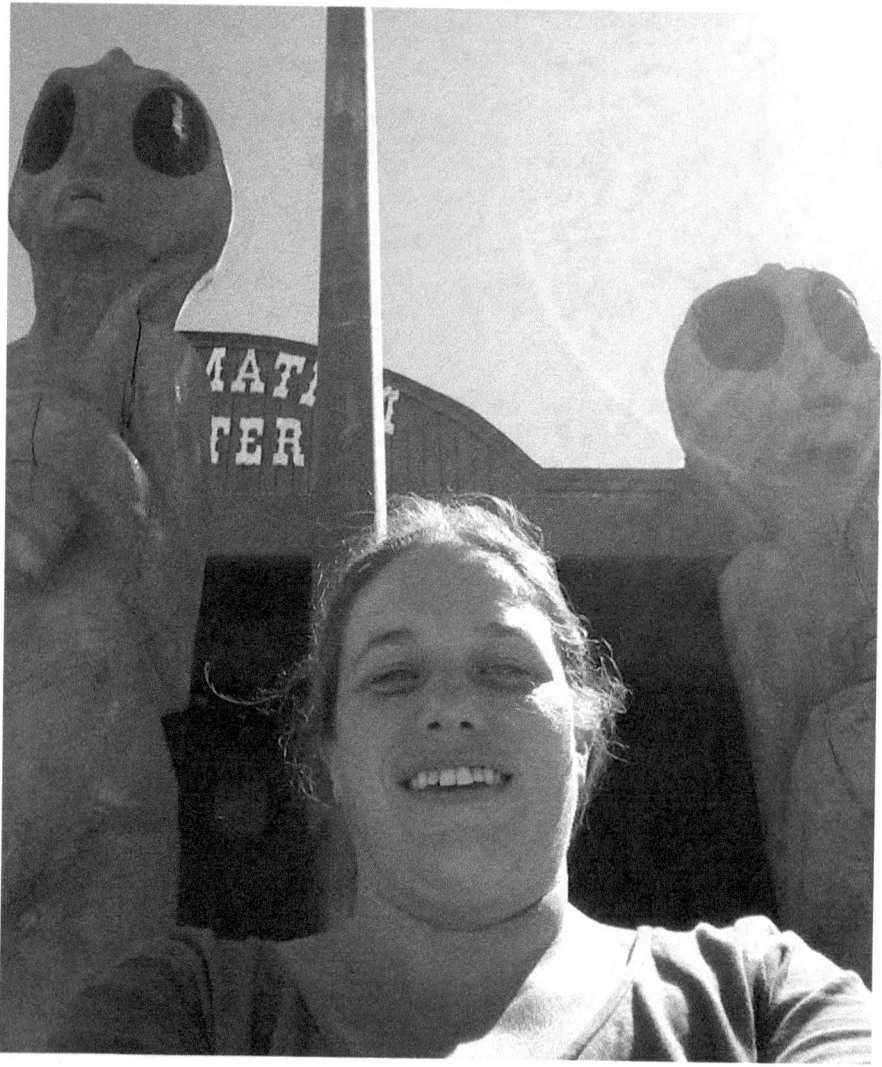

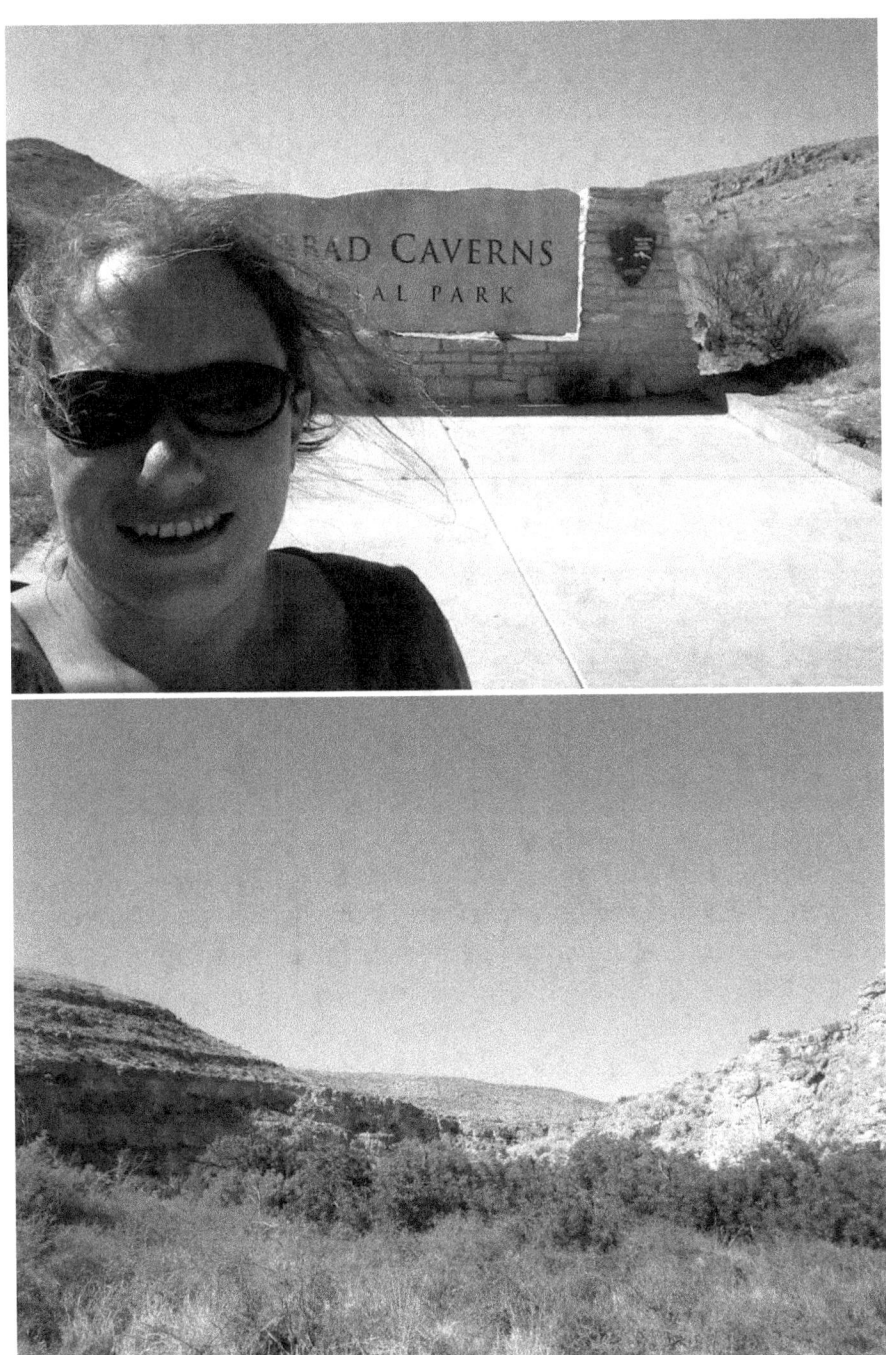

I got to Carlsbad too late... I'll have to sleep nearby and do the tour tomorrow. I asked the cute park ranger at the info counter if there are any free campsites nearby. He pointed me back down the mountain and a few miles down the highway to some Bureau of Land Management land where I could camp. He said I'd see where others have had a fire pit before. Means Rd.

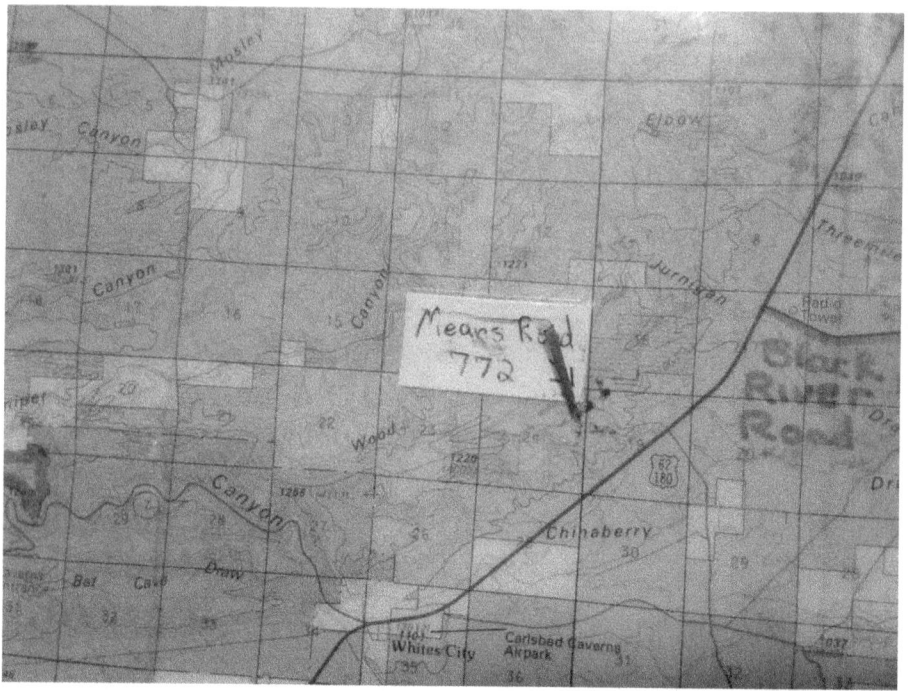

I went to where he said. The road is a bit rough but not too bad. Gertie made it to the first flat and campsite just fine. I didn't push her any farther though. She doesn't have very good ground clearance and I don't want to ask for trouble.

Means Road takes a left and curves up the side of a foot hill. It sits overlooking a work site or something across the highway. After dark, you can see the glow of a city in the distance. I park Gertie with her back to the hillside and facing the view over the desert.

It's dark but there is a full moon. It lights up the white gravel road like a trail of silver or snow.

The sky is so clear! So many stars!

Gerties' back window makes for fabulous star gazing from my bed.

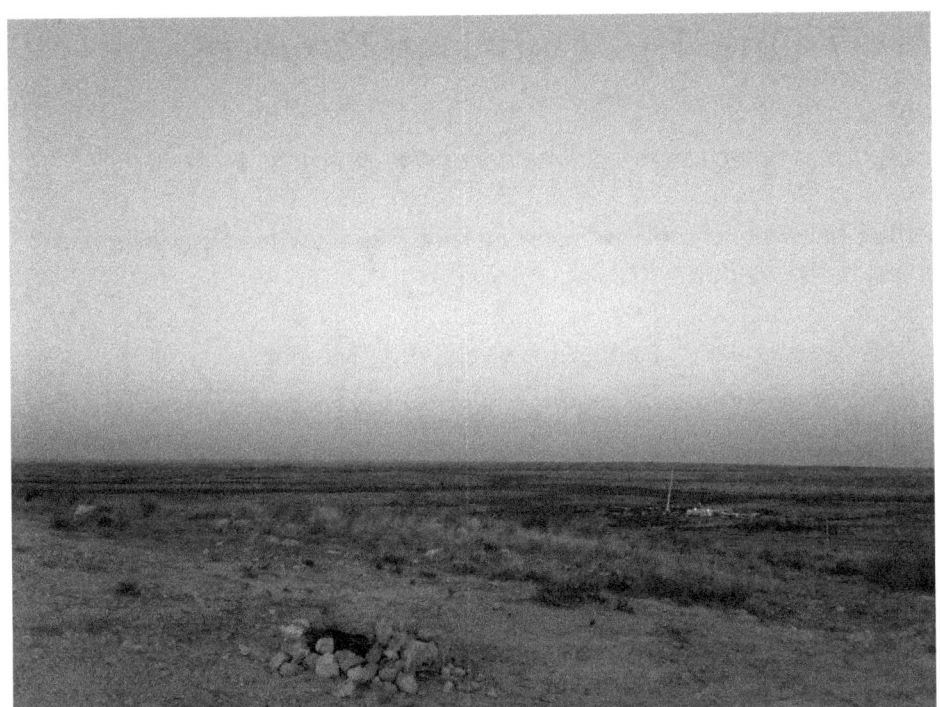

I'm not sure I've had this good of view since I left Arkansas.

Arkansas…

Where am I going to land after this? I don't fucking know…

Tonight, I'll just enjoy this view.

5/1/17 Day 15 - Carlsbad Caverns

OMG!

This spot that hottie ranger told me about was amazing! Perfect!

Perched halfway up a hill with an amazing sky view from my bed and Gerties' hatch window.

The view was amazing! I slept Amazing! I AM AMAZING!

And the SUNRISE! Freaking Breathtaking!

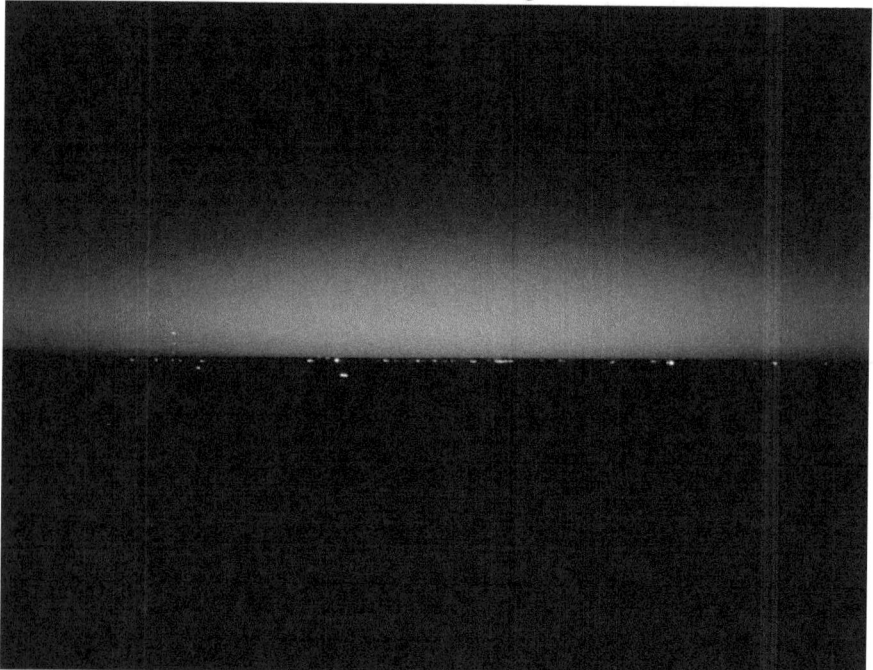

It was clear skies and the colors!
Blue and turquoise and green and yellow and red and orange! WOW!

The sunrise was over, and I was dressed and headed back to the cavern by 6am.

I was starving and needed coffee. I had a couple snacks with me but, coffee. Must have coffee…

The gas station is closed!

Shit!
Doesn't open until 8!
Shit!
Everything is closed!
Shit!

The hotel lobby was open though and they have the standard free continental breakfast.

I debated my next actions for a very long time...

do I ask first? What if she says no...?

What if I just do it and she questions me!?

What if I don't get coffee!?
Coffee...

It's free, but technically, it's stealing. I'm not a guest.

She won't know I'm not a guest. She has no idea who checked in yesterday.

It's free to guests. Surely someone else is skipping their breakfast this morning.

They won't miss it.

wait...

There goes a guy with his own mug!
She wasn't even looking at him!
No questions at all...
I have a mug...
It's just coffee...

It's all you can drink for guests...
This is just one cup...

...

...

...

She didn't even look up!

I walked right in and got my coffee and she didn't even look up!

(So, I grabbed a muffin too)

Pro-Tip: This goes for anything in life... Just look like you belong and sound like you belong and no one will even question you. Also, don't steal...

_____

The ride up the mountain was gorgeous and the coffee was amazing!

Desert flora and informational stops all along the way.

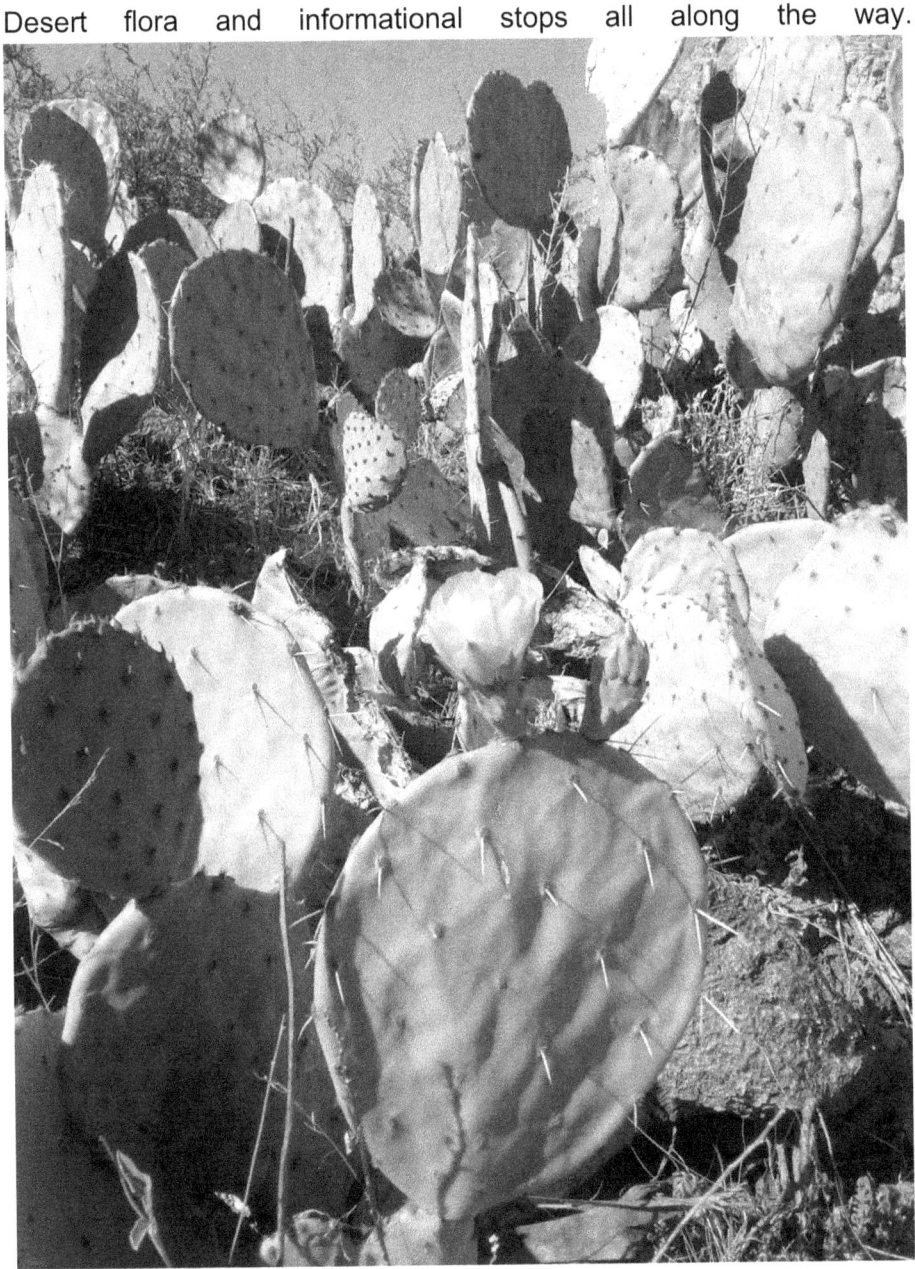

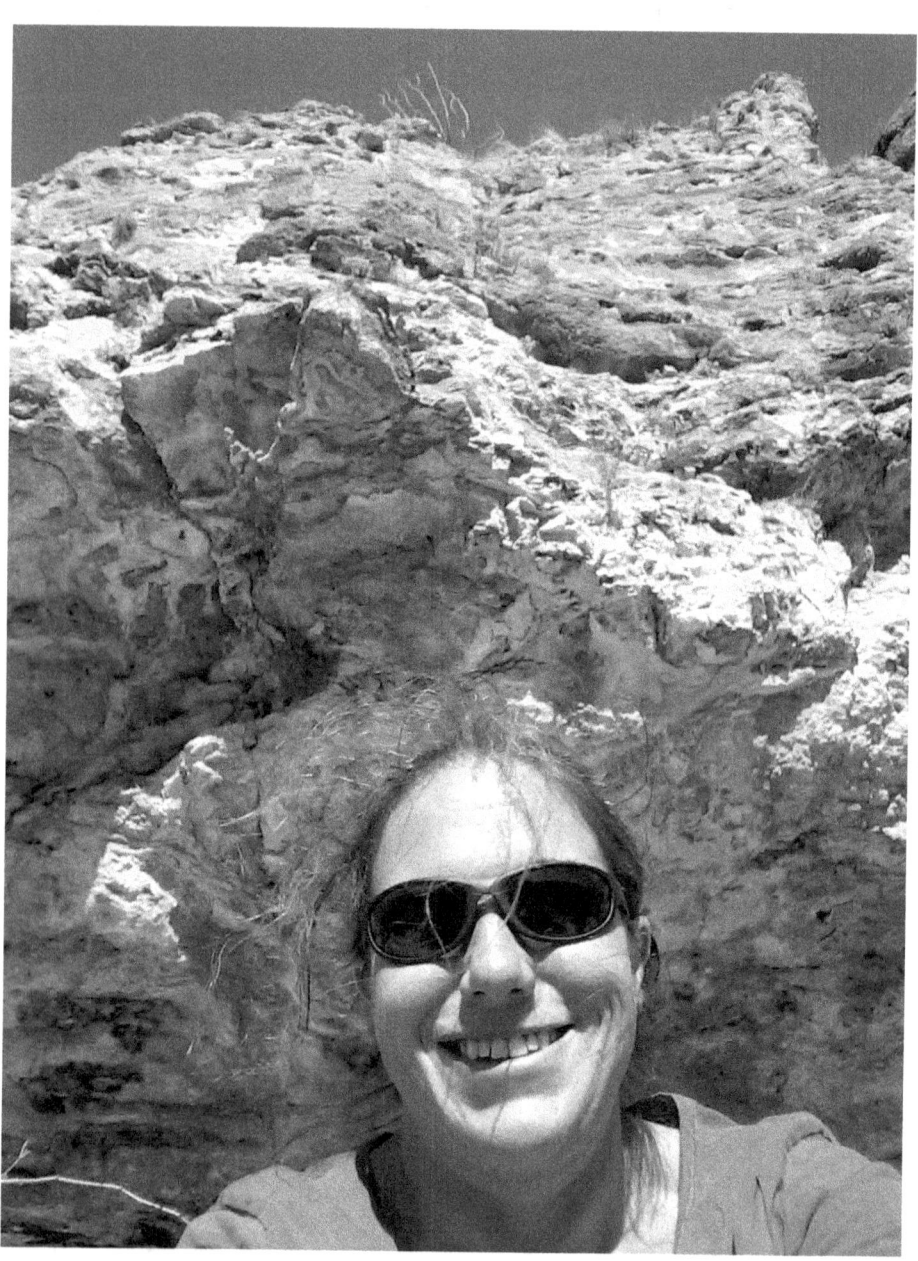

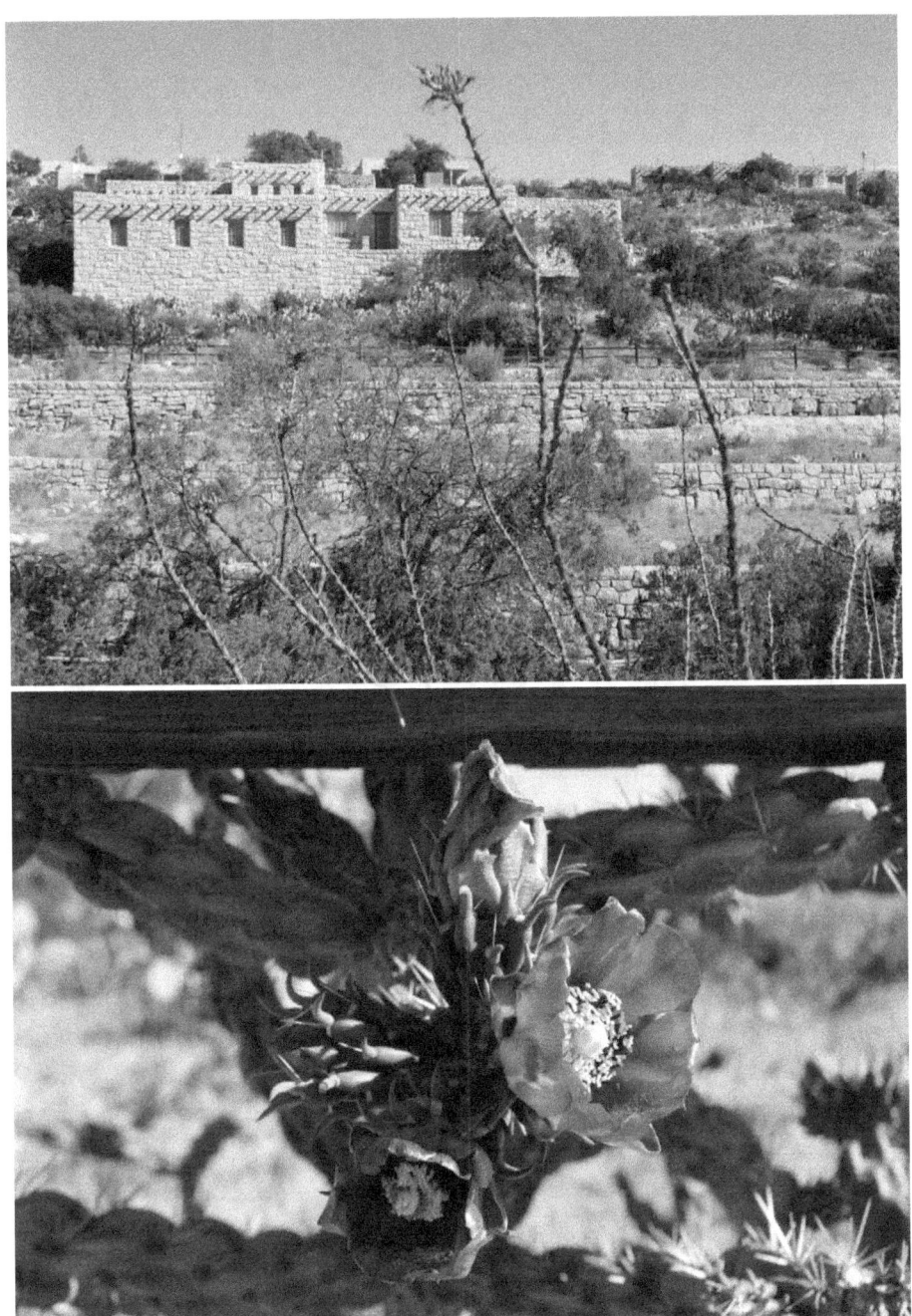

I got to the top before anyone else and the tour doesn't open for another hour or so.

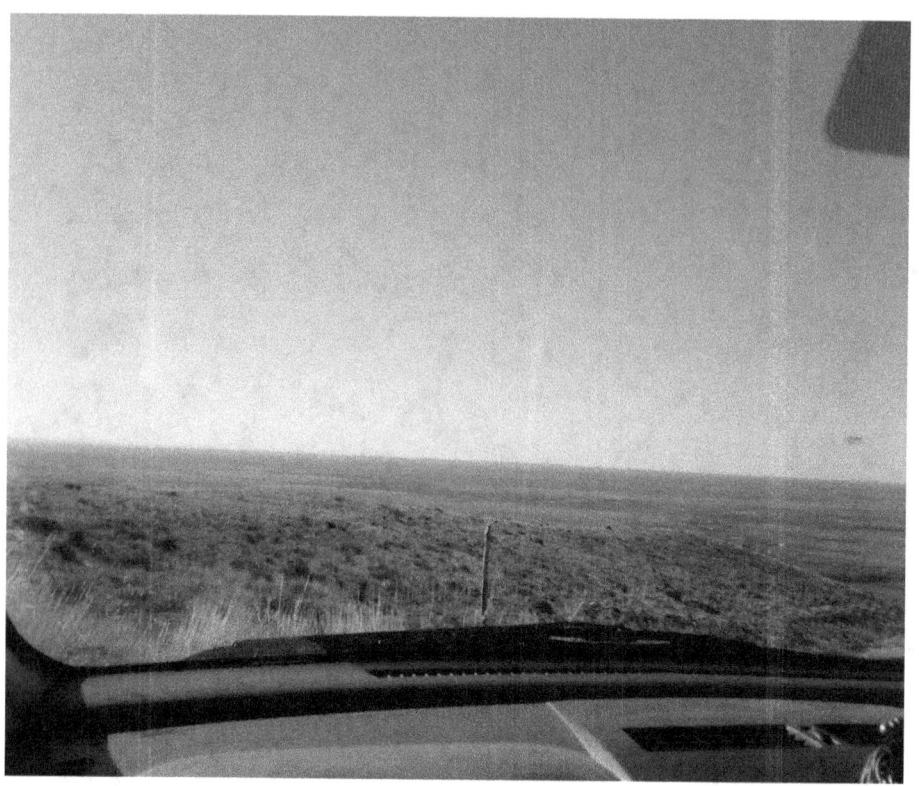

There's an amazing view up here.

I get to sit, think, and meditate this morning with an amazing view and a free cup of coffee.

I've been learning about marketing and branding lately. That's what my conference was.
There is a lot of information to take in.

We've been talking about sales funnels and landing pages and launches.

I could do live painting videos or video tutorials or giveaways as a lead magnet…

Also thinking about my coach. And goals… Uncover and resolve blockages.

I need an assistant... and a social media manager... social feels so hard for me... The resistance is strong... I'll have to flip it...

Social Media is easy.
People who like me and my art want to know what I'm up to.
It's not annoying if I'm not annoying.
I need to put myself and my art out there if people are to see it.
Art must be seen.

After the cavern I'll head toward Roswell. It's hot and there is a campground there called Bottomless Lakes. Maybe I can swim...

I know, I can paint Lace Finch Art on my car! Free advertising. maybe I'll get followers that way!

I can do live paintings when I stop.

opt in for weekly live plein-air on Tuesday, replay on Thursday, auction Sunday.

(present day insert... "At this time next year, you'll wish you had started today" ~ Jen Kem)

On to the cavern...

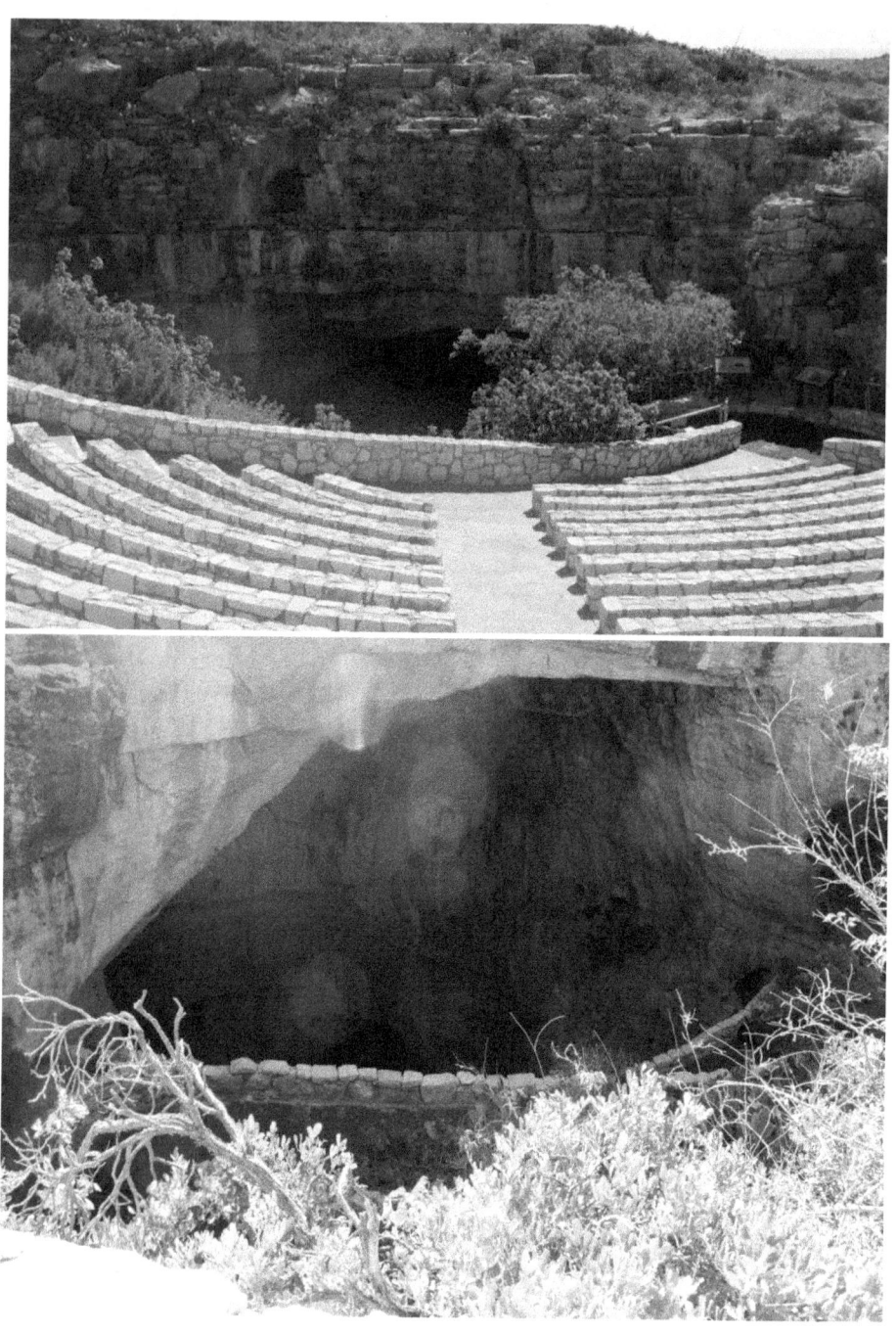

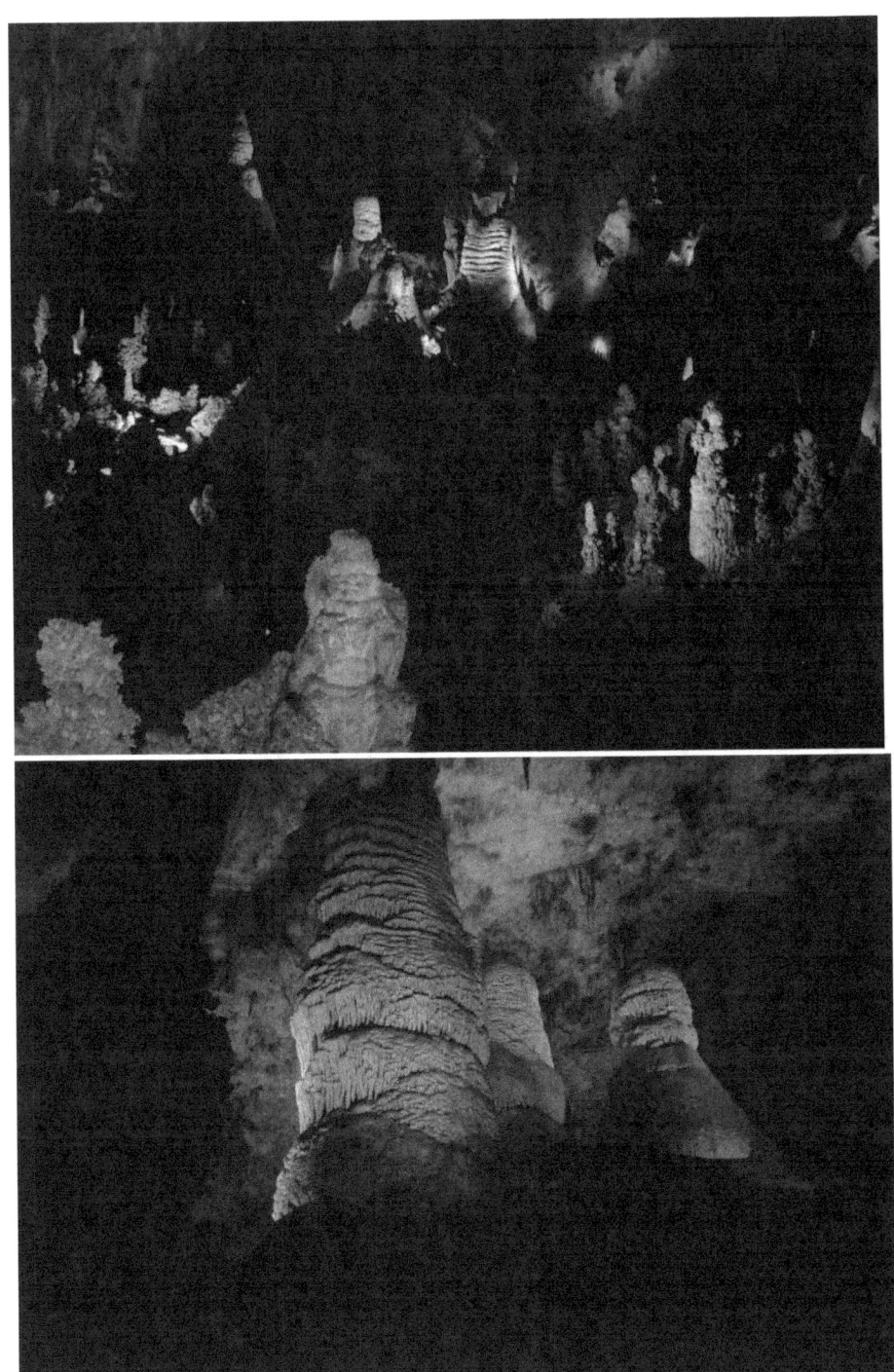

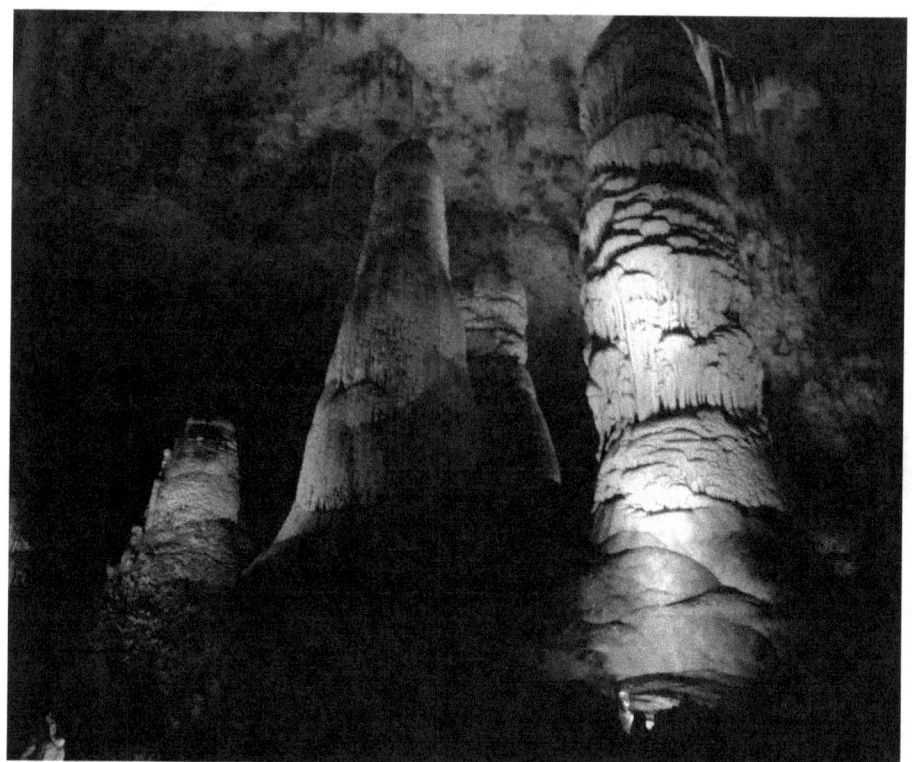

The caverns were neat. Since they are underground, the temperature stays around 50 degrees or so. The cool temp was especially awesome on such a hot day.

These formations, stalactites, stalagmites, soda straws, etc. are kind of amazing and awe inspiring if you think about it. They are slowly formed from the minerals deposited from consistent drops of water over long periods of time.

After the cavern I headed to Roswell. I went out to the campground first thinking I'd get set up, take a dip then take care of business in Roswell tomorrow.

It's like 105 degrees, I'm hot and sweaty and I might stink…

I get to the campground and I'm totally disappointed. The campground has lakes, kinda… But the water is low and the campground is a gravel parking lot with no shade… No way, I'll pass…

95

But shit, now where am I gonna stay!?

Shit! I'm out of data!

I go back to Roswell and spend like 3 hours getting my phone situation figured out and then find out that the next nearest campground is a couple of   hours   away.

The phone part took so long because for some reason I couldn't just upgrade my phone to completely unlimited so I ended up getting a second phone activated. I don't know why... I don't remember...

Phone thing figured out; I race over to the alien museum. I've gotta see something alien while I'm here. Area 51 is off limits, of course...

I thought I was going to go to the crash site but it's actually private property and though they used to let people check it out, they don't anymore.

It's nearing close. I hope the museum will still let me in. I can't leave Roswell without having seen something Alien.

———

They let me in!
It was pretty neat. Interesting documents and pictures and art.

I'm   glad   they   let   me   in.

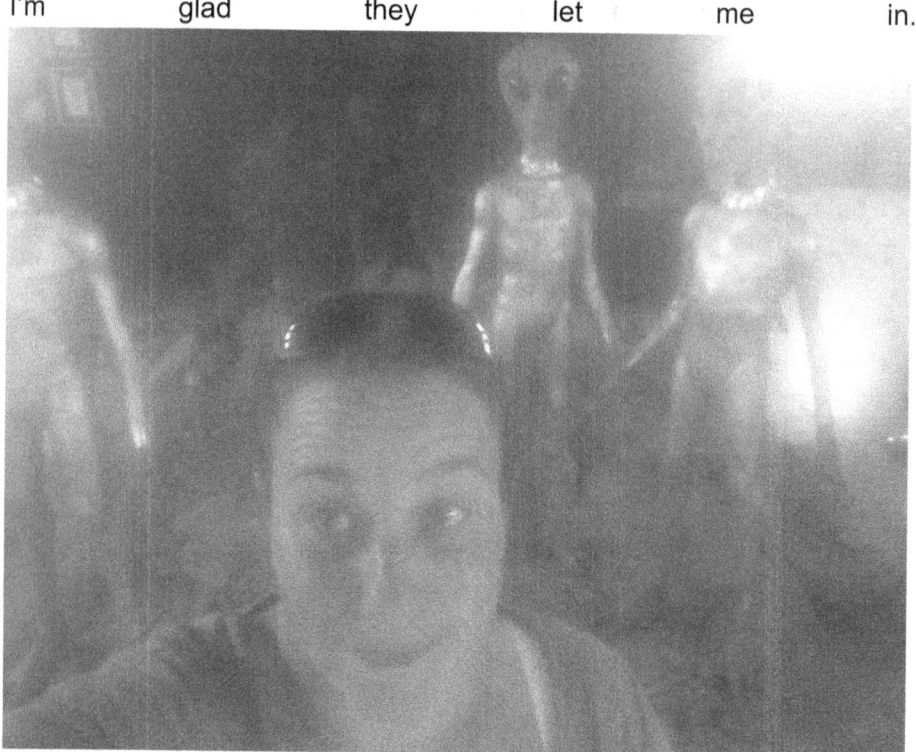

Next stop is now Villanueva State Park instead of Las Cruces.

Be adaptable.

By the time I get thru the museum and get my shit together with the phone stuff, it's nearing dark.

I drove to Villanueva in the dark. I hate driving in the dark; you can't see things. It was an interesting drive though. You could make out the silhouettes of trees and see some fence lines. It felt like big ranch country. At some point you could start to tell we were climbing. And, I may or may not have seen a moose or an elk or a sasquatch or something.

5/2/17 Day 16 - Villanueva State Park, New Mexico

This park is gorgeous!

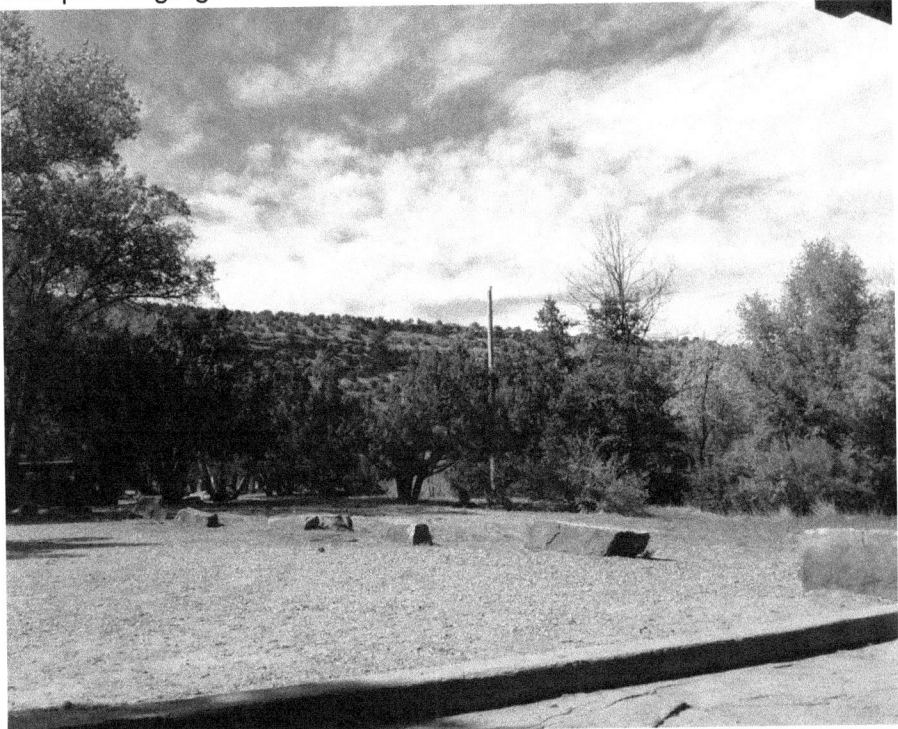

Sitting at my picnic table under an adobe hut and looking out at the Pecos River. It's a muddy red-brown river nestled in between tall rocky bluffs. The best part? There's shade! It's about 3 or 4 hours north of Roswell.

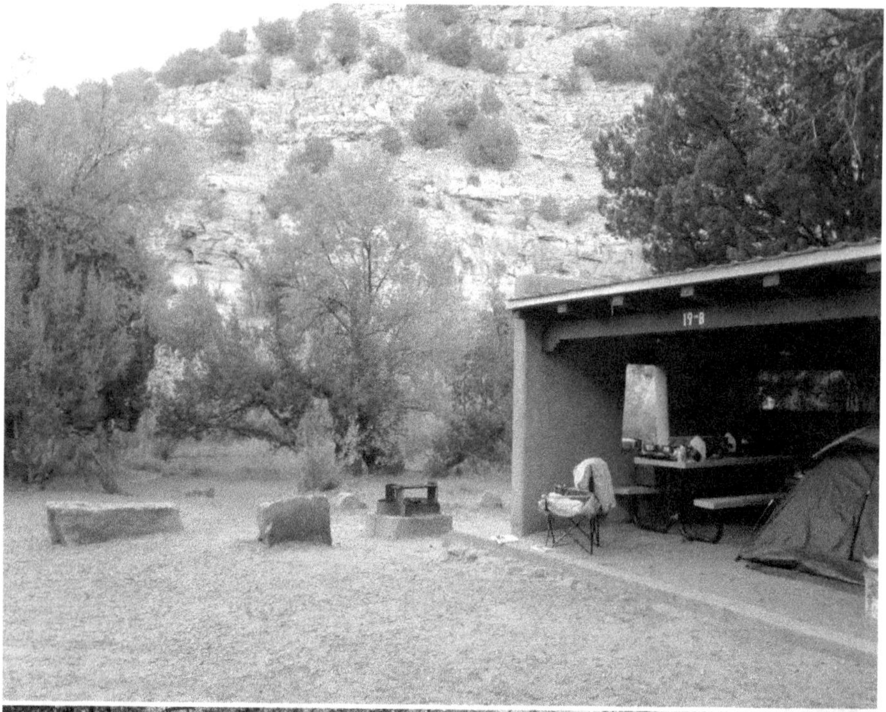

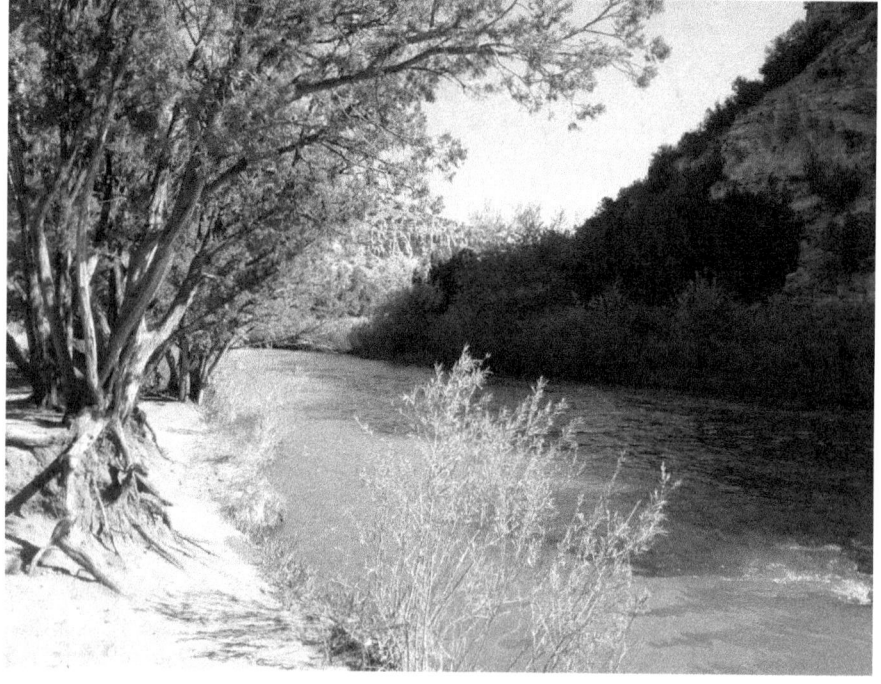

I arrived at the park around 1am and slept at the front gate. It was locked when I got there and still locked when I woke up, so I went for a ride.

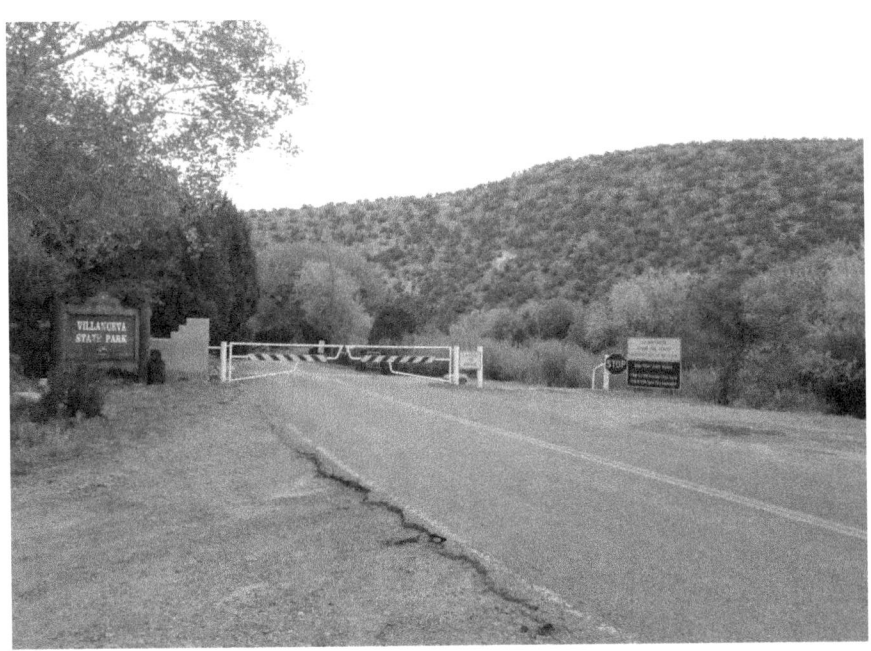

The area is lovely. Red dirt and adobe and small farms. I suspect it's fairly poor around here. It's beautiful though. Might even make it to #3 on my move list.

There's water and hills and the sun is warm but the breeze is cool.

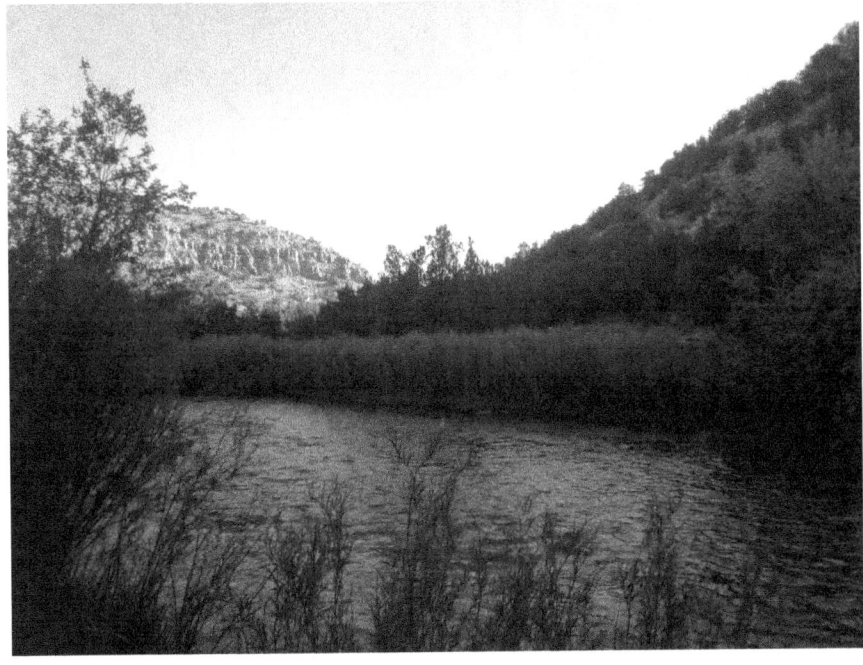

I think I'll paint some rocks this afternoon for dropping along my path.
Rock ideas… Animals, plants, sayings, affirmations…

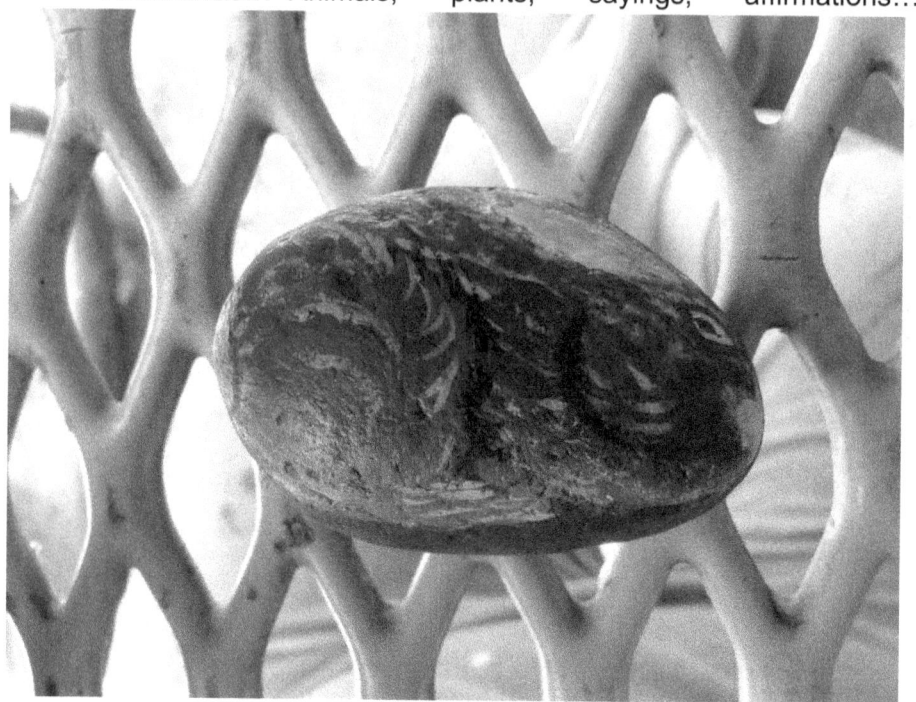

————

9pm - reading Sunshine's book reminded me… Don't forget the rumble strip outside of Albuquerque

Santa Fe - Thurs
Taos - Fri
Albuquerque - Saturday

This book is good - (note to self: look back at the underlined parts)
Ecclesiastes reference
"…the boy who earned her heart…"

That's what a man wants, to earn a woman's love and respect; to win her heart.

"Music is the Soundtrack of life"

"There are two types of men: one is looking for a woman to complete him and the other is looking for a woman to accompany him." Pick one that wants your company, not to feel complete. No tag-a-longs

Thanks   Sunshine.

5/3/17 Day 17

I was up early, watched the sunrise, and made my cowboy coffee. The coffee was pretty gritty, I didn't have any filters. Also, gotta remember to put my taco meat into containers AND baggies. The smell permeates everything.

Pro-tip after the trip I found out about the French press coffee maker and it will be my go-to for any camping coffee I ever make in the future. Going camping? Get a French press coffee pot.

I slept well last night. It was chilly but not near as cold as Marfa. Thank goodness! I should probably grab another blanket before my next stop though.

Money is going so fast.

Also, too much junk food, toxins and sugars - my body is reacting. My telltale rash has appeared and my joints are sore. Better start paying better attention to what I'm eating and start back on vitamins.

I'm going to paint some today and go for a hike.

———

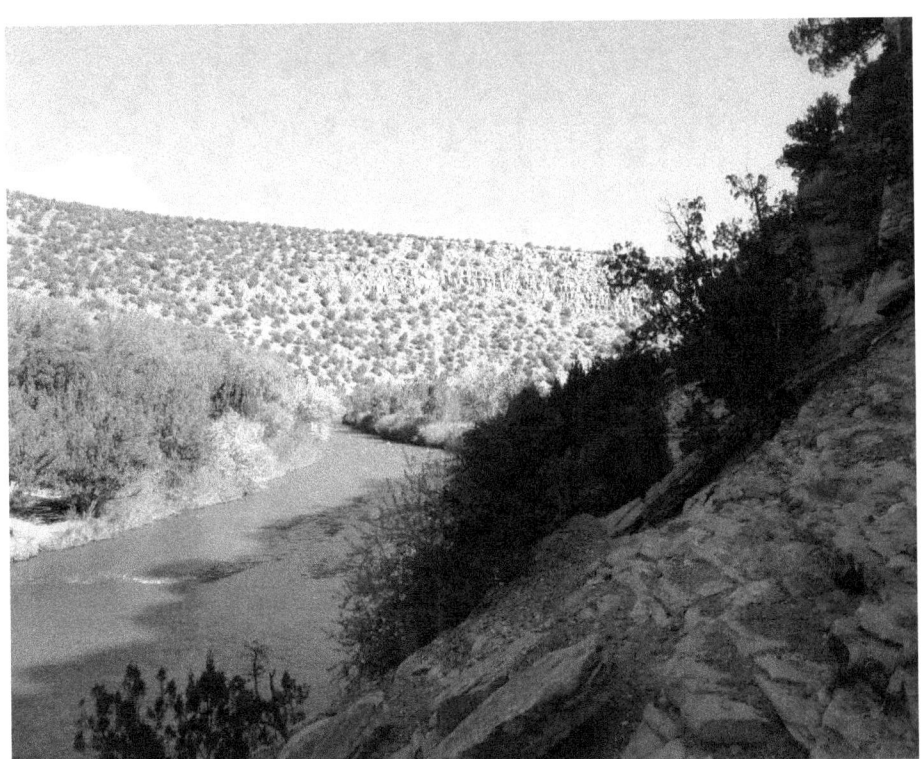

My hike was lovely. I crossed the river and hiked up the bluffs on the other side and had a toke under a bluff. I feel a ton better after the toke. It's still cool down here on the river between the bluffs. The sun doesn't hit much down here and the wind whips through the canyons.

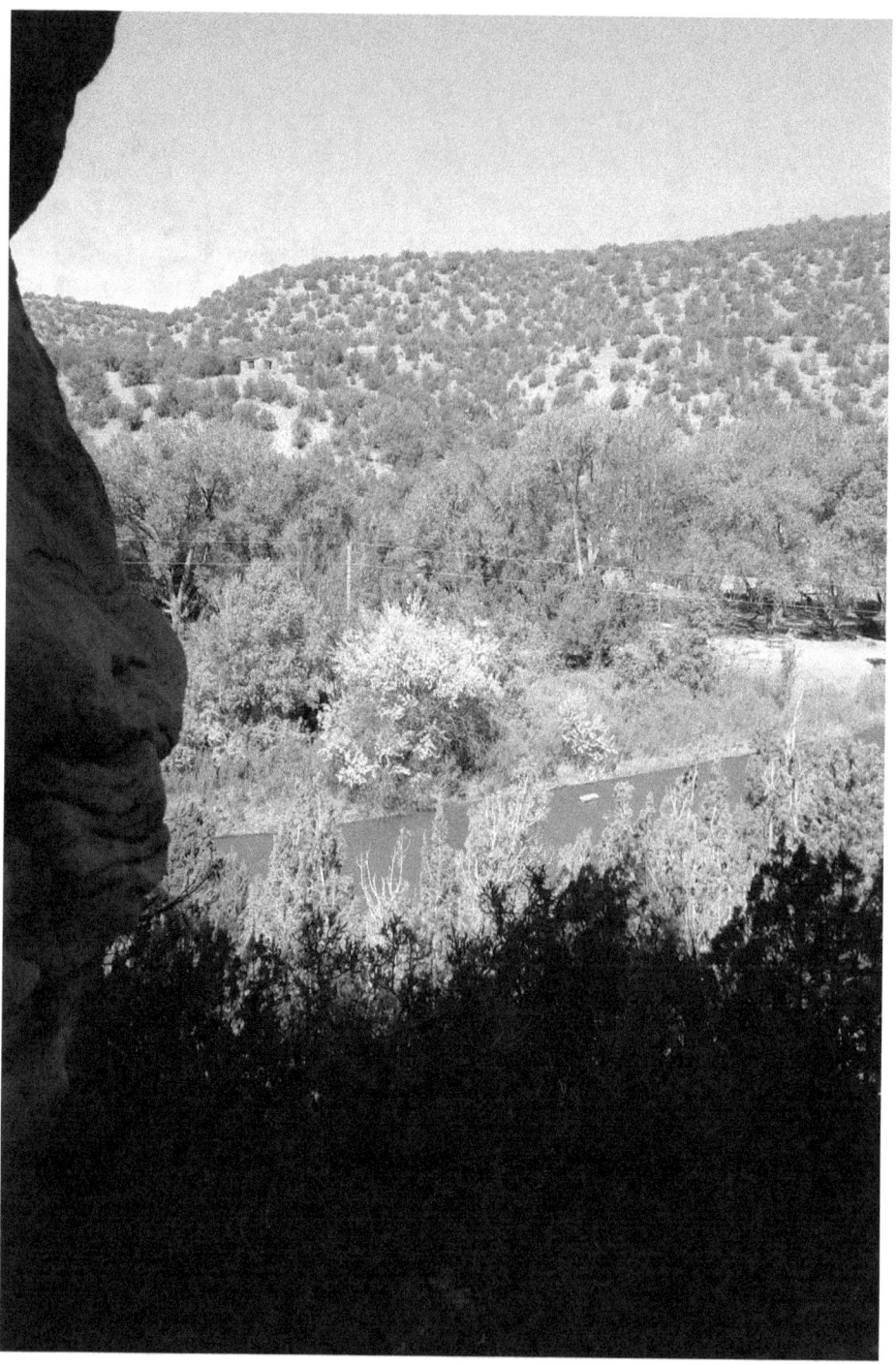

105

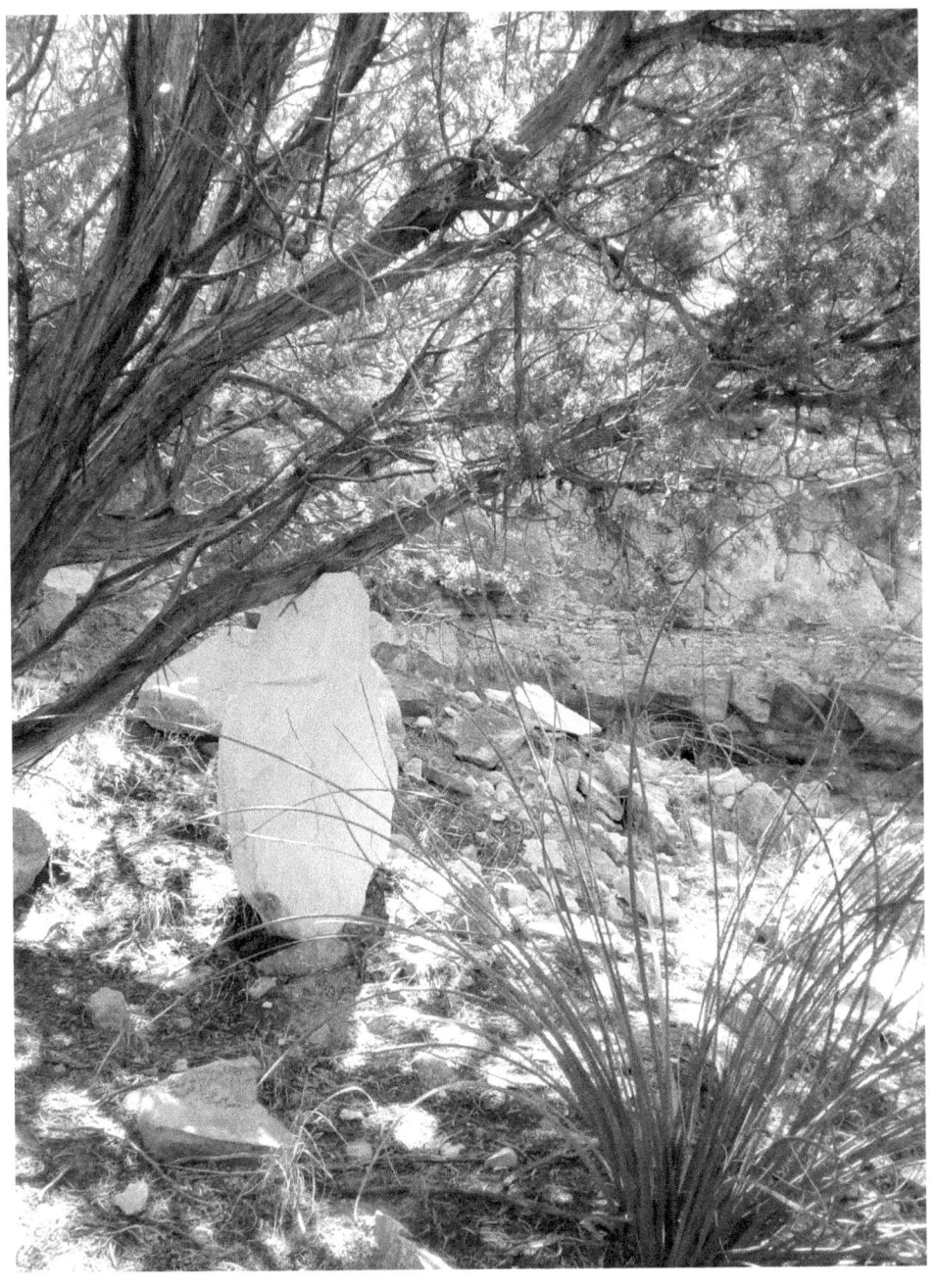

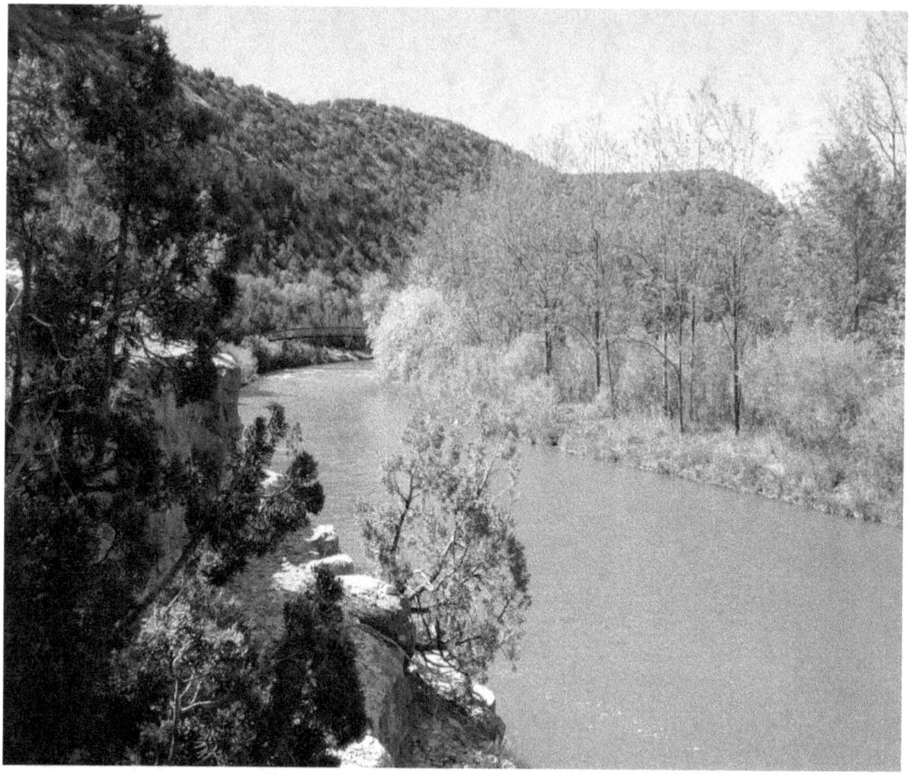

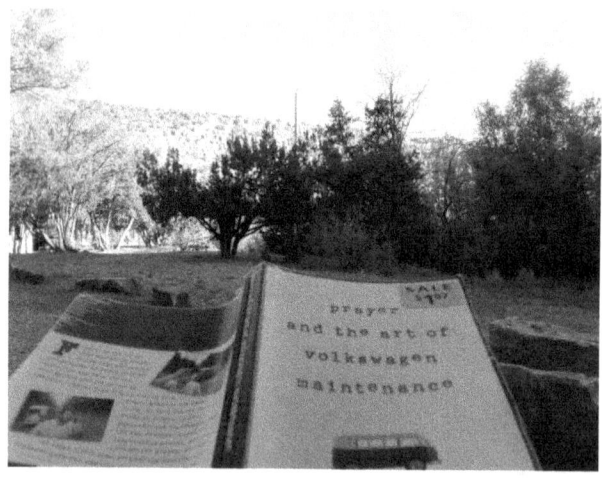

I wish I'd brought a thick comforter, a hammock, hot chocolate, and a solar cell.

I wish I didn't bring the air mattress, lanterns, and so many books...

Really digging this book Sunshine gave me though....

Sitting at my camp site I can hear the river, some low talking, songbirds, doves, wind, and a garbage bag rustle. Except for the garbage bag, this is serenity.

I went for a ride earlier to get signal and succumbed to the loneliness...

I called M…
I know better…
It's hard to break those ties; those habits.
You can do it.
I can do it.

When I got back to camp, I met another camper, "P". P is a Snowbird. He travels between AZ, NM, and CO and might be from either Kansas City or Champaign, IL. He's a Stephen King fan. I can tell he's been on the road for a little while. He'd love to chat all day and hates cities.

It's interesting the people you meet and the info you can gather from them on the road…

Pro-tip Take everyone's opinions and experience with a grain of salt. We all see things through our own life filter. Nothing you see or hear is really real except what you think is real. Don't let others negativity or fears or whatever cloud your experience. Listen for helpful hints.

5/4/17 Day 18

It was cold last night but I slept pretty well. I really need to get another blanket though. I finished Sunshine's book this morning as the sun rose. It's his birthday. I'm leaving today but I'm not sure which way to go. Santa Fe or Taos… Regardless, better get packing. I'll decide on the way.

———————

My gut said Taos first and I'm so glad I followed my gut. This way went thru the Carson National Forest. It's the closest thing I've seen to Arkansas yet. The only drawback is that I arrived in Taos after everything on the square was already closed or closing. No problem. I can see it all in the am.

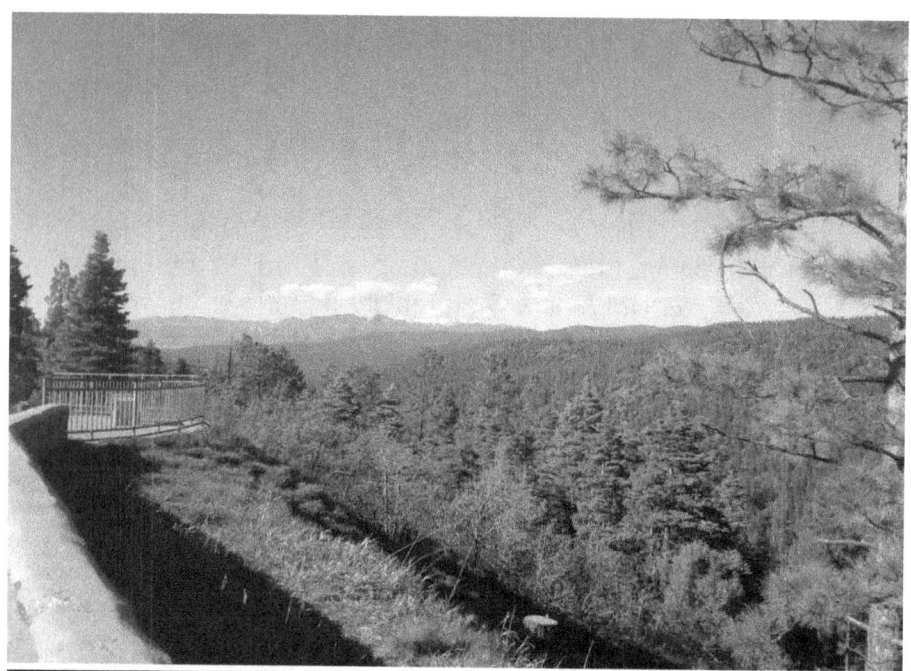

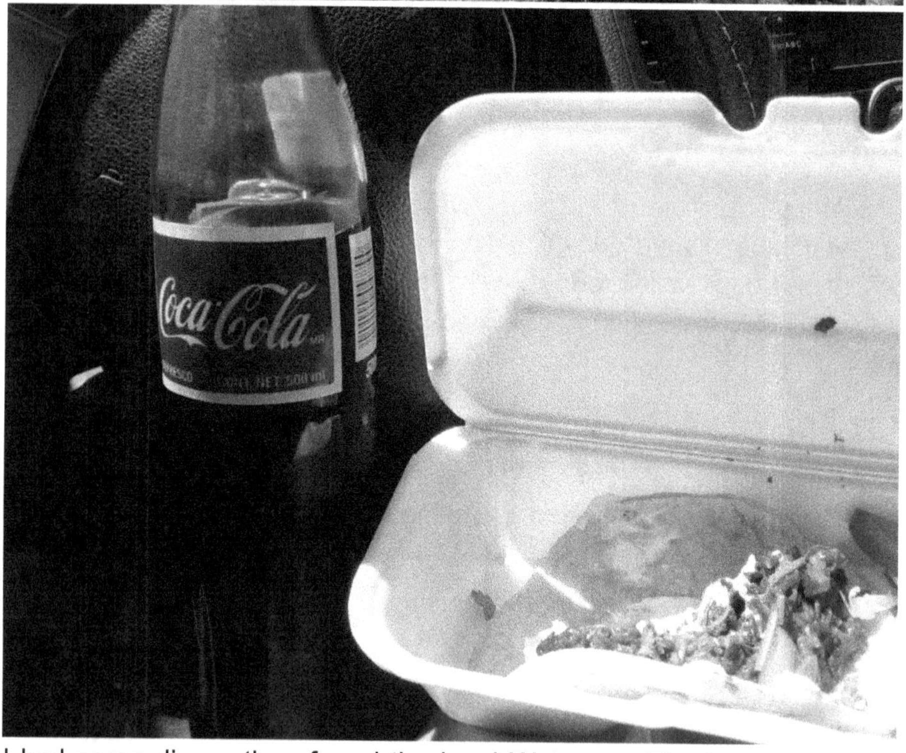

I had some dinner then found the local Walmart. Finally got that extra blanket and another SD card and chatted with Sunshine for a bit. I kinda miss him too. What a sap I am...

I loved the drive today thru the forest though. Snowcapped peaks and winding creeks and little towns in the valleys. Also, pretty sure I witnessed a drug deal at a lookout, lol.

I loved the forest but its sparsely populated so not good for selling art. Taos is neat but there is a lot of traffic and the art is all native styled. I get a vibe that the locals aren't fans of outsiders even though I'm certain tourism is a huge money maker here. I don't know, it just doesn't feel like home to me.

Where the hell am I gonna go after this!?

I realize I won't be headed to Bear Bottom, but Eureka Springs is still my number one choice. I'll be starting with nothing though. That will be hard there. It's kinda pricey... I really don't want to go back to Indiana but if I don't find someplace else that's where I'll land... Where the hell am I gonna go?

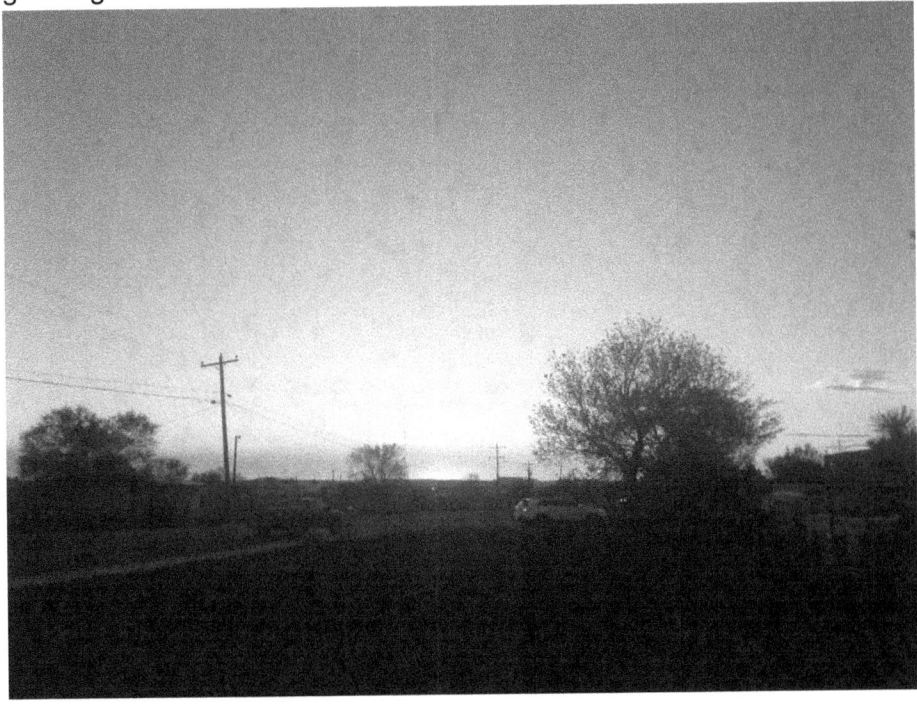

5/5/17 Day 19

I woke up early and wandered around the square at Taos. The shops weren't open yet. I looked in all the windows, but I know it's not where I fit. Some of the art is great. I see a lot of traditional native American style.

Would my style fit? Stand out? Which is better? Do I even have a style yet?

I also saw some rafting outfitters. Cougar would like that. She'd really like Austin though, I think.

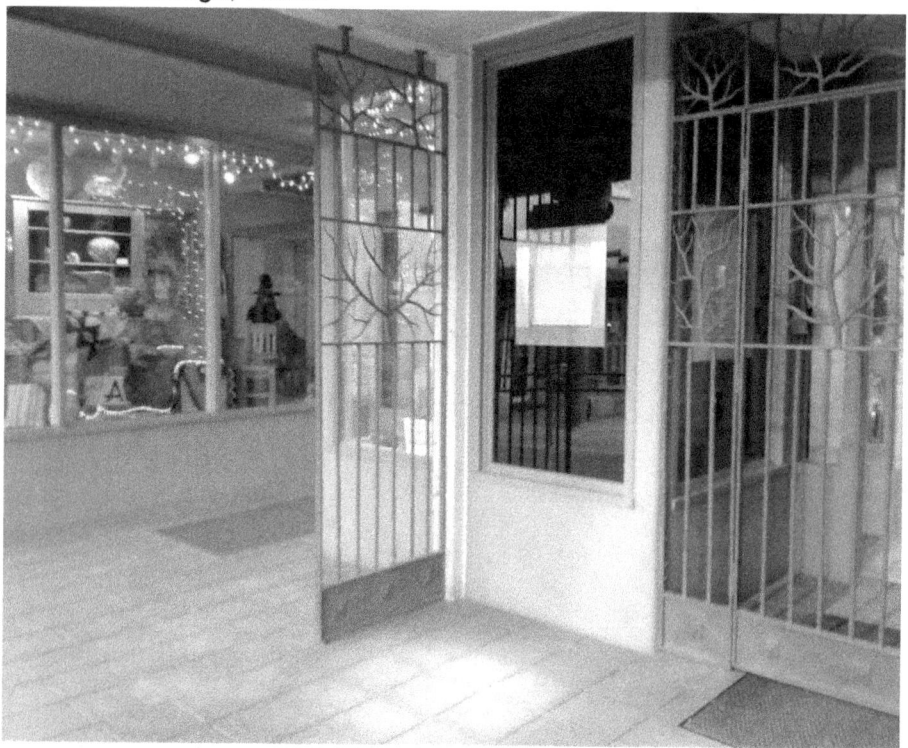

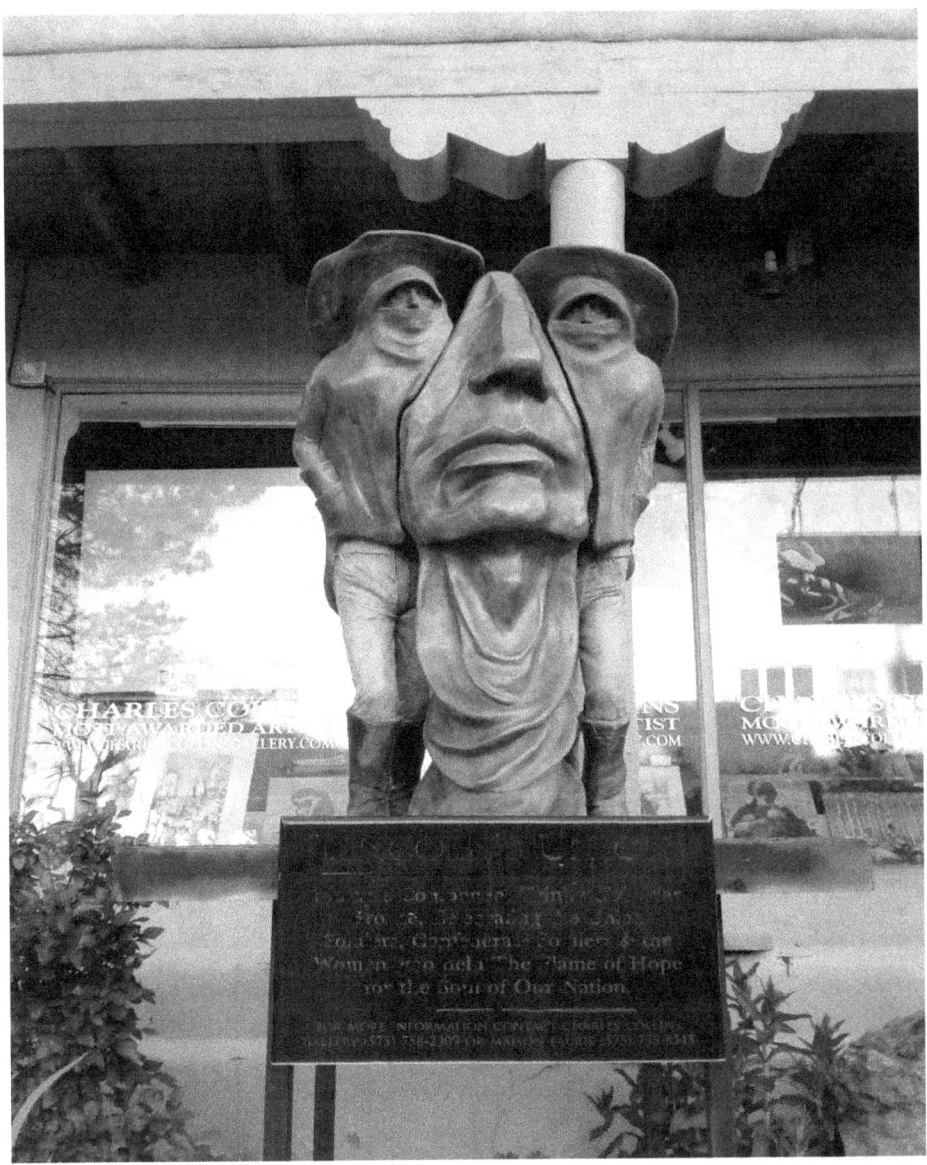

I left Taos early and headed for Santa Fe. This drive was also lovely. I had my first coaching session while I overlooked the Rio Grande. I particularly loved all these questionnaires she gave me. They were helpful to see where I'm really at with myself. They rated things like my relationships with people, money, whether I'm taking action. Her whole premise is that we are a whole system, so all the parts of the system have to be working well so the whole system works well.

We set some goals for me for the next week:

1. Talk to some gallery owners
2. Work on my branding course material for 2 hours
3. Journal more reflectively. How do I feel, what do I think, etc.

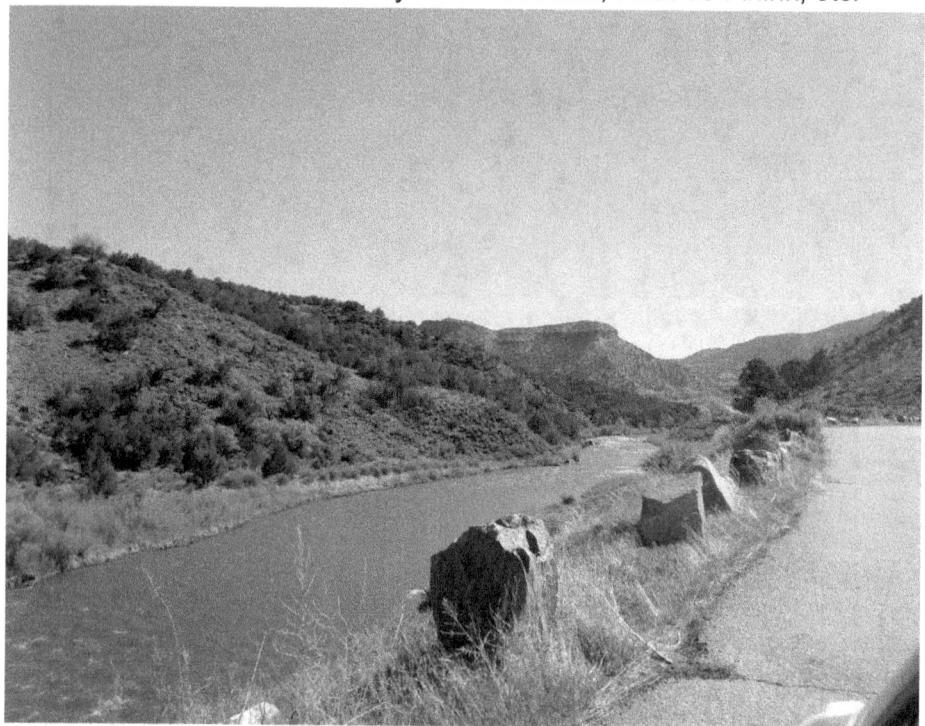

After the call I got my fly-fishing gear out and fished the Rio Grande for a few minutes until a bunch of rafters showed up. I had fun while it lasted.

———

Santa Fe was neat. It's a lot larger than Taos. I could have spent a couple of days there and still probably not have seen everything. But I know the money is going quickly and I still have to make it to California, at least.

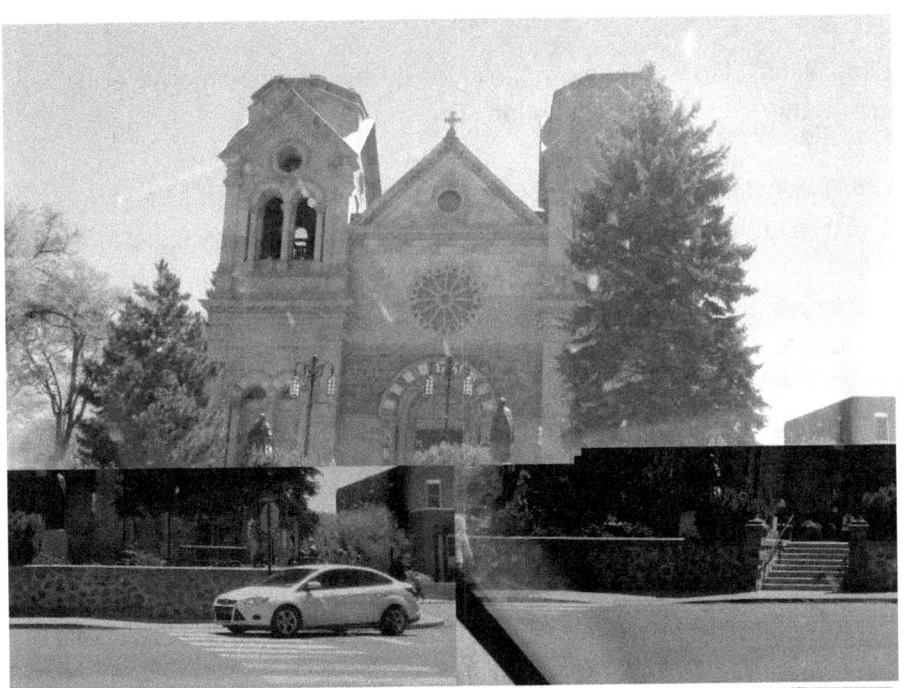

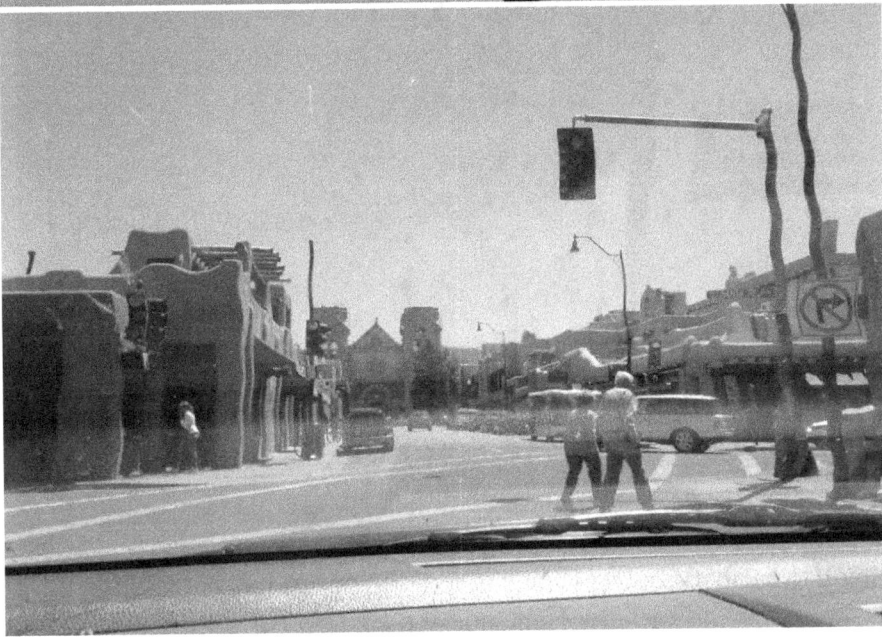

There was an art show on the square and at the Governor's Mansion today, so I checked out those artists as opposed to trying to find all the galleries. I ended up buying a lovely wire bracelet from a Native American woman at the Governor's Mansion.

I'm feeling a little claustrophobic in the cities these days; too many people, too much traffic, too much stimulation. Too much.

I thought I might like New Mexico but it's hot and dry and doesn't feel right for me. I don't think I'd fit well here.

After Santa Fe I headed toward Albuquerque. I found the musical road but had to circle back to catch the rumble strip. I also stopped at the Petroglyph National Monument. It was too hot, and I was too tired and hungry to hike.

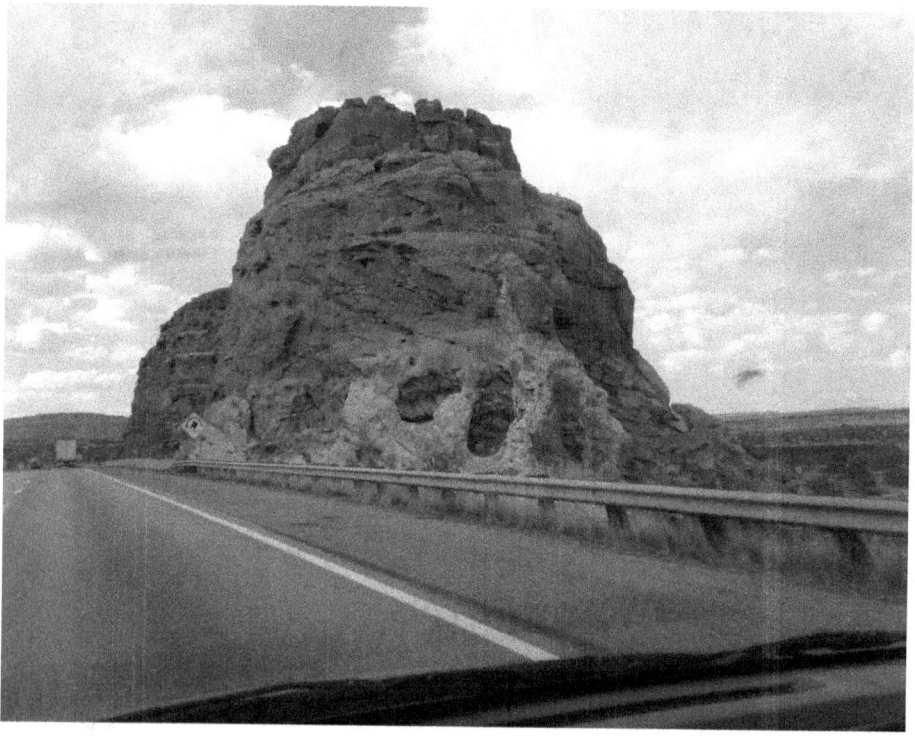

I was going to try to make the state line tonight, but something told me to turn at Grants, NM and go see a volcanic ice cave tomorrow.

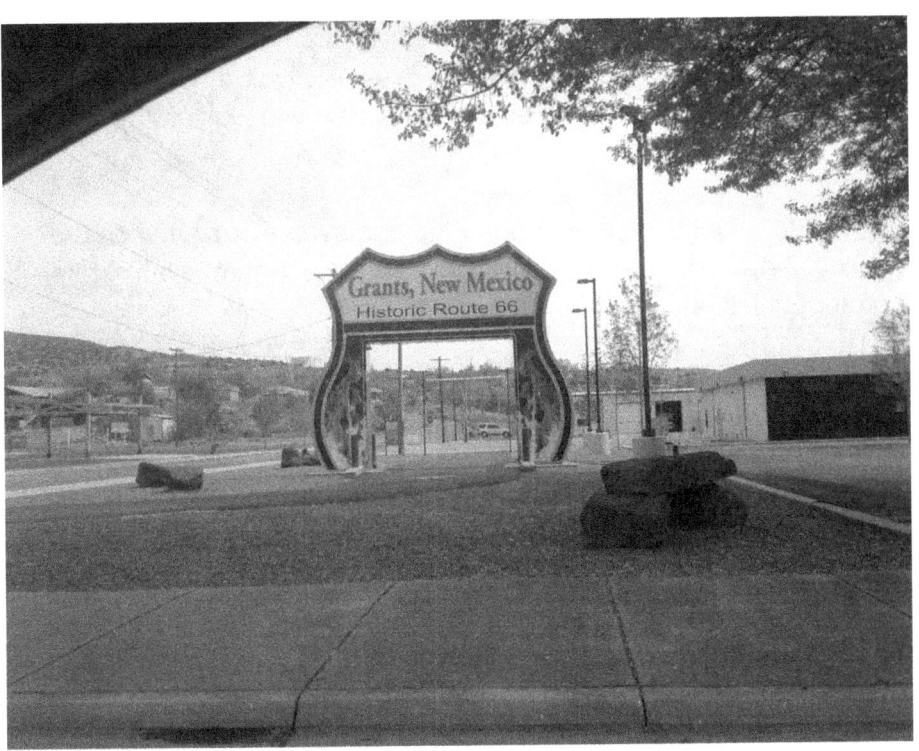

My ass is kicked. I decided to stay at a hotel tonight. I'm so hot and wore out. I need a shower, some good food, air conditioning, and a comfy bed. I can tell I'm worn out because when I got to the hotel, as I was standing in the lobby, my whole body was still rumbling like driving and my tongue didn't   work   well.

Tomorrow I'll do some laundry, get an oil change, see the volcanic cave, and probably be in Flagstaff by evening.

———

As I'm driving across this country it is very clear that 1% owns the other 99% or, at least, 1% owns 98%. I believe there is still maybe 1% that might mostly own themselves...

There are so many homeless, drug addicted, and impoverished. So much ignorance and stupidity and hate.

It's also very clear that the general population could give a shit about our environment. All these amazingly beautiful and seemingly secluded places and they all have one thing in common…. TRASH. I've had moments on this trip and in my life where I've felt as though I were standing in a place where no one else had been only to look around and find   trash   at   every   turn….

I'm thinking up a painting series on the topic. Maybe call it America the beautiful but the landscape images will be made up of cigarette butts, pop cans, water bottles, and beer bottles.

With all of that though, it wouldn't be accurate if I didn't comment on the contrast. With all the negative that I've seen, I've also seen so much LOVE. Tiny pockets and single individuals full of love for themselves, others, their culture, their community. It's amazing really. In a single moment and sometimes in a single individual. A mother, hugging their child with their one hand while throwing their cigarette butt or water bottle on the ground with the other.   Maybe that is the painting…

_____

Where the hell am I going? What am I doing? What do I even want!?

I want it all… I want a studio/gallery and apartment in the city and I also want a wilderness retreat center. I also want to do the Adam-Eve show and travel.

But I feel so much resistance within me to each of these things.
Big is scary! Do people even care? About anything?

Garbage lines every road and trail and creek in this country. There are garbage islands in the ocean. Do people care about anything?

5/6/17 Day 20 New Mexico - Arizona

After 20 days on the road, last night's bed might have been the best ever. It was barely even clean but OMG so much needed!!

After laundry and an oil change, I hit the road. On the way to the ice cave there is a national monument. When I stopped at the welcome center, the ranger asked if I was headed to the Zuni festival. "No, but I am now!"

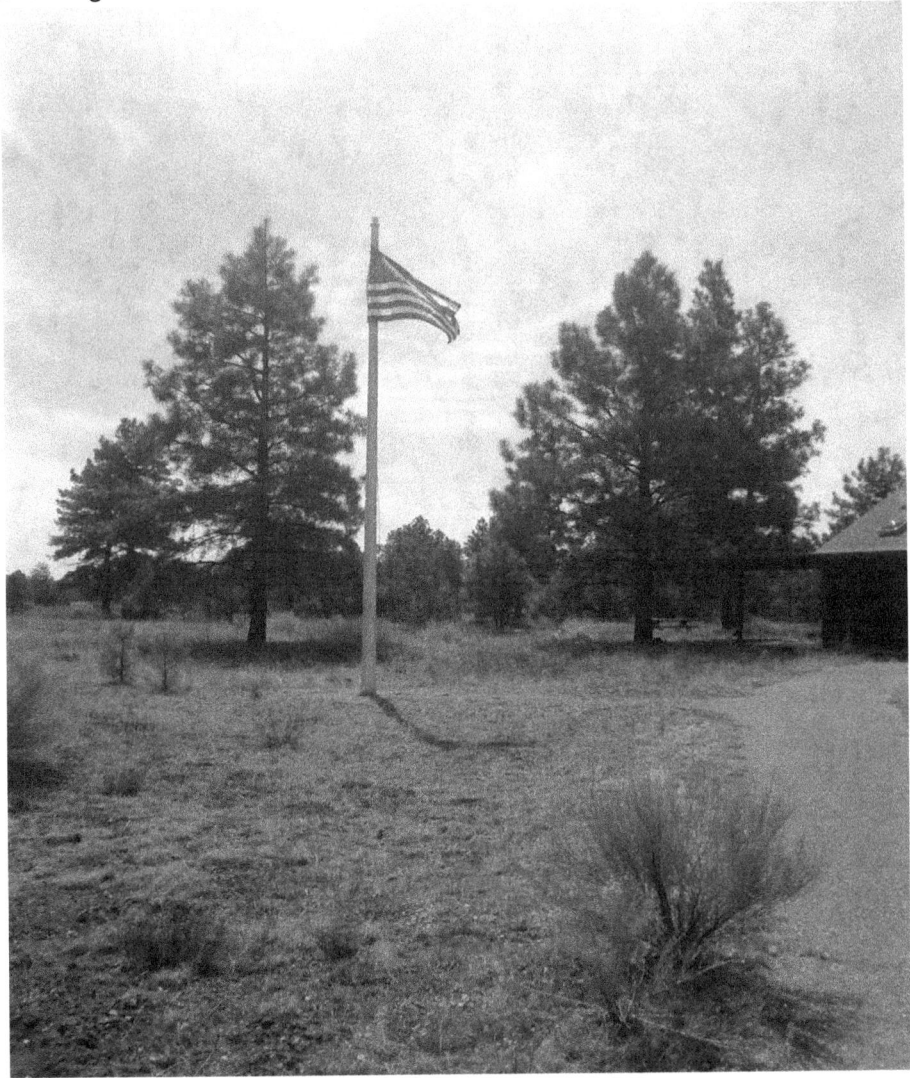

First though, I went to the ice caves. It is a private property in the midst of the national monument property. The property has been in the owner's family for four generations and now she and her sisters run it. Ironically, she and I also discussed trash. It's a headache for her too.

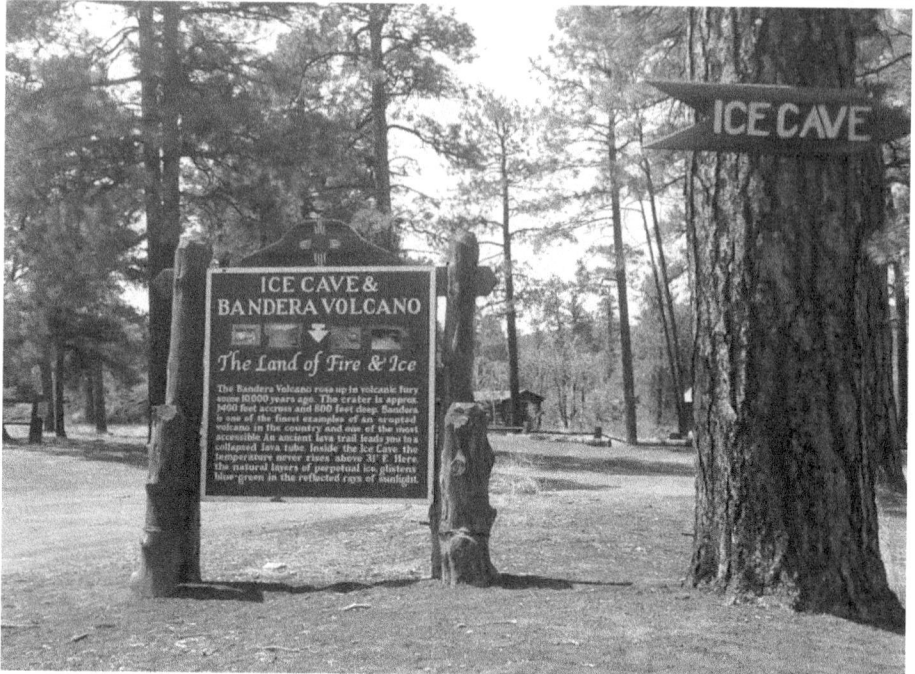

There is a little hike to the ice cave, but it wasn't difficult. The stairs at the cave's entrance were a bit steep but there's a stop halfway if it's needed. The cave is situated mostly underground and opens to the north so there is little to no sun on the opening which keeps the temperature inside the cave cold enough to keep the ice from melting completely.

119

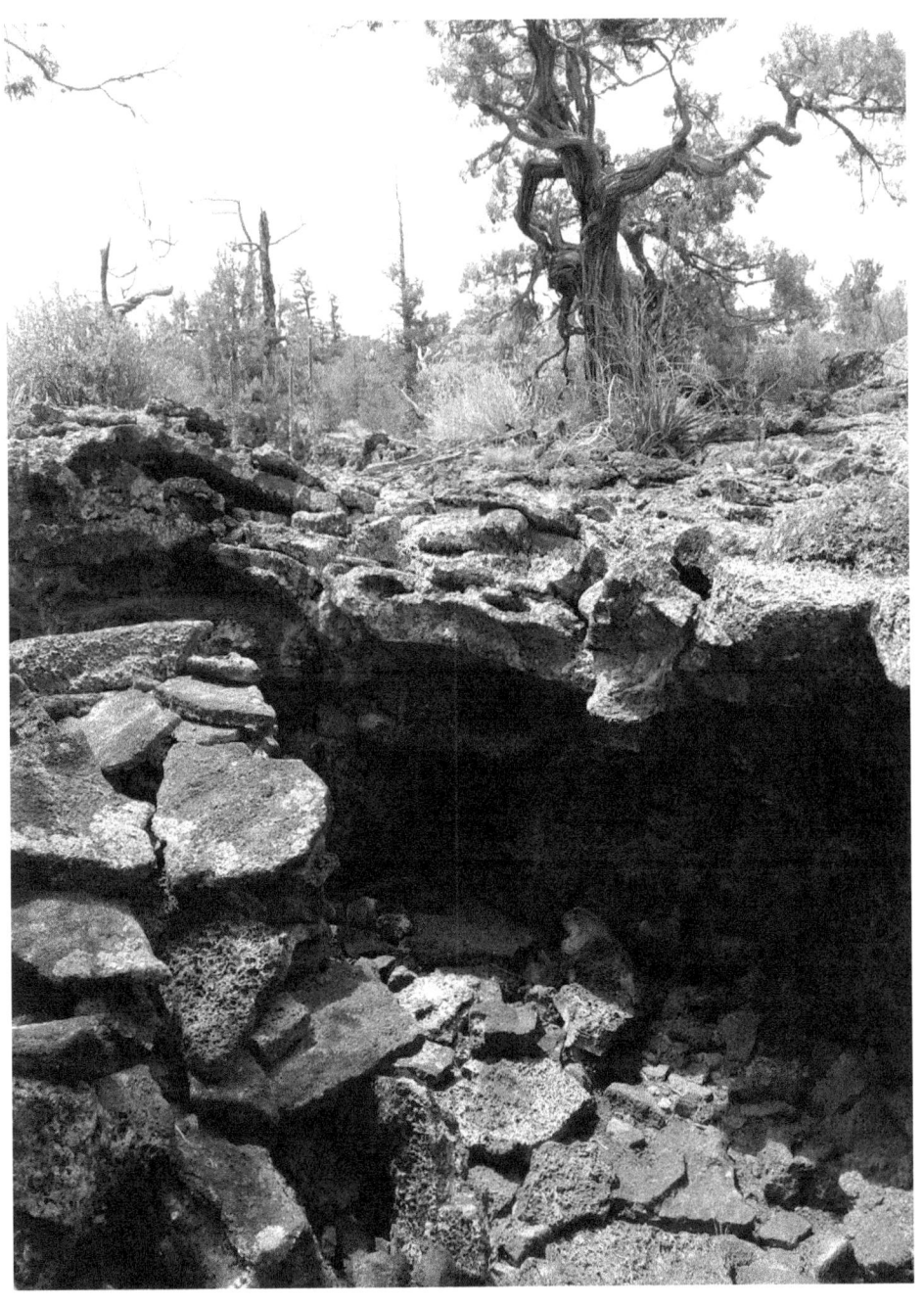

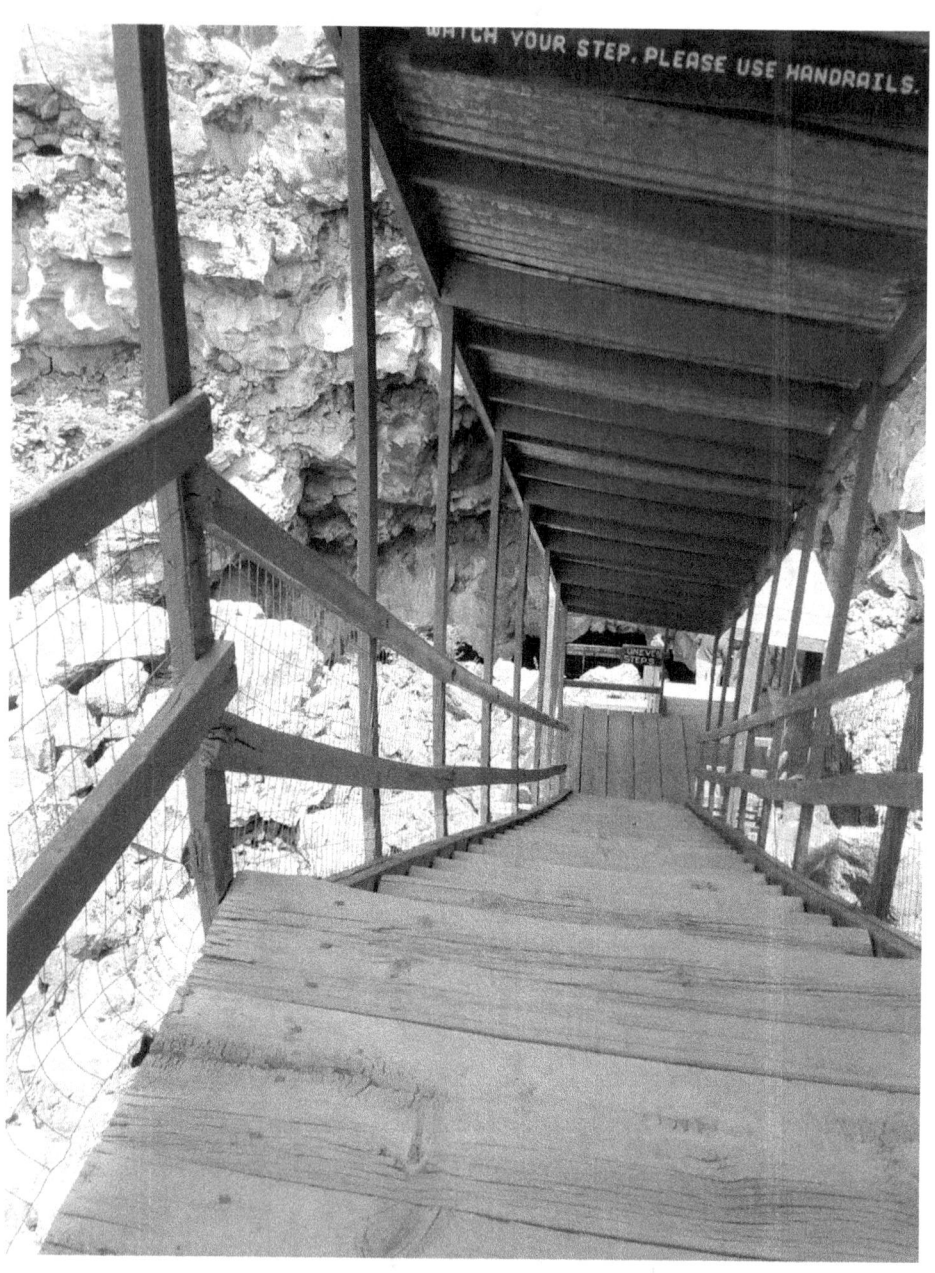

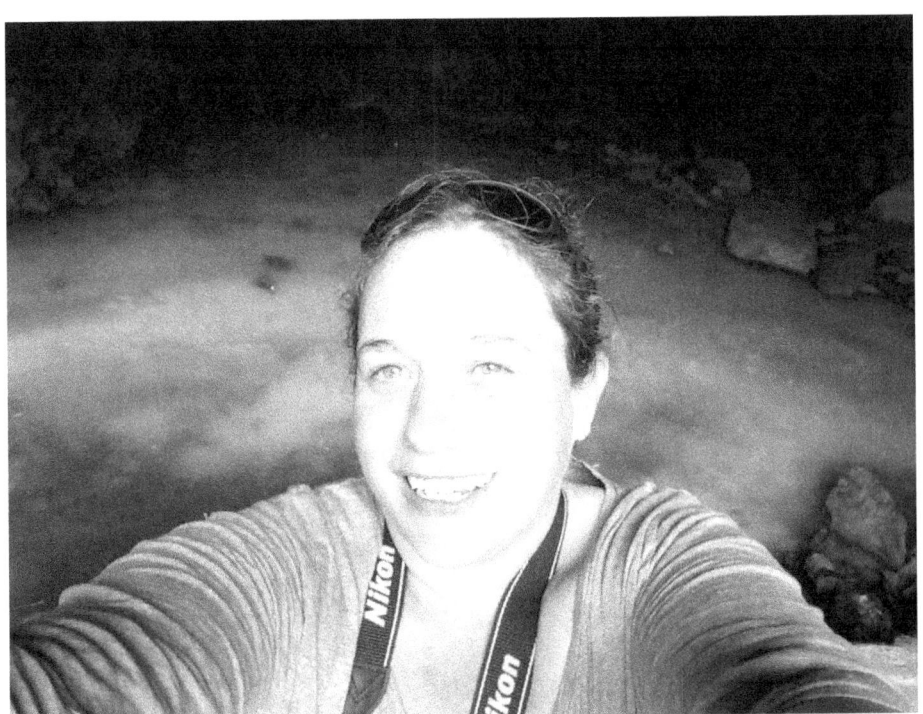

While at the cave I met a couple who are from Gallup, NM. The woman is an art historian and an artist. She has a studio/gallery there in Gallup. I promised to stop and see her studio on my way thru and I did. I was able to peek in and see a few works in progress. If you're near Gallup, stop and say hi.

Between the ice cave and Gallup was the Zuni reservation and their festival.

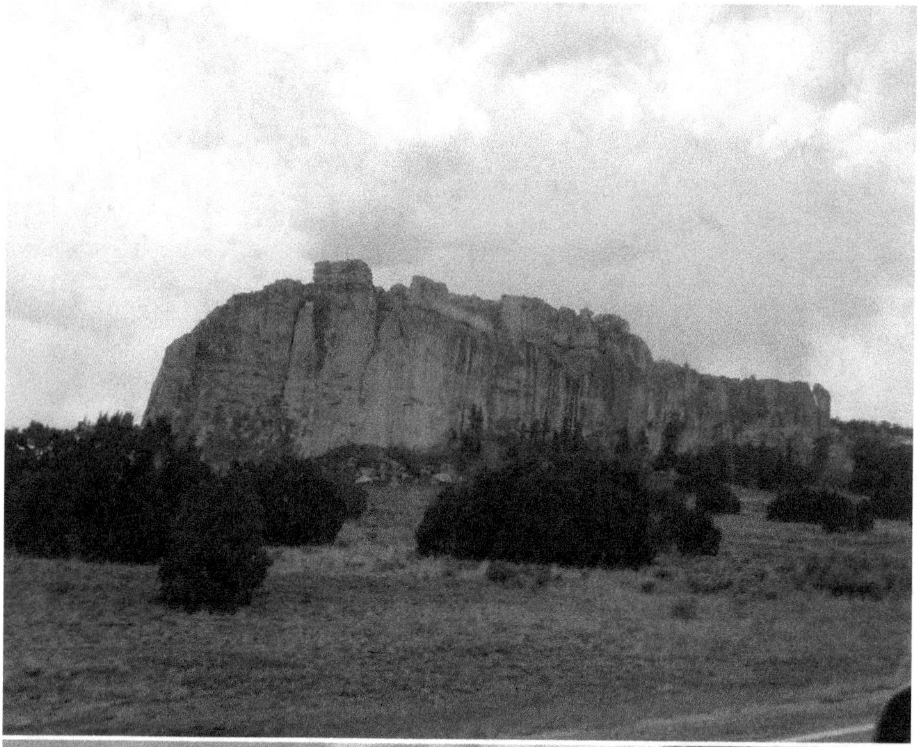

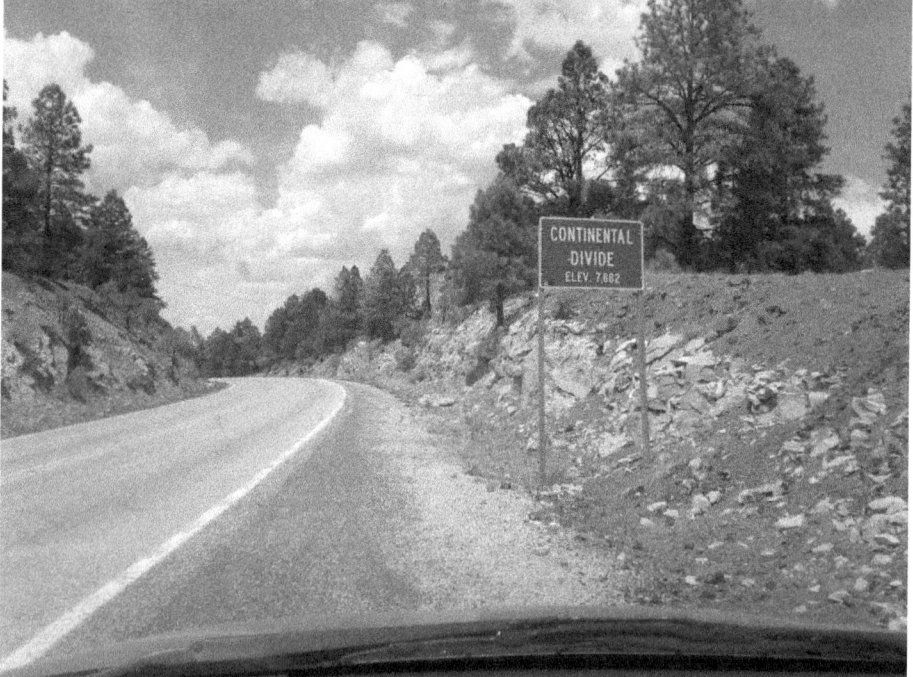

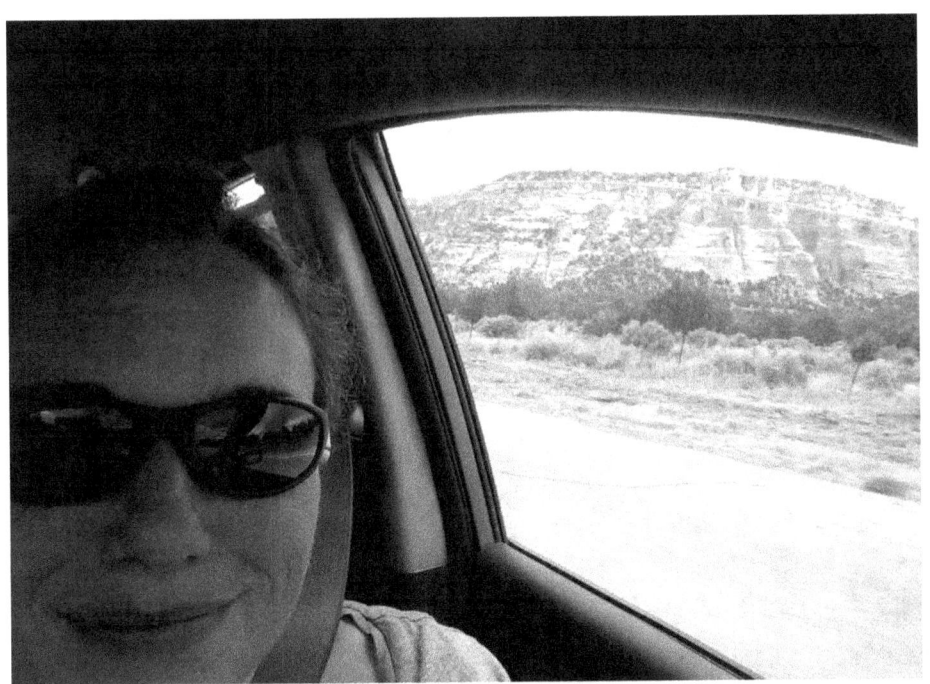

The Zuni fest was neat! They had lots of dancers and some native drums and native flautists. I loved getting to see the show. There was also a carnival for the kids and native artists. But there was very little food! I was really looking forward to food.

I took a bunch of pictures at the fest that I really wanted to show. Pictures of the musicians and dancers mostly. But, I'm not sure if that's ok…

I wish I could have bought some of the artists' works but rather, I spent $5 on a little stainless rainbow ring (probably from China, ha!). I liked it and it was within my budget, but I bought it as a gift to myself. I'll wear it on my left hand as long as I need to. It is a reminder to myself that I am committed and want to remain committed to myself. To my healing, clarity, and growth.

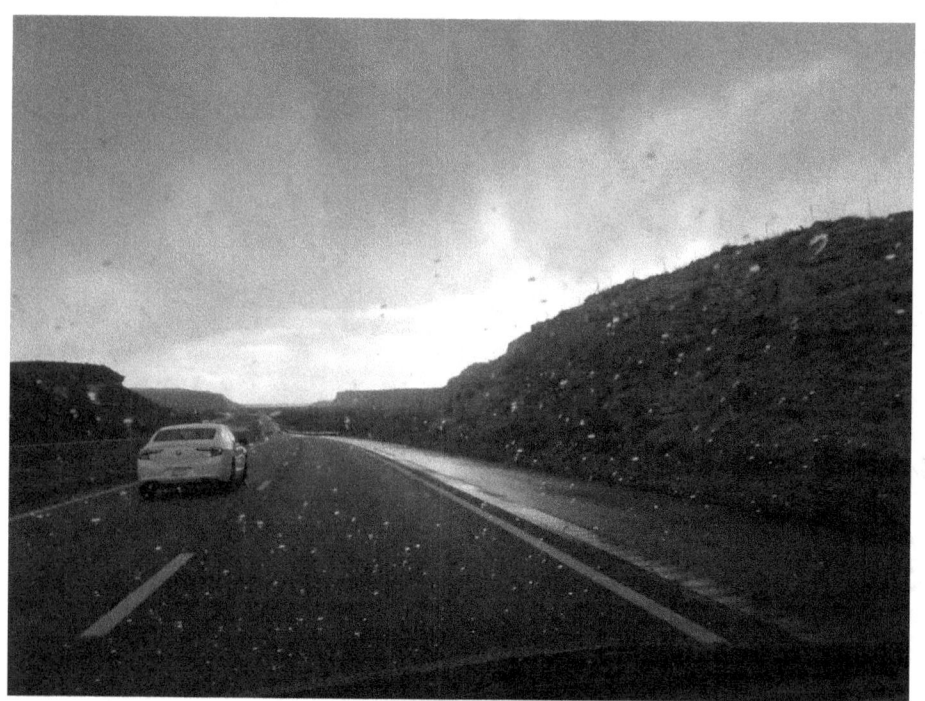

It was raining when I got to Gallup. I stopped for gas and there was a homeless man with one shoe asking for a drink. I gave him what was left in the handiest jug I could reach then went into the gas station. The gallon jug was about half full. When I came out, he asked me for a drink again. I didn't give him anything else. Should I have? I probably could have dug for another partial bottle. I could have handed him my bottle. I don't know. I felt good about giving him the first jug. When he asked the second time and I looked up at him, he seemed to not even really see me. He didn't register that I'd given him the first one. I don't know... I answered, "I gave you what I had. Sorry."

I want to help people. I love seeing people thrive. It's amazing to witness someone being able to do a 180 in their trajectory and move from drowning to flying. I love seeing people happy. I can't make everyone happy.

After Gallup I made a B-line for the Arizona state line... I was ready to be done with New Mexico.

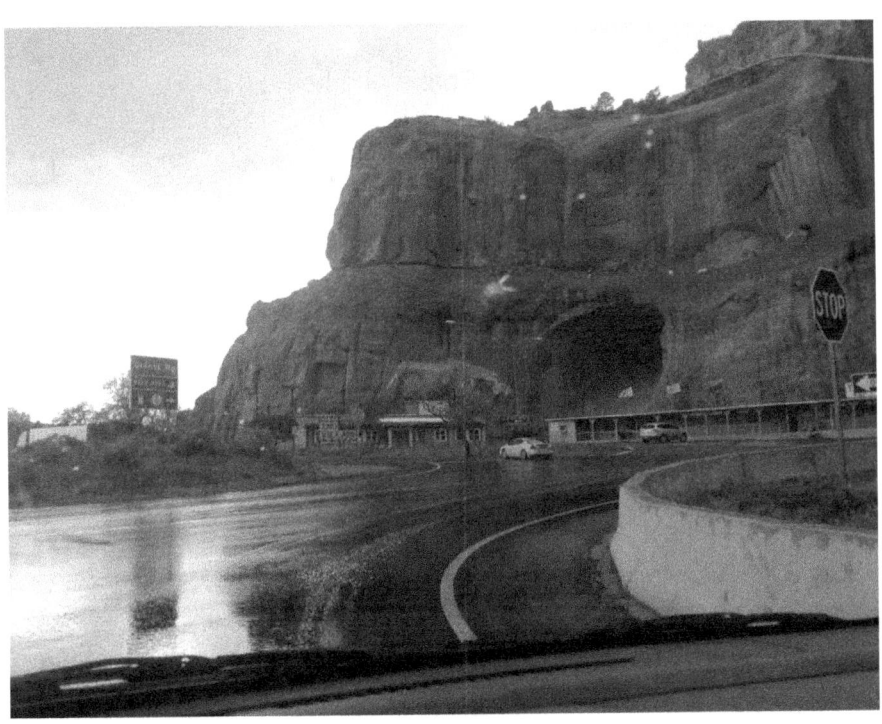

At the state line is a Teepee gift shop and tobacco outlet. They had all sorts of neat things. I bought an interesting bag of tobacco and put a quarter in the Zoltron/Medicine Man machine. It said my life will change with the receipt of a letter and that I should wear amethyst.

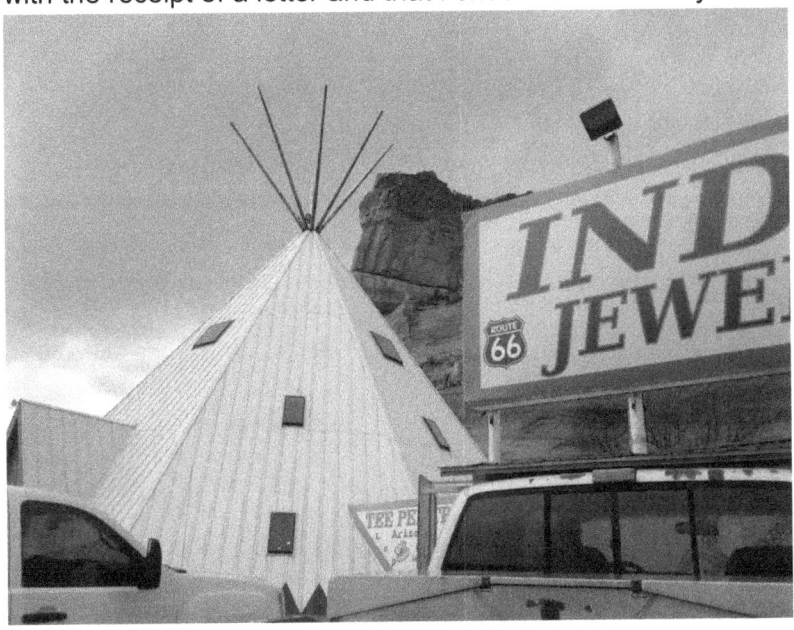

After that I saw a sign for the Petrified Forest and headed there.

The Petrified Forest is a 25-mile road with lookouts and hiking opportunities along the route. I took tons of pictures including one at Lacey Point. How could I not? It's actually spelled right!!

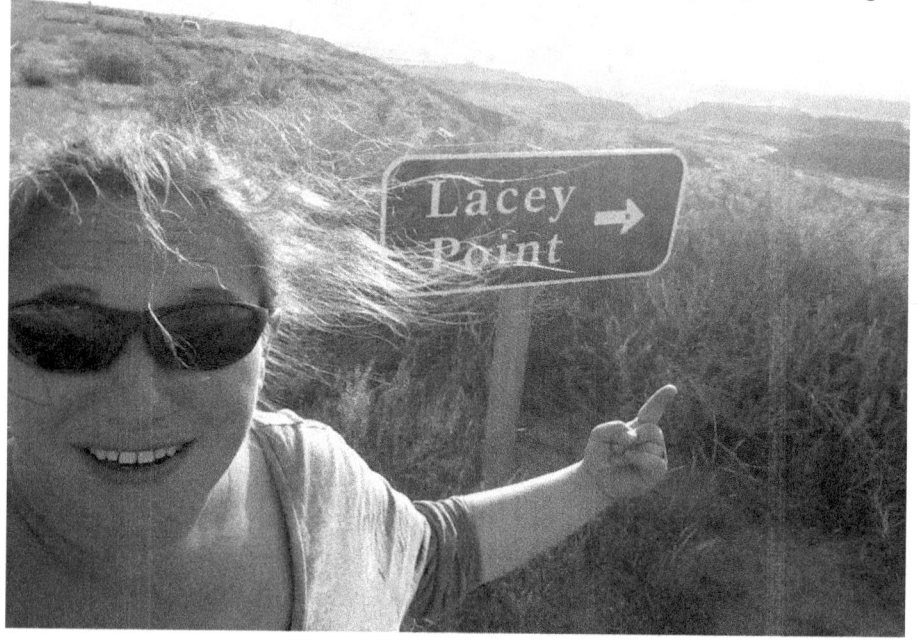

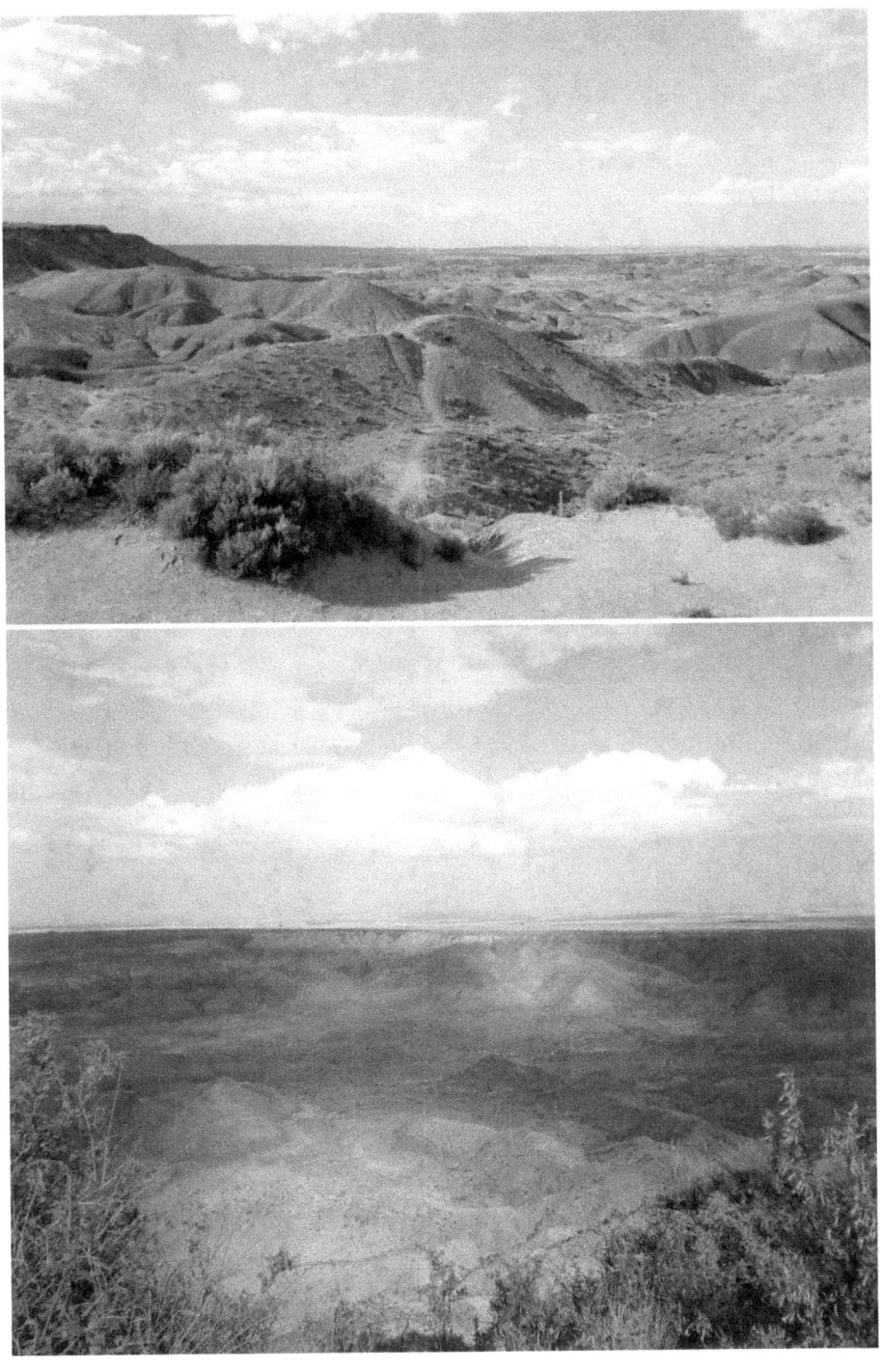

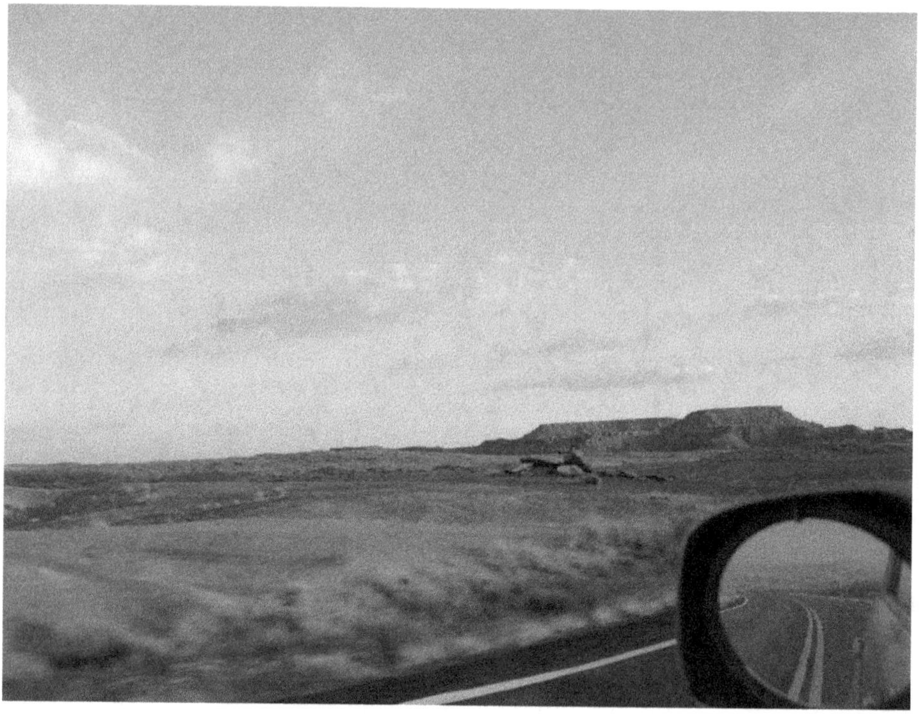

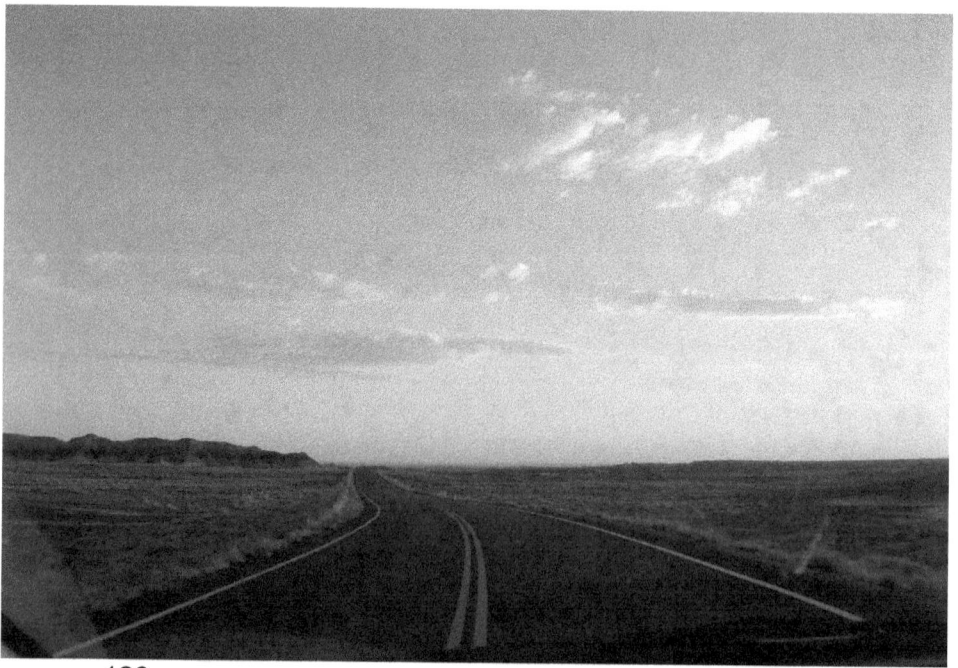

I loved seeing the colors of the hills! I didn't really see many petrified trees though. I think you have to go on some of the hiking trails to see them.

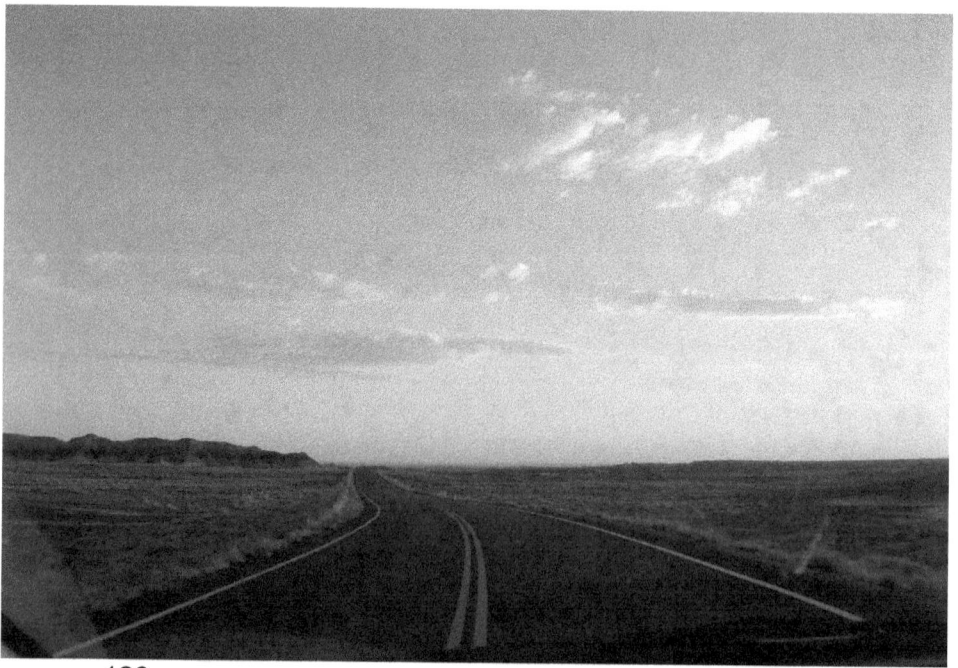

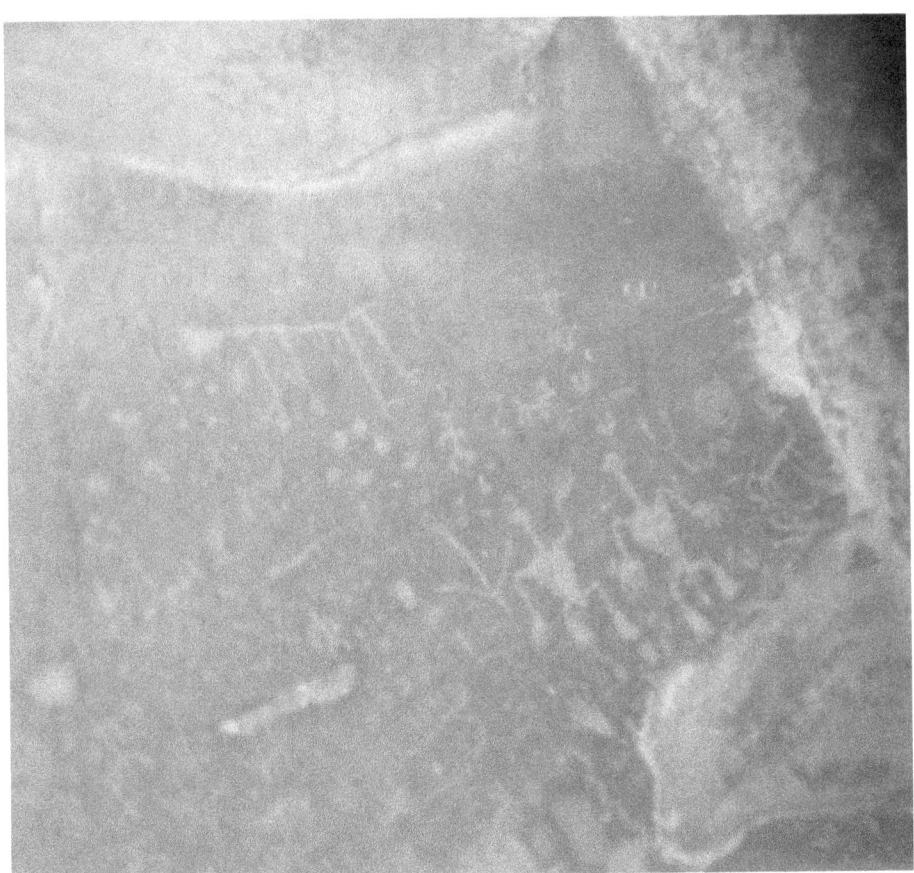

My favorite thing might have been the Petroglyphs though. The petroglyphs are on some rocks below a lookout. You have to look through binoculars to see them. I did my best to get a picture through the binocular thing.

What do you think it says? I see a deer and maybe a man and woman? Corn?
maybe a snail and a coyote on the right? Maybe it's aliens, haha.

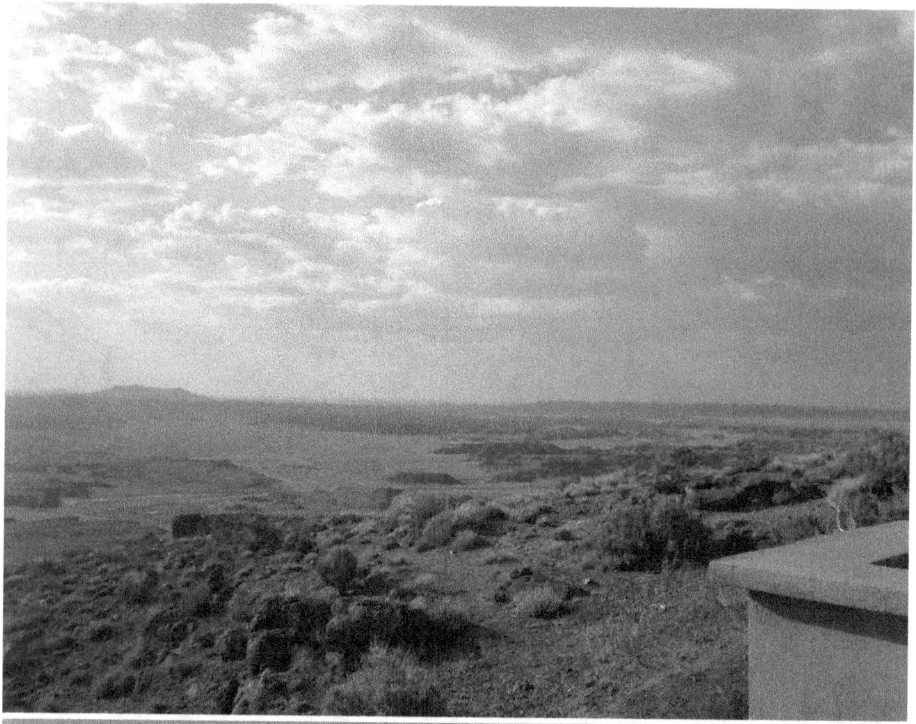

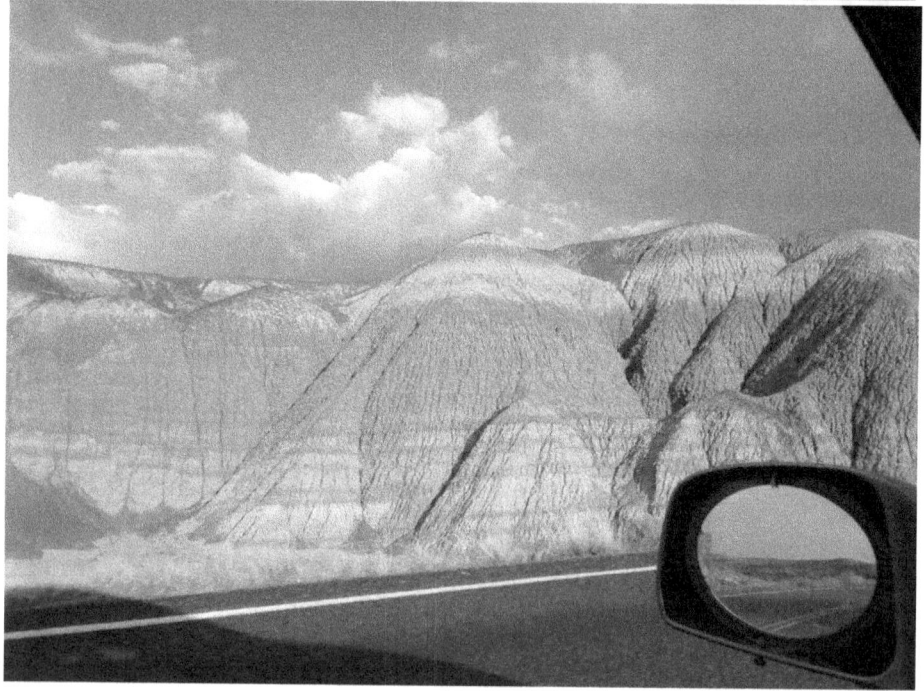

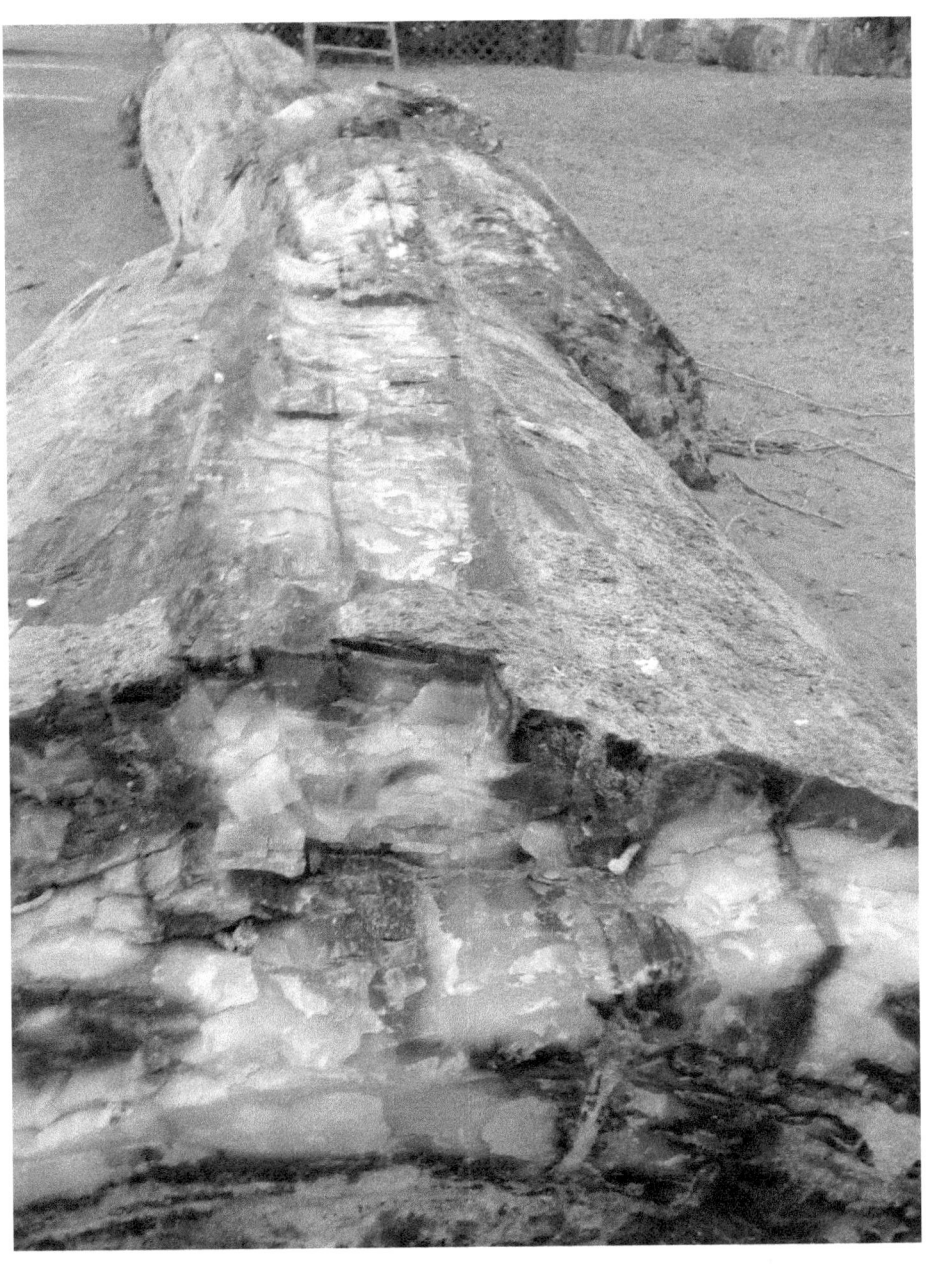

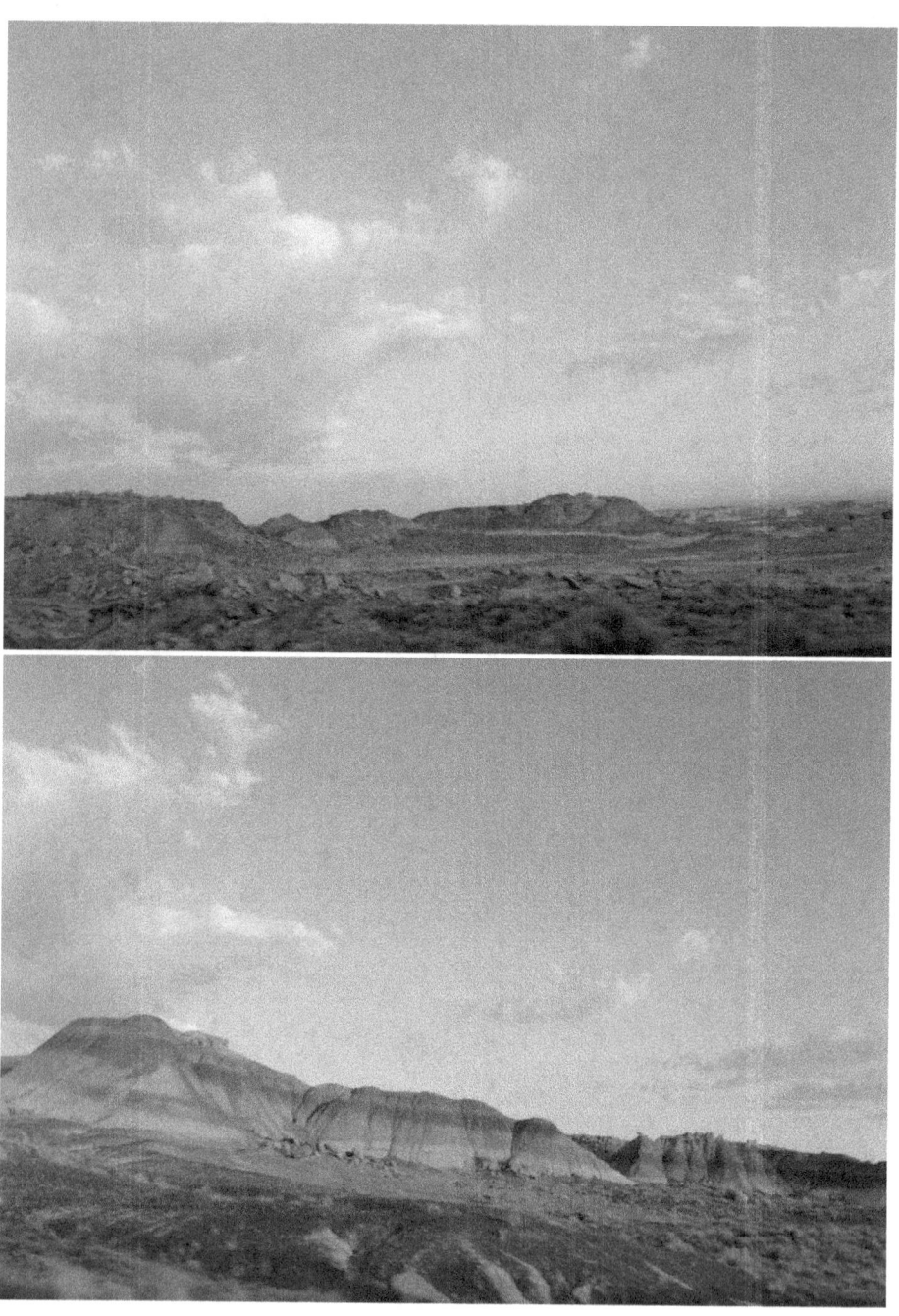

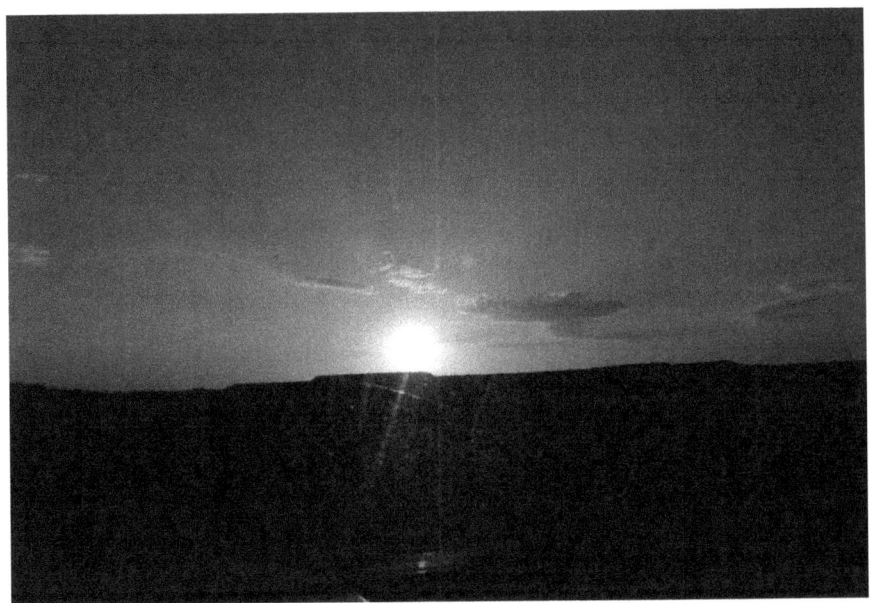

At the end of the 25-mile road is a rock shop/tourist trap that allows overnight camping in their parking lot. I was lucky enough to catch the sunset at the park gate just before pulling into the parking lot for the night.

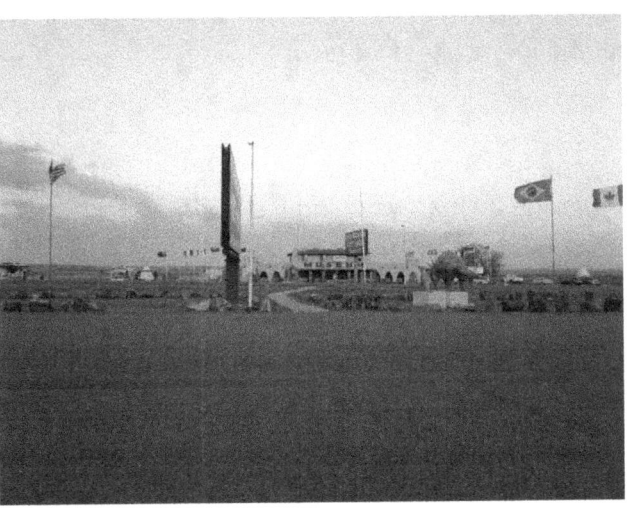

What an amazing day this was! I awoke in an air-conditioned room and had waffles, coffee, and a shower. I saw an ice cave in a volcano, Native American dancers, and trees turned into rocks. Then, I finished it off with an amazing sunset over the dessert. How could this day possibly get any better!?

I saw so many things it's hard to comprehend them all. I'm in awe.

As I'm sitting here contemplating the awe-inspiring amazingness of our world, a youngish couple pulled in and started to unpack. I watched them try to get their Eddie Bauer tent up in the desert winds. They finally got it up, turned their backs, and it started to blow away! Ha! I know I shouldn't laugh but I can't help it. I'm sleeping in my car and having the best freaking time and these two are pulling out their expensive brand name gear and cursing the whole time.

Life is funny...

Oh shit! It gets better! They're in there making out with the light on! Do they know they're giving me a show!? Bahahaha! It was quick. They soon ate dinner and turned off the light and went to bed. I turned on some music and watched the stars.

I'm so grateful for my life right now!

_____ some late-night rambling_____

I'm sitting here in my car watching the stars and having a toke and I just had a thought....   God is Magnificent!   This universe, nature, God, creation, it's magnificent! I saw in the sky in this place of prehistory all these things, at once… sun, moon, clouds, and rain. And then, a rainbow! And now, the clearest night with tons of stars. What an amazing and powerful day this has been!

Curiosity   Gratitude   Adventure   Amazement   Kindness
        Humor   Grit   Openness

I believe these things are essential.

5/7/17 Day 21 - Grand Canyon

I'd planned on waking this morning and going back into the Petrified Forest to see the museum however, as usual, I'm up with the sun and it doesn't open for 2 hours. I can be halfway to Flagstaff by then...

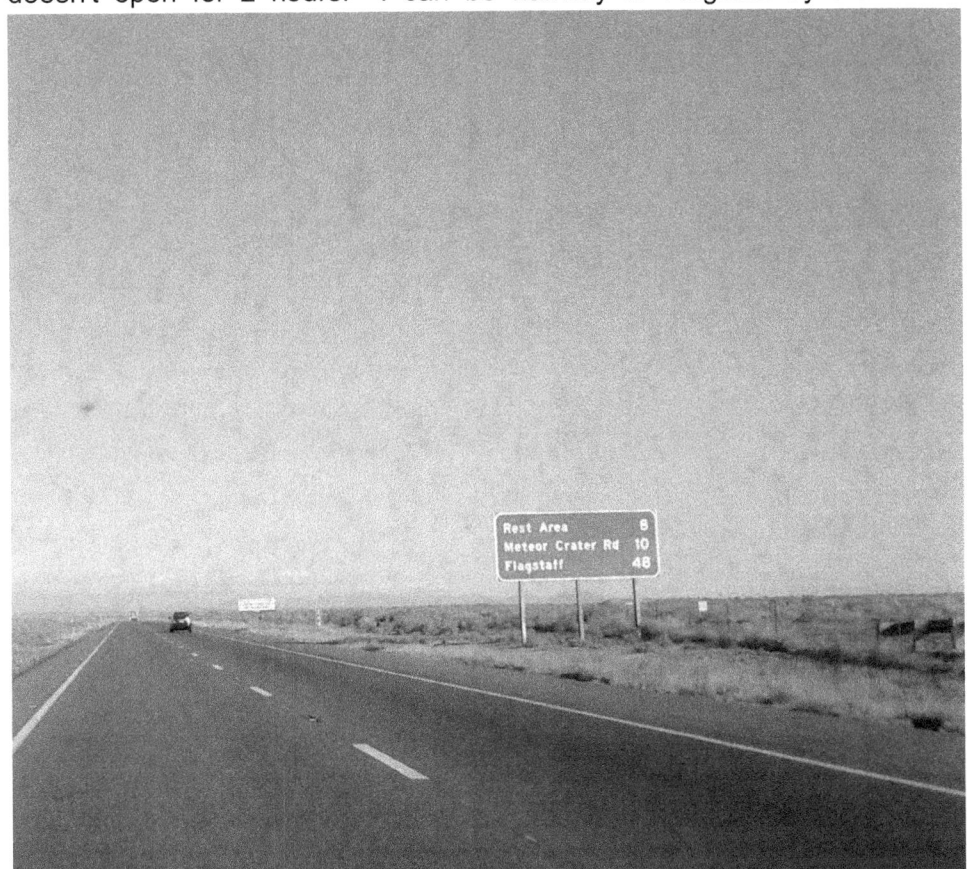

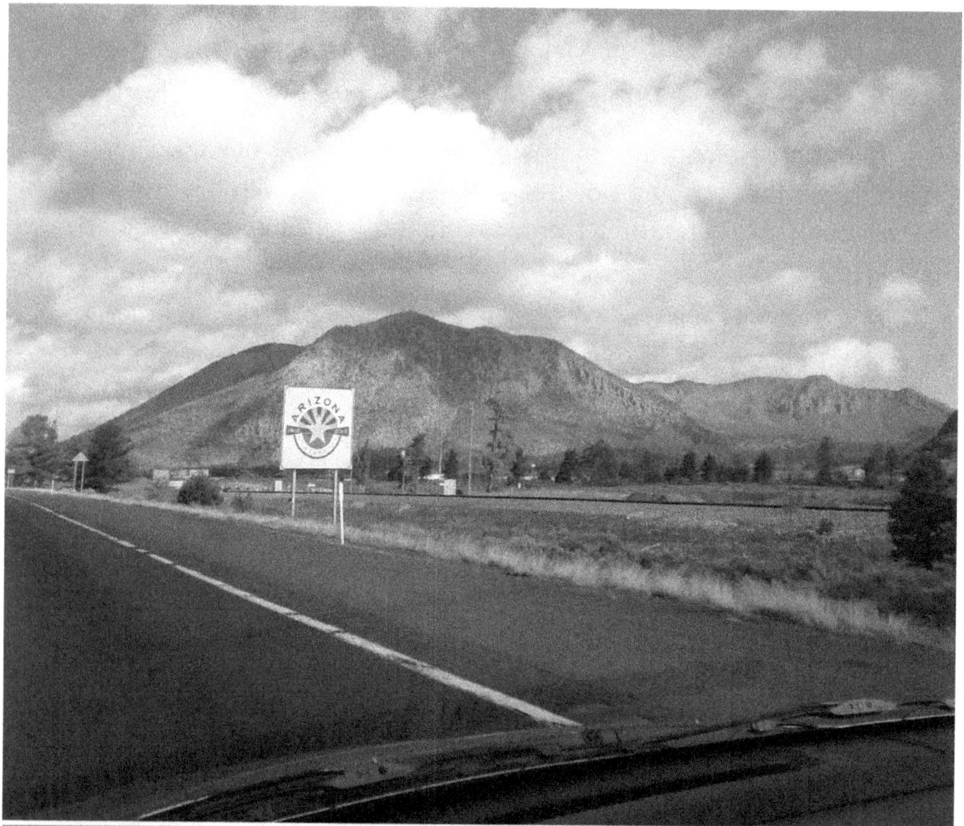
ARIZONA

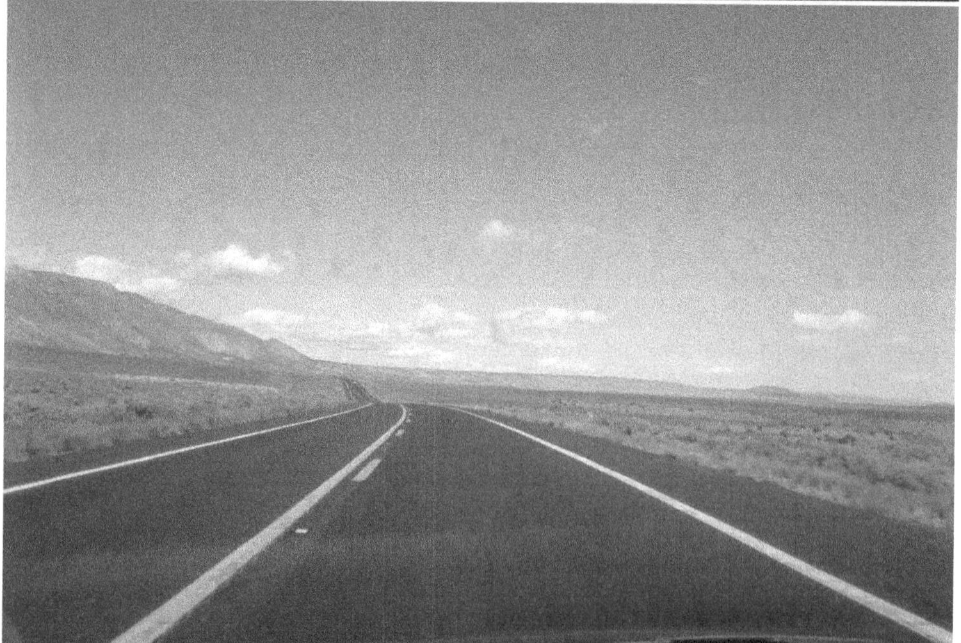

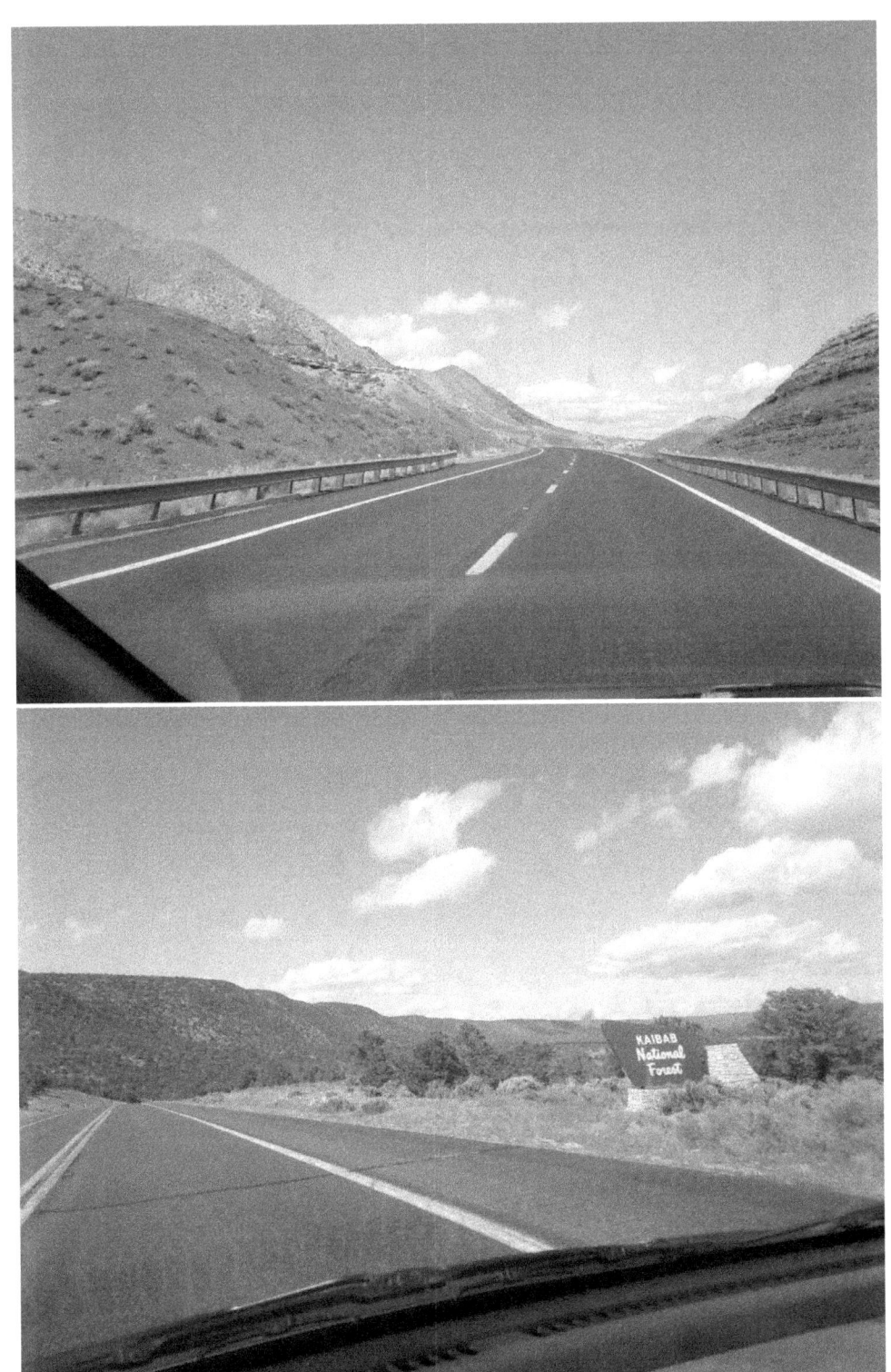

From Flagstaff I headed up to the Grand Canyon.

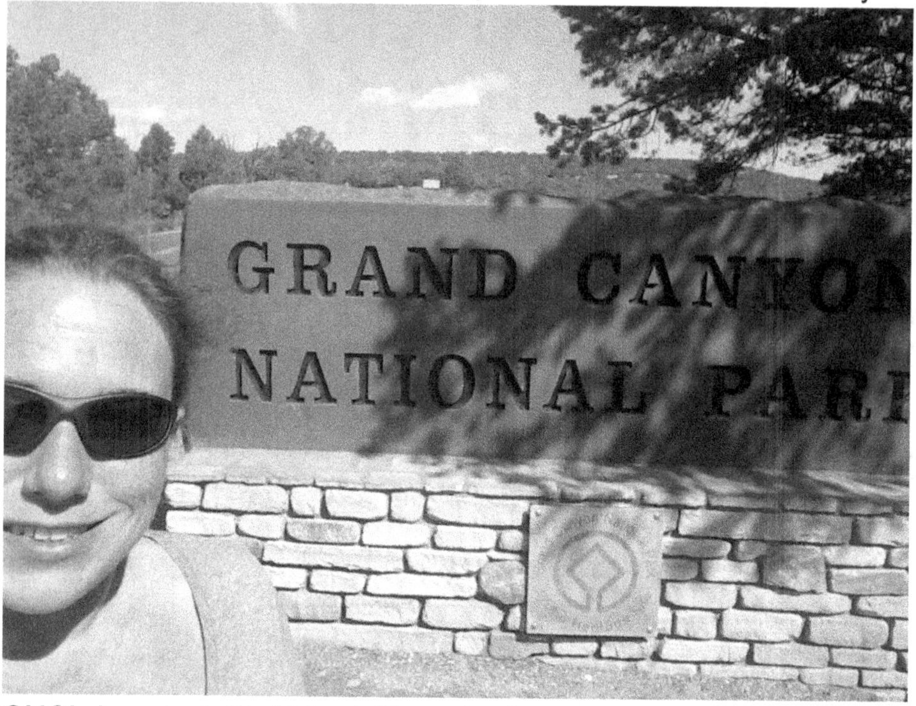

OMG! Amazing! That View! The colors!

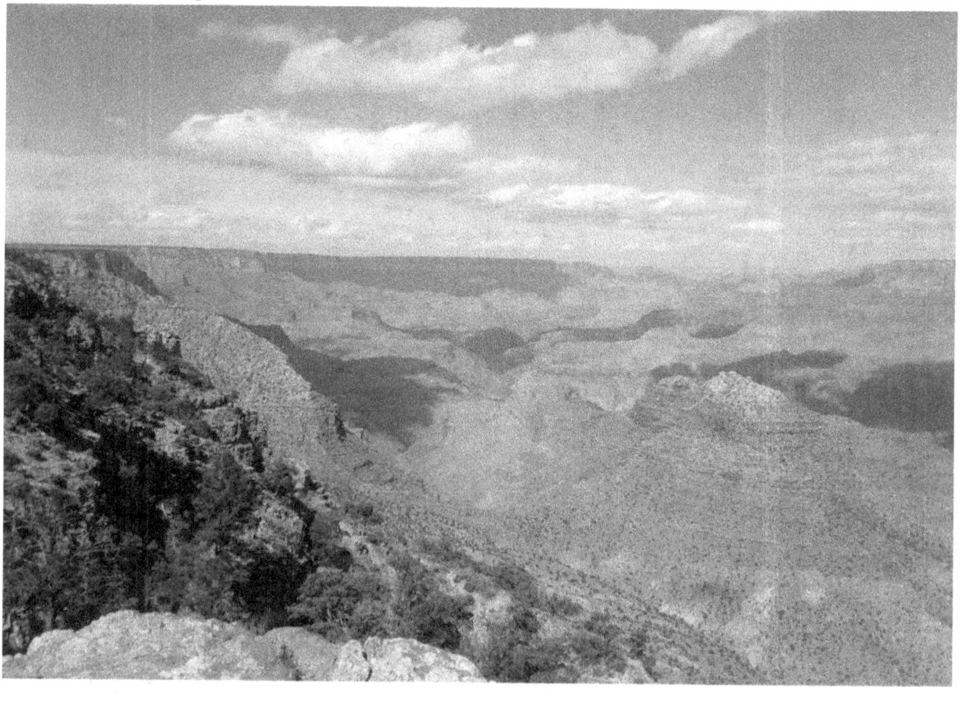

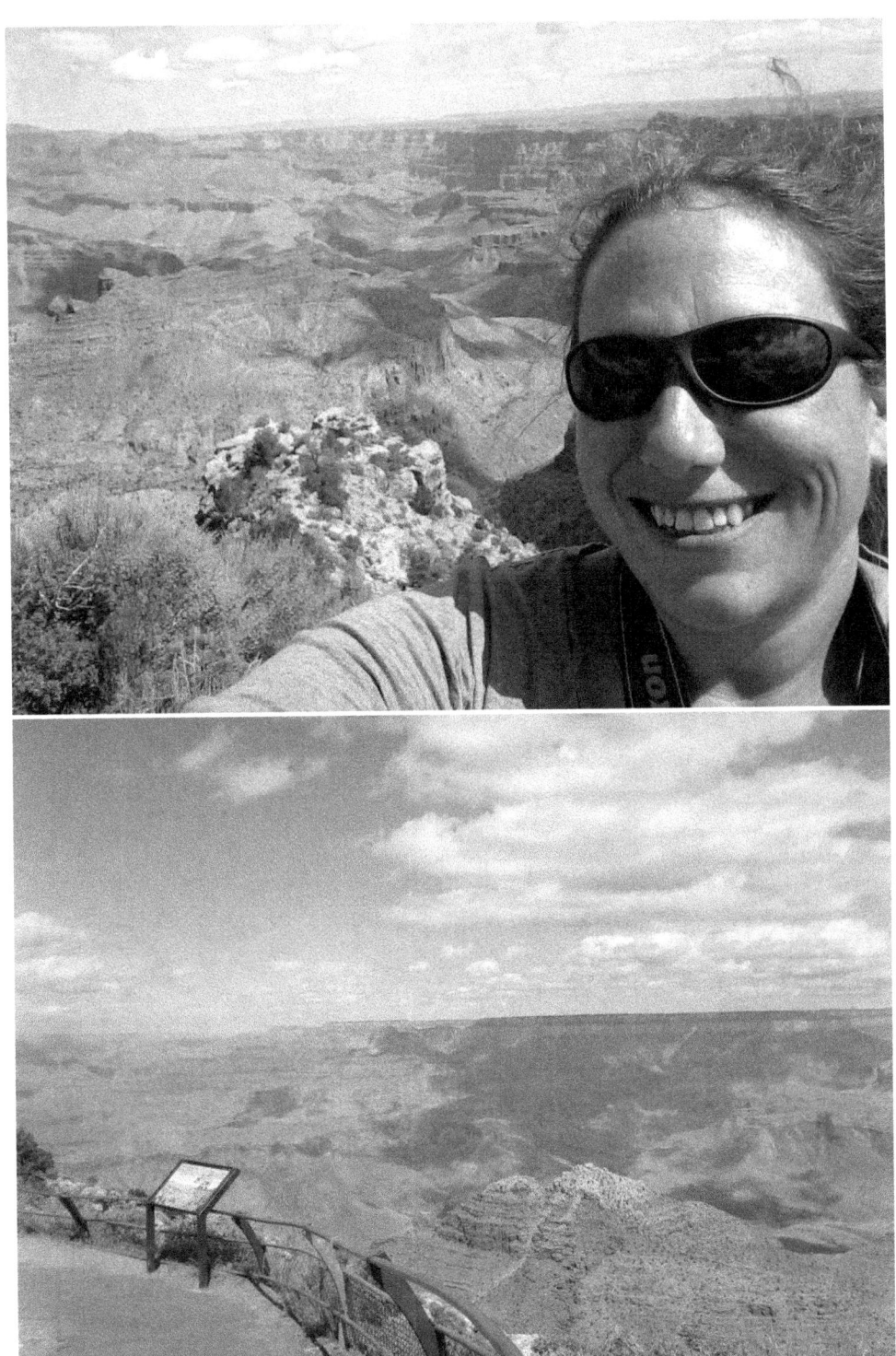

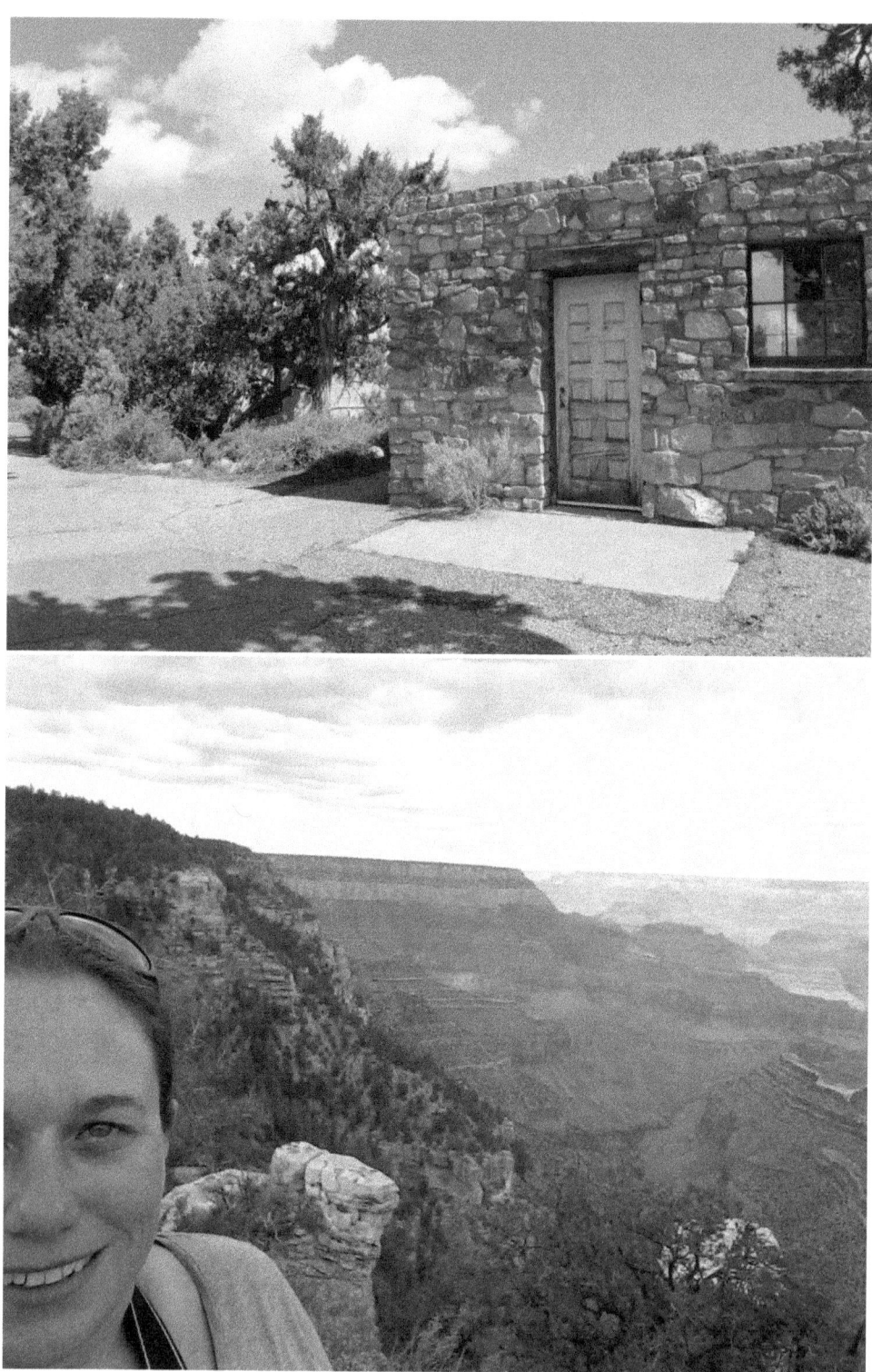

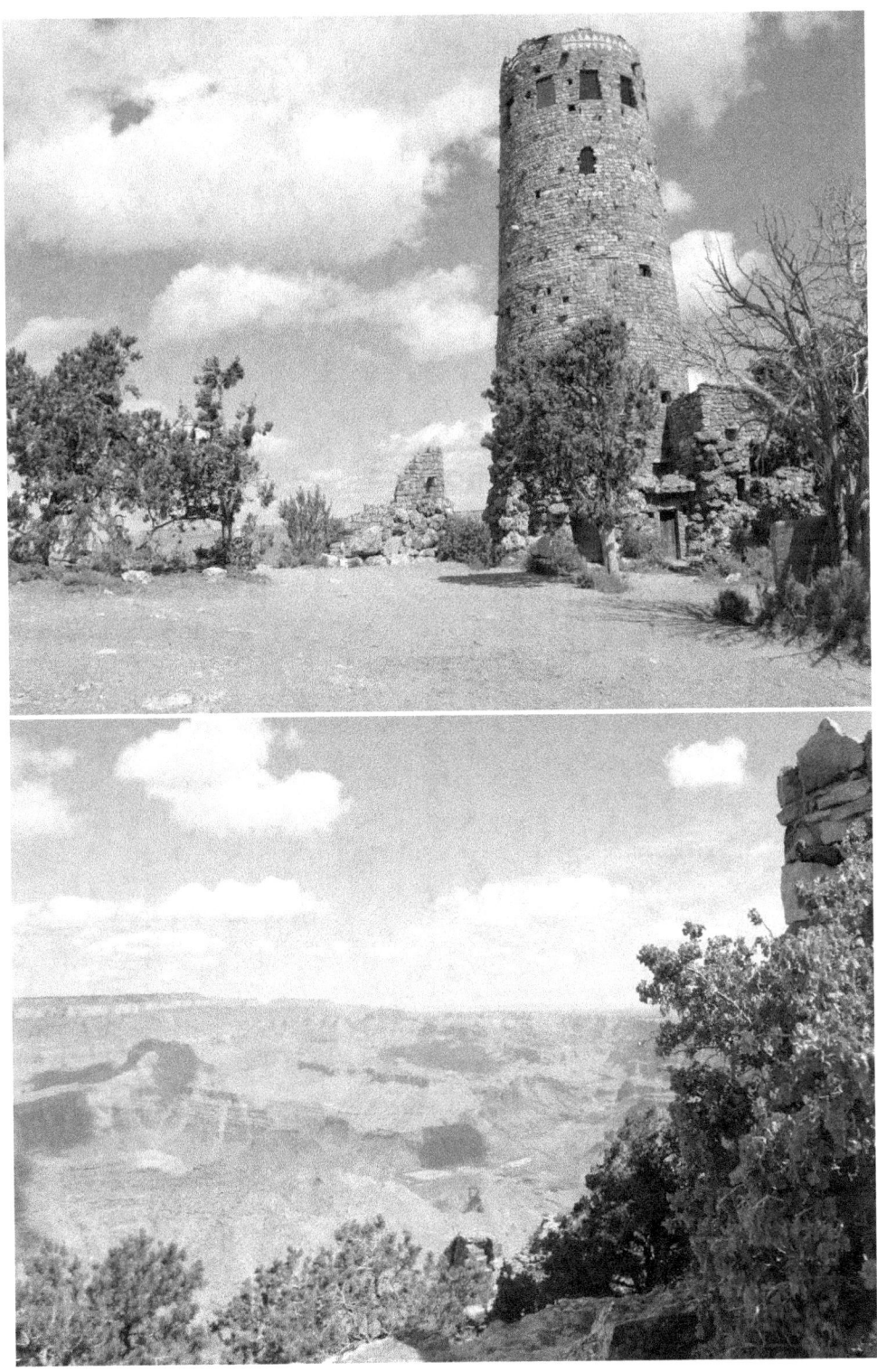

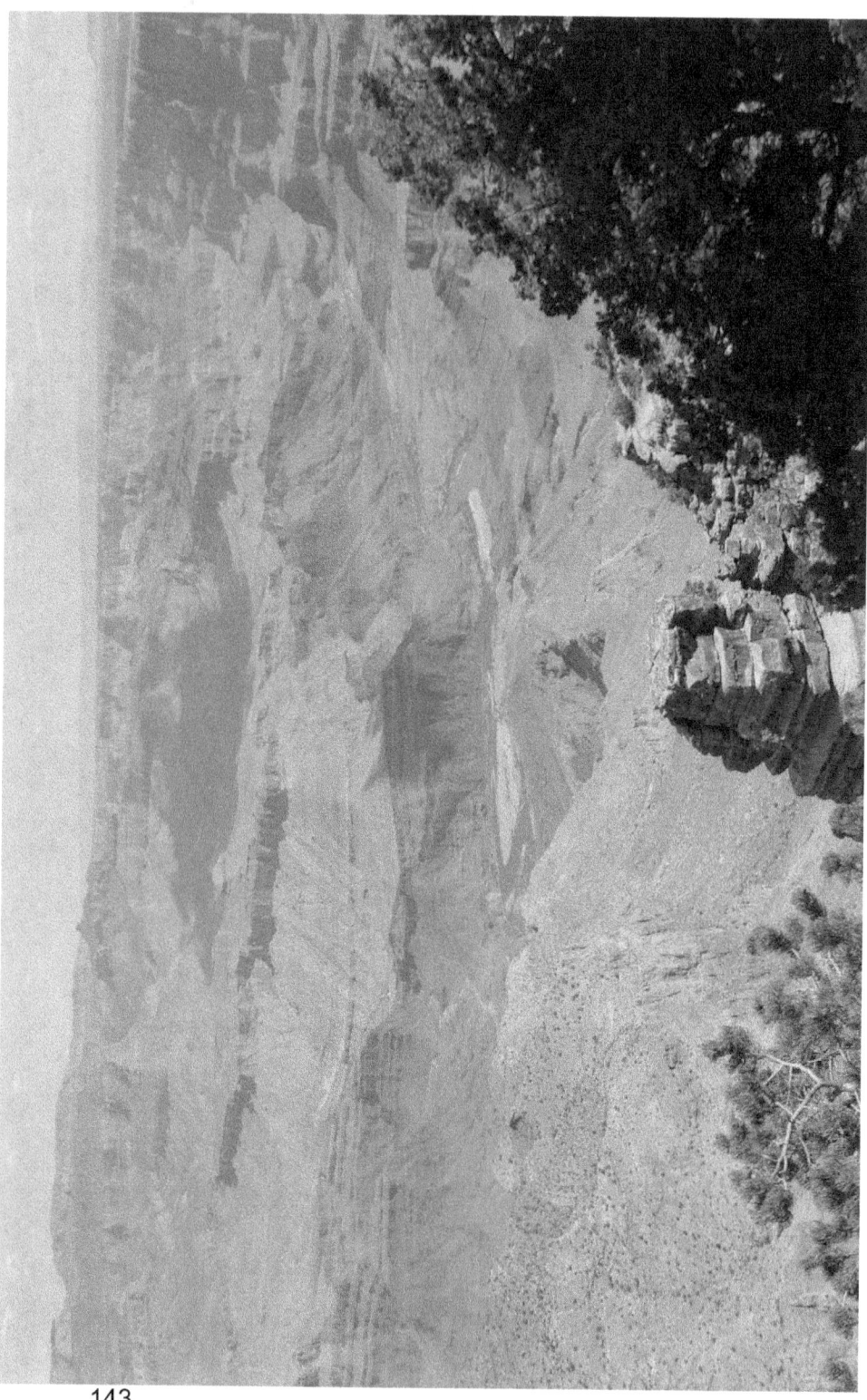

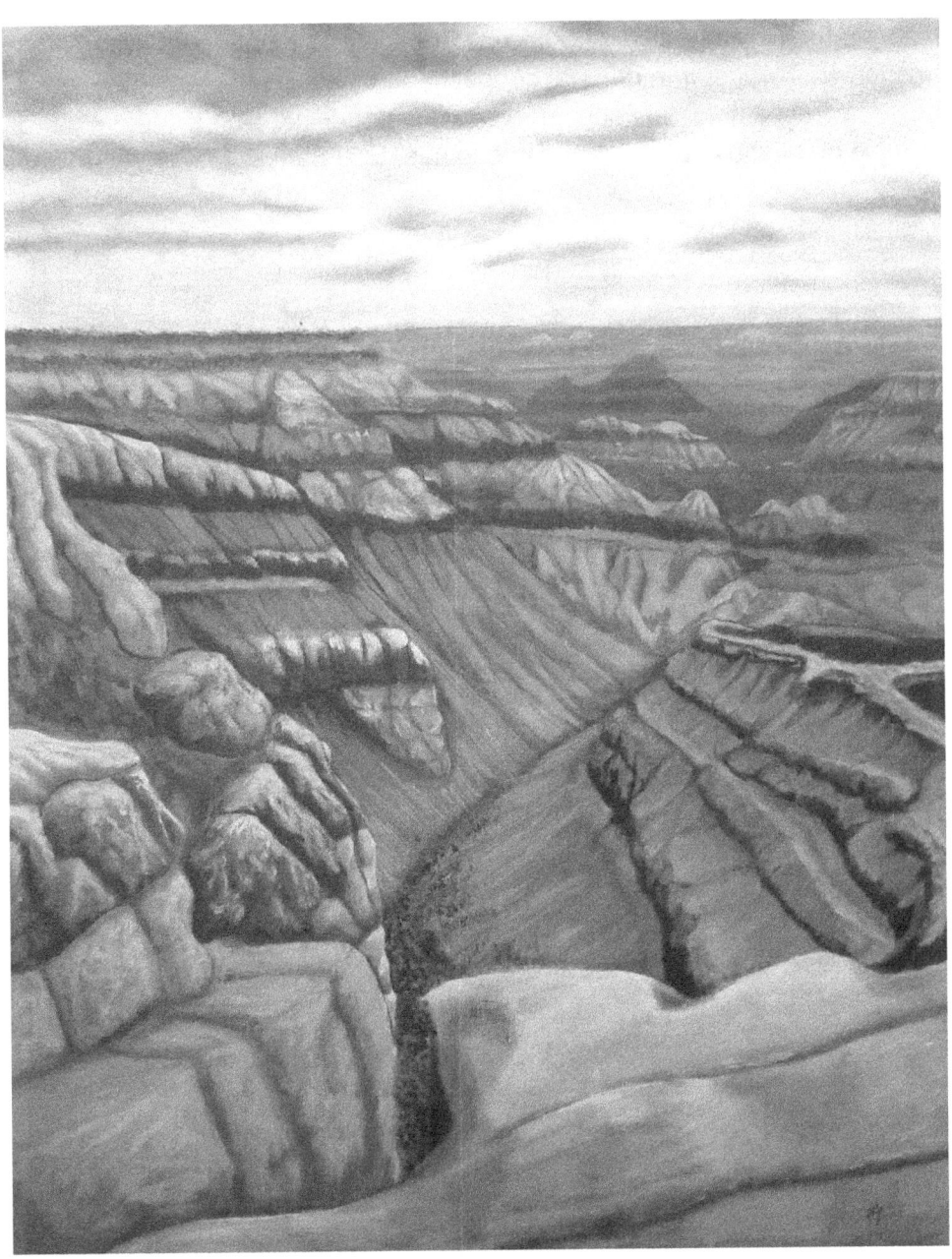

I'm in awe of the canyon!

I'm also disgusted. So many people! A term I heard recently was "cone licker" or an old term "touron". Now, don't get me wrong, just because you visit a tourist destination or are on vacation, doesn't automatically make you a "touron". You are a "Touron" if you wander around with a map/phone in your face and bump into people or, if you leave a trail of trash in your wake or in general conduct yourself in such a way that you have no respect for anyone or anything around you and completely trample on all the cool shit you came to see. End Rant...

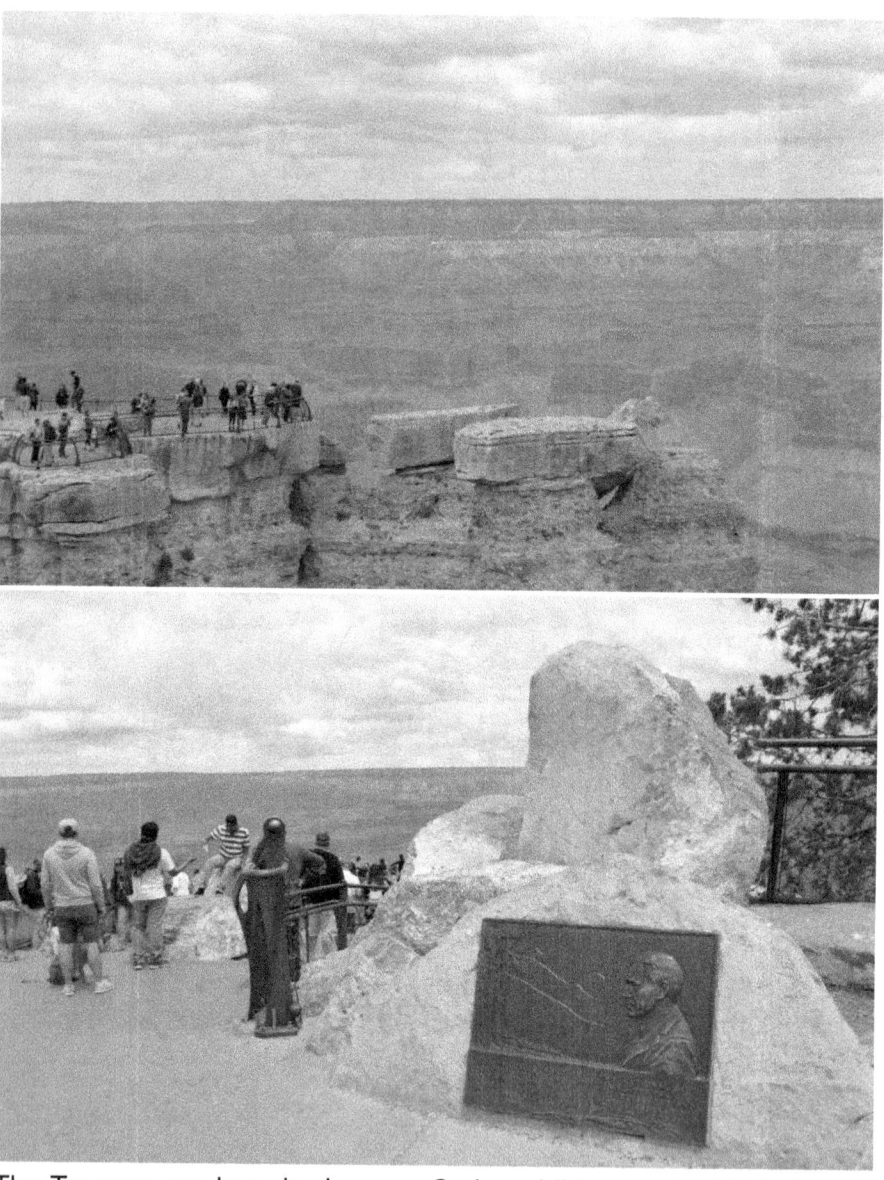

The Tourons are here in droves. Crying children and old blind dogs... Trash, stupidity, disregard, and disrespect. People on your tail pushing you through the park.

145

Slow down a bit! Enjoy the view! Be polite! Pick up after yourself!

There's something worse though. Ol' Gertie is making some strange noises. I'm not sure what it is but it's getting worse. I first heard it up on top of the canyon. A knocking sound coming from my transmission area. Shit.

It goes away in neutral or if I press the clutch. Shit. That sounds transmissiony.

I'd heard about some National Forest land that you can camp on up here and I was planning to stay the night but with this sound I think I should head down… a tow truck up here would be hella-expensive…

———

Back at Flagstaff and I'm no longer hearing the sound. That's a good thing. Bank account, on the other hand, not so great. I'm spending money quickly. I'm over halfway thru my funds and not even to California yet. There are so many more stops I'd like to make!

Can't really think about that now… Just gotta watch my pennies… It'll be fine…

5/8/17 Day 22

I'm a bit nervous about my car and my money today…I'm supposed to meet a friend in Sedona tomorrow. The car isn't making the noise now though so no reason to stop at a shop here in Flagstaff. Sedona is my next stop.

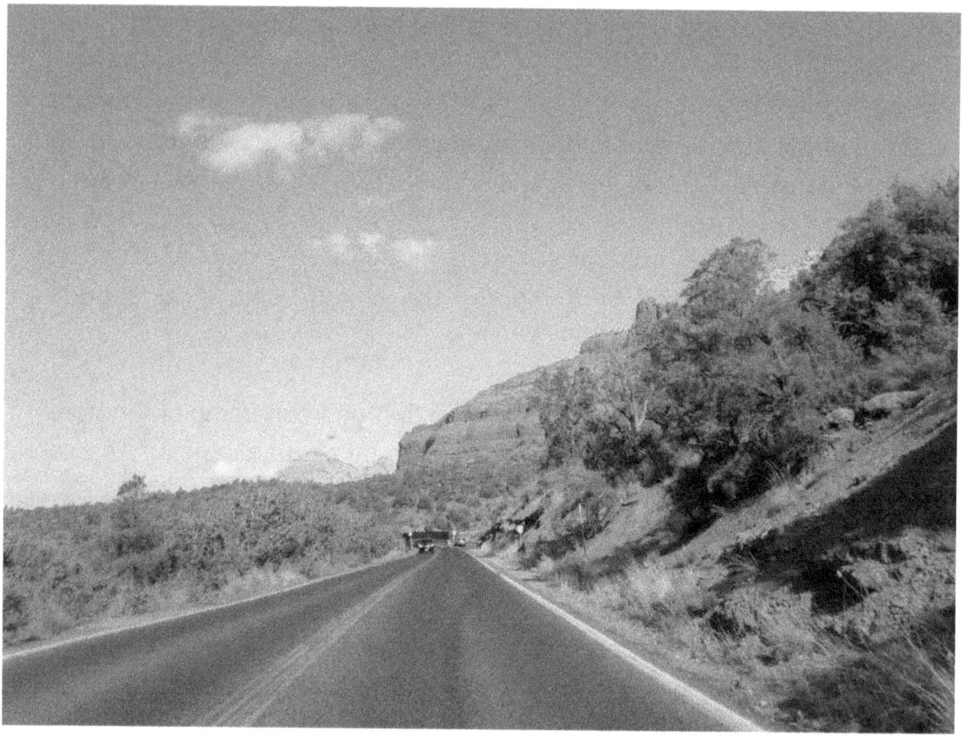

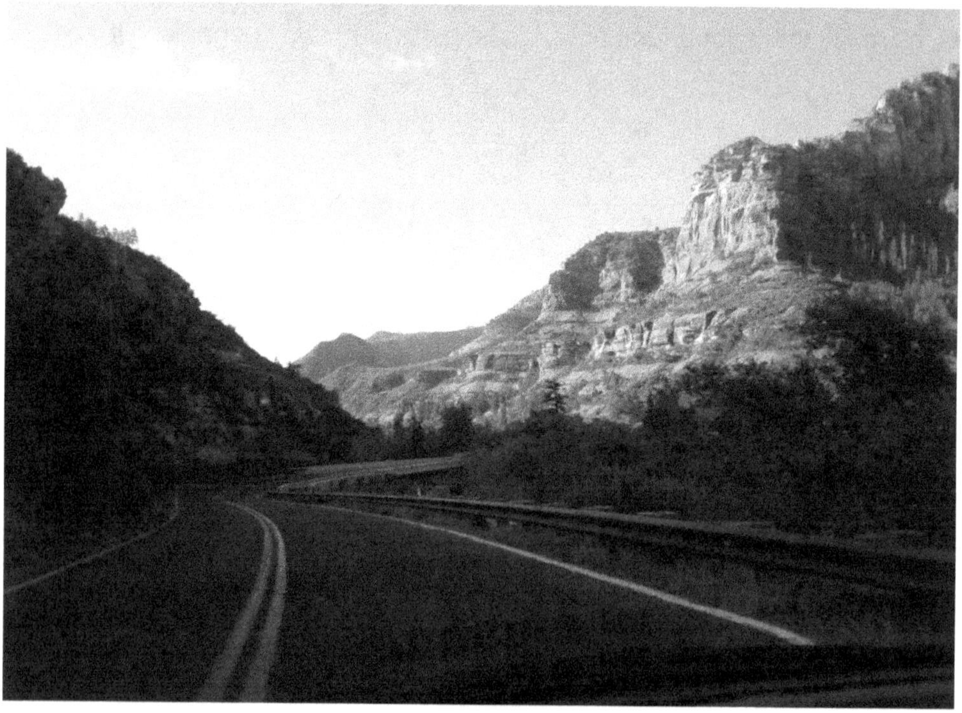

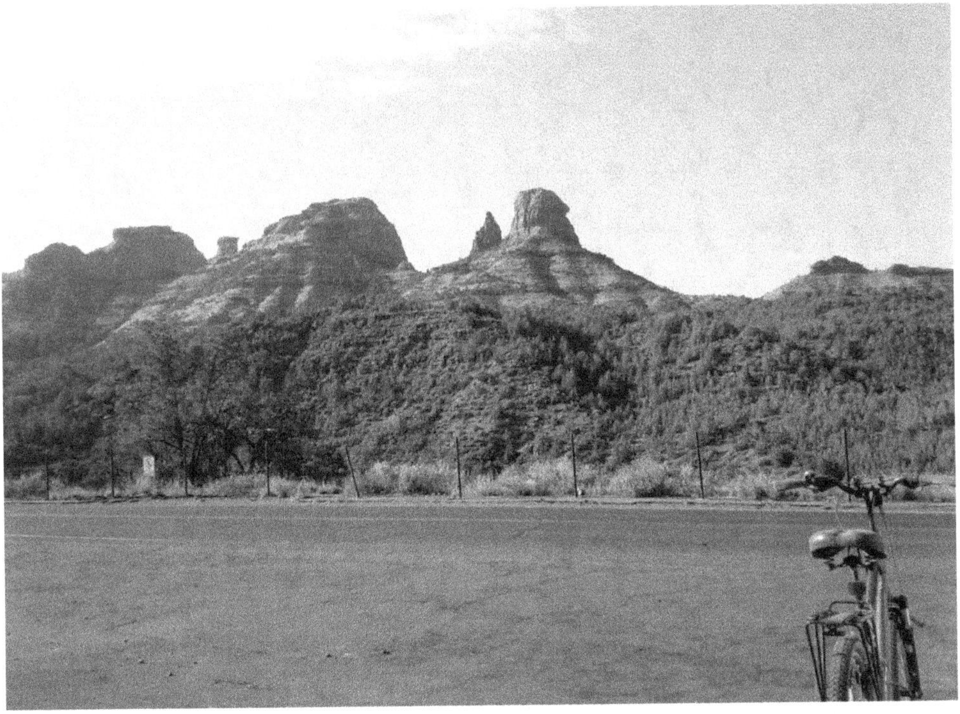

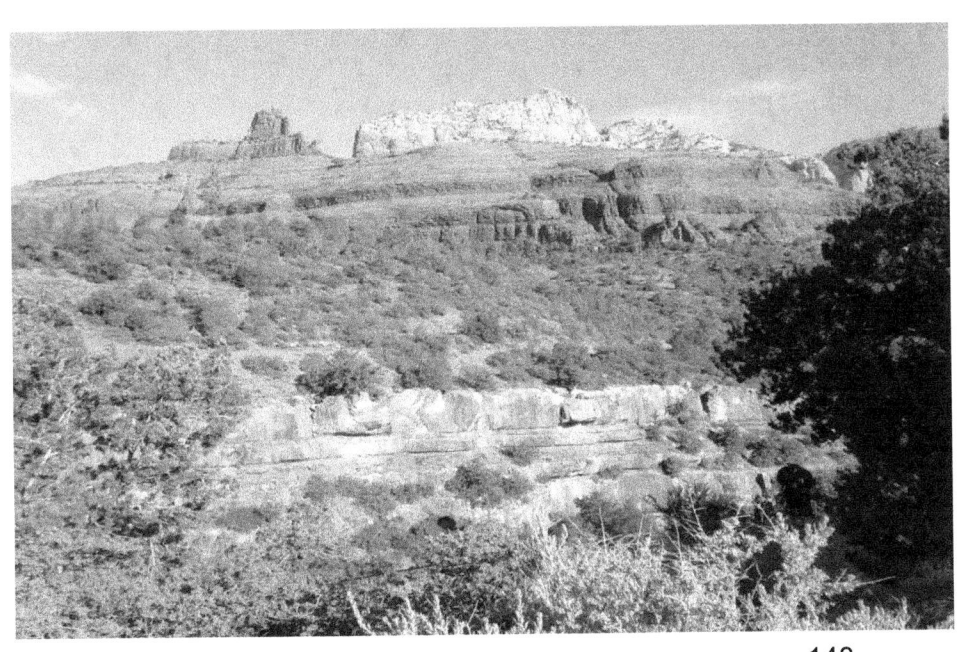

The drive to Sedona is amazing! That color! I've never seen rocks that color! I stopped at several over looks and then wandered around town for a bit. It's quite warm here today.

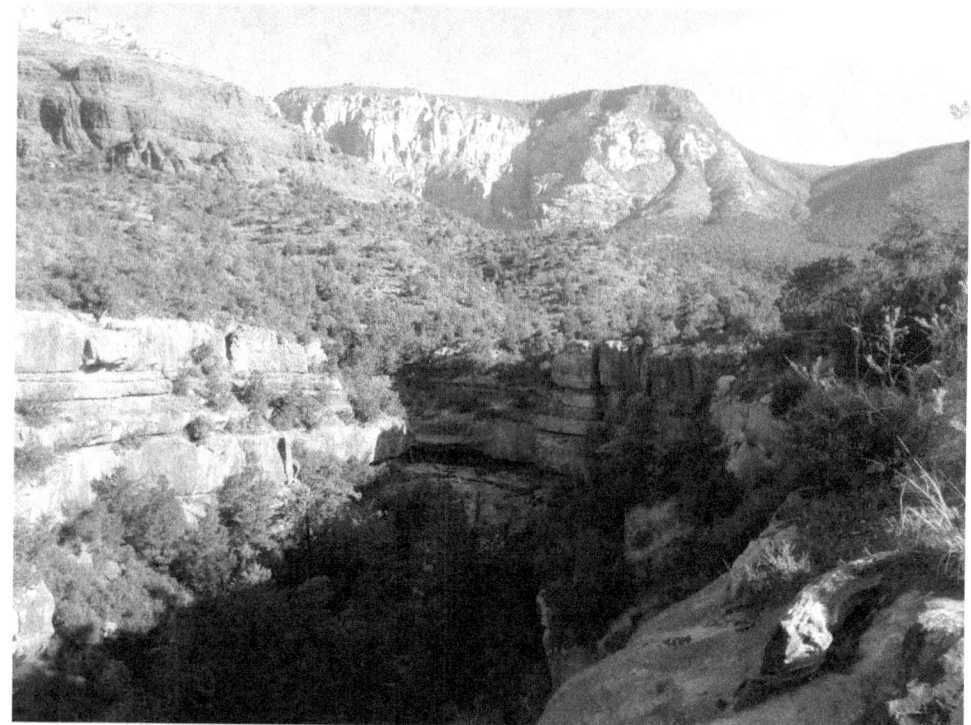

Sedona is gorgeous. It's very unique and there is a lot of art. It's also quite expensive here and I haven't found a free sleeping place yet.

I'm not feeling good today. Anxiety is high and I feel very out of place. I'm not feeling social and I don't really want to stay the night here. Ugh, I'm gonna feel bad if I cancel for tomorrow but I'm not feeling it. I just want to keep driving. I'm gonna cancel. So sorry friend.

I'm feeling all sorts of anxious at the moment. I'm getting nervous and getting low on funds. I don't know where I'm going yet but I've gotta get to the coast at least. Even if I just make it to LA. No, I wanna see the whole coast. If I'm gonna stop where I land, I hope it's at least northern California or further north. So much I want to see still.

Keep going… don't stop, just keep going…

Heading toward the Hoover Dam and Vegas. I'd hoped to get there to see the lights on the strip at night. Oh, but I'm not feeling it. The anxiety is starting to settle in my stomach. Now, I am running. That's how I really feel today.

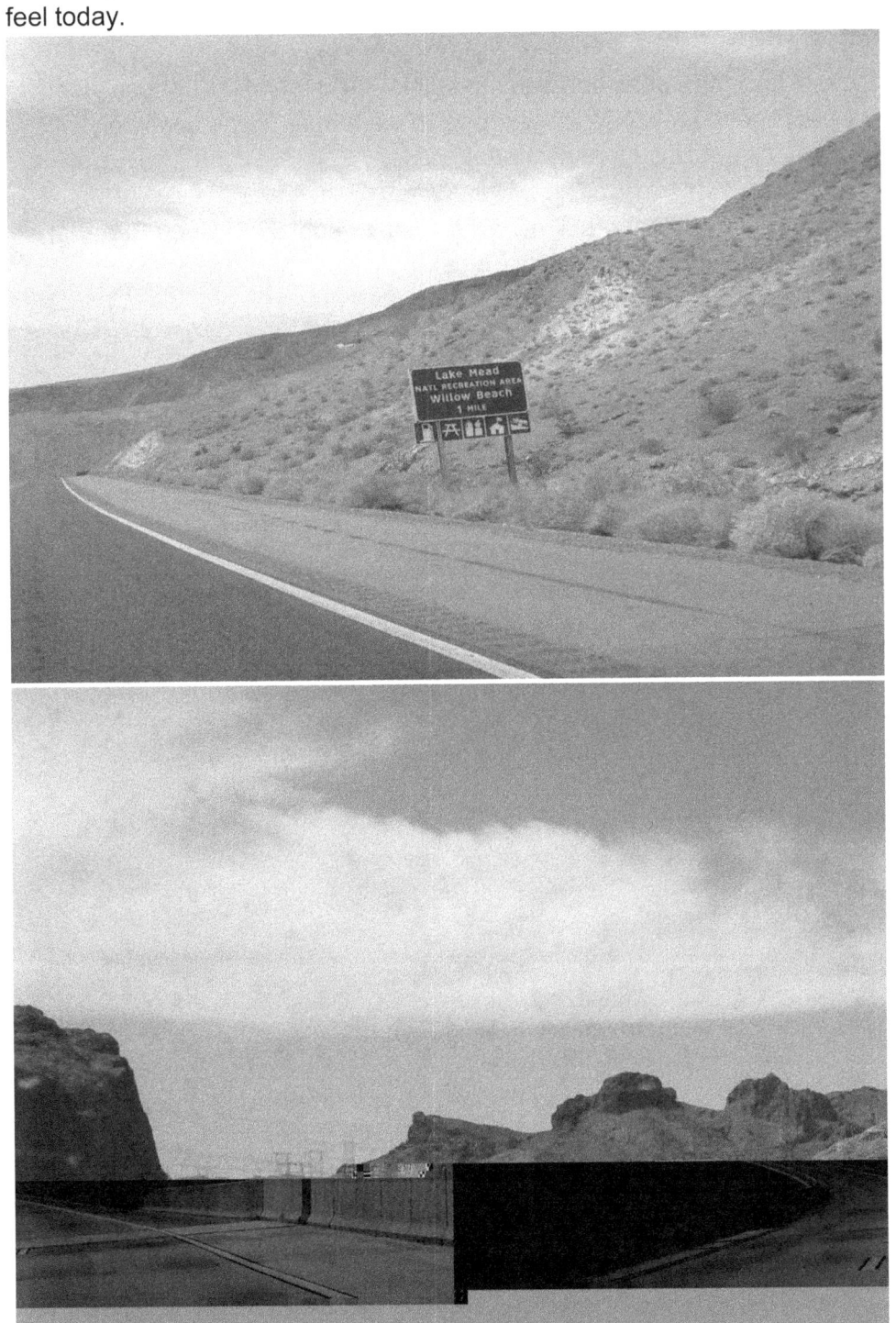

What the hell am I doing!? I don't know…. Just keeping on keeping on.

Straight through Vegas, too early for lights. And the traffic… I don't feel like peopling today. I had enough people yesterday. In the car by myself on the back roads is more comfortable.

How am I ever going to sell my art if I can't people!? Deep Breathe, Lace. You'll be fine. You'll figure it out…

Rolling on…

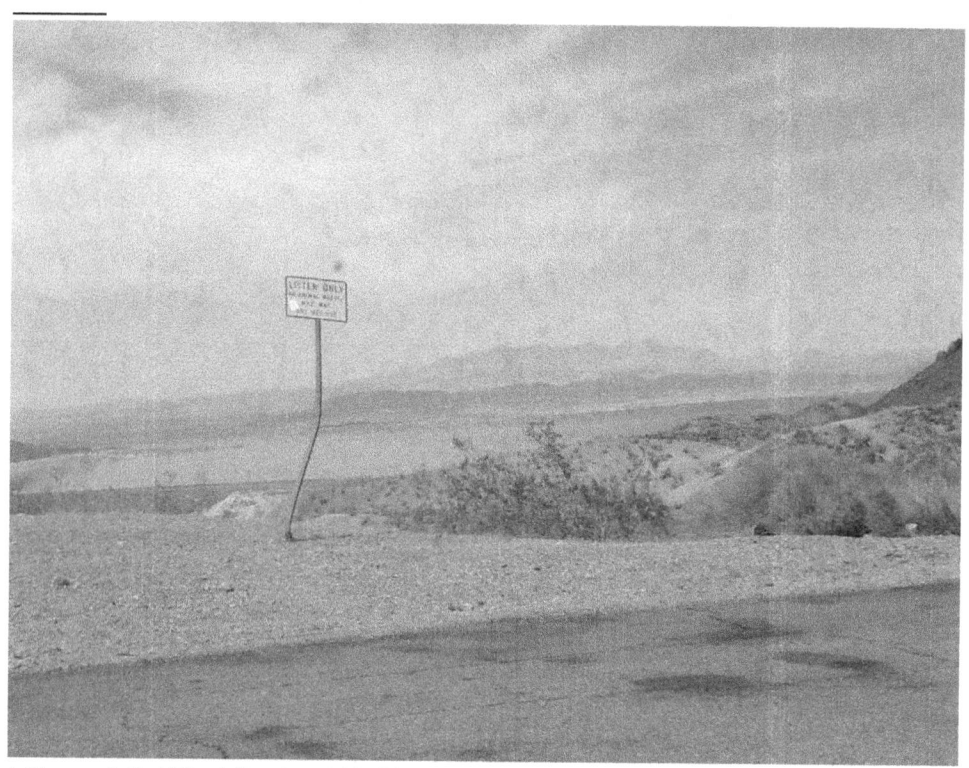

Litter only? What the heck!? How about no littering!

I made it to Barstow, CA tonight. I'll be sleeping at the Walmart. It's loud and bright though, and hot. I hope I get some sleep.

As if I wasn't feeling stressed enough today, M called. He's freaking out about something. Is that why I'm feeling like this today? Am I still that programed and connected? Maybe but my problem today is money. And, I'm scared…

Relax, Lace, you're just fine. Trust the process. Follow the plan. What plan?! Do you even have a plan!?

You'll find a place. No, the desert isn't it, but you already knew that. You already know that you like trees and rivers and mountains. You'll find your place. Keep going.

5/9/17 Day 23 - L.A.

I woke up really early today… 3am! I've got a terrible headache too. Can't let that stop me though. I'm headed into LA today. I've got an Airbnb reserved and I need a freaking shower. When was my last shower? New Mexico!? Shit. that was 5 days ago… Today's goal? SHOWER!

———

My drive from Barstow to LA was mostly in the dark. But then I came up over a mountain pass to a sea of lights. First San Bernardino then LA. I thought San Bernardino was it at first. From darkness to this lake of lights but then you come up over the next mountain and THERE it IS! A SEA of lights on a backdrop of blackness. Past LA is the ocean, I know, but right now, it's pure darkness.

So, I drive down into LA and start trying to find my way around. I found my Airbnb. As it turns out, the Flower District shares its corner with Skid Row. NOPE, not staying there! There goes that 30 bucks. Found the arts district but, nothing opens until Thursday at 11am. Today is only Tuesday. Shit… Now what? I need to regroup. I need a shower and a place to sleep. Screw it. I'm going to the beach.

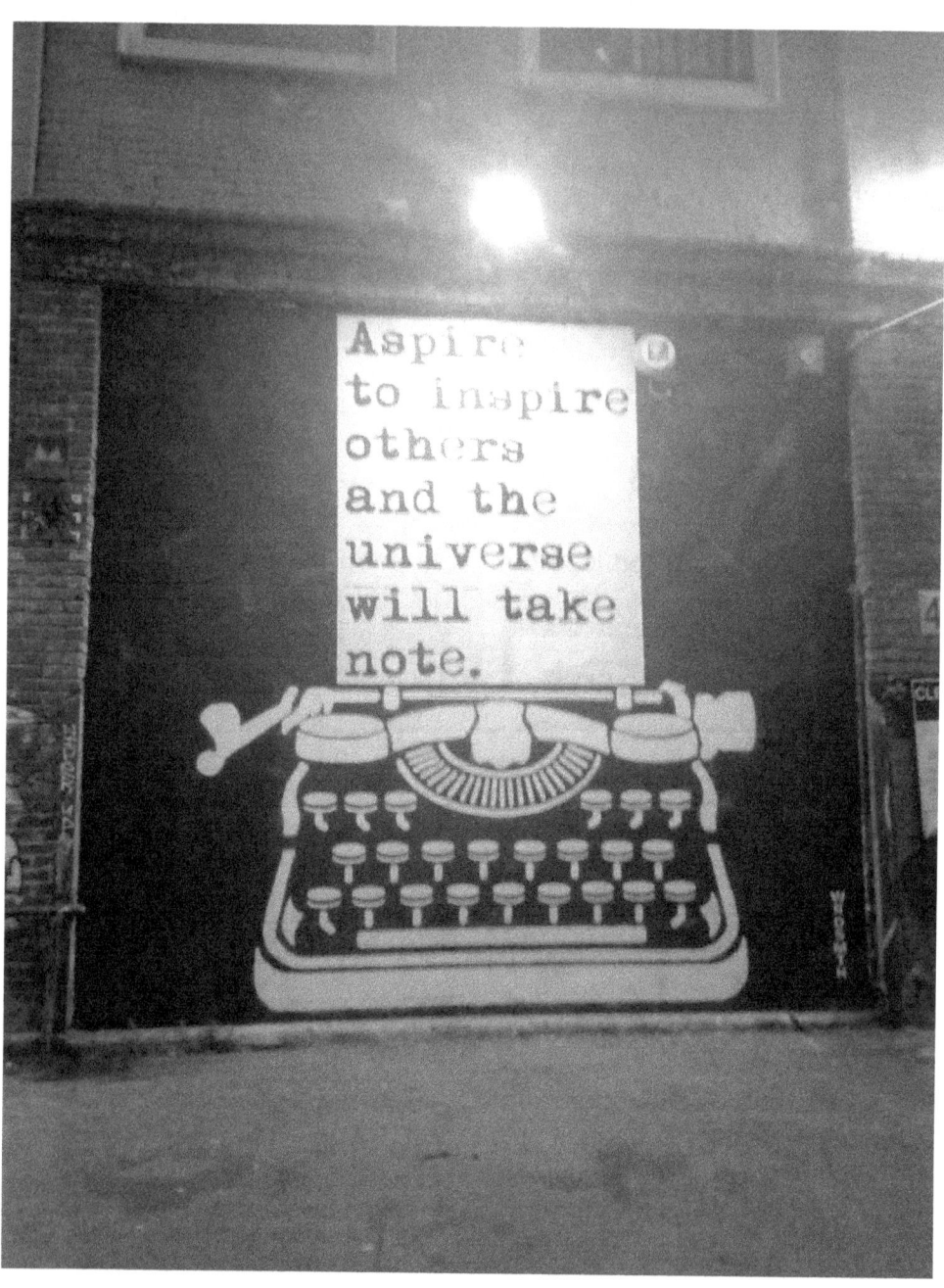

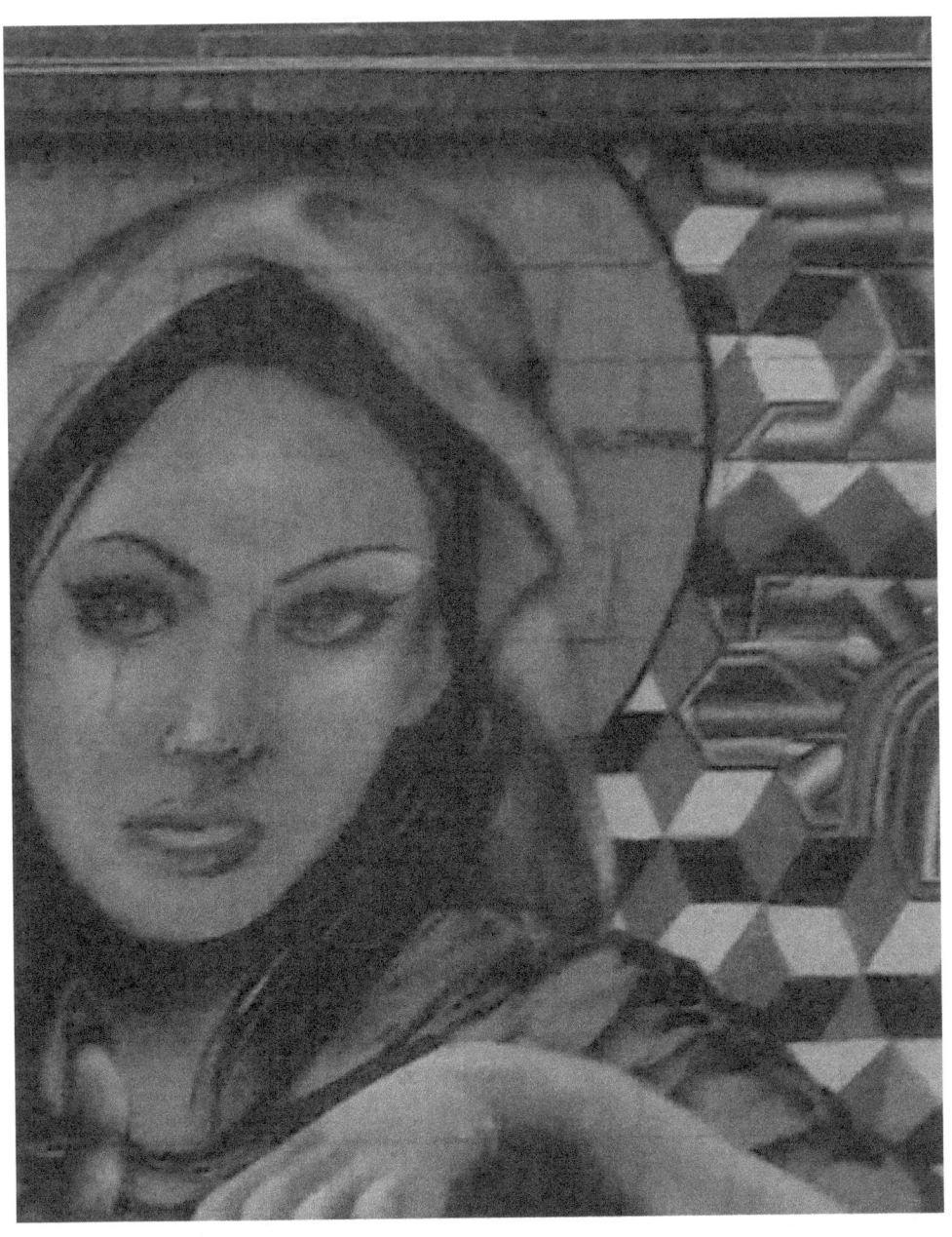

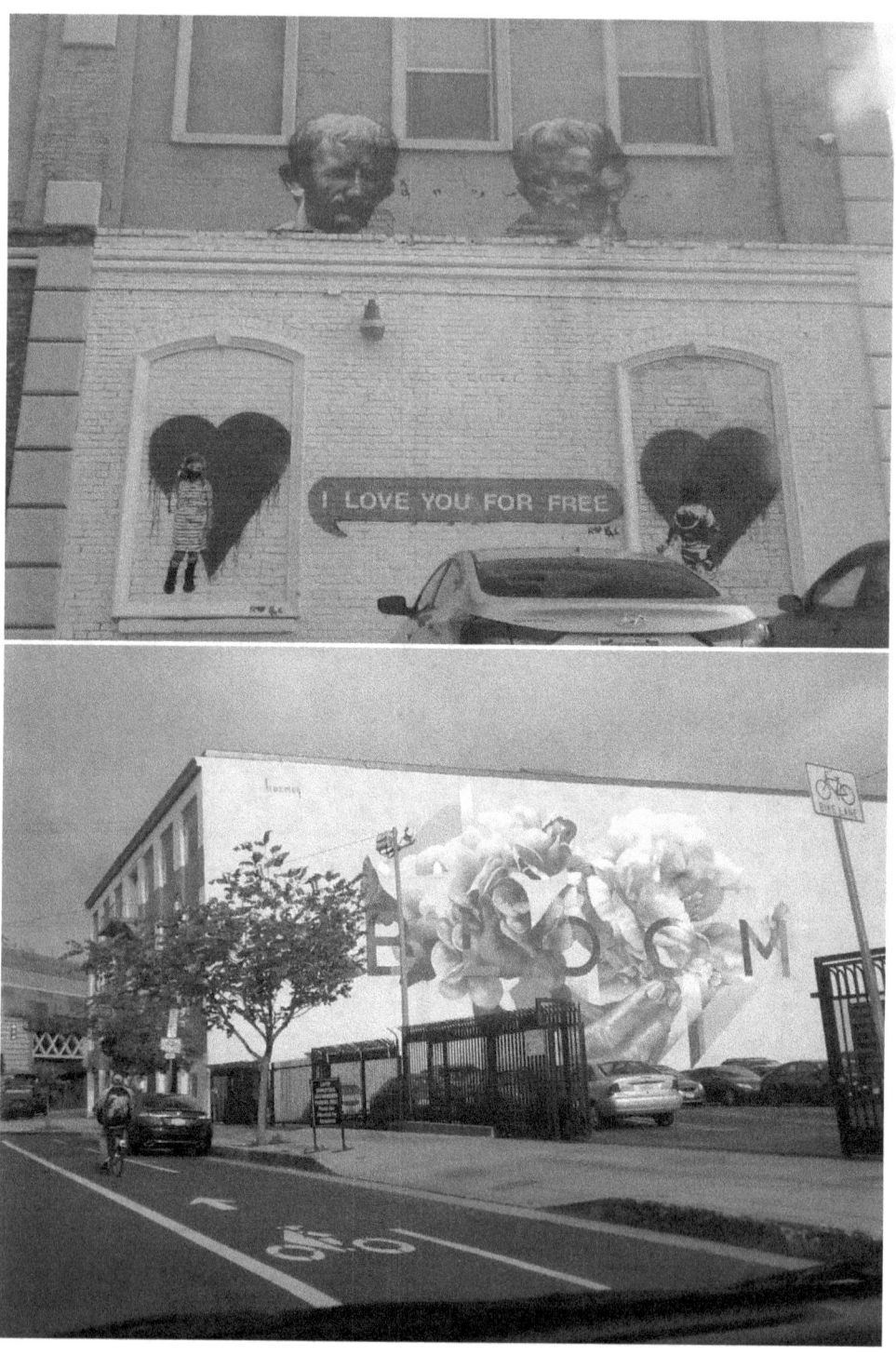

Ya know, I've never been a city person… I grew up in an urban area about 45 minutes outside of Chicago, but I've always felt more comfortable in the country, in the woods. Traffic in the country is a horse on the driveway or a slow-moving tractor. Traffic in the city is bumper to bumper in a sea of exhaust.

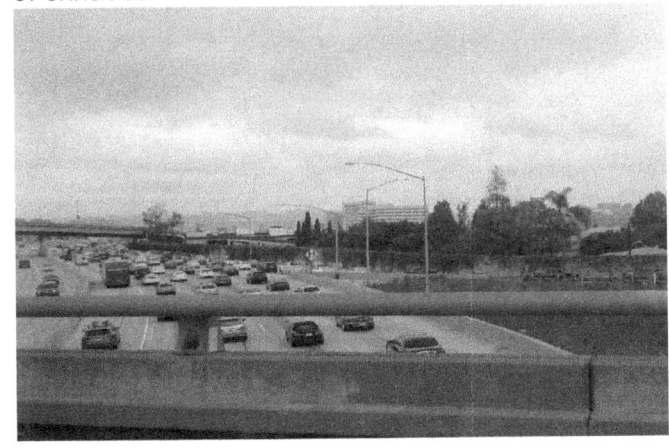

Santa Monica pier is 15 miles from the arts district in LA and it took 1.5 hours to get there.

INSane! My calf, clutch, and brakes got one helluva workout. And a homeless man started to ask me for money then did and double take and instead asked if I was homeless too. Really glad I've got my car...

_____

At   the   beach   at   last!

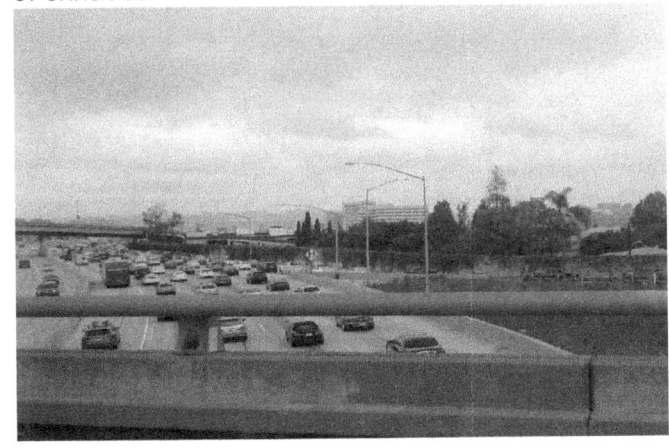

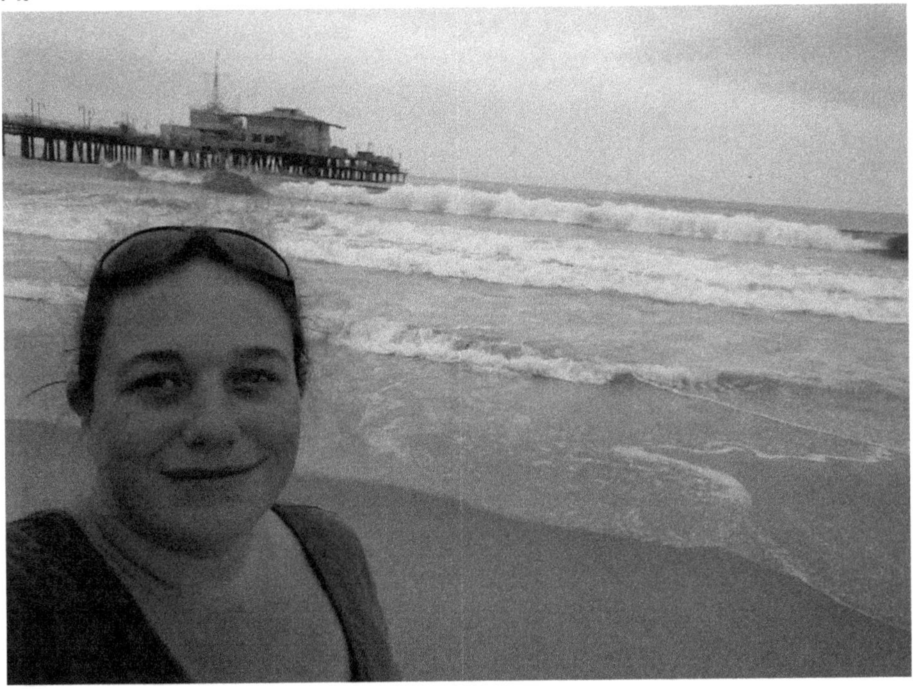

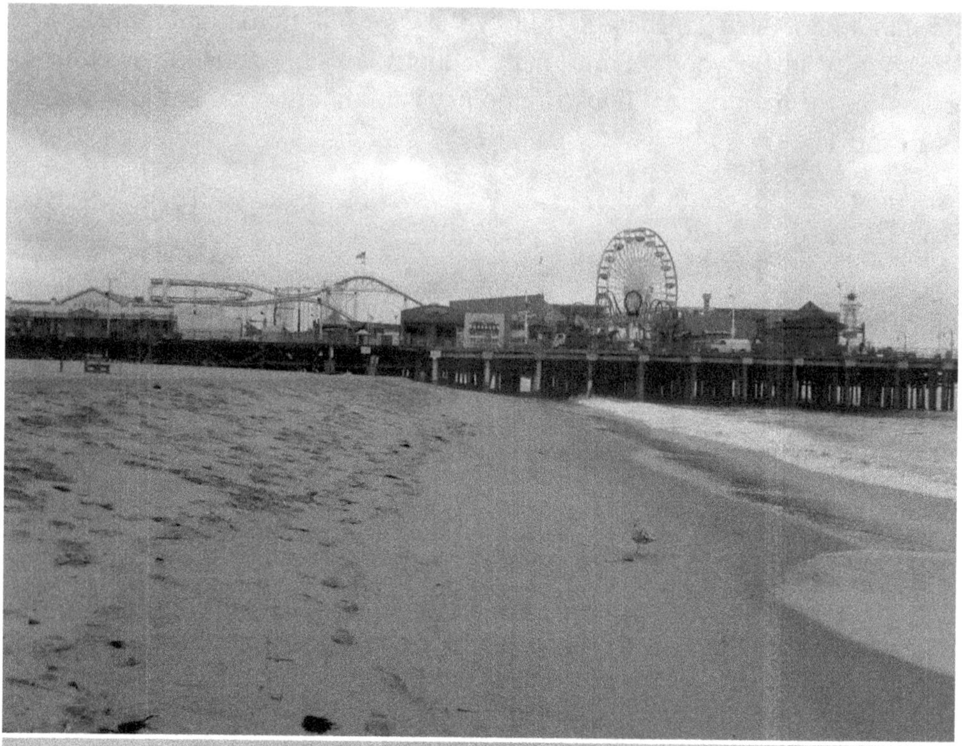

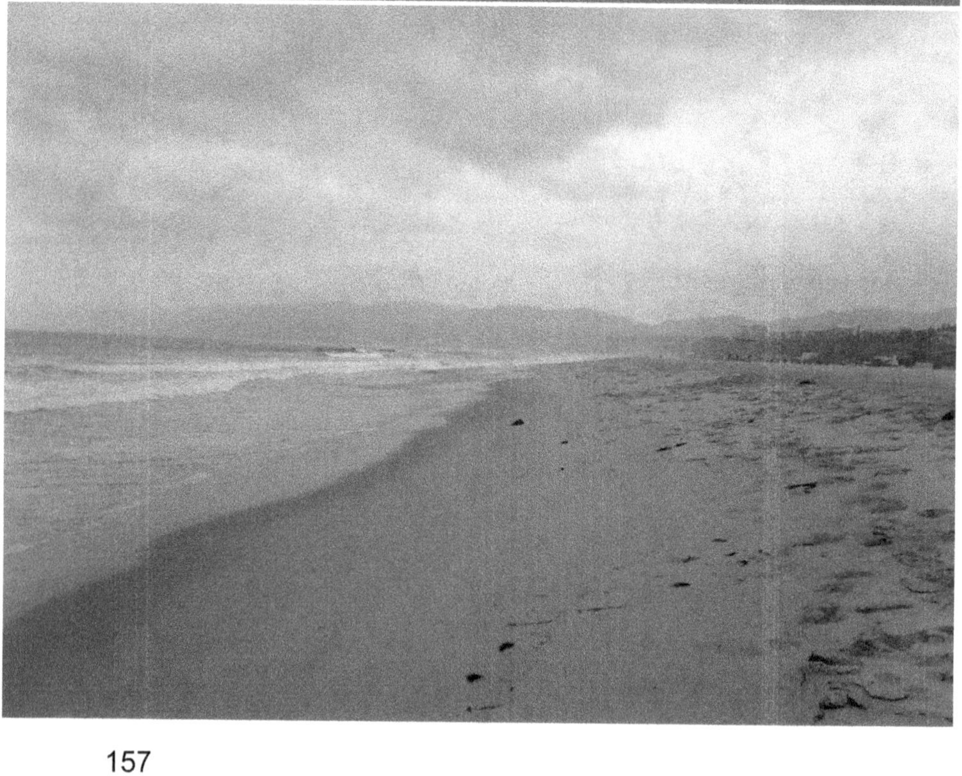

157

It's a foggy and cool morning. The sun hasn't cleared the mountains yet. The beach smells like salt and fish. And nobody is here.

It's perfect.

There's an empty bench at the end of a small boardwalk. I sat down there to ponder my life and watch the waves and whatever else might be moving this early.

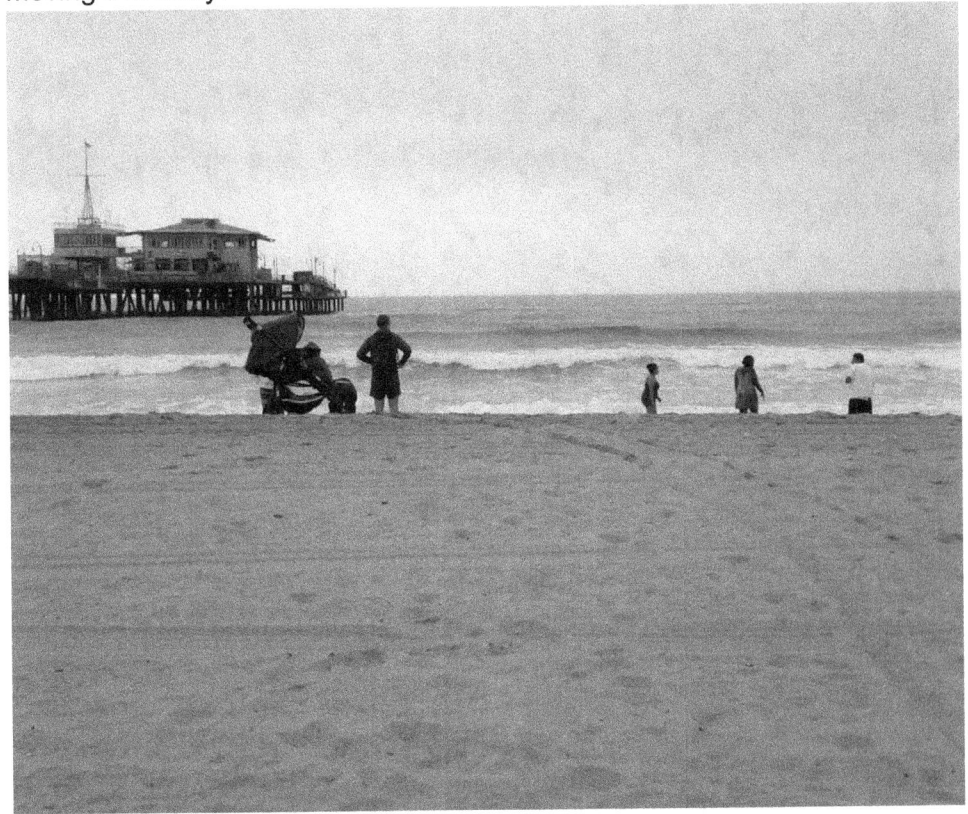

Before long a sweeper comes up behind me. I'm out of his way but still get sand thrown on me. Time to check out the pier and have something to eat.

.

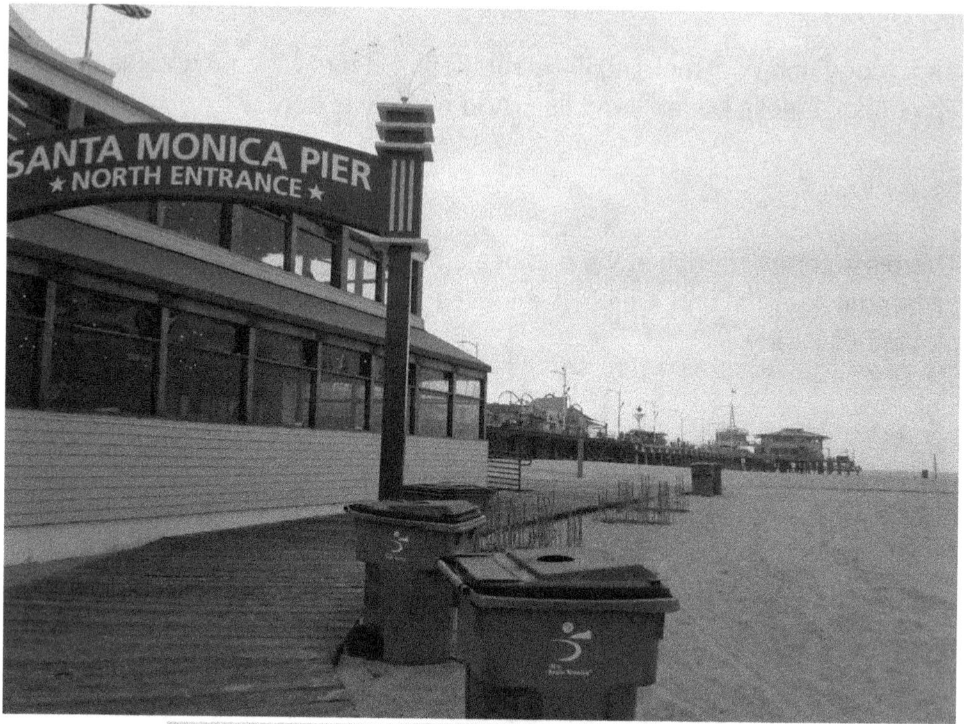

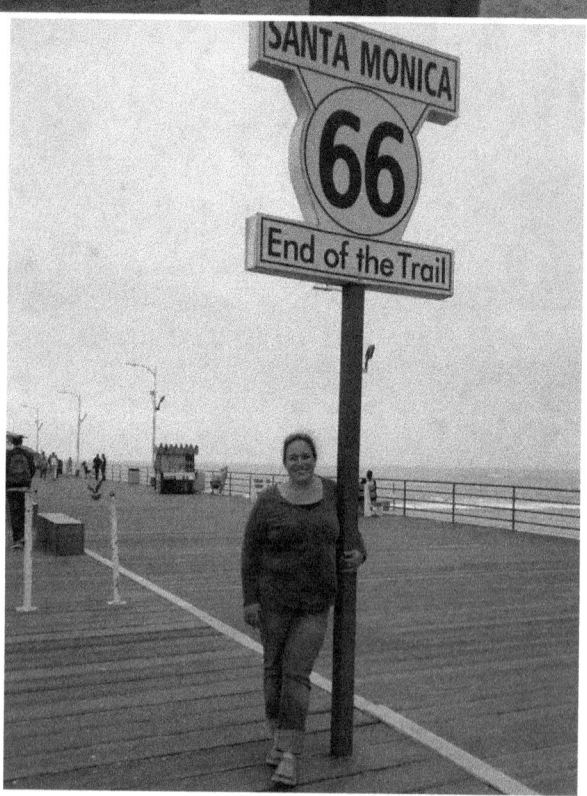

159

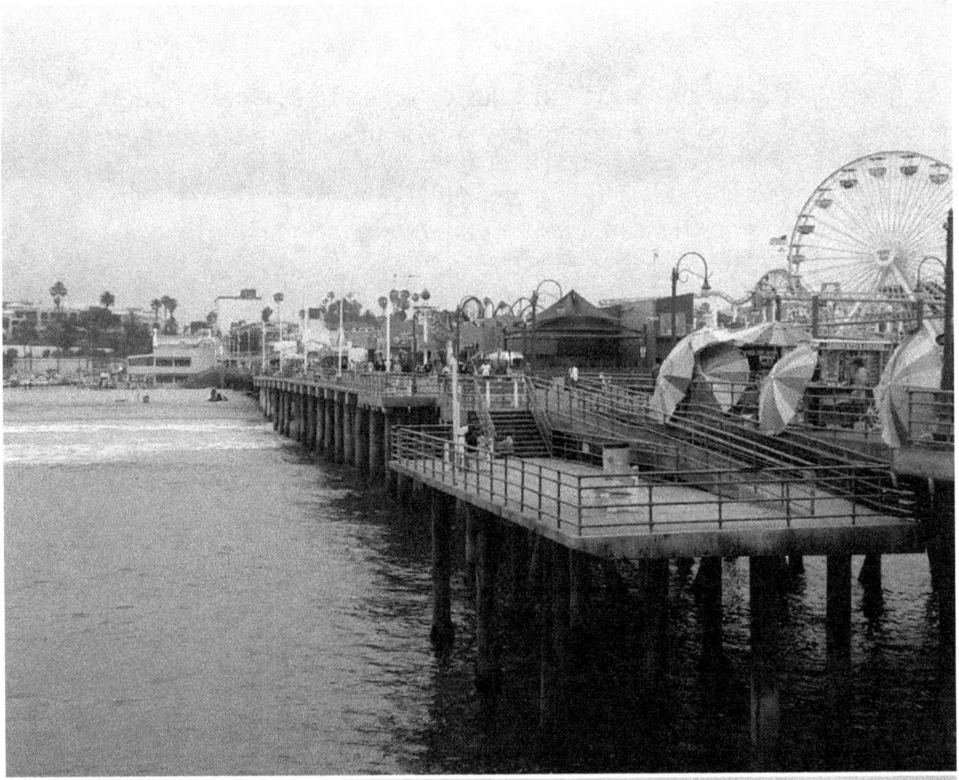

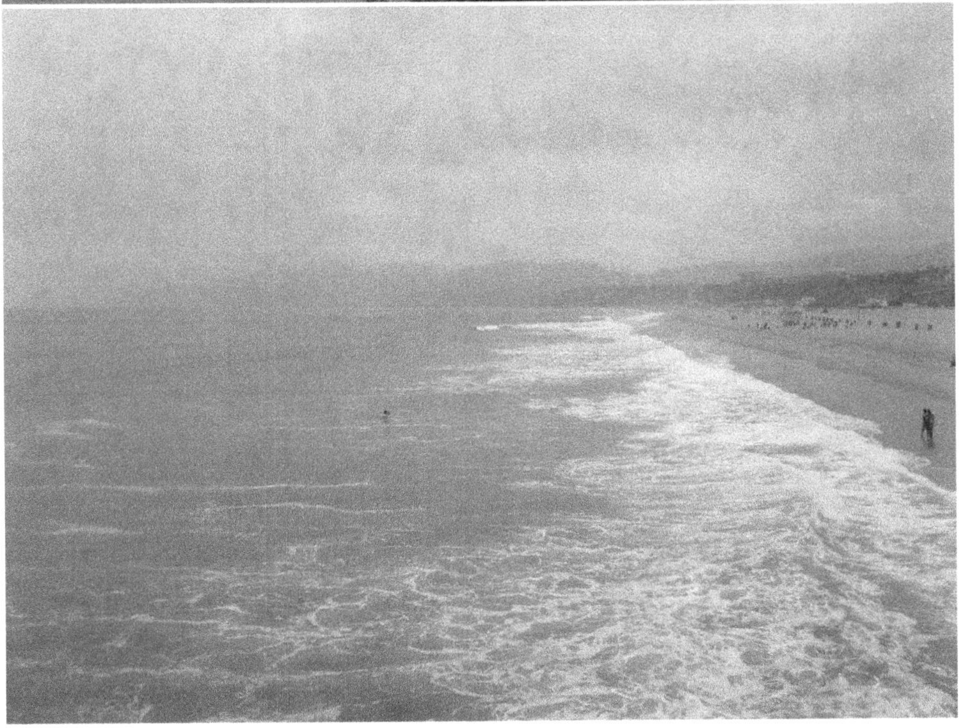

My goals for today are simply a shower and someplace to sleep. I'm gonna head up Hwy 1 and see what I see on the way to Monterey.

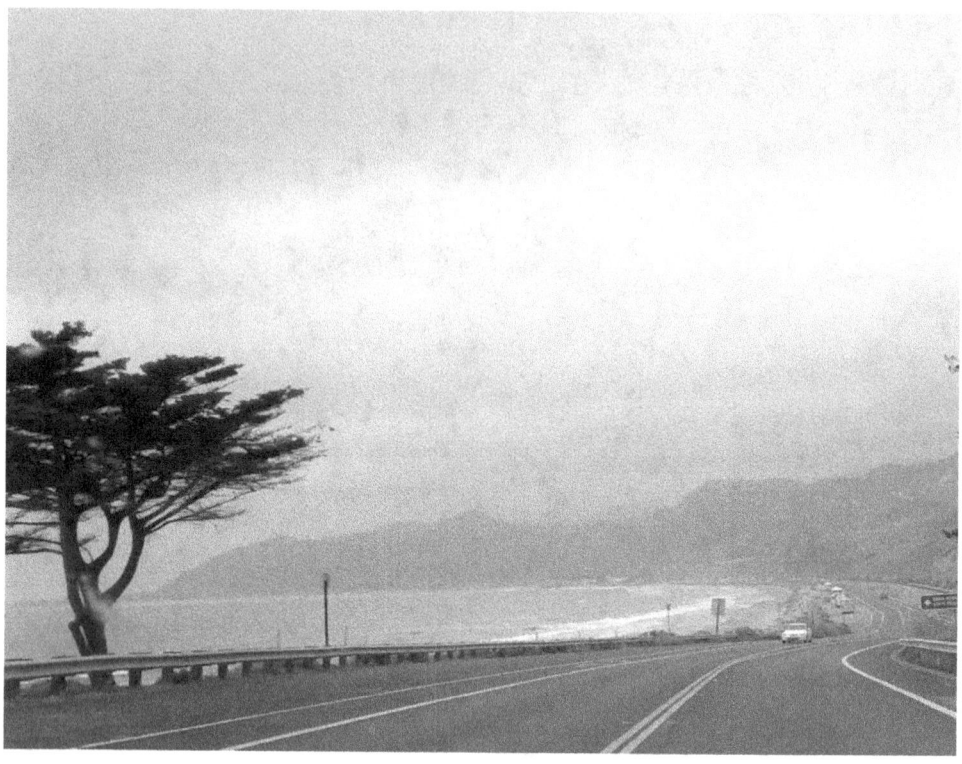

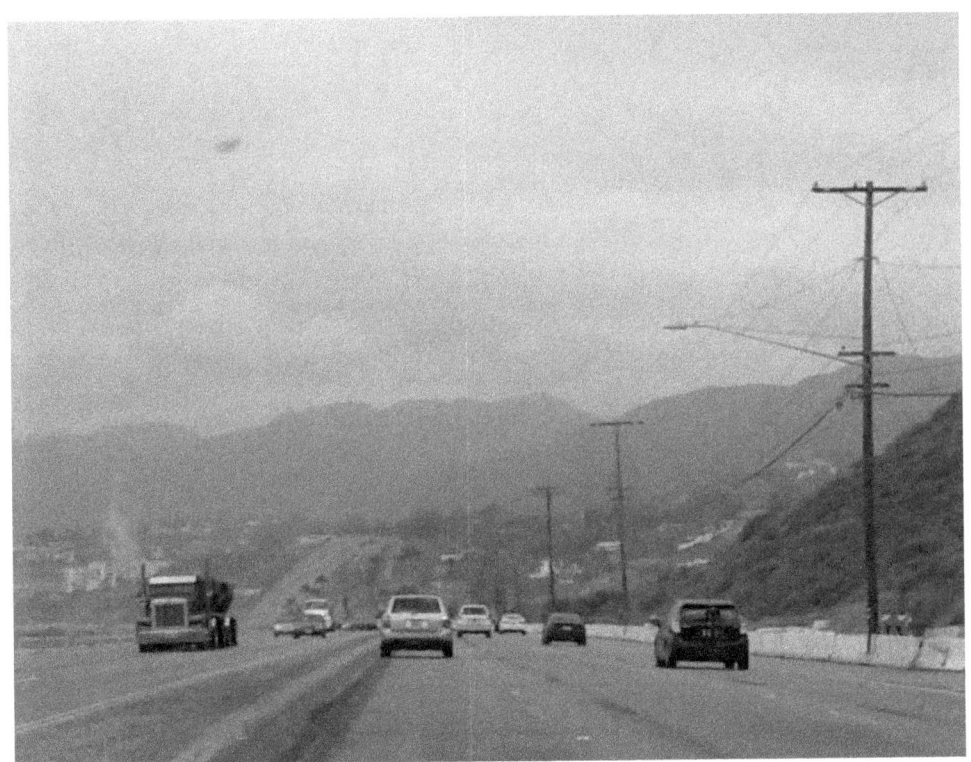

Along the drive I'm still researching for someplace to sleep and shower. I finally find a place that may or may not have a spot by the time I get there; I'm unable to make a reservation.

Seriously flying by the seat of my pants these days…. But I've got a feeling…

This campground has a shower and is $30 a night. It's the cheapest I've found that still has a spot and a shower. Ordinarily I would be able to take Hwy 1 right to this place, but the highway is currently closed at either end of this 9-mile section where the campground is.

There were fires and landslides that have the road closed. The only way to get to this section of HWY 1 is to drive inland an hour and a half and back out again. On the map I can tell the road is winding. Surely no one else will make this trek without having a reservation. What if I get there and there isn't a spot? My gut (I'm learning this feeling is my intuition) is telling me to go. Just do it. GO! It says…

Here I go.

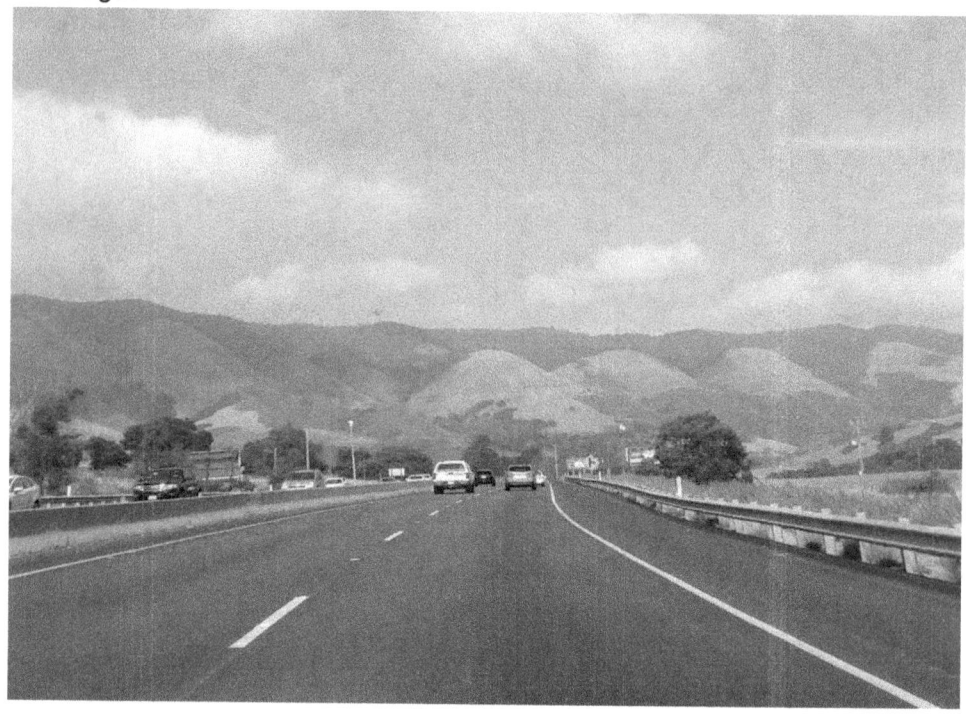

Nacimiento-Ferguson Road and Lime Kiln State Park

I follow the GPS and it tells me to take this Nacimiento-Ferguson Road. At one point it has me turn into a military base or test ground or something. I'm a bit freaked out. I know the GPS will cut out eventually, but it doesn't really matter. Once I'm on this road, I'm on it till it comes out at the ocean, at HWY 1

———

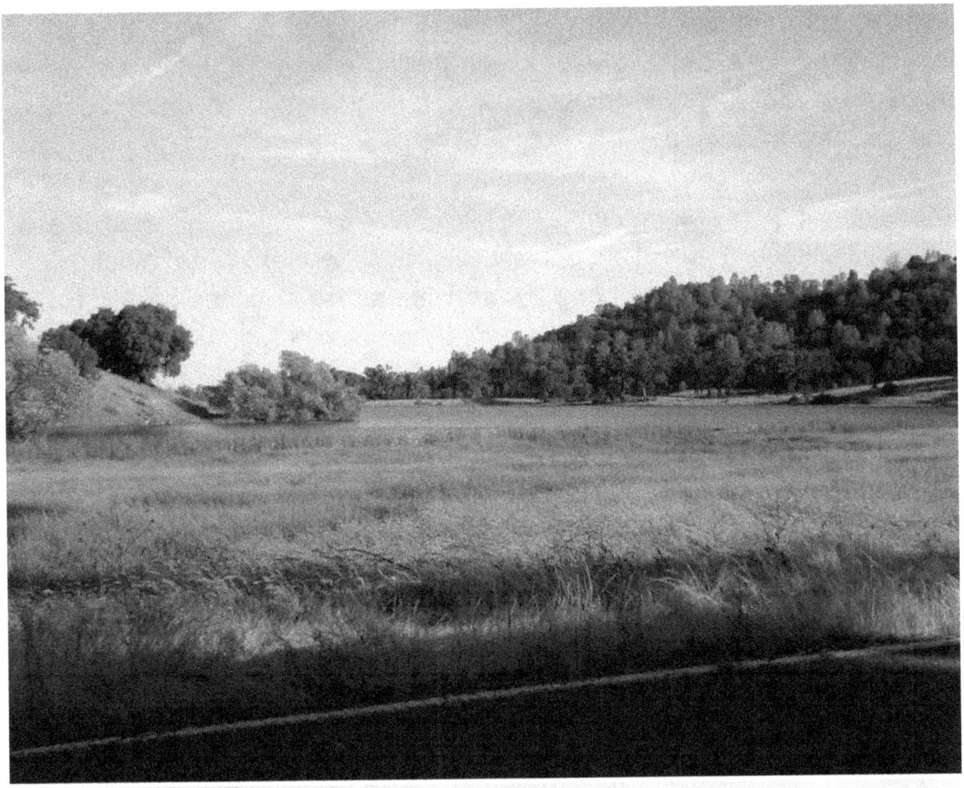

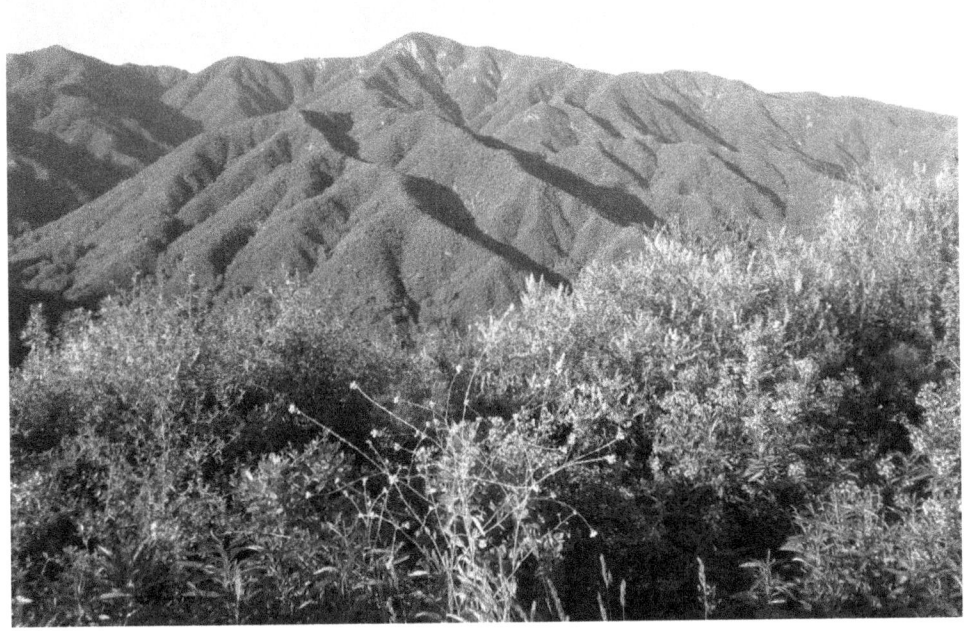

Shortly after the turn off, the road starts to head into the woods and up the mountain. It's pretty. There is a surprising amount of traffic coming out. Lots of rent-a-RVers. (does that mean they went in, found no spot, and are leaving? Hope not.)

There's a car on my rear pushing me hard. Way too fast for this road. As the road climbs it starts to get skinnier and twistier. The windiest, skinniest road ever. It's barely 2 cars wide and it switches back on a dime! You've never seen a blinder curve! And there's fog! And this dang car keeps pushing but there's no pull outs! I'm on the edge of my seat and going uncomfortably fast. A pull out! I skid in and to a stop. "Fuck! Ass Holes! Slow down!!"

Yeah, I really did holler at them. Shaking my fist and all! Lmao.

And right in front of this biker who passed me on the way in. Doh!

But, OMG! This view! This view! It's gorgeous!

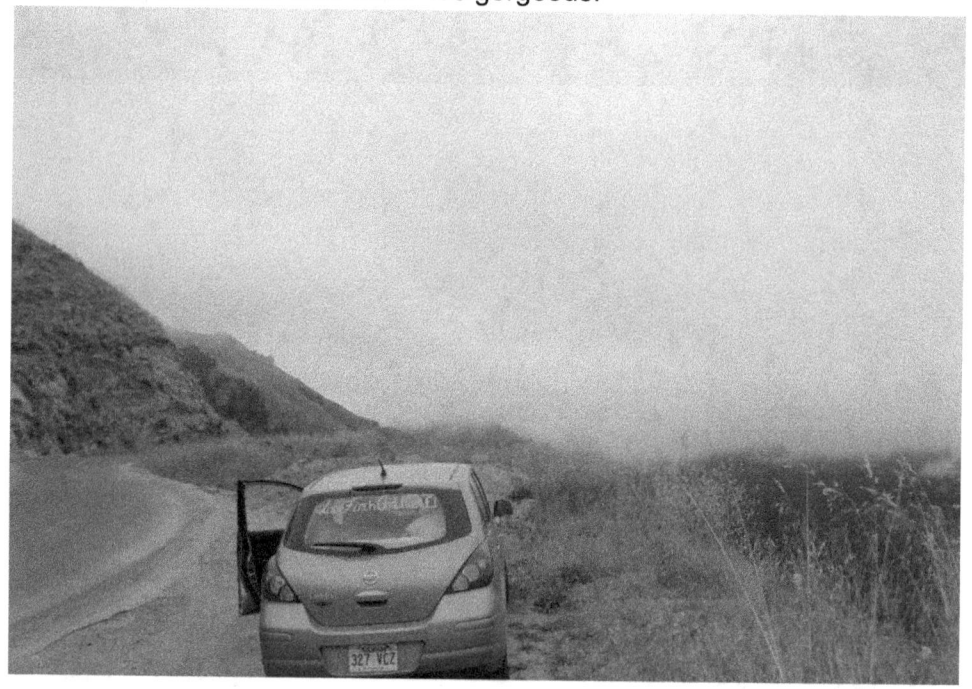

I roll on. It's getting foggier. I'm so glad that car isn't on my ass anymore. Soon I come up to the top of the mountain. I'm above the clouds! No shit! Above the clouds! Probably just above the fog but still it's spectacular!

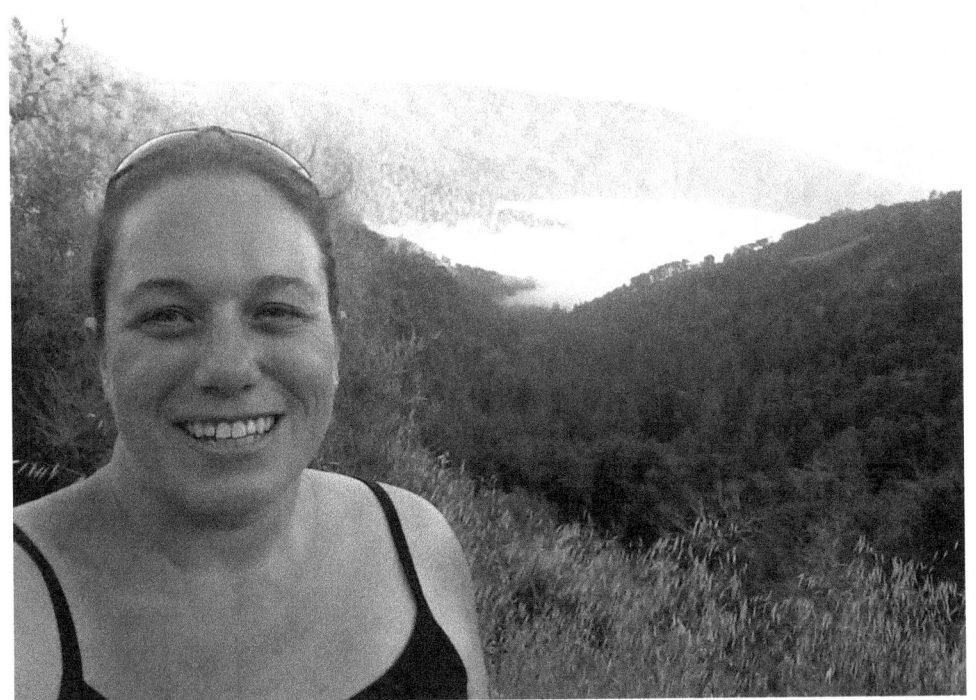

I'm so glad I made this drive! This drive is amazing! It doesn't even matter if I've got a spot at the end. This view! This drive!

Down the mountain now, trying not to go too fast. If you drive a stick, you probably already know this but, put it in a lower gear to go down so you don't have to use your brakes so much. This drive in a stick takes a bit of talent or skill and certainly a little luck. Down especially...

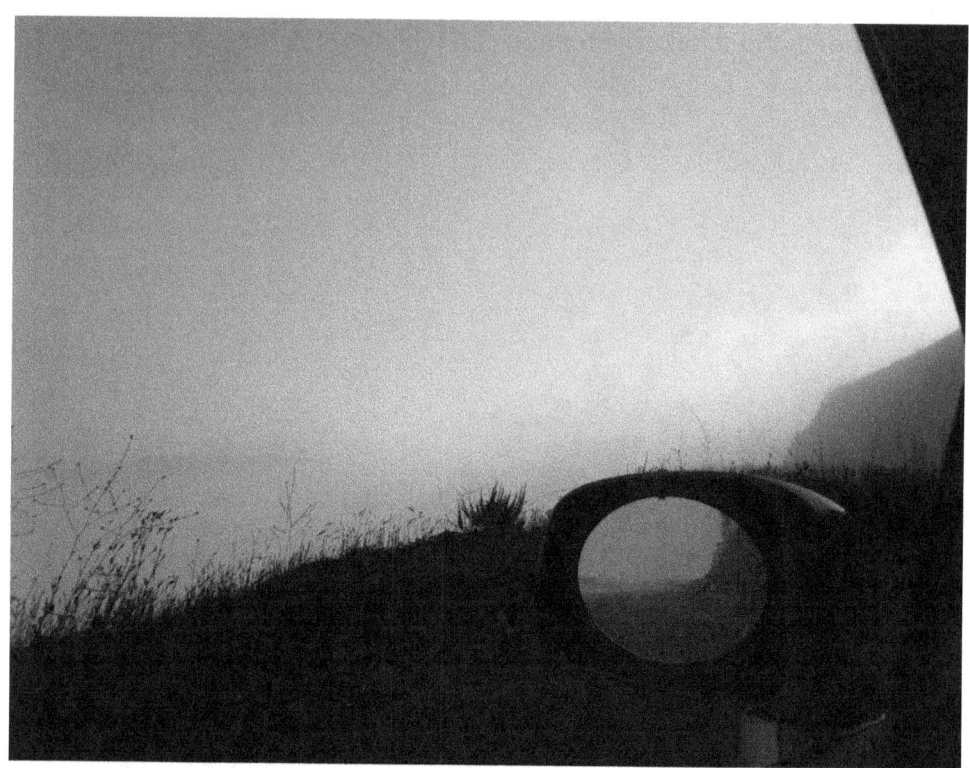

Down through the fog, switchbacks, blind corners and rent-a-rvers... the adrenaline is high and, OMG! There it is! The ocean! This crazy amazing drive ends at the ocean! Oh, the rewards for following your gut! I've had the GoPro going the whole time. I wonder if the videos will show how amazing this is... I wonder if I cut out the cussing...
https://youtu.be/atOkW96IBzE

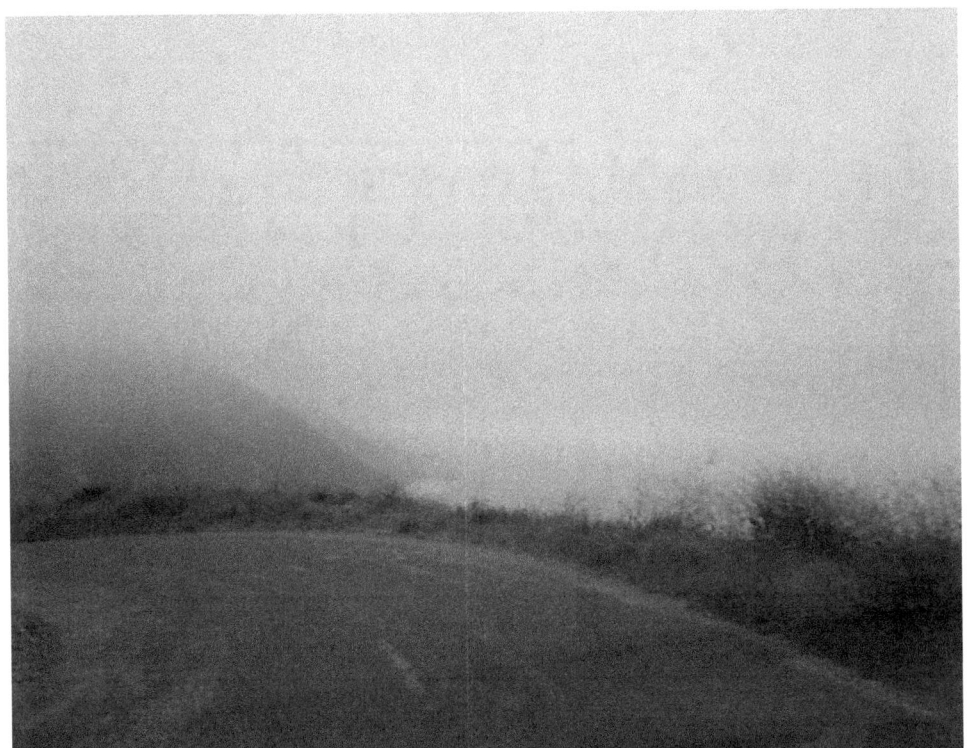

The first park I come to is directly across the highway from where Nacimiento-Ferguson comes out. Oh, and here's that biker again. I tell him "I thought I was crazy taking this road but you're crazy!" And then we meet a bicyclist! We look at each other and laugh, "Nope, He's crazy!" pointing at the cyclist. "But not stupid!", he says, "I'm getting a ride back out tomorrow."

I ask them if they know who to talk to about a site and they tell me It's full. Shit!

But wait! Turns out this isn't the park I was headed to anyway! Yay! The other is just down the road.

A few miles down the road I come to the park and the start of a bridge that is closed from the landslide. Thank God this place isn't closed! They have a spot too! And a shower!
Oh, the rewards!

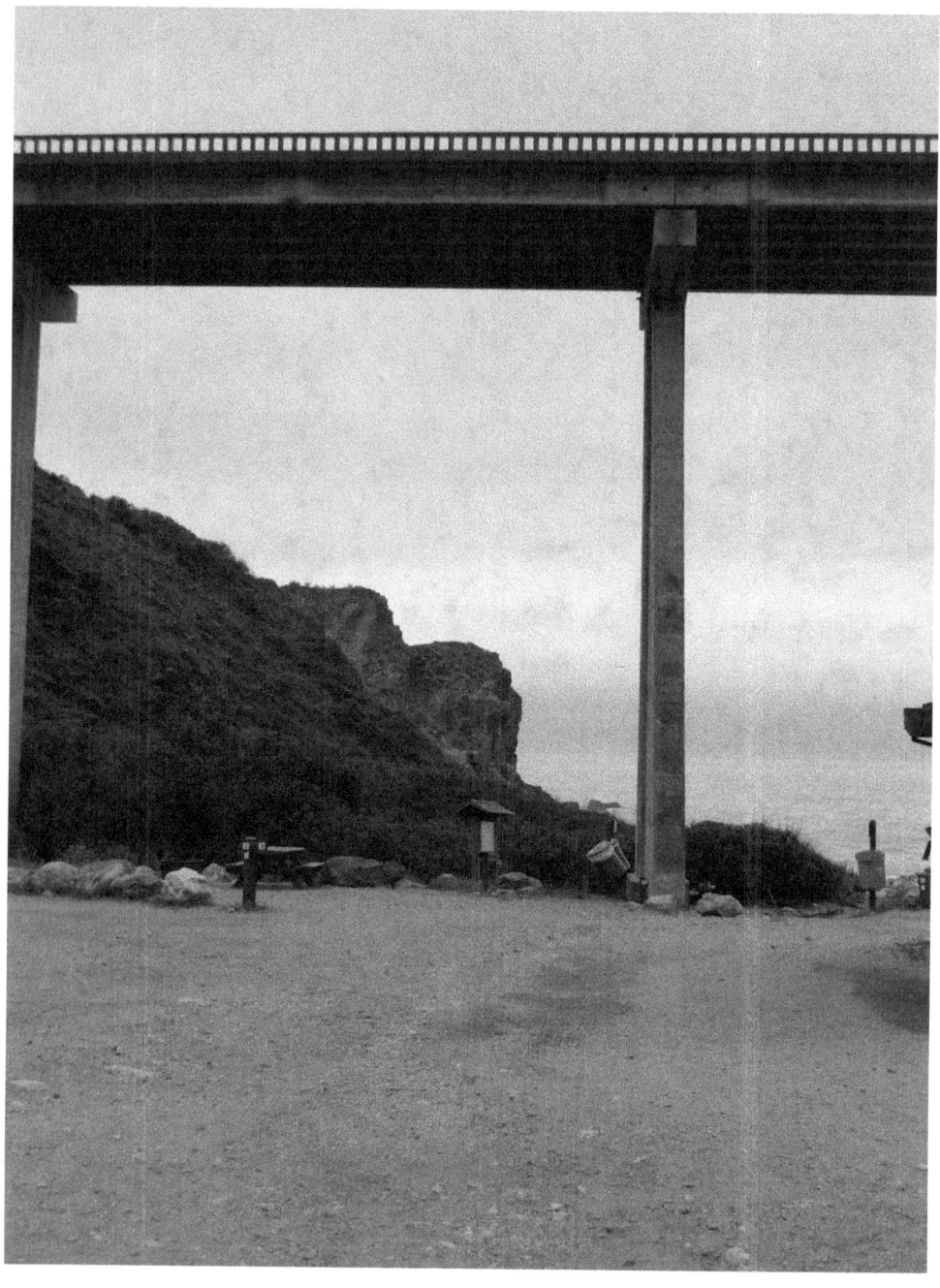

I get my choice of staying on the ocean or up in the woods. I chose the woods. It's chilly on the coast. The woods are redwoods. Not the huge kind, but redwoods anyway. And, there's a creek too! It's perfect! I have to hurry and get a shower though, they cut the water off in thirty minutes!

Thank goodness my intuition shouted at me this time. Thank goodness I listened!

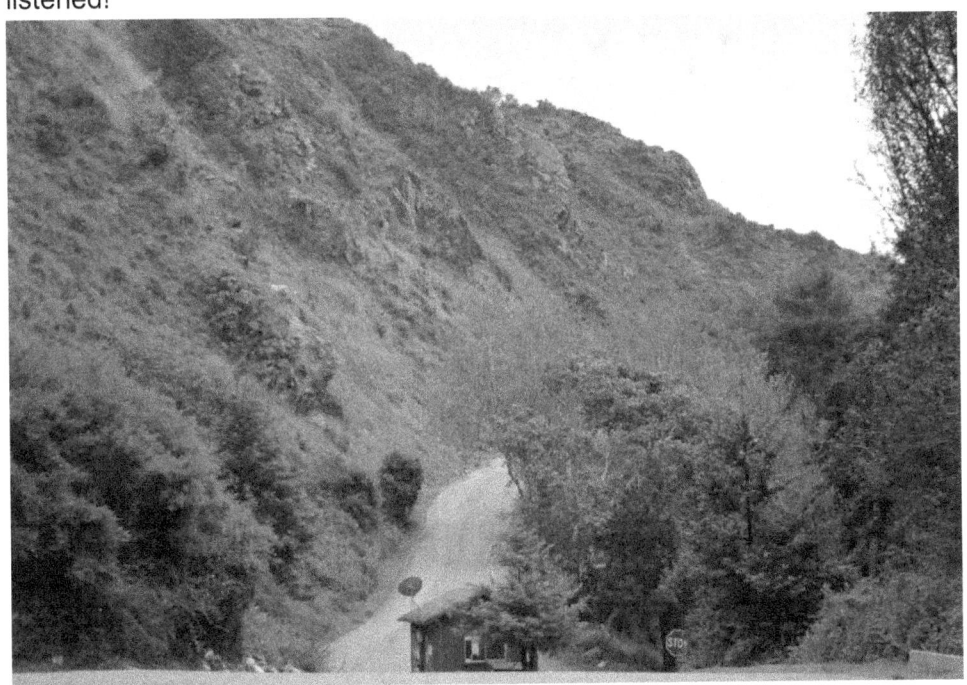

After my shower I run in to the biker again and sit and chat with him for a bit. His name is Morgan and he's a mechanical engineer from Ventura County. He laughs when I'm secretive about my smoke. He says he doesn't smoke but it's not a big deal. I'm sure I talked his ear off, but he didn't let on. He's headed a similar route to me tomorrow. Maybe I'll see him again…

It's getting late. Since I'm only staying one night and it's chilly, I decide not to put up my tent and slept in the car again. I'm starting to get used to sleeping in the car. It's actually pretty comfortable. Tonight, will be extra perfect here under the redwood canopy listening to the creek.

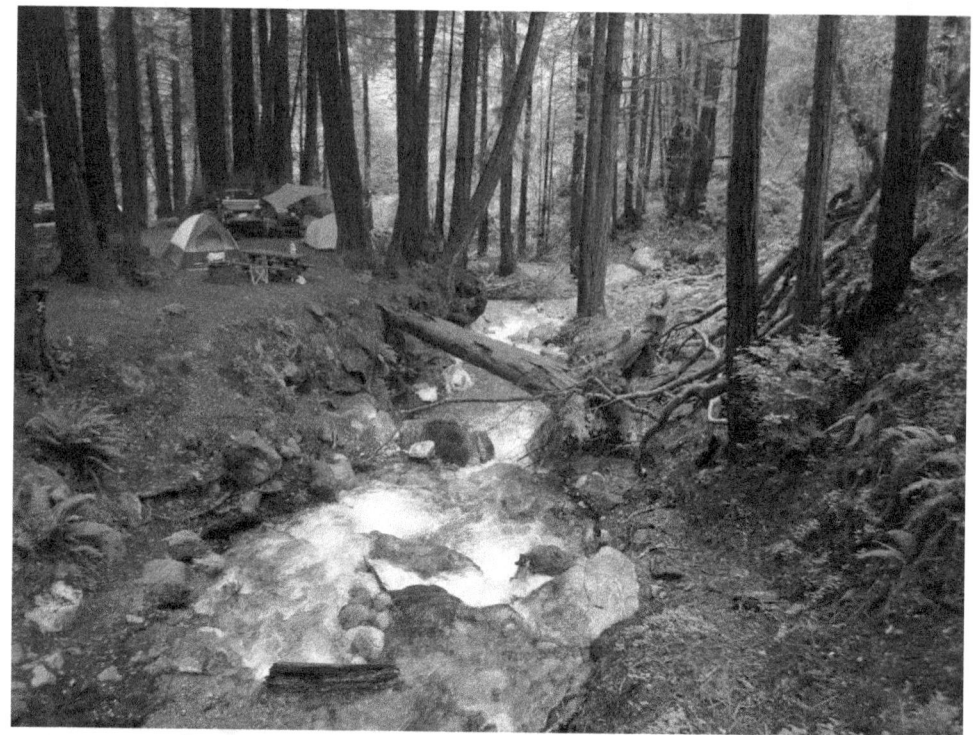

What an amazing day! And I got a shower!

5/10/17 day 24

Wednesday. I slept beautifully last night. And I'm lazing around this morning enjoying myself. I wandered around the campground and took pictures of the ocean and the woods. This is a perfect little spot...

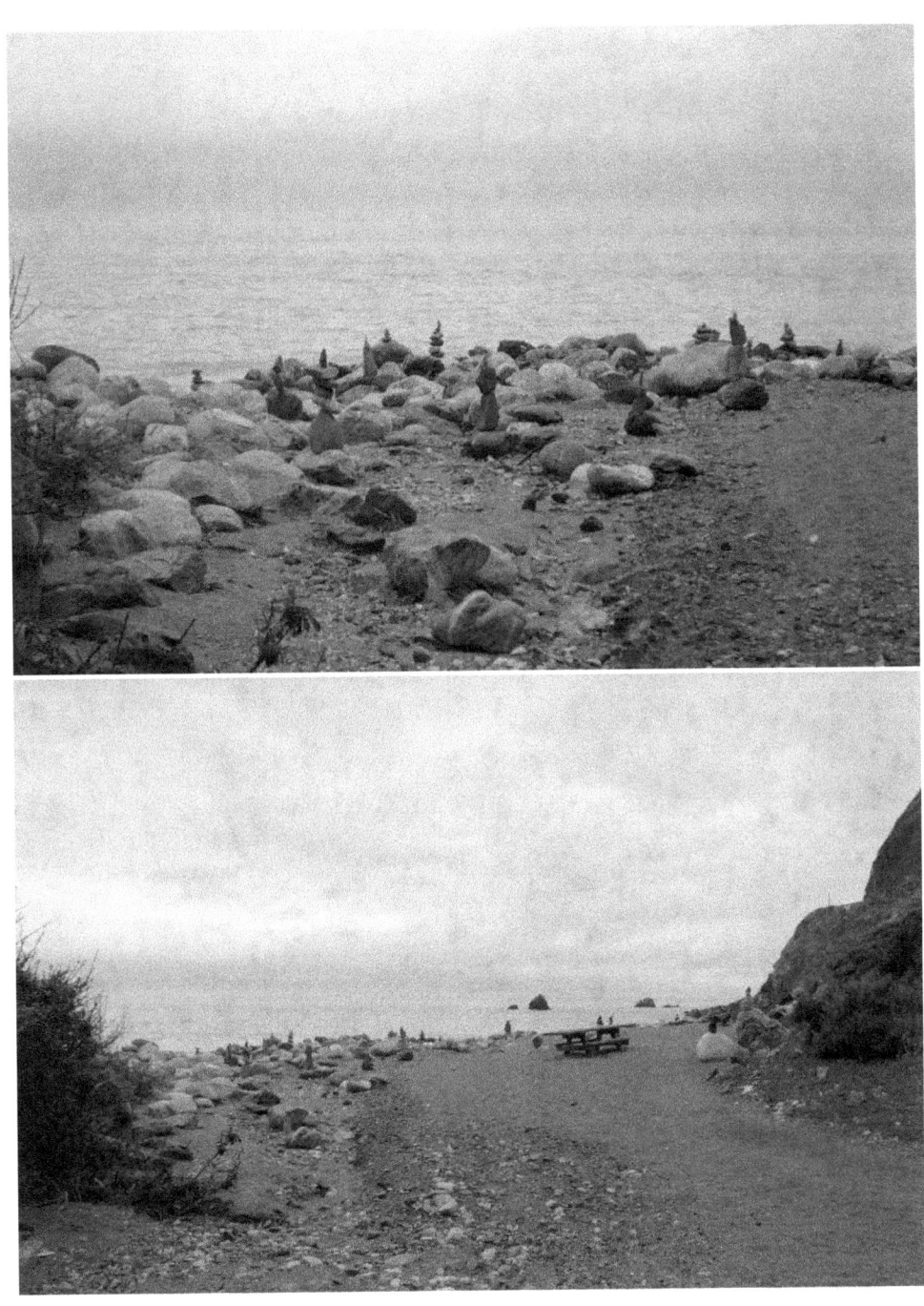

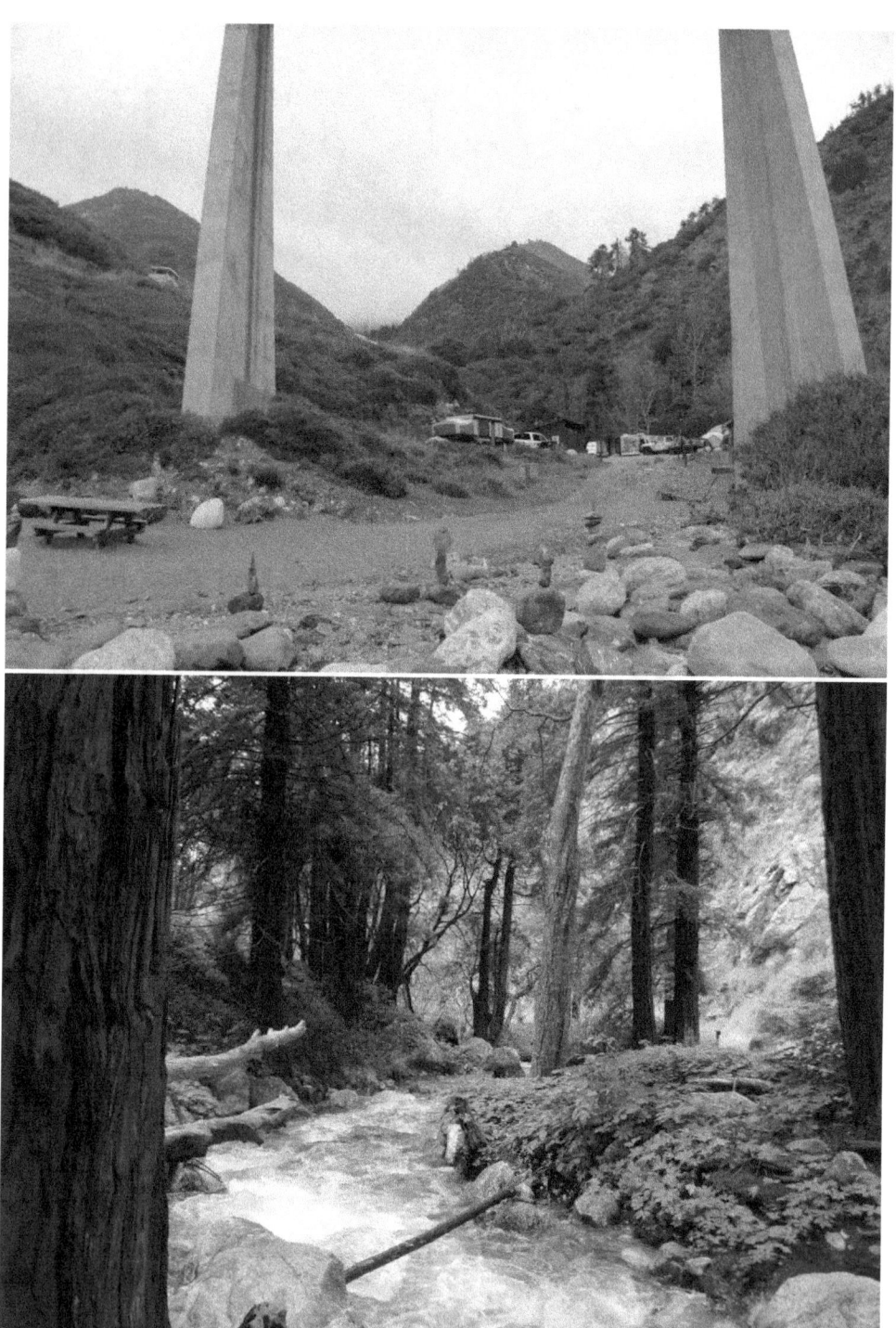

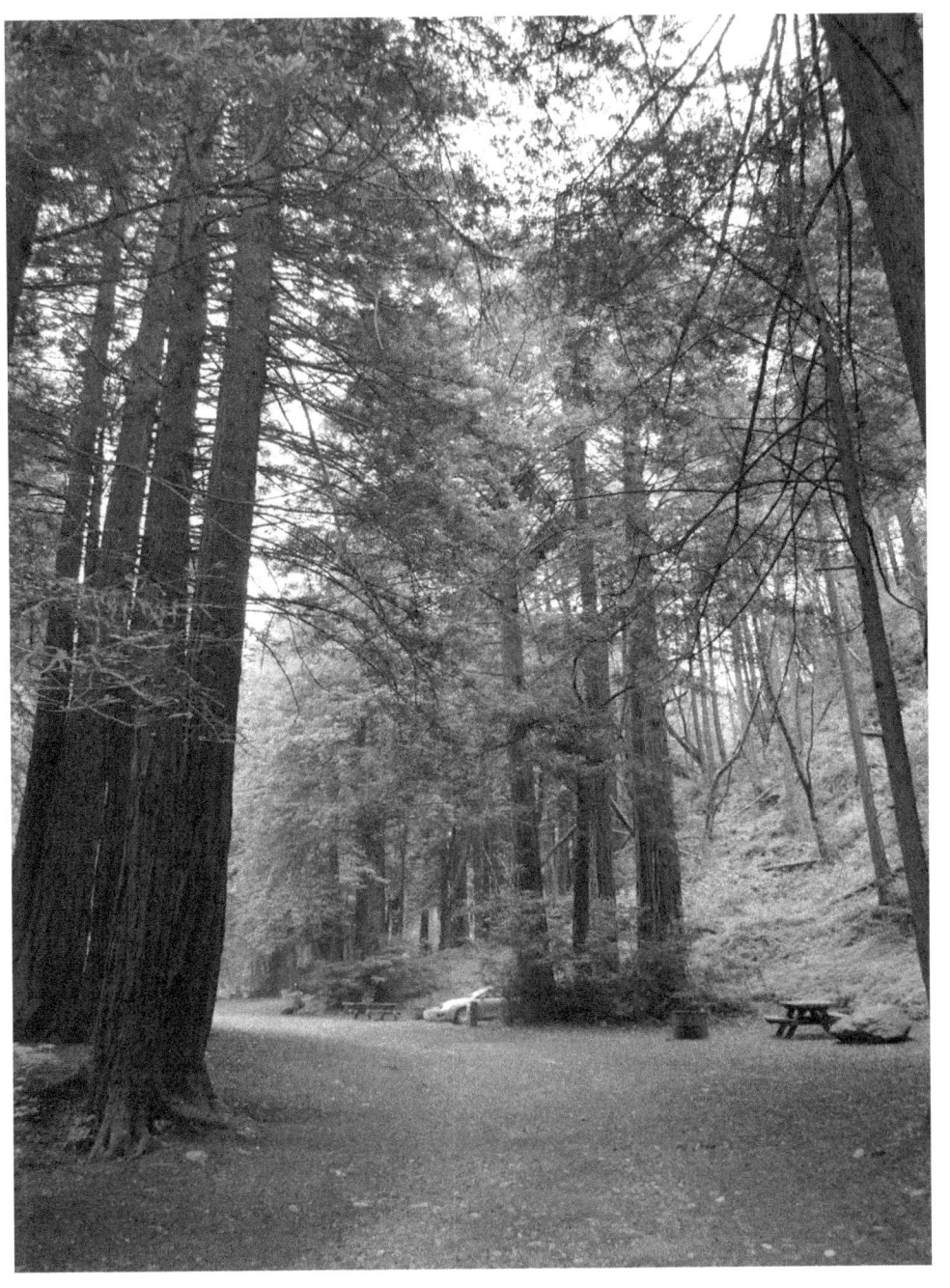

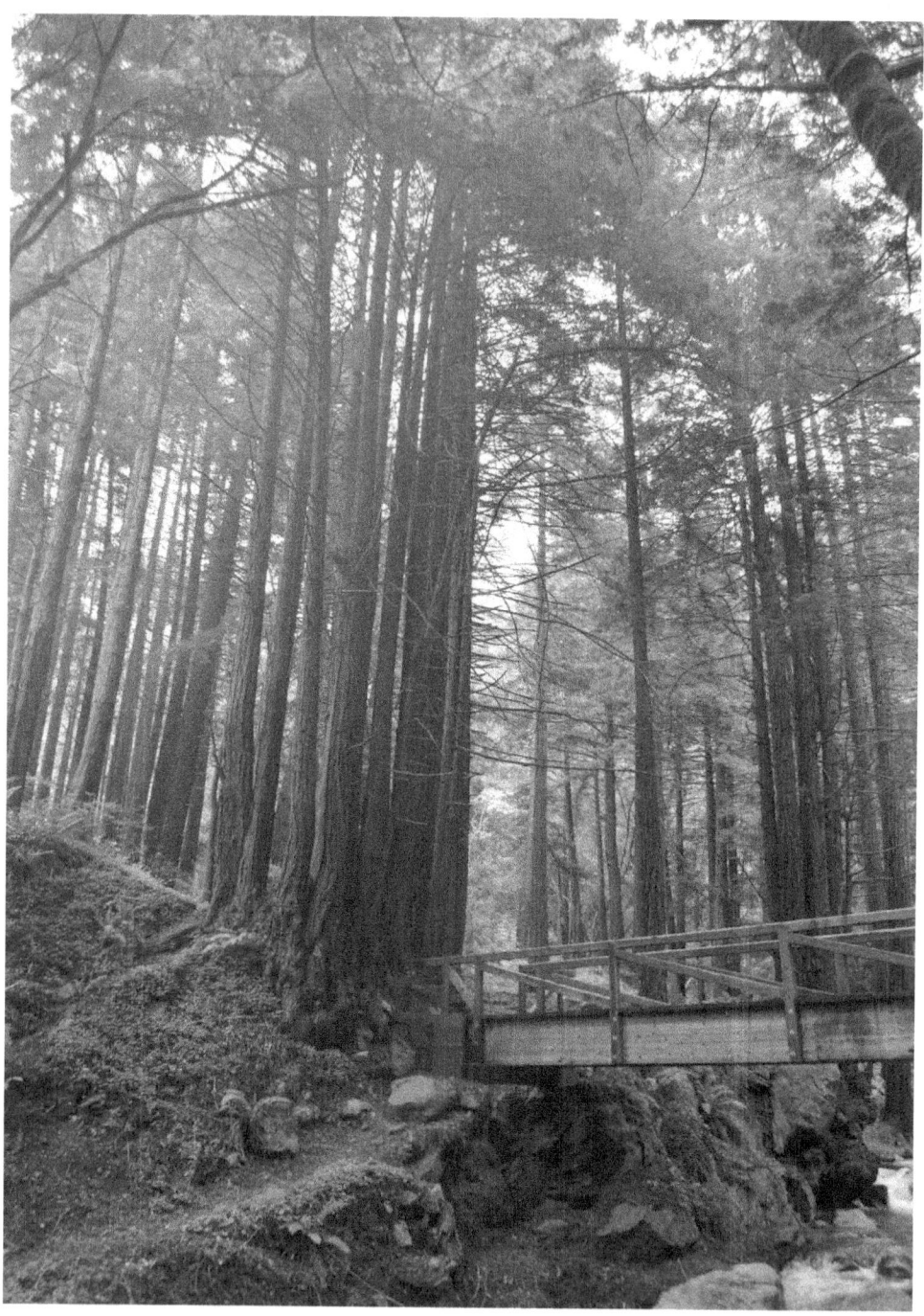

Now, turn the book sideways and flip
through the next few pages
to catch the waves
;-)
(unfortunately, this trick doesn't work the same on the eBook version)

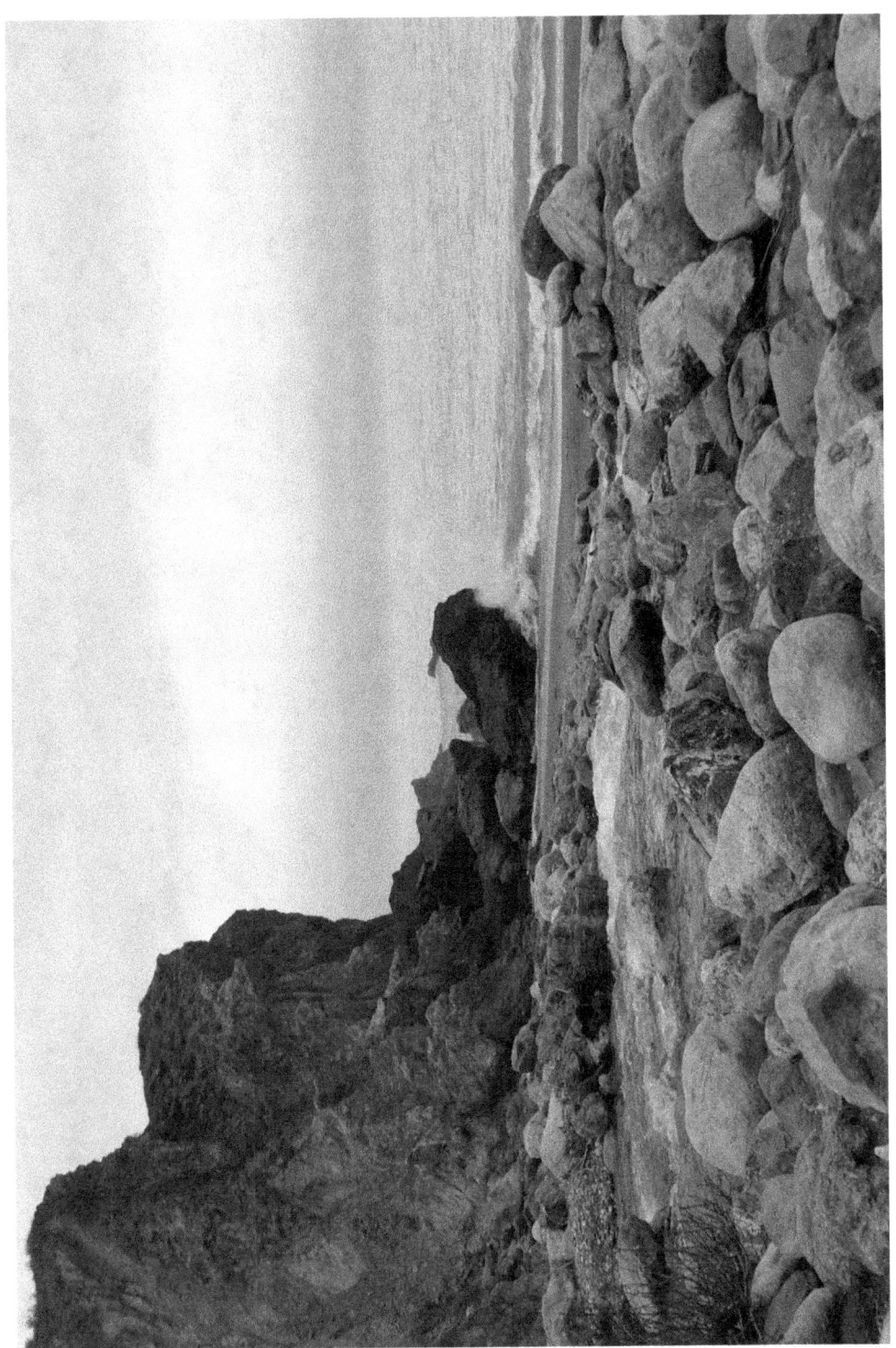

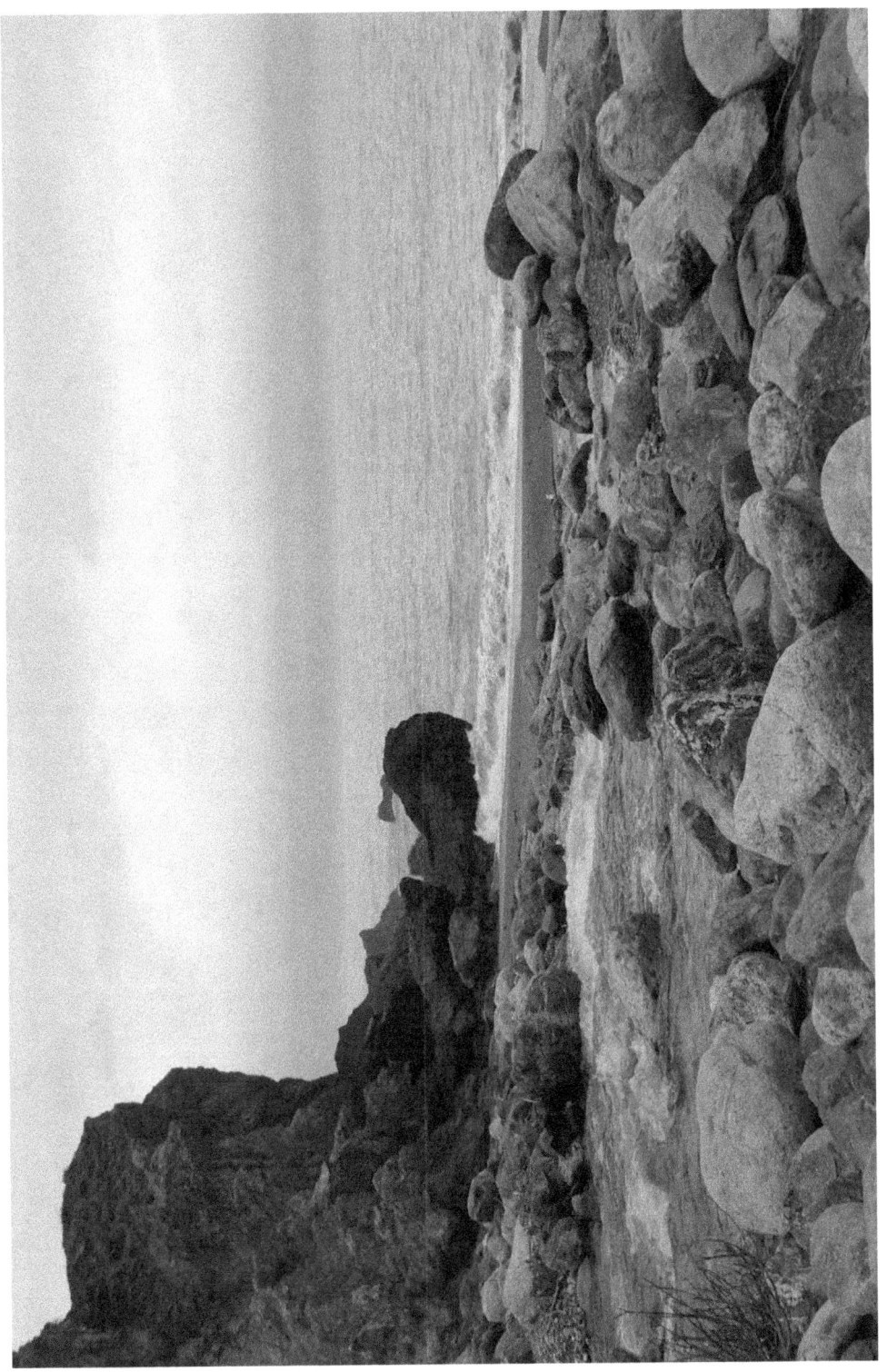

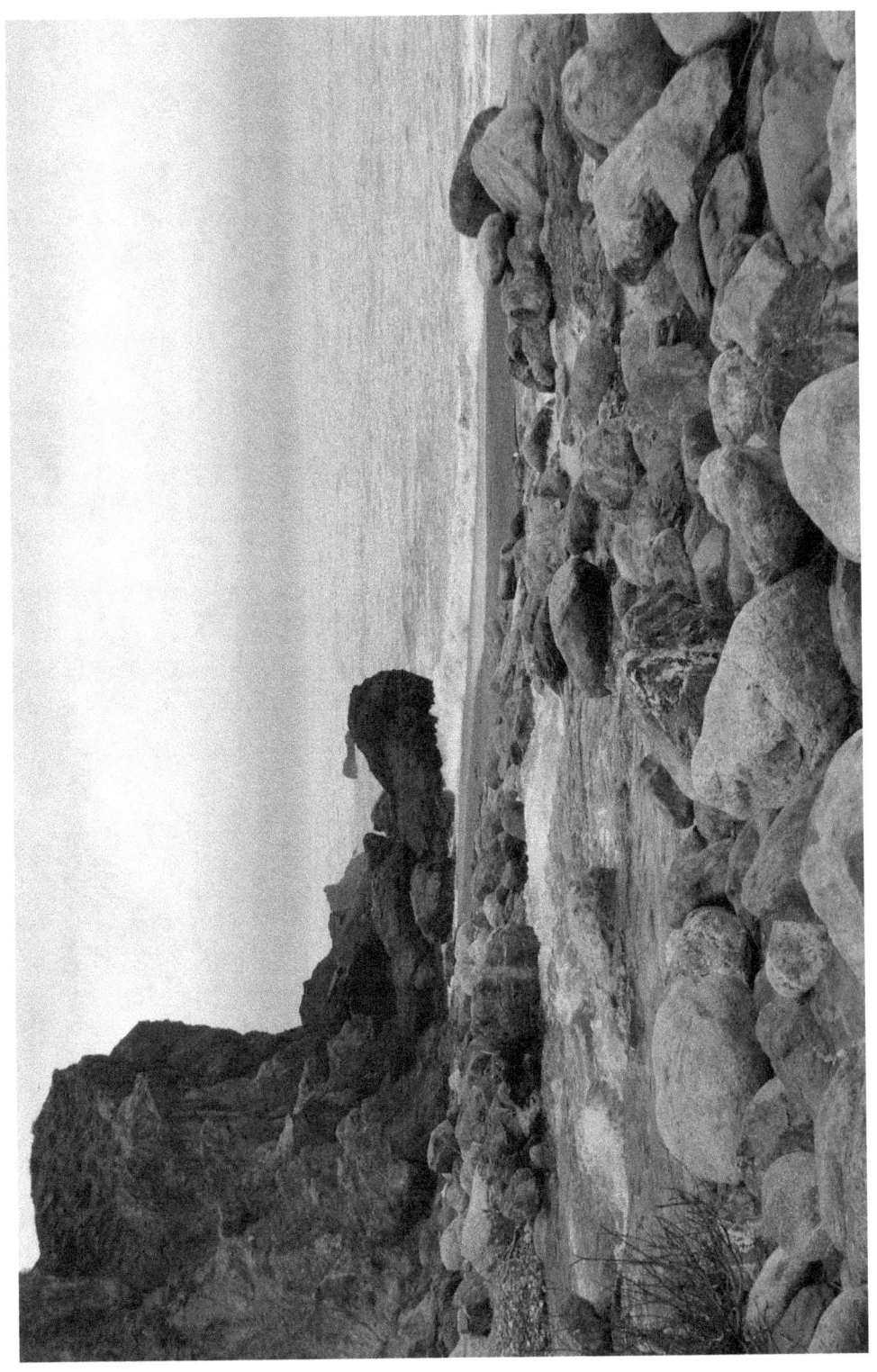

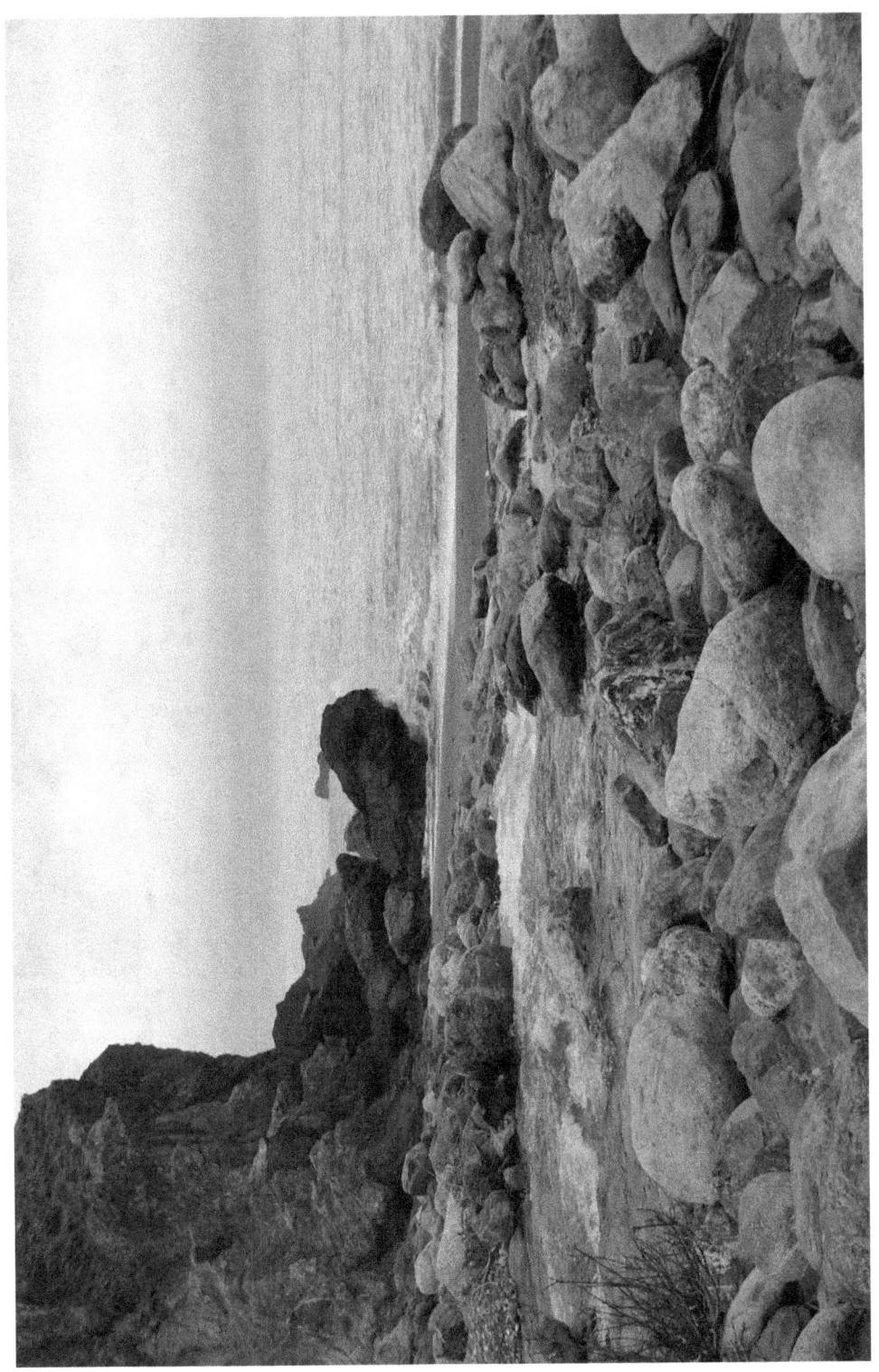

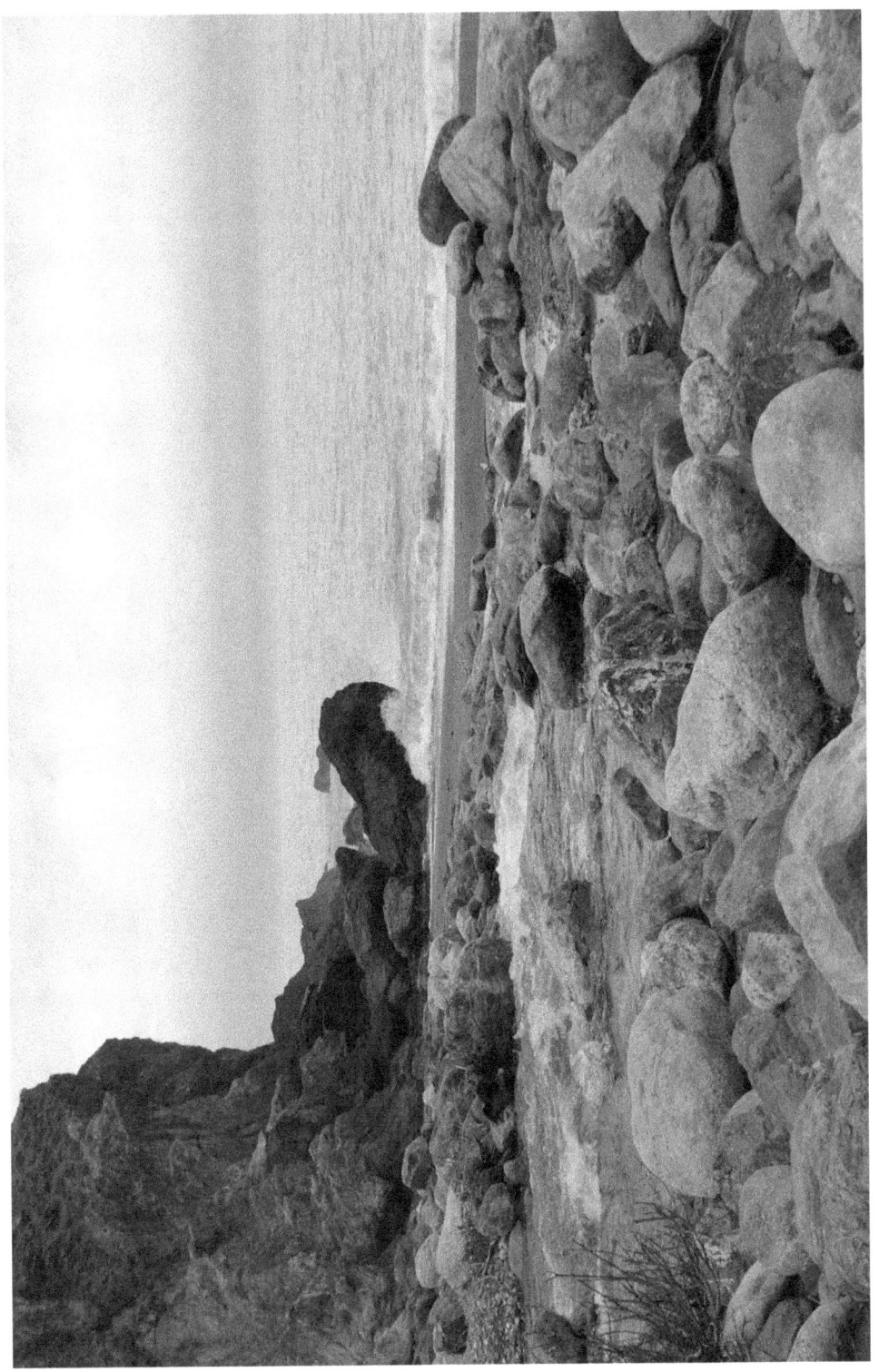

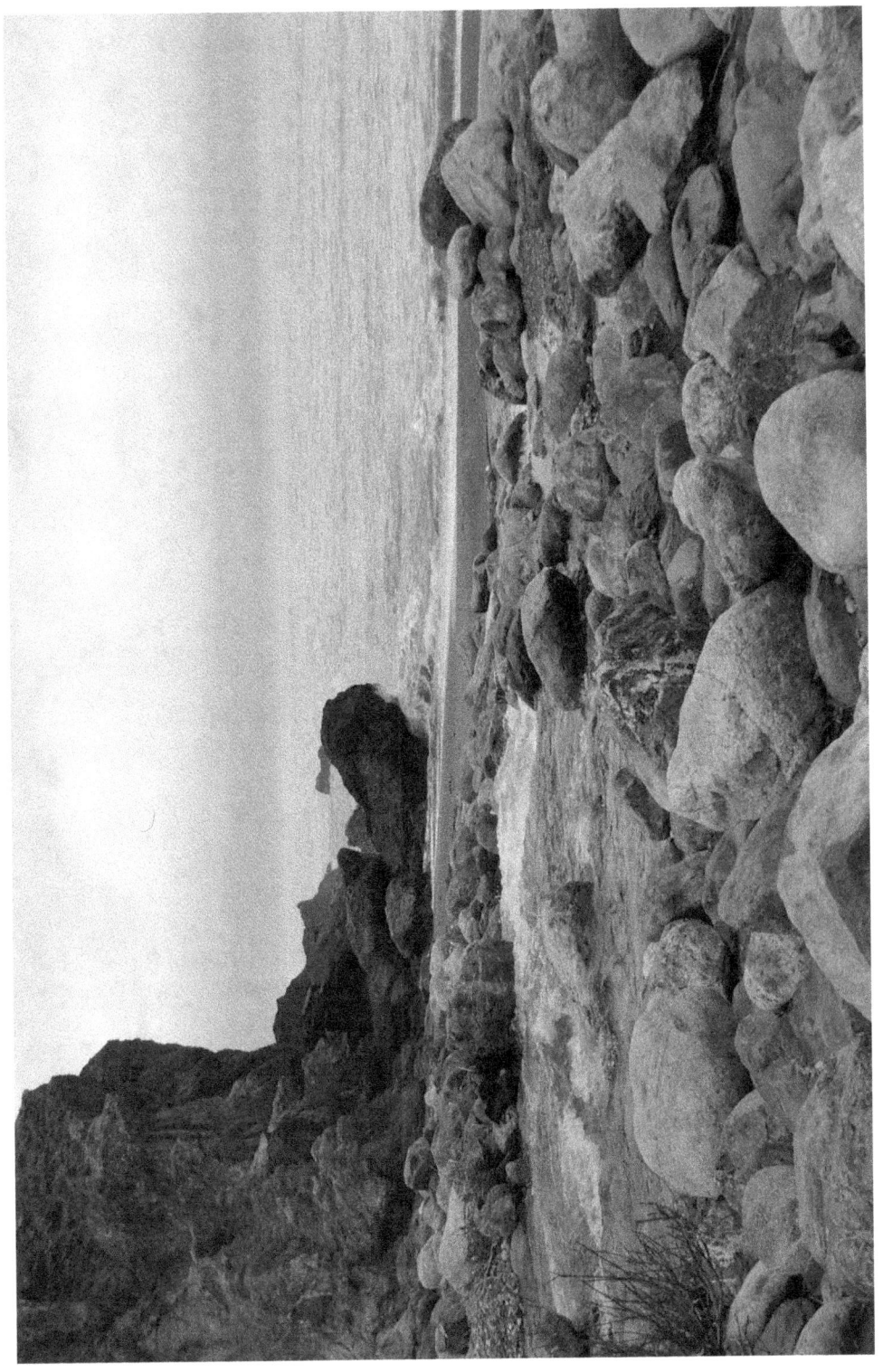

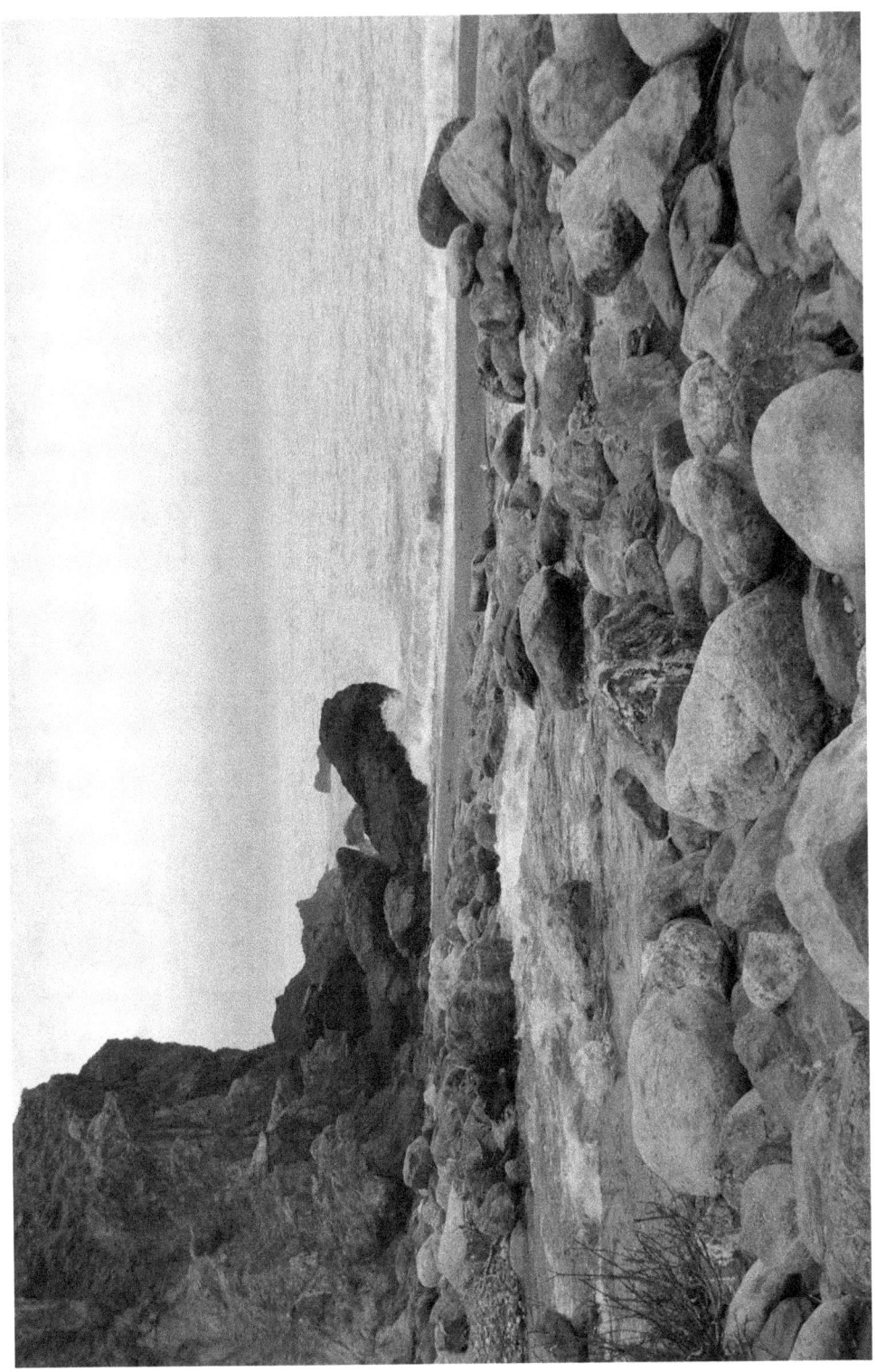

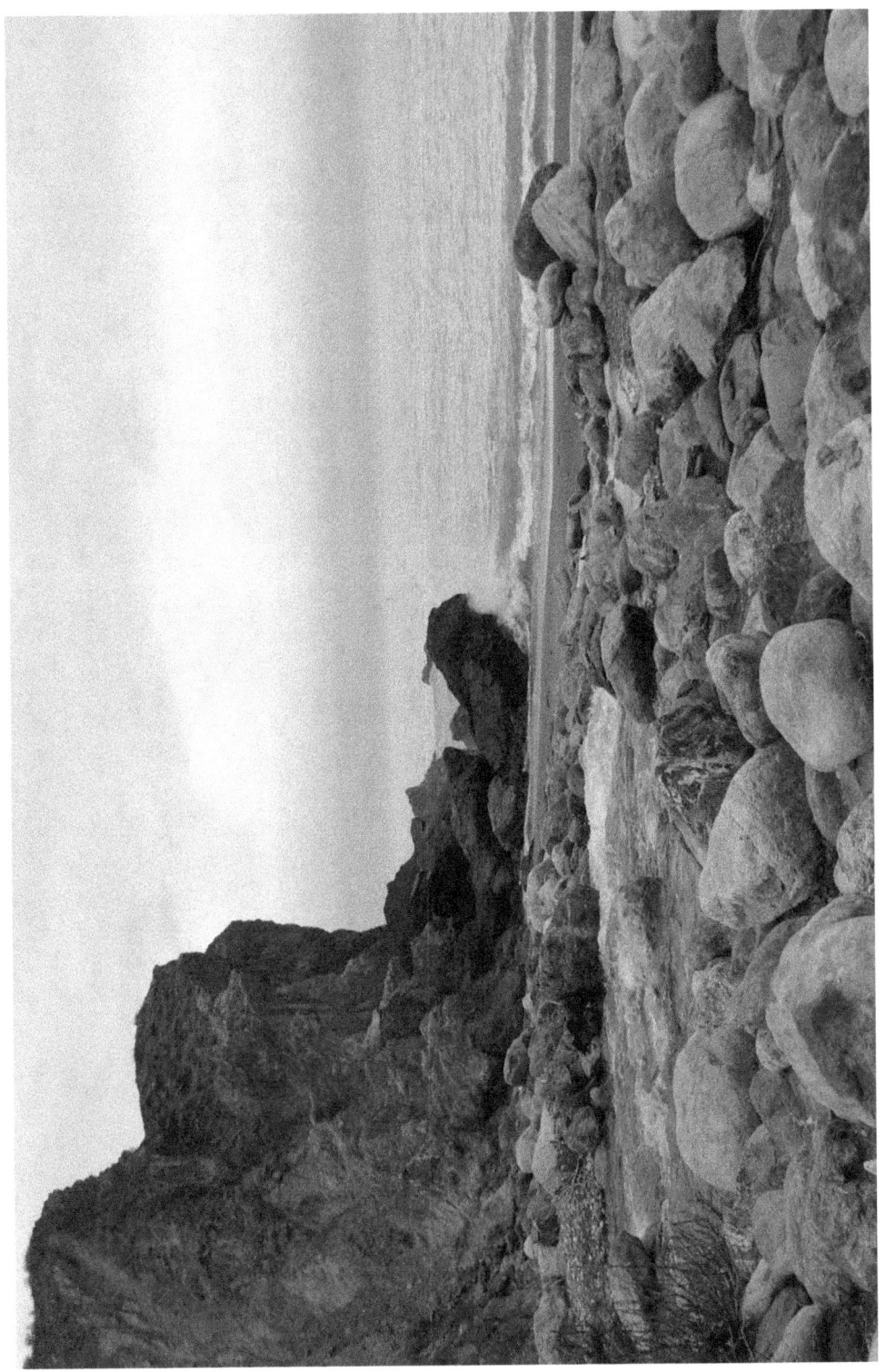

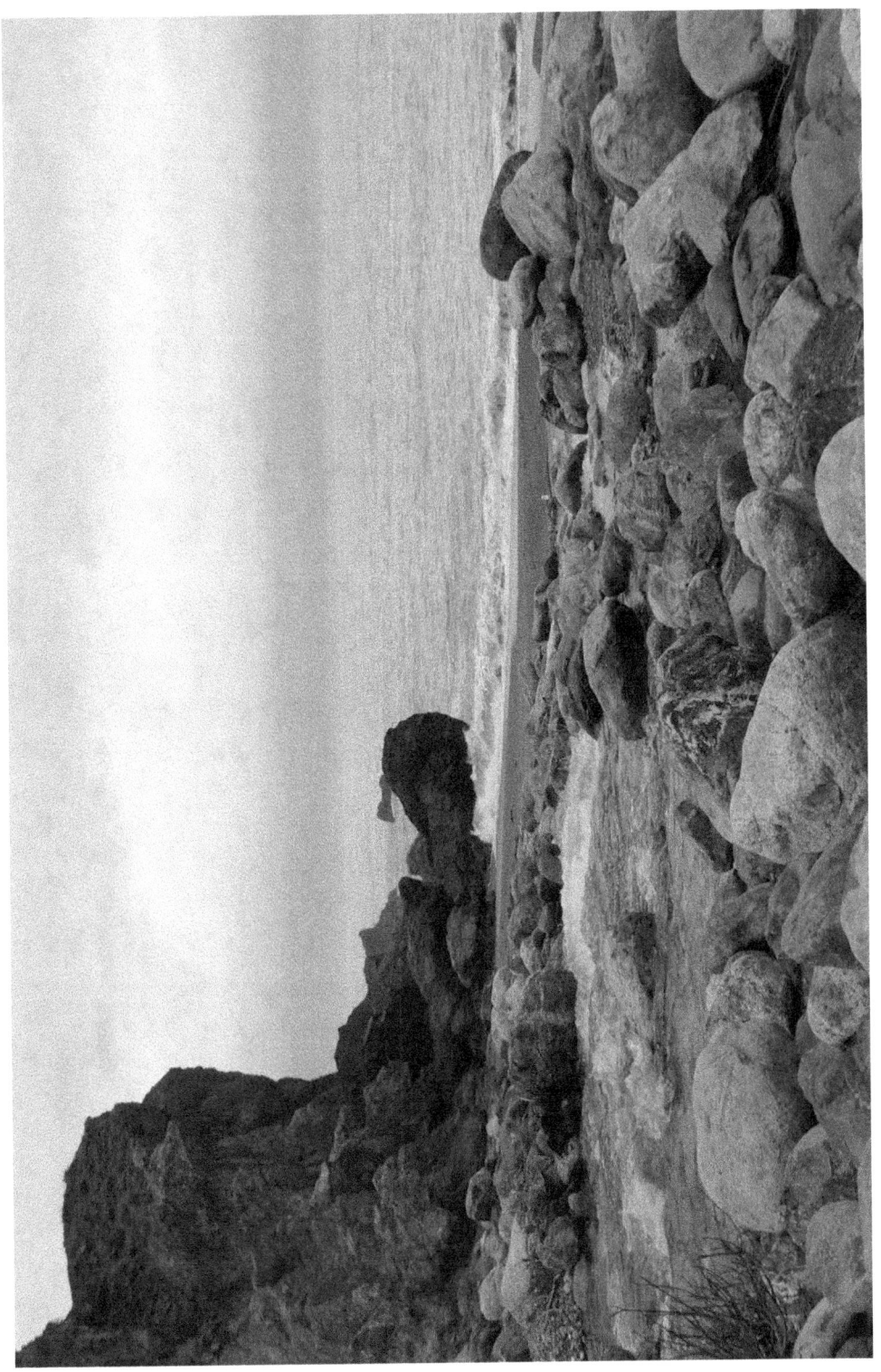

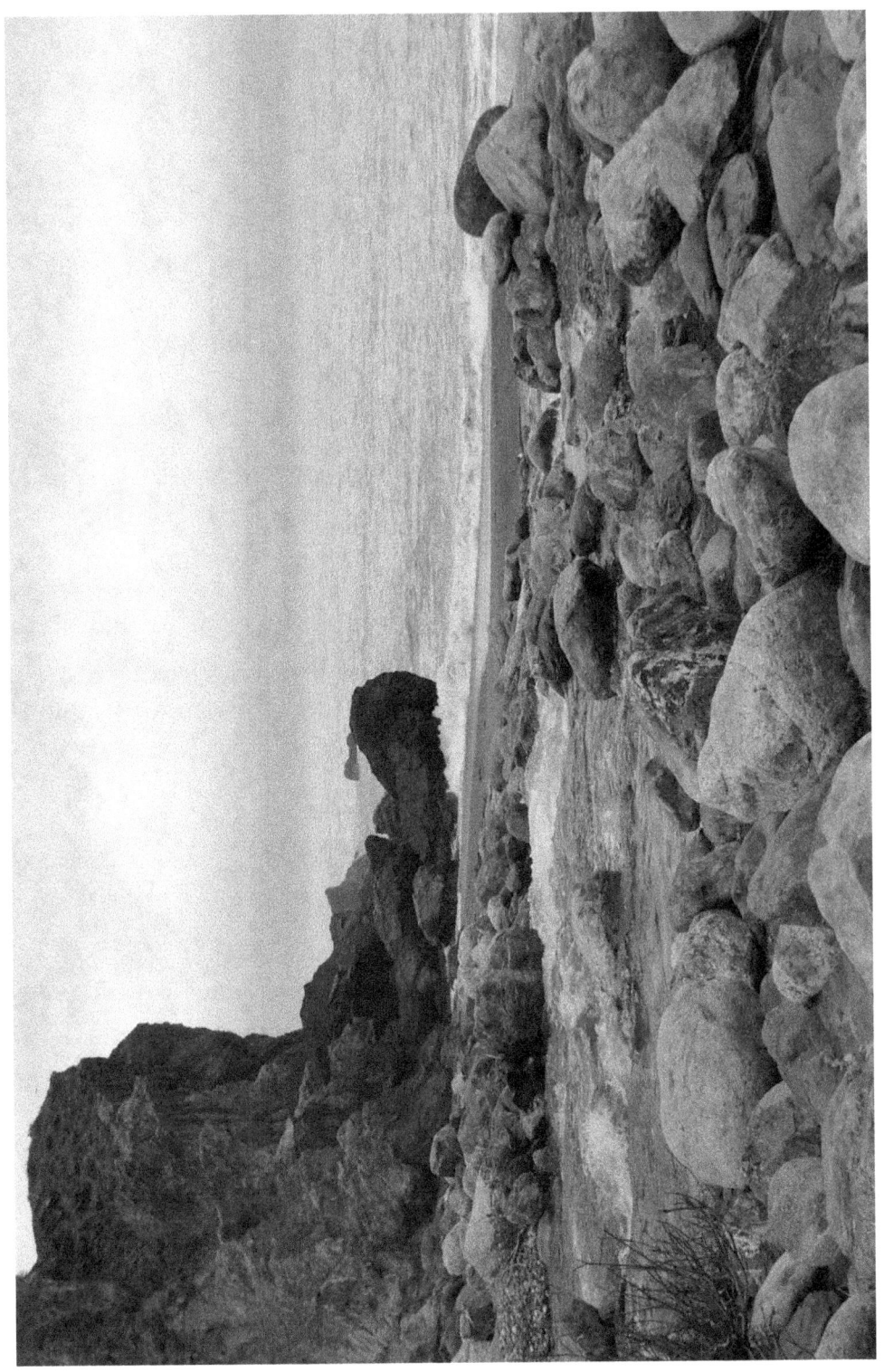

You're welcome.

Today I'll head toward Sequoia, tomorrow Santa Cruz and Monterey. First, I'll drive to the other end of this section of Hwy 1.

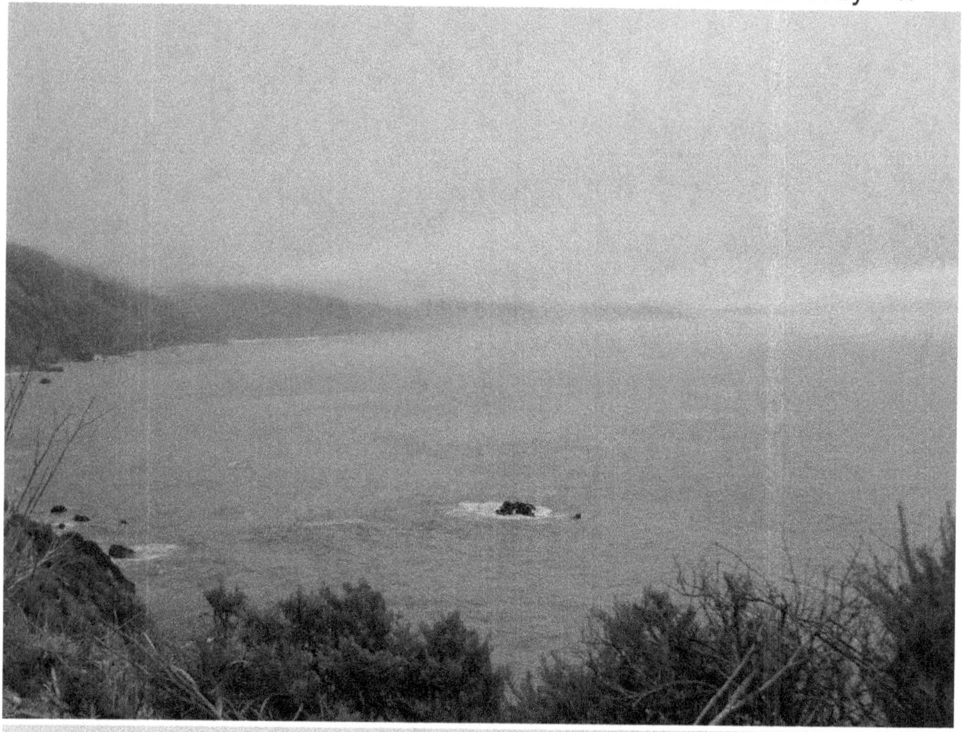

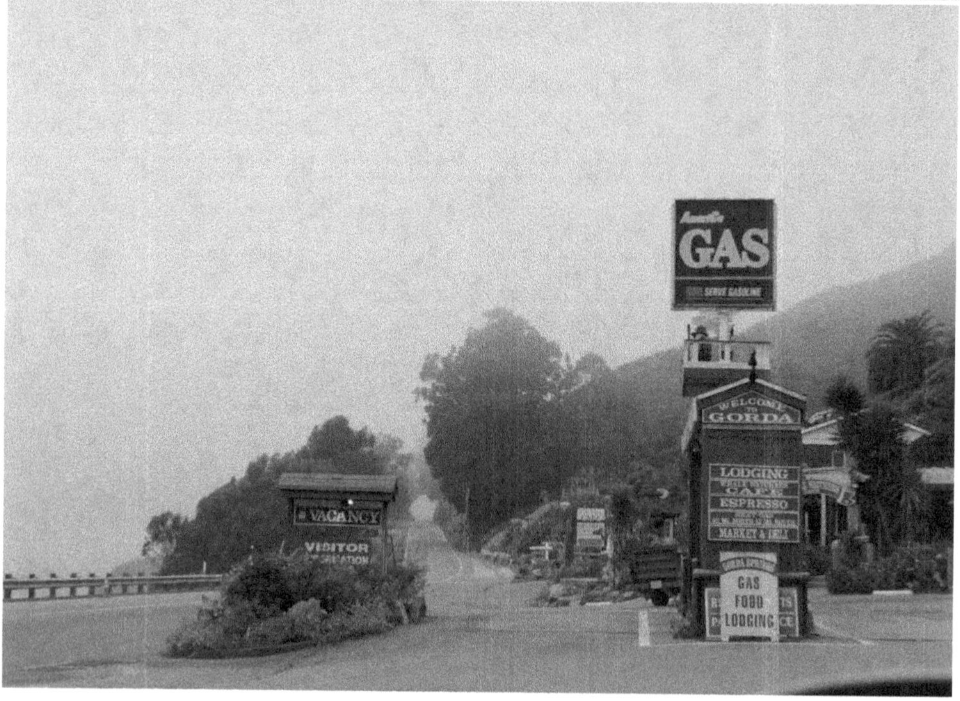

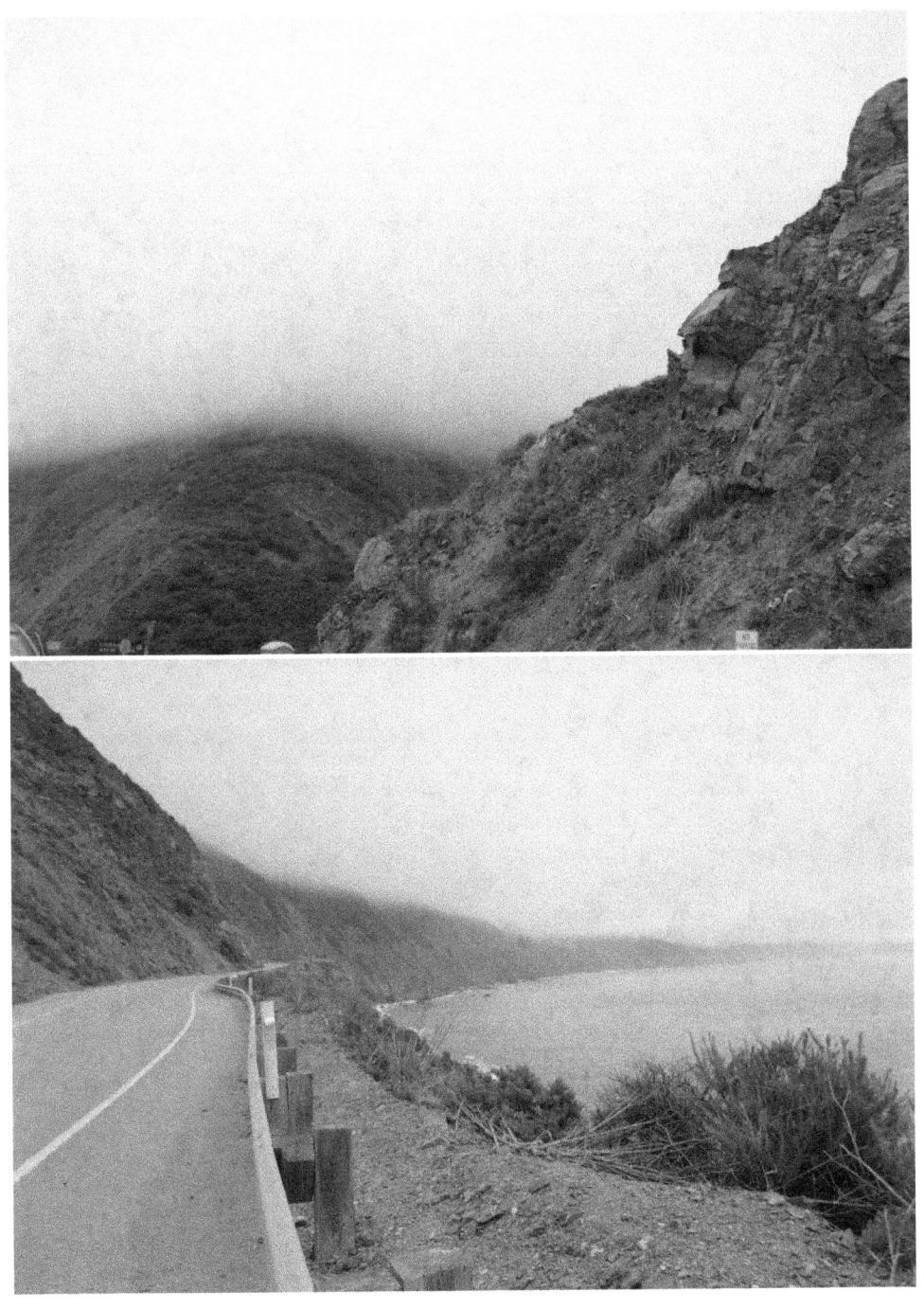

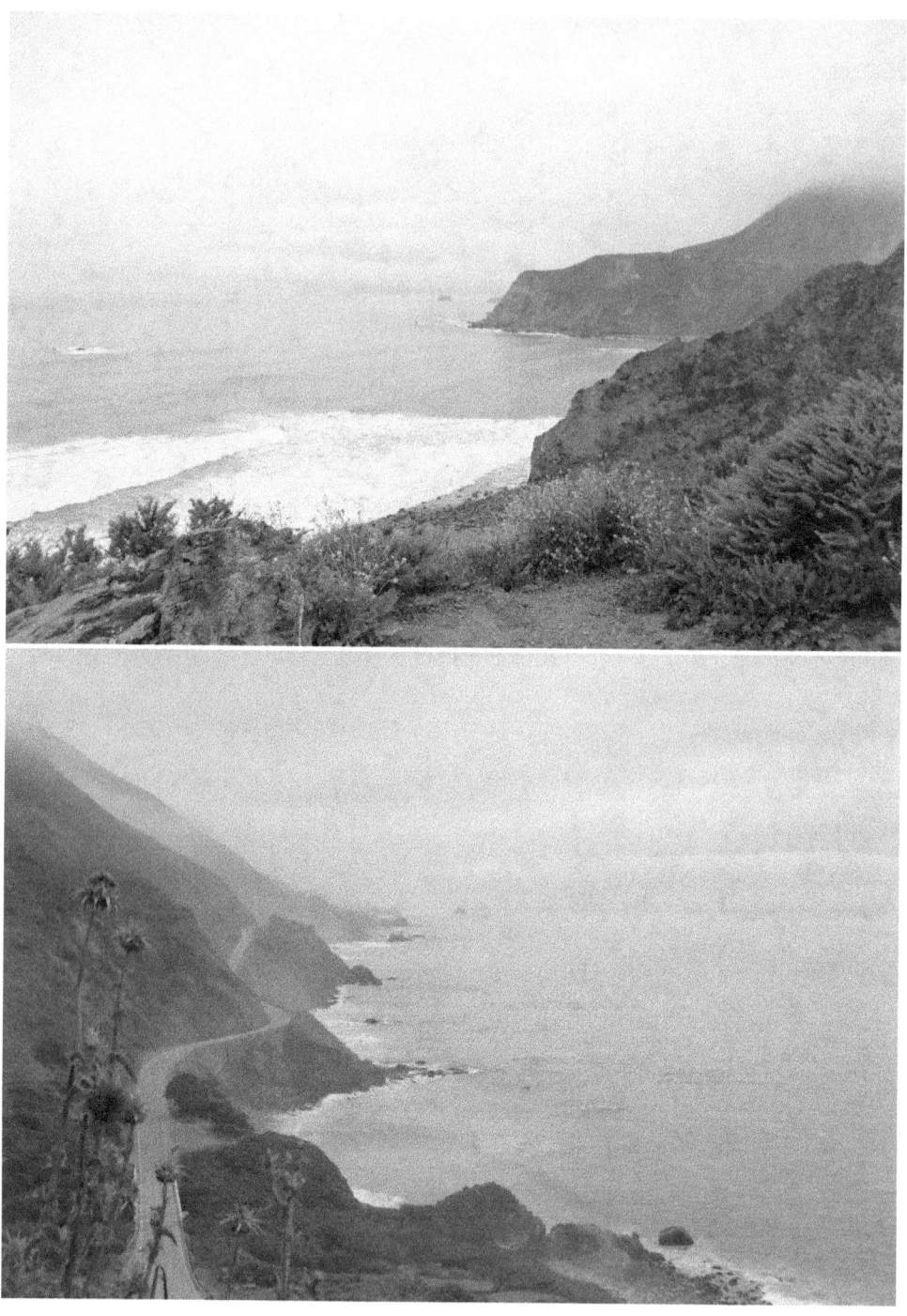

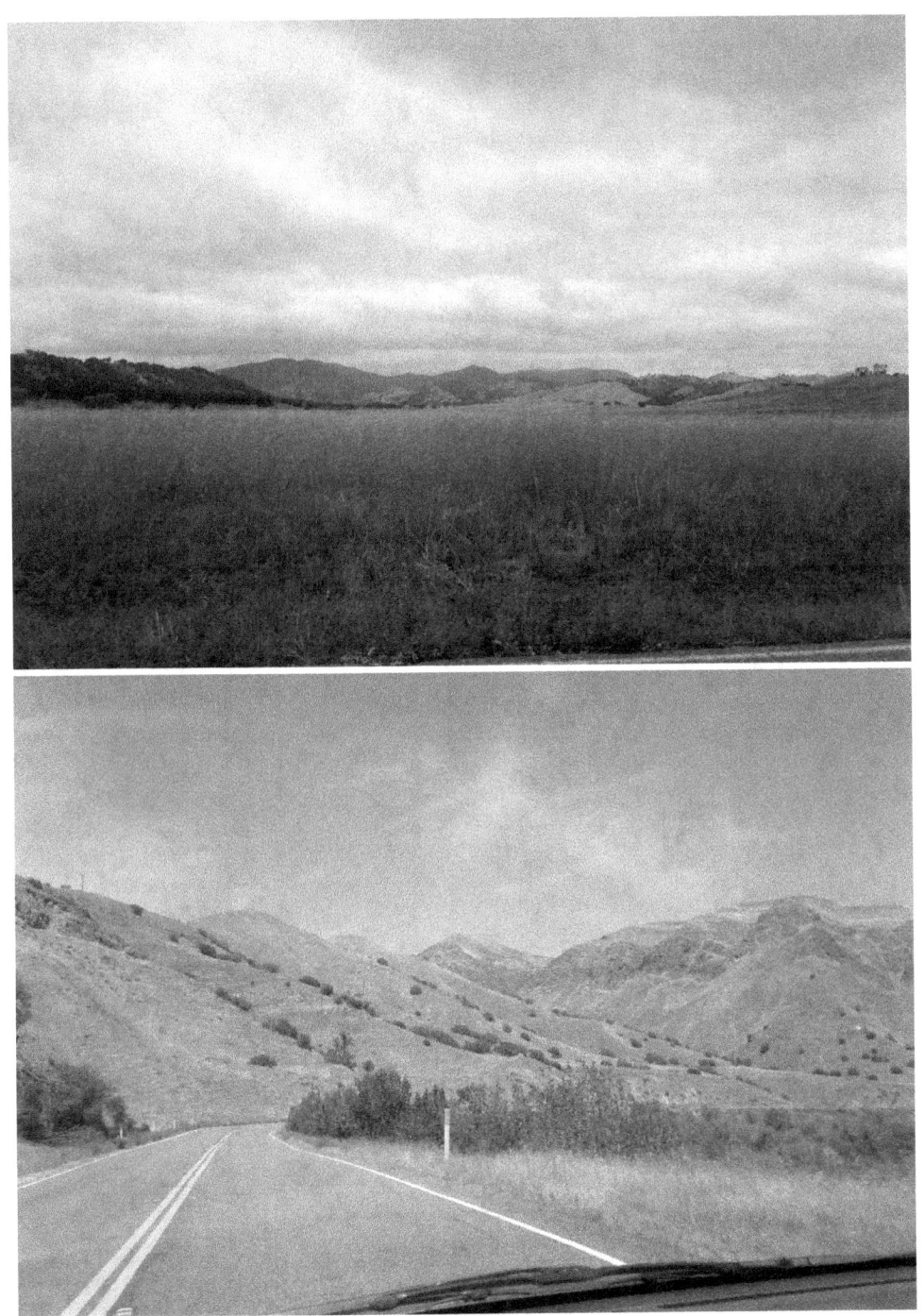

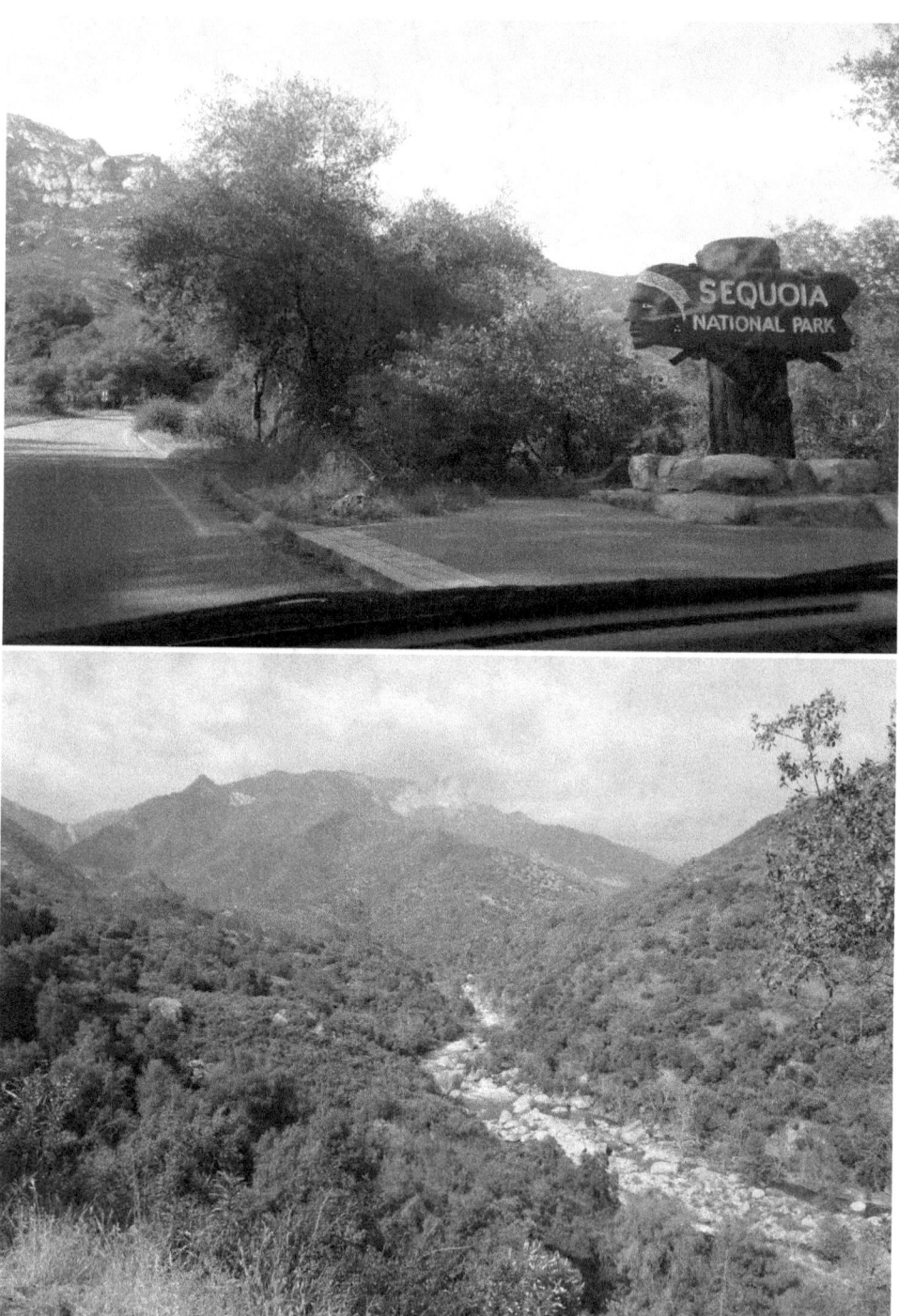

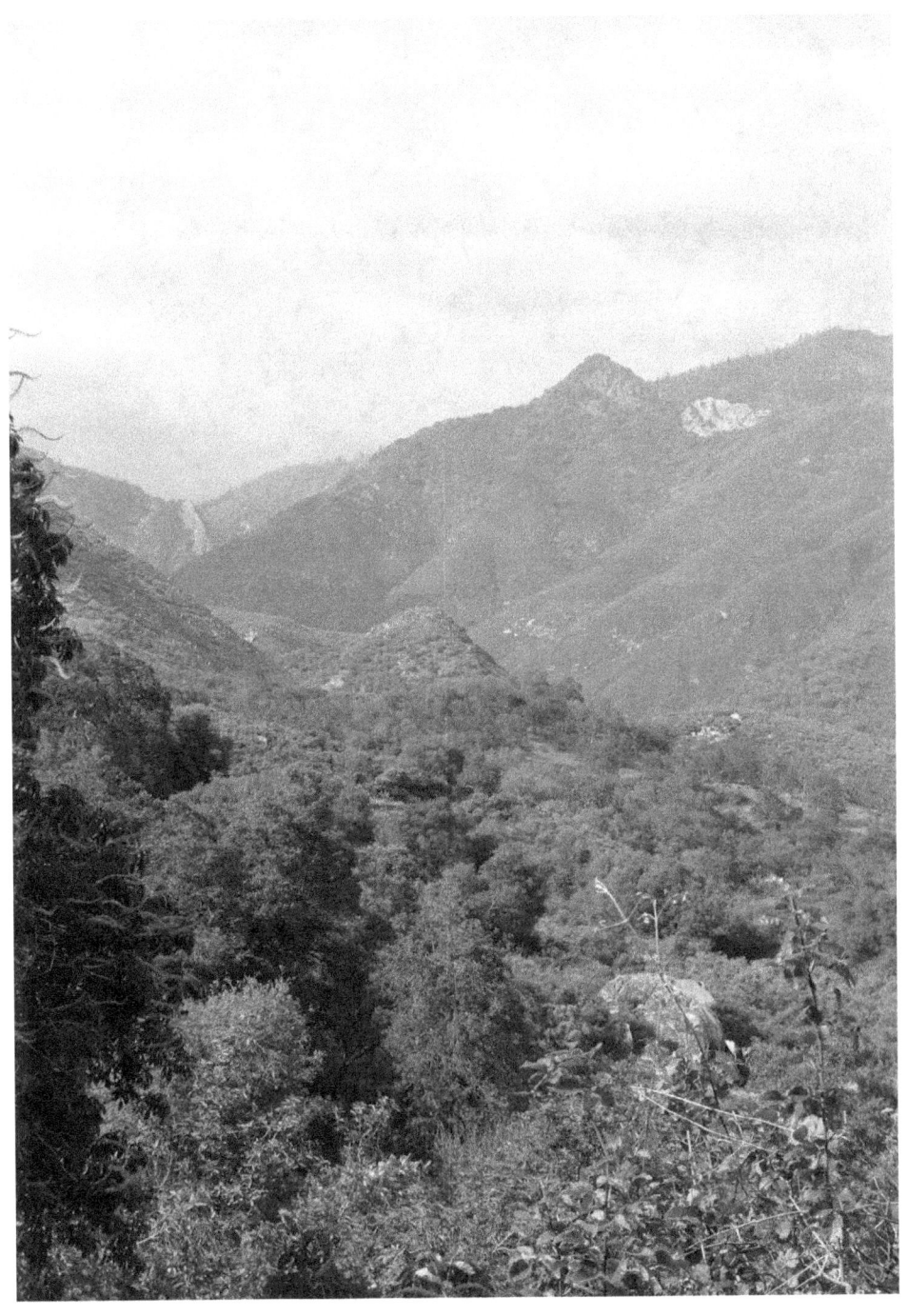

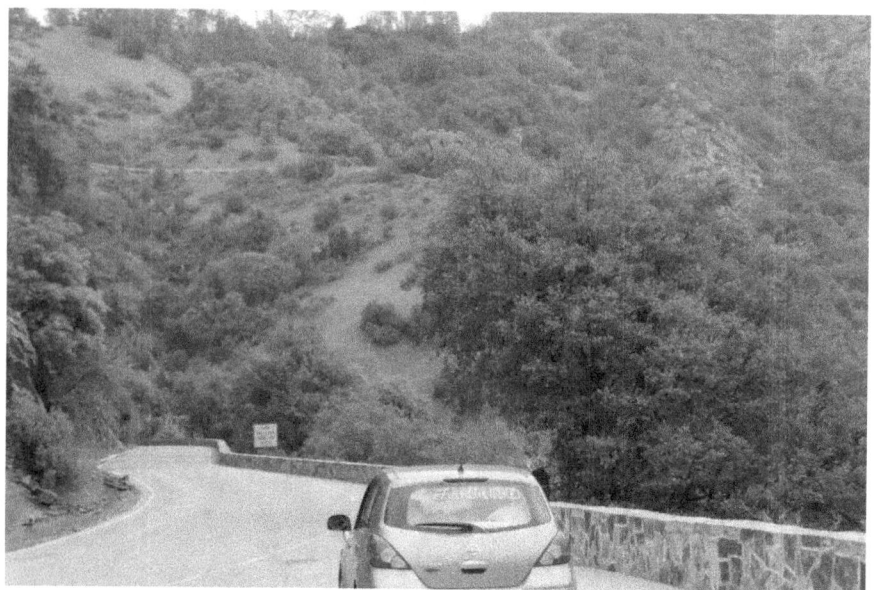

Shit! My main card got declined today! That means I'm down to my last $500 bucks. Shit!

Guess that means I'll be eating a lot more hot dogs and peanut butter. But I've made it in to Lodgepole in Sequoia and can camp here for the night. -$22

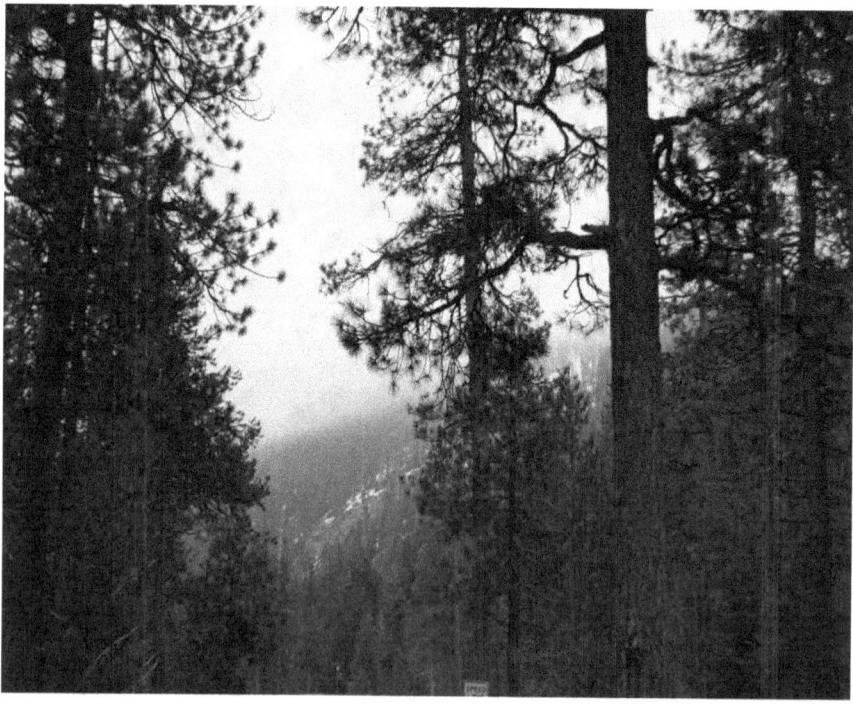

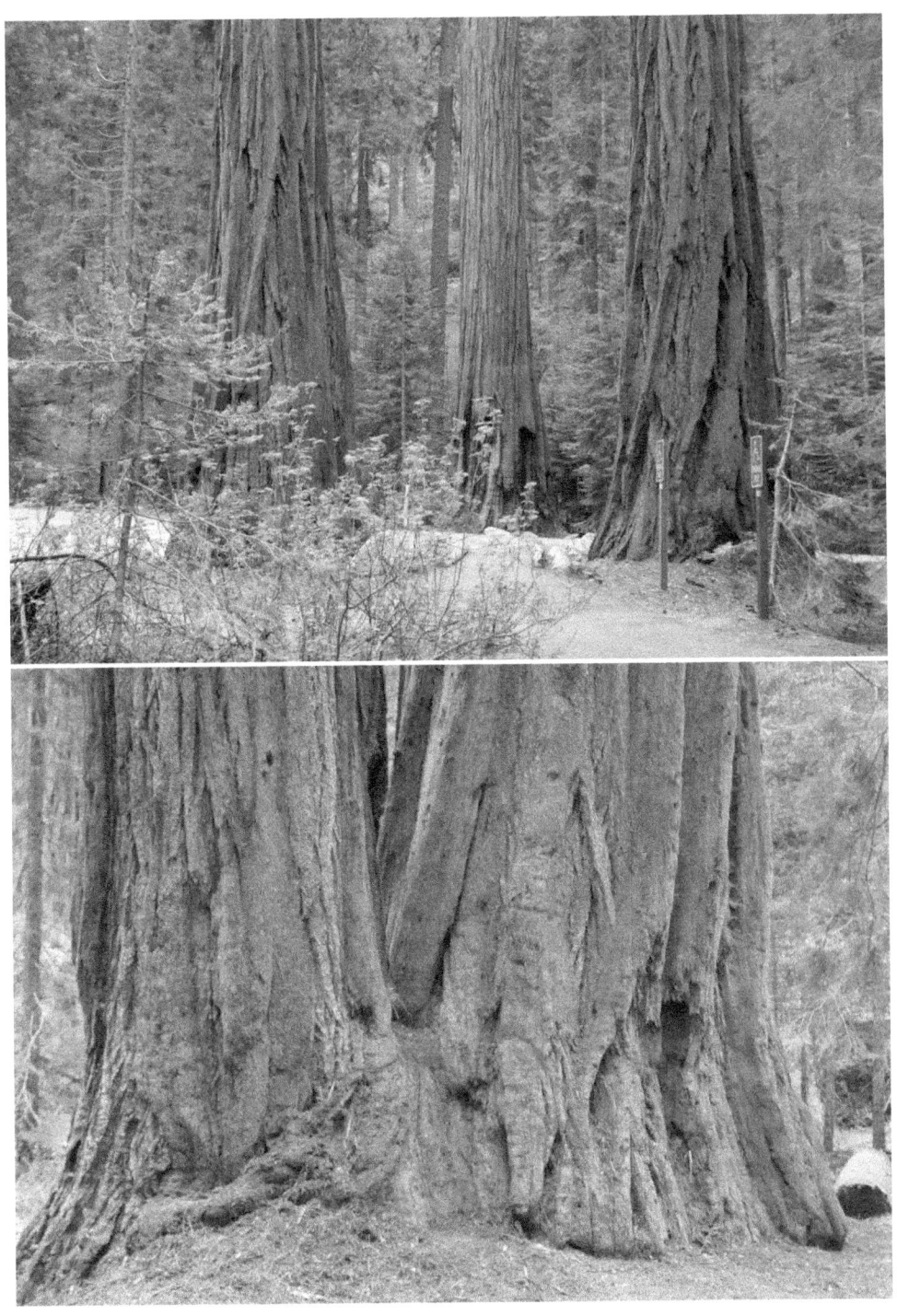

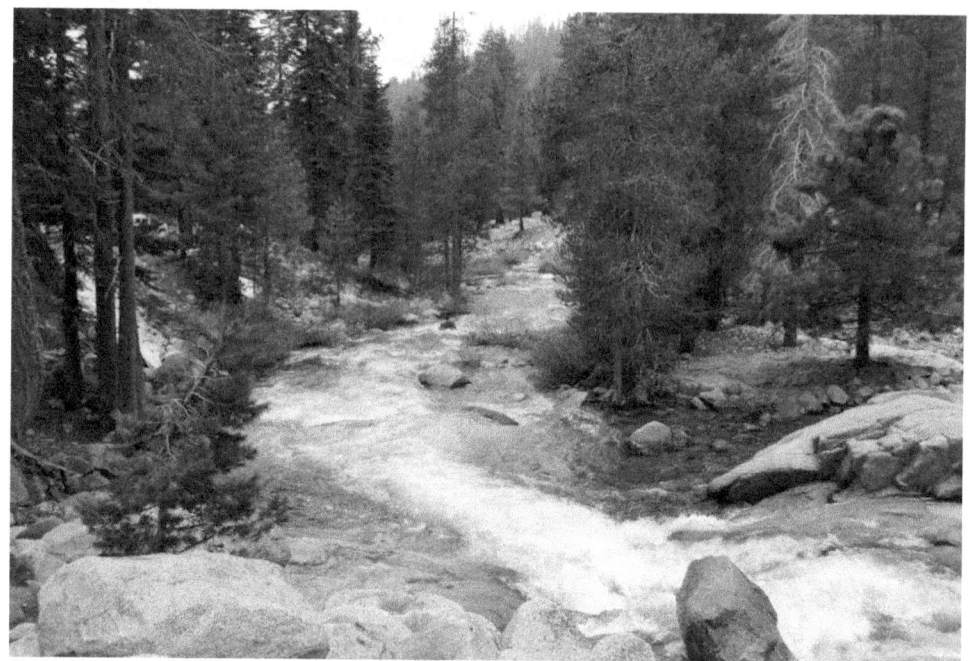

I met a guy here who lives in his vehicle permanently. He said he has two vehicles. He lives near LA most of the time, in a van, but comes up here twice a year to reconnect. Here he's got a Subaru. He said there is another BLM land up the road that I could have stayed at. Too bad I already put my fee in the box. He also gave me a tip about when I can't find a place to stay.

When he can't find a place in the city, he'll pull into a dark, quiet neighborhood with street parking. He'll sleep for the night then leave early in the morning. He also said if for some reason I do get stopped just to tell them I'm traveling through and got too tired, so I stopped for a nap then roll on my way. Wow. I hope I don't need that info.

———

I'm feeling a bit defeated. I'm nearing the end of my funds and haven't hit my objectives; I haven't made it to San Francisco (Really, Portland and up to Glacier...), I haven't sold art, and I haven't found a place to land. fuck... And who am I kidding? I didn't even paint anywhere along this path except that one place in Texas.

But wait! I'm not done yet! I still have time! I still have hope!   I can still sell art!

I will sell art tomorrow. I'll head back toward Santa Cruz and Monterey Bay. I'll find a place to set up and paint. Find a place to sell.

How much do they even sell for? By the square inch? By time and materials? And what's the multiplier? 18"x24" =432; $1 per square inch? Less? More? Or is it 18+24? How do I decide? The one I did that size I sold for $450. Is that good? Is that the right price?

"... Do not ask me where I'm going, as I travel in this limitless world, where every step I take is my home." ~Eihei Dogen

I had been feeling very at home out here traveling in my little car. But as the money runs out, I'm beginning to feel very lost, nervous, and homeless. I know I'm just out here running. Am I running to or from? I said I was running to my dreams but, I suppose since I don't know where I'm going, I'm actually running from. No! I know where I'm going. Artist. Author. Art studio. Retreats. Nature. Peace. Water. Woods. I know where I'm going.

5/11/17 Day 25 - Car Trouble Fo'real

It's chilly up here still. There is still some snowpack even. The giant sequoia are huge! The base of some are bigger than the car. And, the rocks are granite. When I see this place, it's easy to imagine dinosaurs.

The campsites all have bear boxes to lock up your food and anything that might smell like food to a bear, i.e. shampoo, deodorant, dirty diapers…

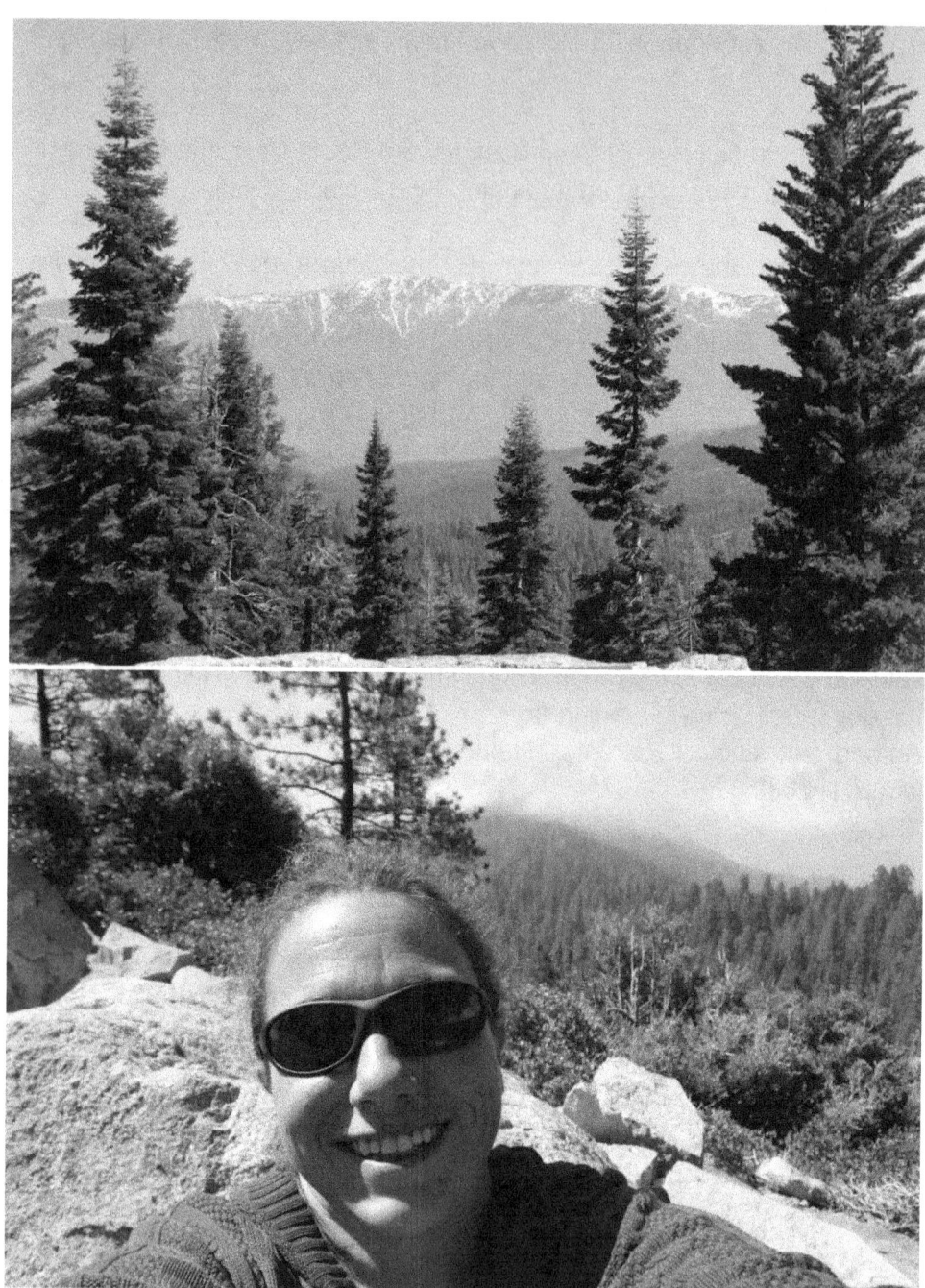

Last night I sat by a campfire for the first time since that $6 a night campground in Texas. It was nice but I did get a bit spooked. The anxiousness has my senses turned up too high, I guess. I could hear things rustling in the woods nearby. The campground is fairly empty and there is no one camping very near me. My mind kept telling me "oh shit! It's a bear!" It probably wasn't. Maybe, but probably not.

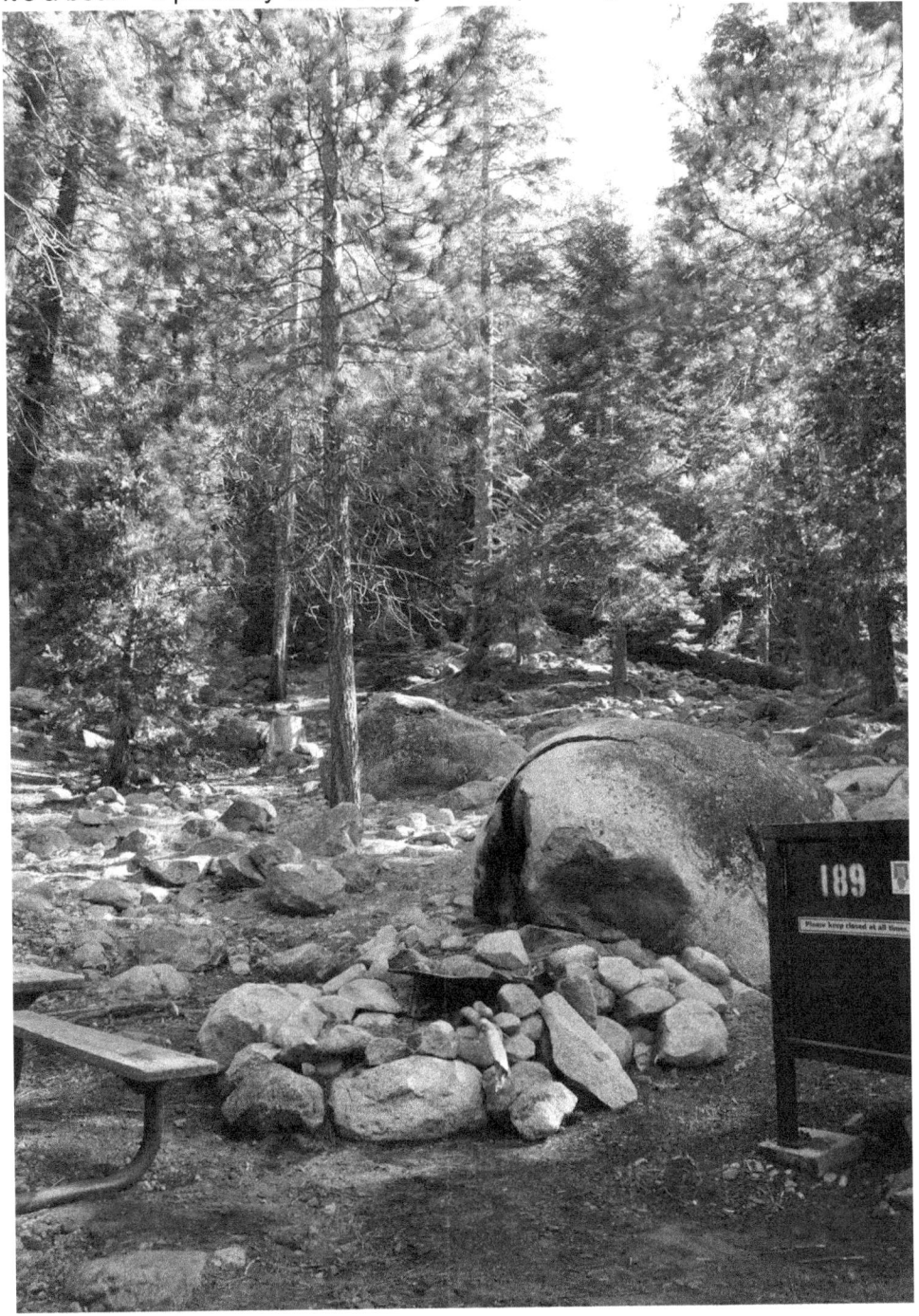

My coach told me I should have been painting at all these places. She's right. I probably should have been. I did the one though. It took all day and looked terrible. No, I'm doing fine. This trip was to see as much as possible. To collect data. To think. To regroup. To heal and grow. To make it as far as possible before my moola runs out.

In fact, it's time I get rolling again. My plan was to head straight up into Yosemite, but the road is closed. I have to go out to Fresno then back into Yosemite. Bummer.

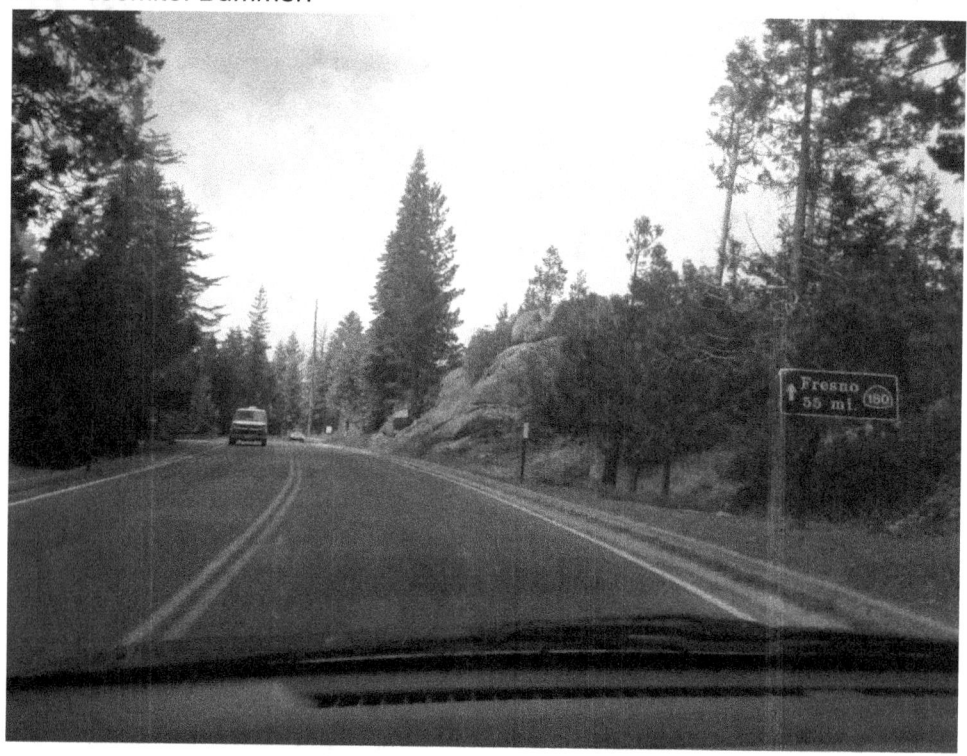

_____

Uh oh, the sound started again. And this time I've also got a flashing check engine light. I stopped at AutoZone in Fresno to get it scanned. Misfire. Ok, fine, I think. I'll just change the plugs. I've got the tools and plugs are cheap. No biggie. As I started taking off all the plastics, I happened to notice a hole in my belt. Nope.

Pro Tip: A flashing check engine light is usually a misfire. If you run the codes, it will probably say random misfire on a certain cylinder, but it might say random multiple misfires. Either way, a misfire is not always plugs or wires. A misfire on a single cylinder might be a plug or a wire but, Random Misfires or Random Multiple Misfires is NOT your plugs. While it could be several things, it's probably a vacuum leak. To Look for a vacuum leak: With your car running, spray some carb cleaner near all the hoses under your hood. When the sound of the engine changes, you've found your vacuum leak.

The guy at AZ recommended a mechanic on mechanic row, but that mechanic wasn't there. I stopped at the only shop I saw that sounded like a white guy: Sam's. (forgive me... I don't know. Who else do I go to? This is like trying to find a mechanic in G.I. it's mechanics row. There are a hundred! Where do I start?! I don't know about you but for me, I start looking for one that looks like somebody cares about it and that they'll speak English.) So, I go into Sam's. Turns out Sam is Asian and doesn't take credit cards. Doh! I finally see a shop that looks like it's got it's shit together. (probably going to be the most expensive too)

They don't hear the sound. The diagnostic is $70 +$150 for a belt and can't do it until morning. That's ok. I had to call mom and dad to see if they can help. Dad said he would, and they sent a Western Union. I got there just before it closed. They sent a little extra, so I had Chinese next door for dinner. It was good and I feel a little better.

After dinner, I was sitting in the car and heard the sound again. When I investigated, I found a broken motor mount. Shit. there goes the little extra.

5/12/17 Day 26

When I woke up this morning, I took the car back to the shop and showed them the motor mount. While they were fixing it, I walked to a laundromat and had my coaching call. My coach helped me come up with a game plan.

While at the laundromat I noticed a help wanted sign on the wall for fruit pickers. I saved the info. Worst case, I could do that for a minute and then keep going.

I also looked for shows. I'd rather sell art than pick fruit. That's how you sell art, right? At a show?

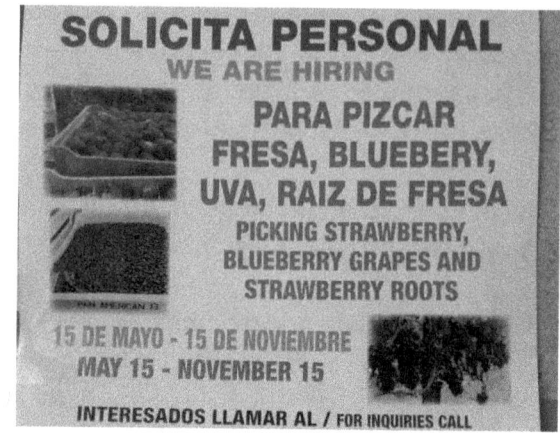

I found a show in San Francisco. I emailed. The show is in two weeks. I can do that. If I'm accepted, it's going to cost me $300 to be in the show. But I've still got some credit available. I can do this. Where will I stay? I can get an Airbnb and use some of the credit for that too.

Adam-Eve and Waterbodies will be my big showpieces but, maybe I can put together a few other things as well. Also, biz cards and bio. I'd need to find a library.

I go back to pick up the car. I barely make it out of the parking lot and hear a different but even more horrible sound. Way worse than the original sound! It sounds like something is about to vibrate off. How did they not notice this!? Straight back I go. Thankfully, the tech quickly heard the sound and found it. The weight on the end of the new mount was loose and vibrating. They fixed it quickly.

In the meantime, I heard back from the show and I've been accepted. That was quick! (is that a red flag?) It's expensive (another red flag?) But, you've gotta spend money to make money, right?

So, slight change of plans, no Yosemite. Maybe it's good I couldn't go straight thru.

Trust the process. Everything happens for a reason.

My coach suggested I go to Carmel-by-the-sea as it's an artsy town. So, I head that direction (back out to the coast) on my way to San Francisco.

On the way, I stopped at Casa de fruta and did a short Facebook Live announcing my show and showing some of the pieces I'll be showing. Then, I had a little nap.

I got to Carmel during the golden hour just before sunset. It's gorgeous. It's also windier and colder than I expected but with the sun on my face, it's lovely. I sat there on the beach taking a few pictures and people watching while I waited for the sunset.

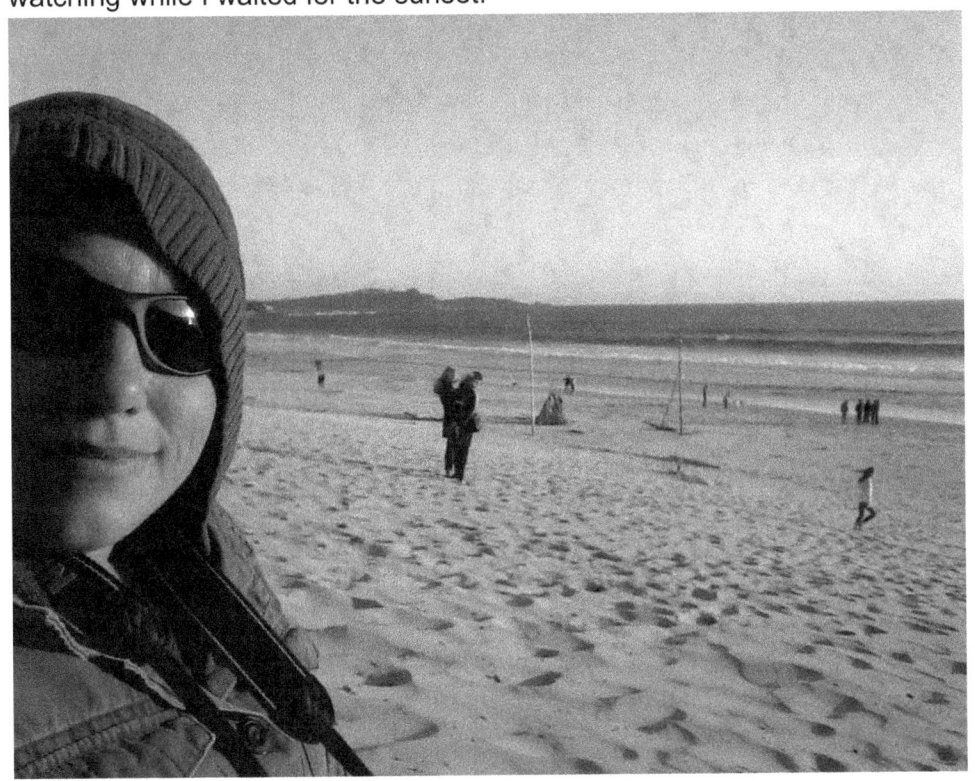

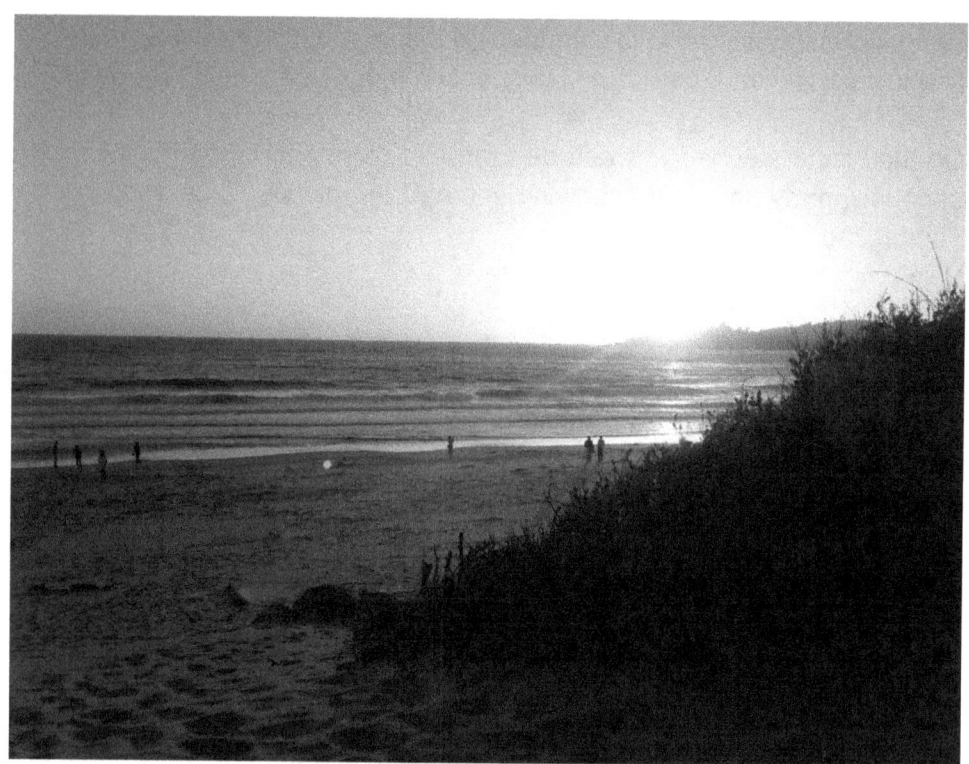

Carmel is a very rich tourist town on the beach. It was founded by artists and writers. The main street is lined with buildings that are reminiscent of some European village. There's definitely no Walmart or sleeping on the beach. If I weren't feeling so dirty and homeless, I might really like it here.

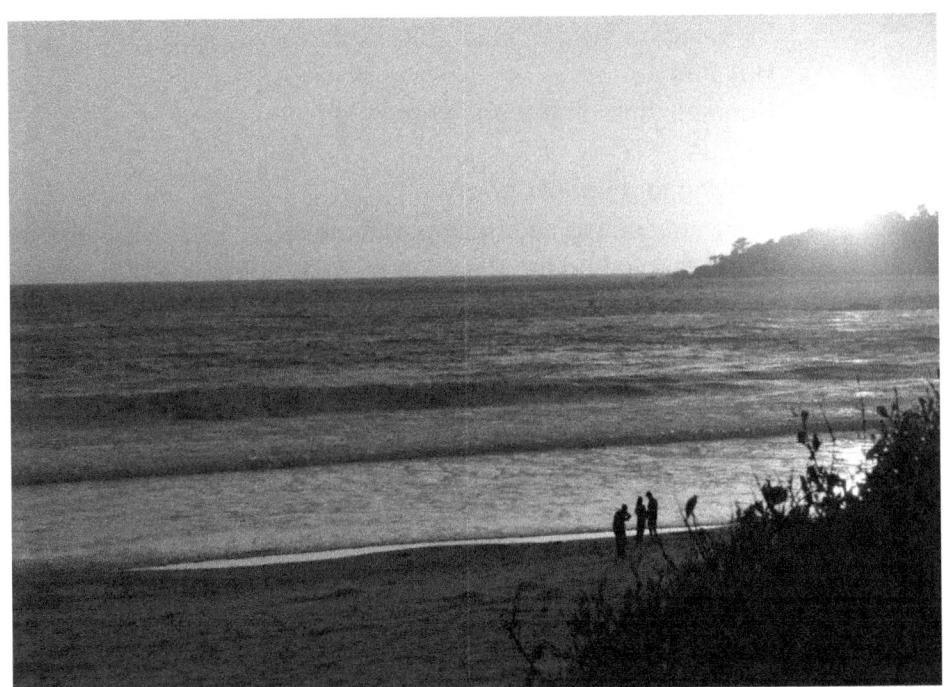

I watched the sunset then wandered around until long after dark before finding a Home Depot parking lot. There are several campers here but not the nice retired RVer kind. These are older models. I wonder if the one in front of me even still runs. There is also a car nearby with a couple people in it. I suspect those two won't actually be sleeping. There isn't any room in that car to sleep and just barely a few inches to recline their seats.

As I sit here watching, there is a guy that comes up to the gas station in front of me. He pulls a blanket out of his bag, spreads it on the ground on the side of the building, and lays down to go to sleep.

> "Sunshine beating on the good times
> Moonlight raising from the grave
> String band playing worn out honky-tonks
> Pretty young thing going dancing in the rain
> High heel lady spitting at the nickajack
> Businessman with a needle and a spoon
> Coyote chewing on a cigarette
> Pack o' young boys going howlin' at the moon
> Hey darlin'!

Sleeping on the blacktop
Hey darlin'!
Running through the trees honey
Hey darlin'!
Leaving for the next town
Less'n my sense catches up with me."
from Sleeping on the Blacktop by Colter Wall

The camper in front of me has a bicycle parked by its back bumper. A guy with a broken arm walks up, gets on the bike, and rides a way. A second later, a guy comes out of the camper waving a gun. The thief is already gone. I'm officially freaked out. Should I leave? I don't know where else to go.

As I sit finishing my left-over Chinese from yesterday, a cop pulls into the gas station. He fills his tank and leaves. He says nothing to no one. Wow….

Tomorrow I'll head back to Carmel and paint. I've also found a park nearby with a shower. I found a $30 /night campground with no facilities, and something about a road that people can park on overnight. I could maybe stay another night around here. I'll probably shower and roll on.

Despite this past few minutes and the money for repairs, I feel pretty good today. I am hopeful, and grateful I'm not sleeping on the blacktop.

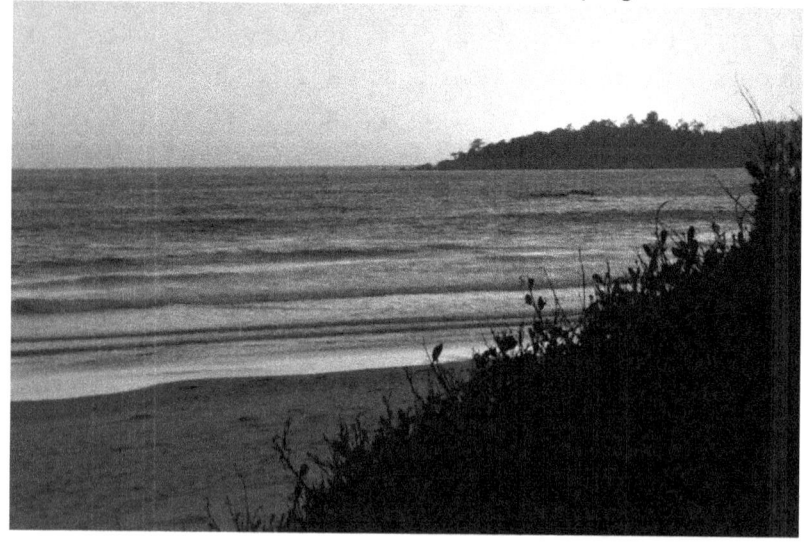

5/13/17 Day 27

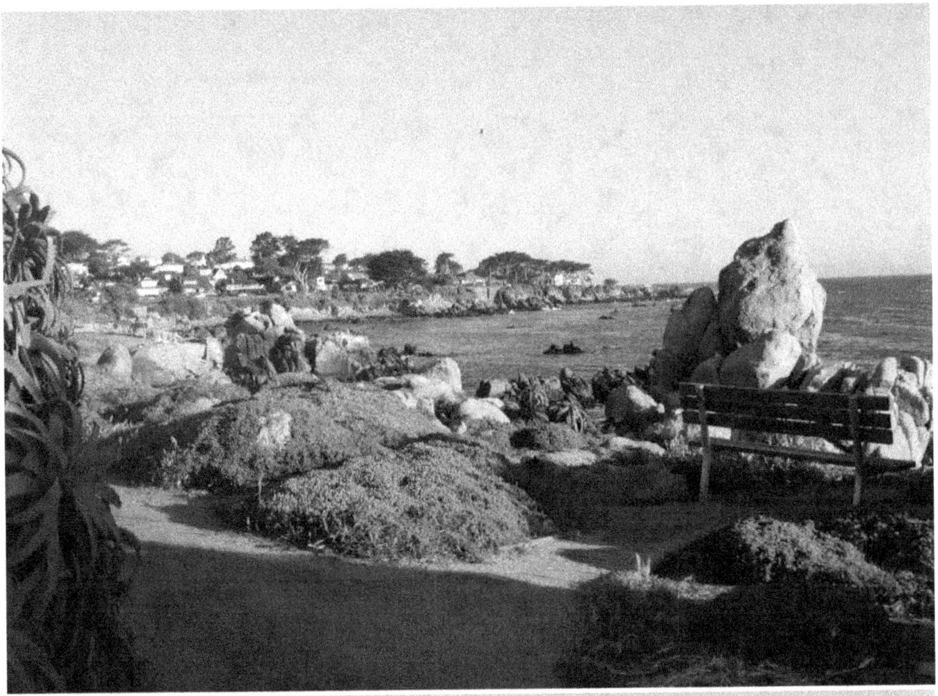

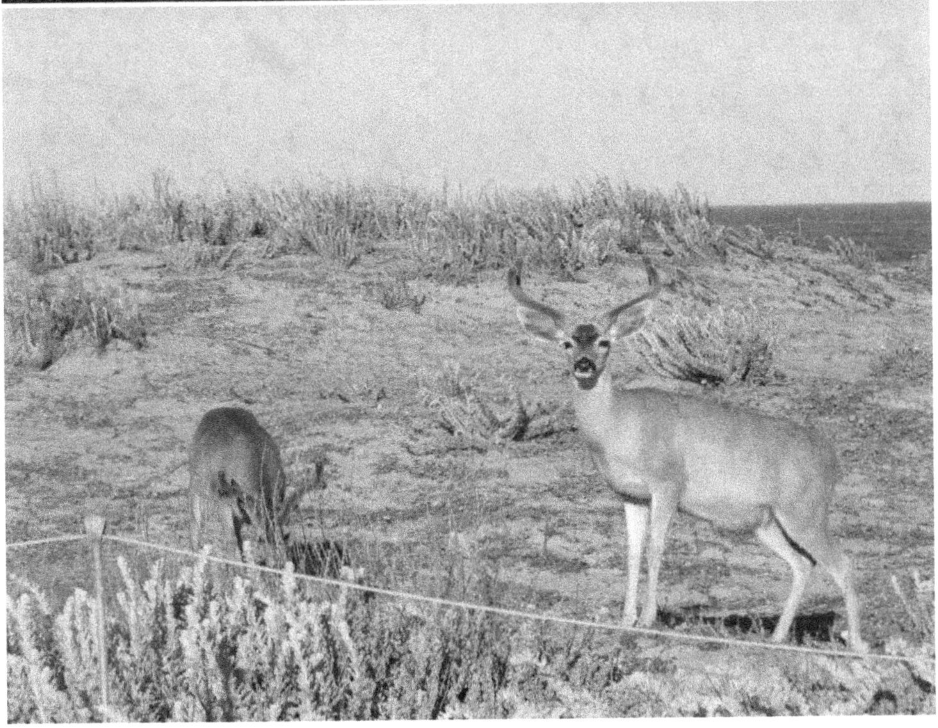

I went back to Carmel this morning after a drive on the coast in that area. I sat and painted on the beach near where I was sitting last night. It was super windy and kinda chilly. My paint was drying very fast but, I managed, I suppose.

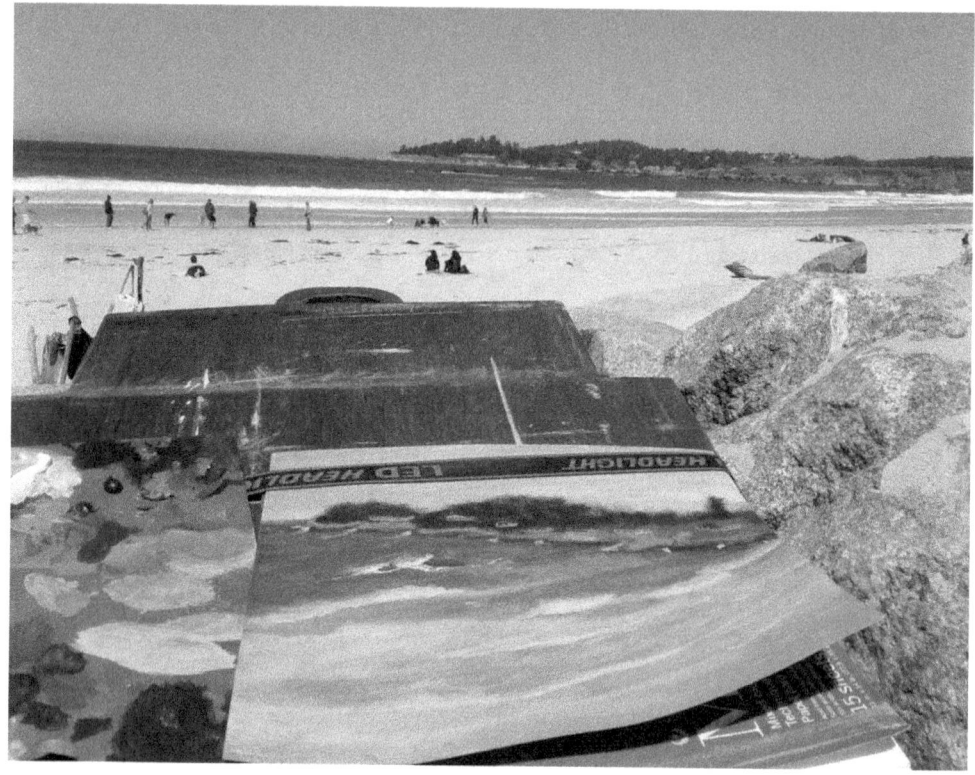

I found a roll of film while I was there. How can I find the owner of it, I wonder?

While I was painting, I got a phone call from someone important to me. I almost never answer the phone when it rings but I did this time. I thought it was going to be a nice phone call. Turns out the caller was calling to scold me for showing my Adam-Eve paintings in my Facebook video yesterday. Because "someone might have their kid on their lap while they are scrolling through and might accidentally see it" I basically say this sounds like a personal problem. maybe they should be doing something with the kid instead of scrolling Facebook. The call is short and puts me in a sour mood. But then I look up and remember I'm painting on the beach. Fuck that... Oooommmm.... Or, at least I try. I'm still kinda sour.

After painting I drove toward Santa Cruz. There are lots of pull outs along the shore and even some camping until you get to Santa Cruz county. Then, all of Santa Cruz county is no sleeping on the beach. Santa Cruz itself is large and busy. It was a tough day and I'm a bit frazzled.

I pulled into this windsurfer beach to watch the sunset.

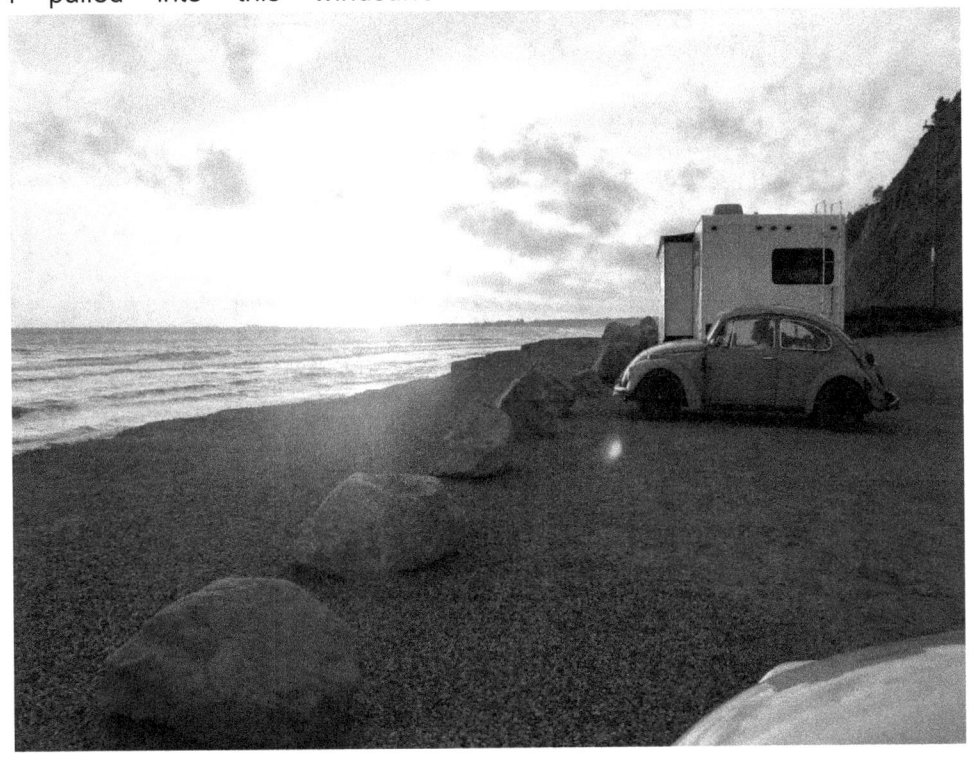

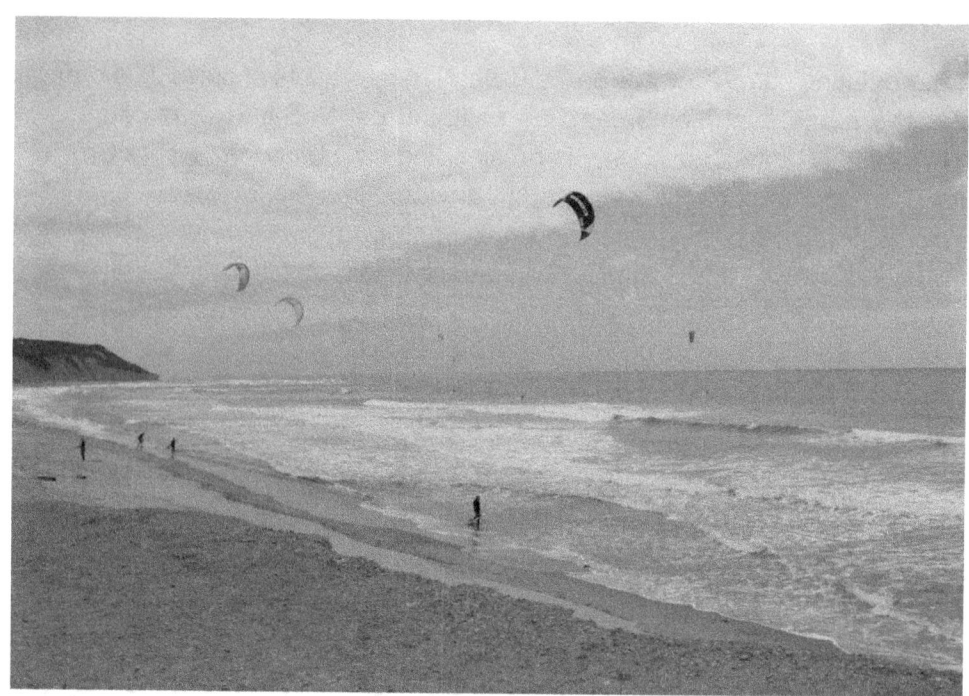

The sunset, the beach, it was all really lovely. I was really enjoying watching the windsurfers and the colors change. Then, some family in a GIANT rent-a-bus pulls in next to me. They block me in. This irritates me, but I tell myself not to worry. I'm not leaving yet anyway. (But what if I was!?) Then, the door opens, and all 15 of them get out for pictures right in front of where I'm standing, with my camera, obviously taking pics. I was quite perturbed.

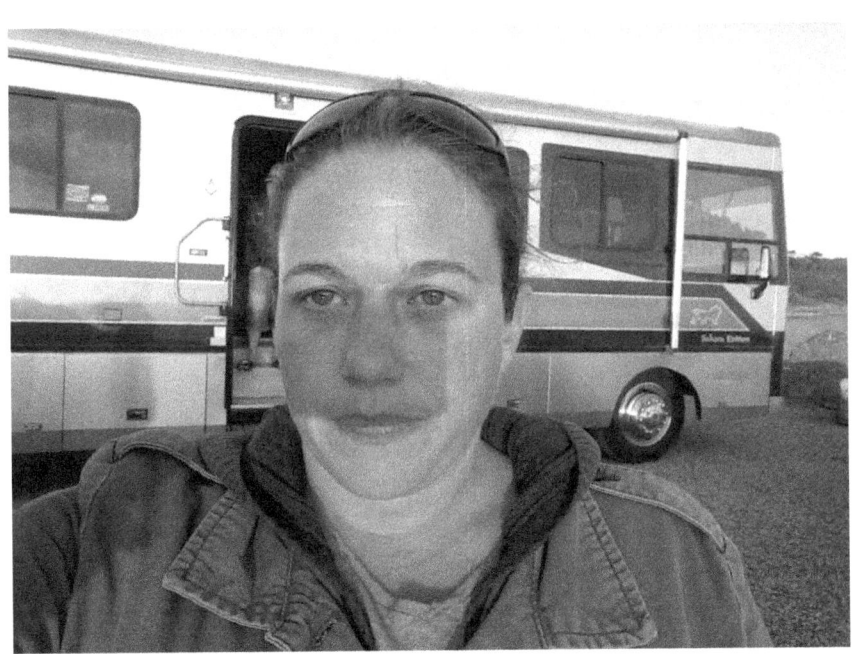

5/14/17 Day 28

I stopped at a bunch of beach spots today and made it all the way up to Palo Alto and San Mateo, but I've got too many days left before San Francisco so, I headed back to Pascadero and the beach.

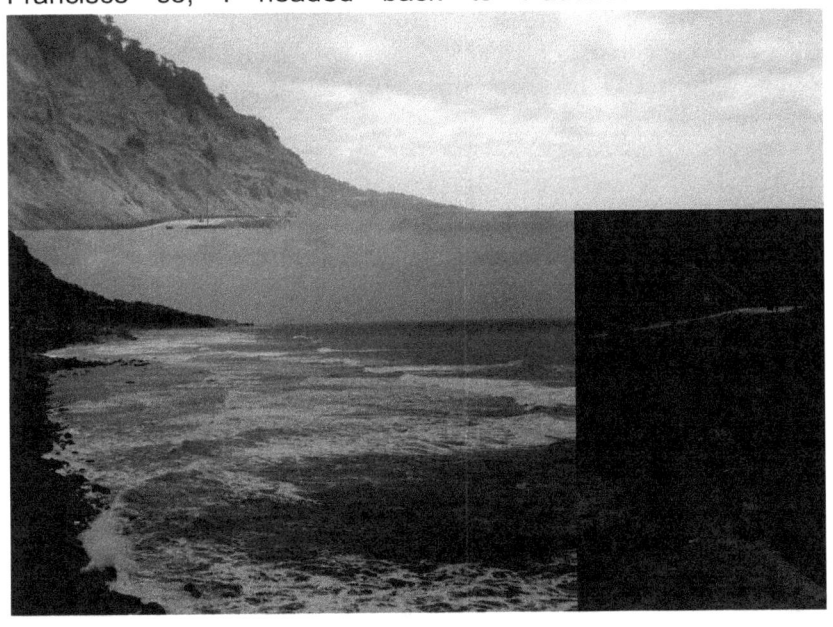

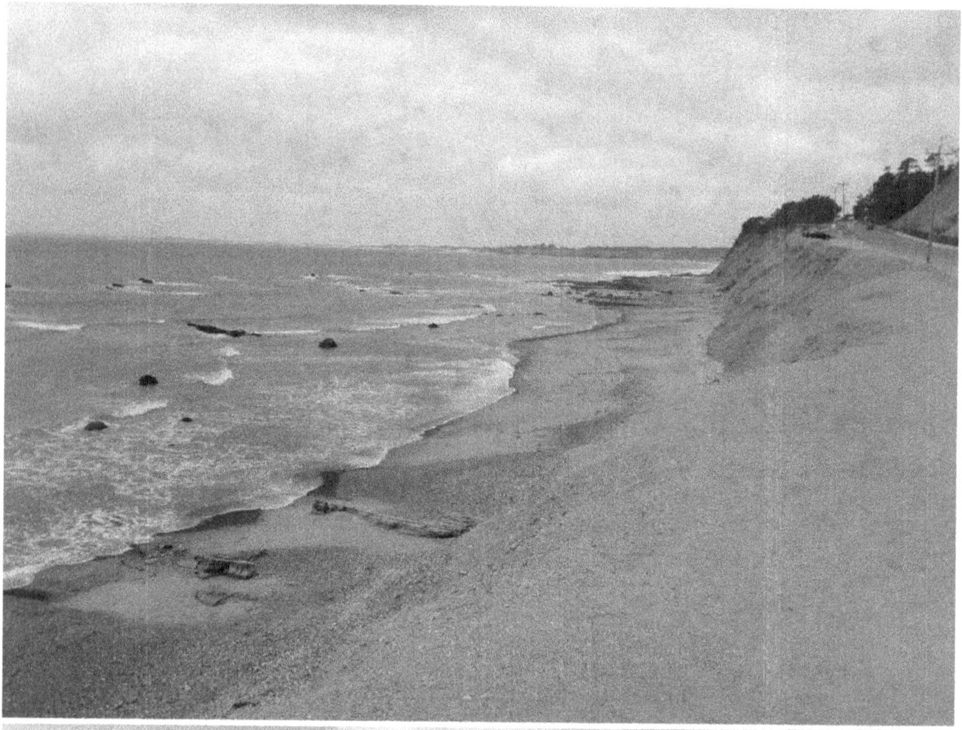

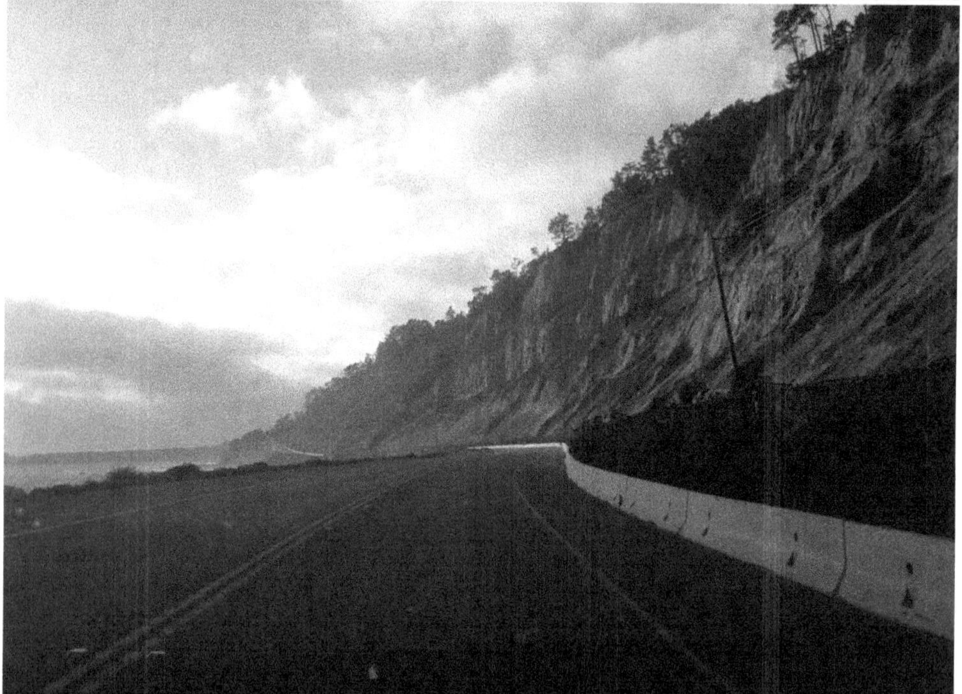

223

I sat and painted at the windsurf spot for a while. There was a lady there hollering about the white flecks being dolphins. She was completely excited. They looked like waves to me.

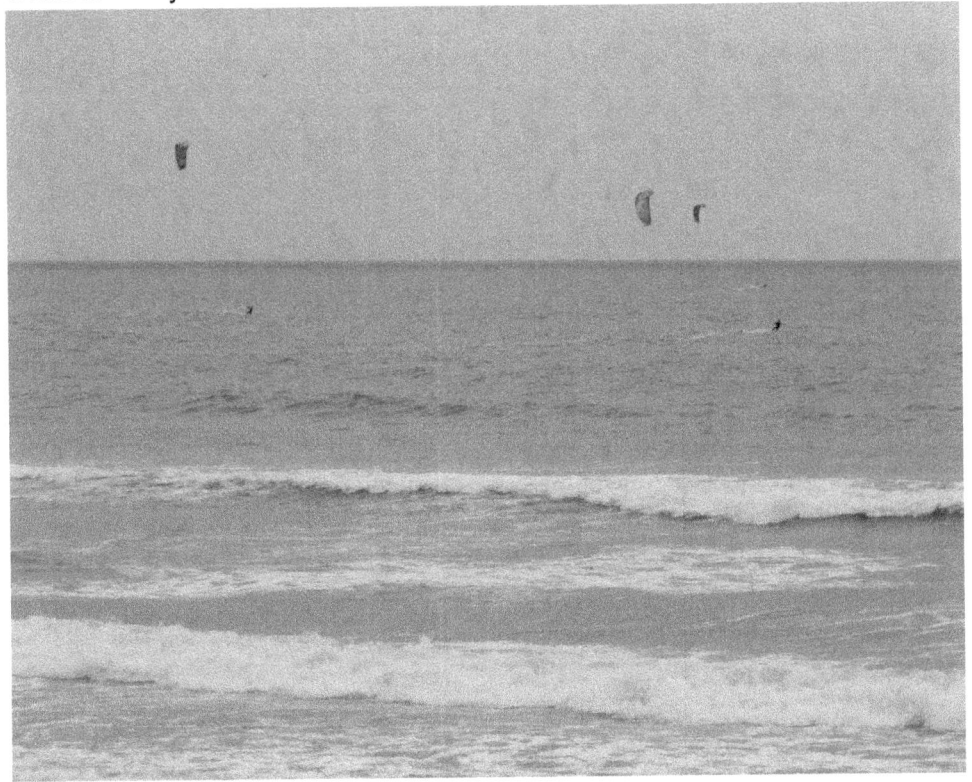

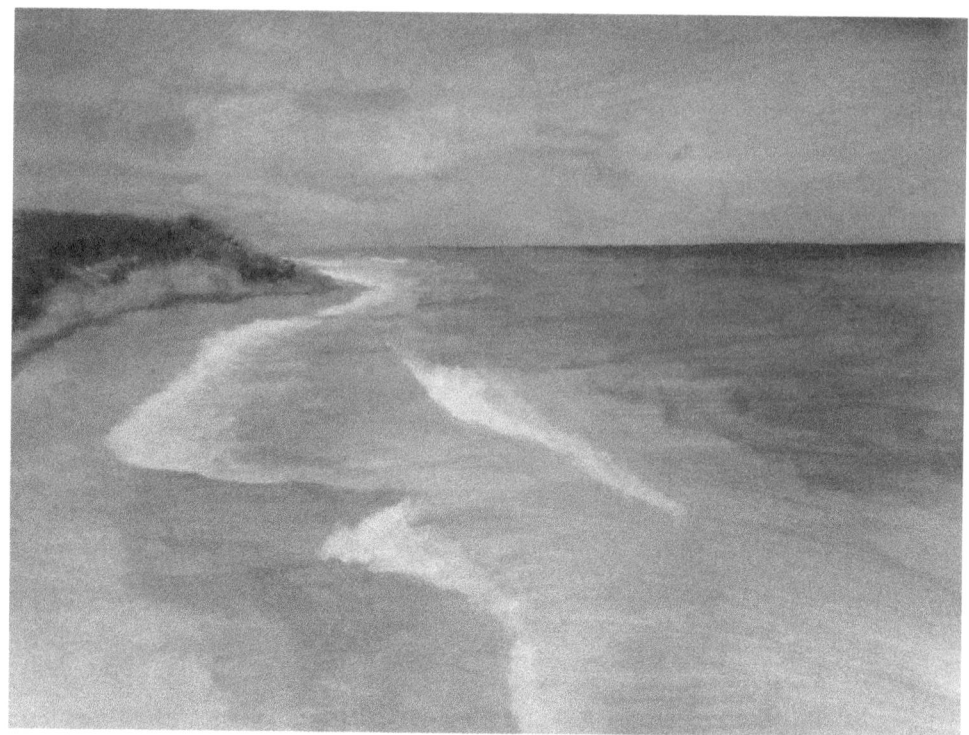

After painting I back tracked some more to the hippie beach and backed into a spot to take a nap.

I'm somewhere between awake and asleep when these hippie kids roll up blaring some awful music. I hollered at them... They got out and went down to the beach and I got a nap.

When they came back, they offered me a dab. I don't know anything about that stuff... I just smoke green. We chat for a bit. They had been down on the beach digging crystals. (what!?! I wish I knew that before!) They also tell me about sleeping on the beach and getting something to cover my windows better. Their sleeping advice? "If a cop stops you, just tell him you got too tired and didn't want to drive off the road, so you stopped for a quick nap."

―――――

I still don't know where I'm going after this show. Eureka Springs is the one I'd like the most but if I don't make a sale, how? It's really looking like I'm headed to Indiana. I'm not ready to call it yet though.

225

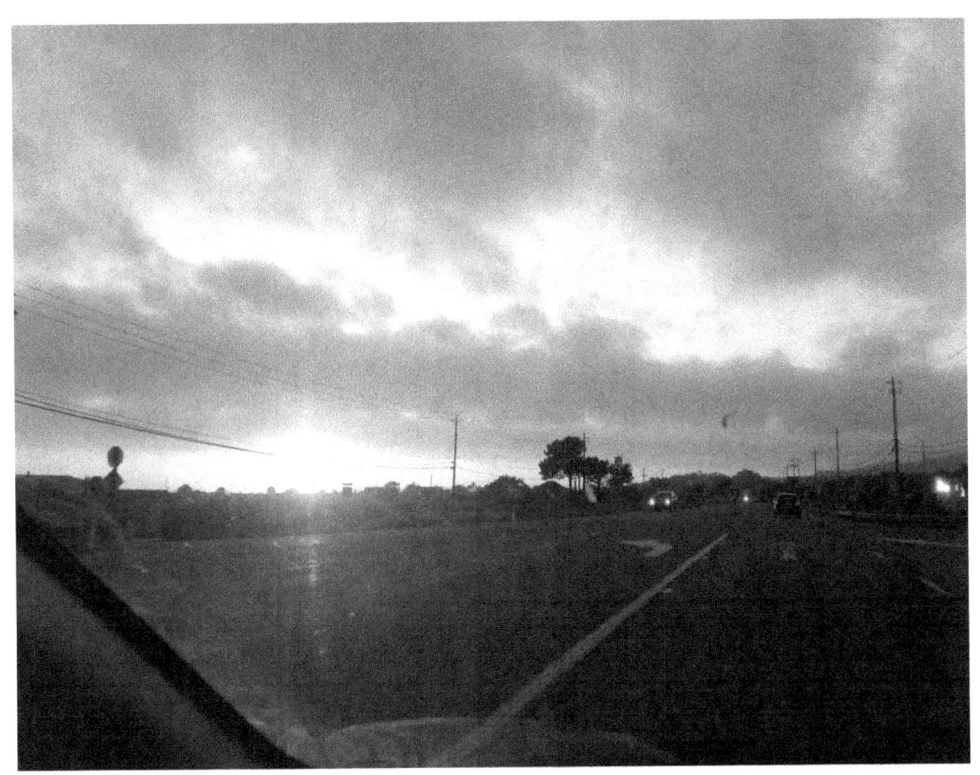

5/15/17 Day 29 - San Francisco

Well, much of the strange advice I've been given paid off last night. I was too chicken to sleep on/at the beaches with the "no overnight…" signs so I ended up driving well after dark. The only Walmart I could find turned out to be a Walmart headquarters, not store. I then tried sleeping at some other store parking lot, but it was so bright, I couldn't sleep so I left.

I drove around for a while and looked for some other reasonable option and found nothing so, it was time for the last resort plans. I ended up finding a dark and quiet street in some neighborhood. It might have been on the back side of an airport or rail yard? I'm not sure. Didn't matter, it was late, quiet, and dark so I locked the doors, put up my window blocks, and crawled in back. Thankfully no one bothered me, and I was able to sleep, mostly. I'm pretty sure I woke up every time a car drove past.

When I woke up, I headed into San Francisco. It was too early for my Airbnb check-in, but I drove past and checked it out anyway.

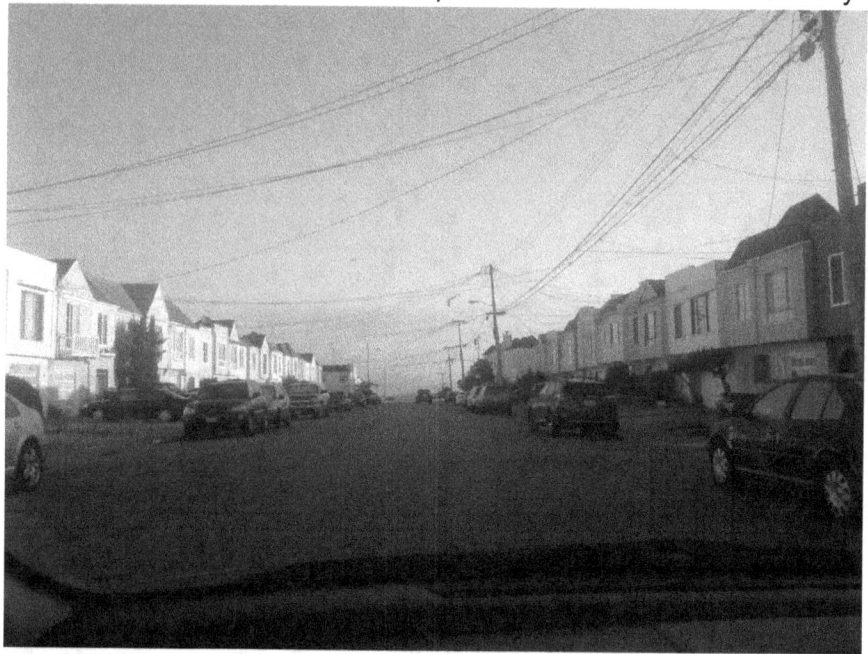

Thank goodness it looks normal and not freaky like LA. I can't check in until this afternoon, so I checked out the city.

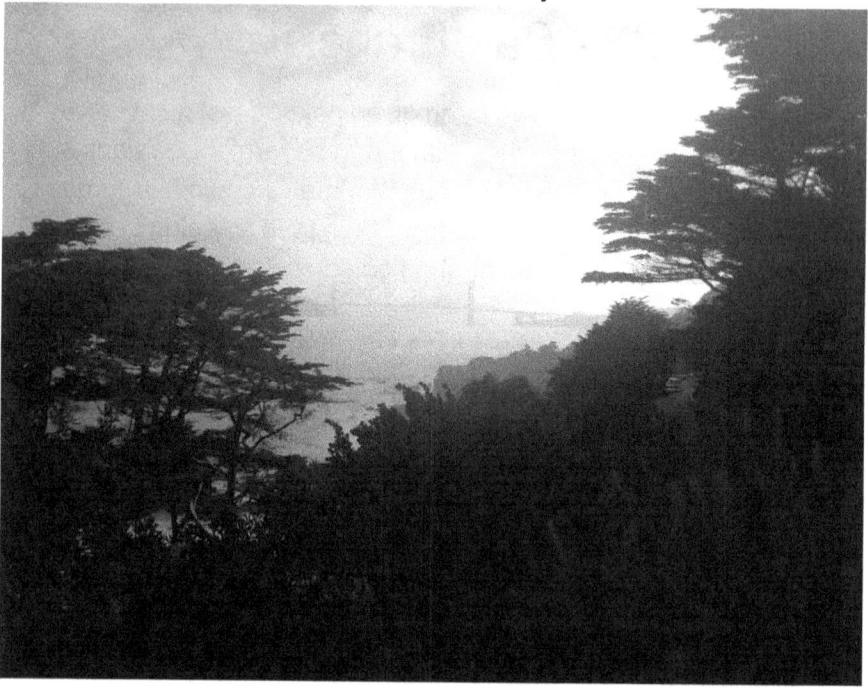

I first went down and sat at the beach and watched the waves and the people for a bit. It was really windy and cool. Also, there was lots of trash at that beach.

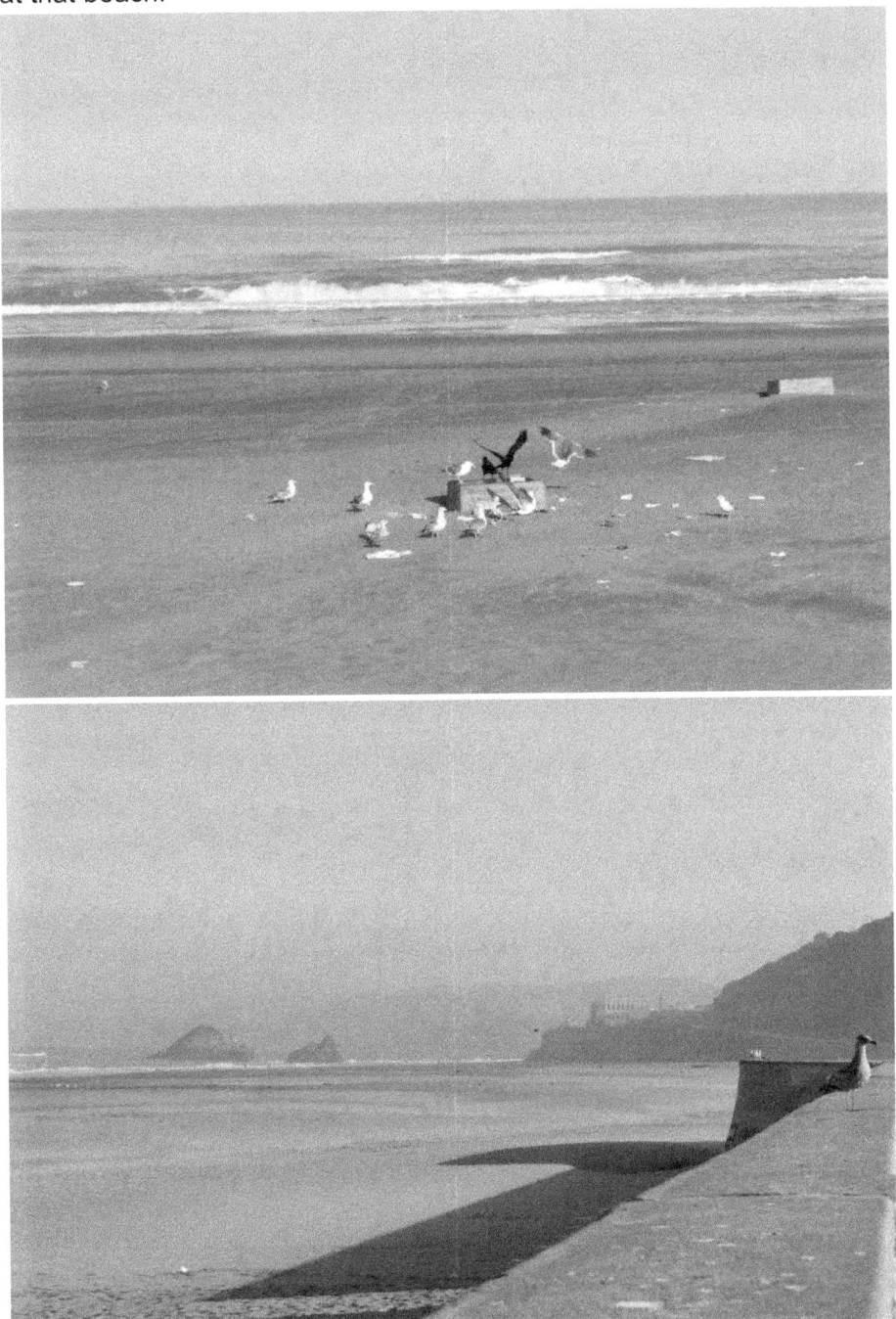

After a bit, I went and checked out the park below the bridge then went up to the lookout park above the bridge.

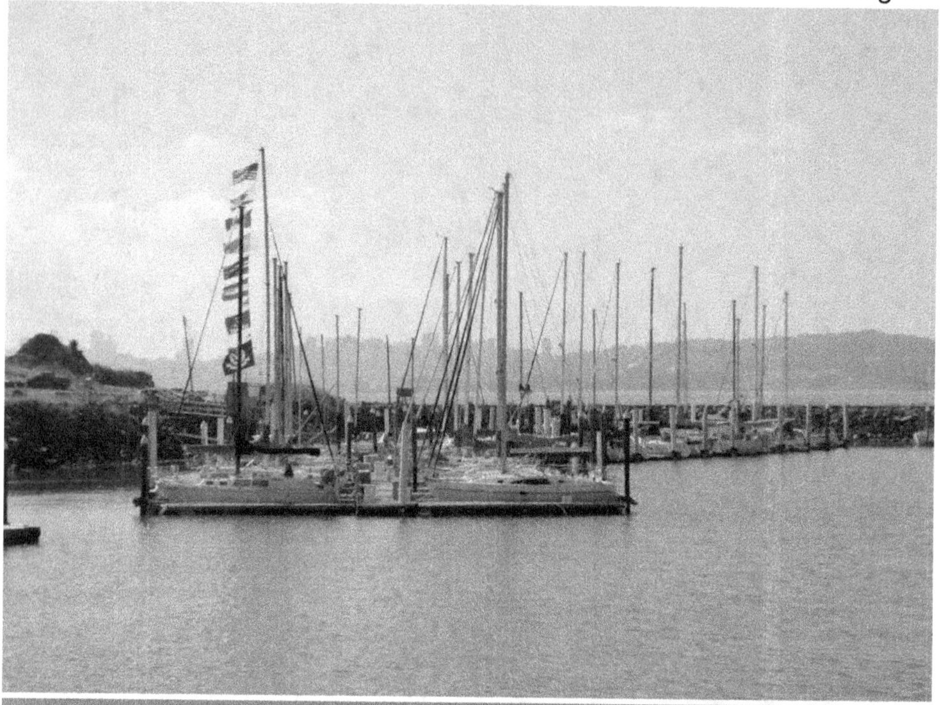

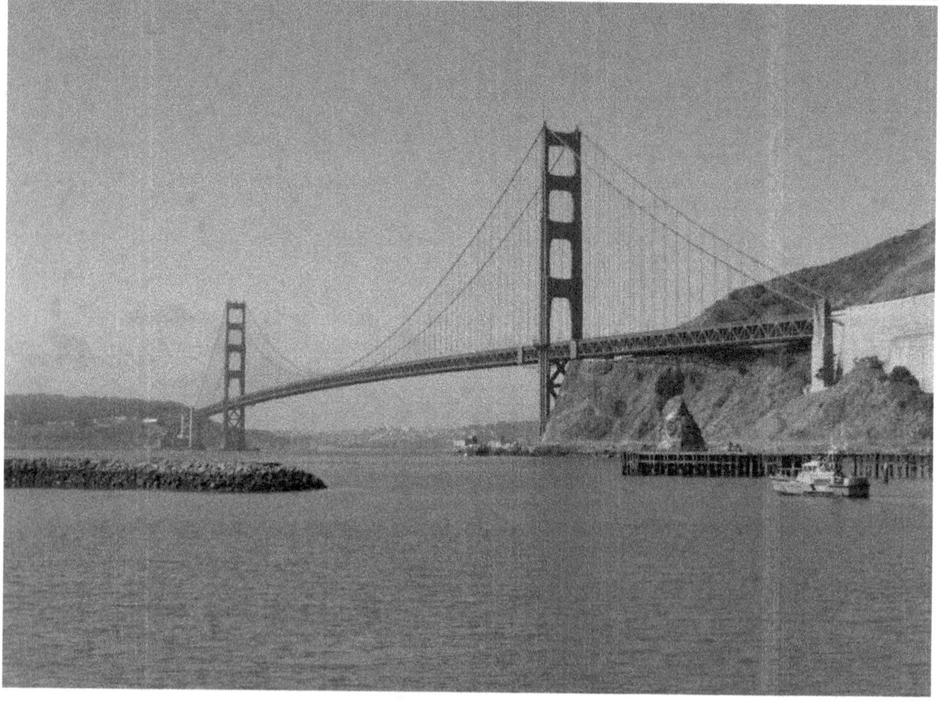

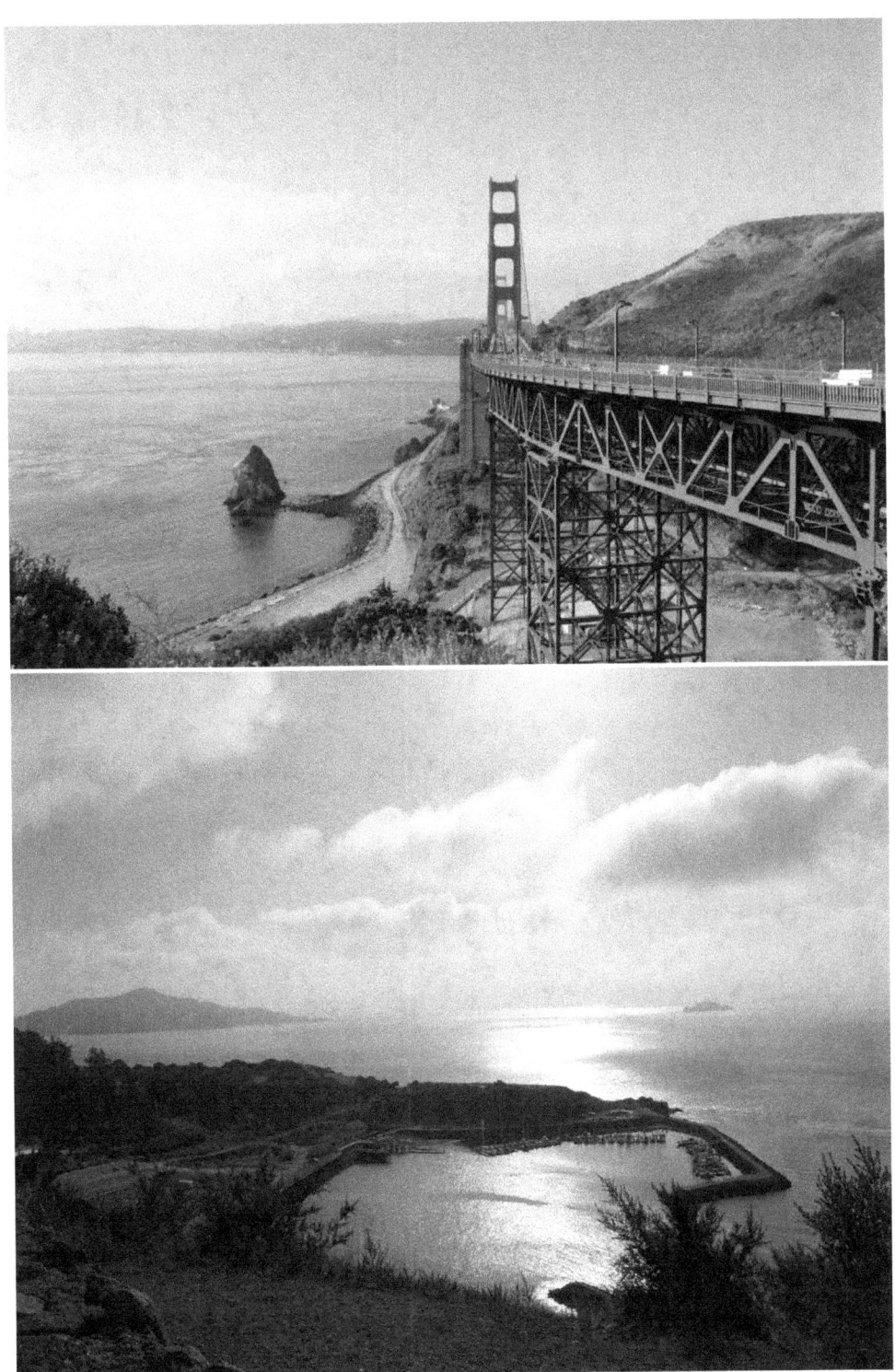

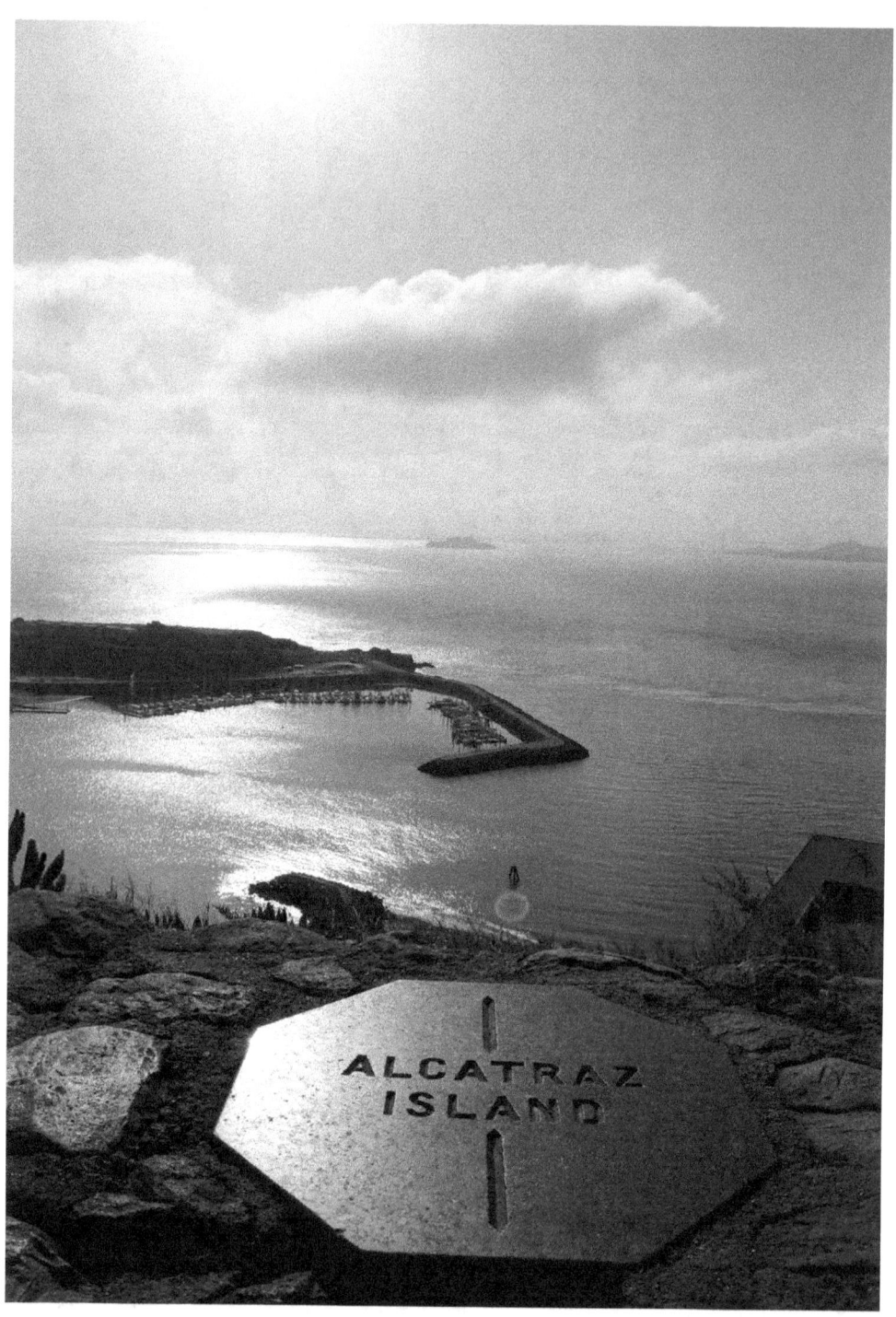

After that, I drove across the bridge to Sausalito.

231

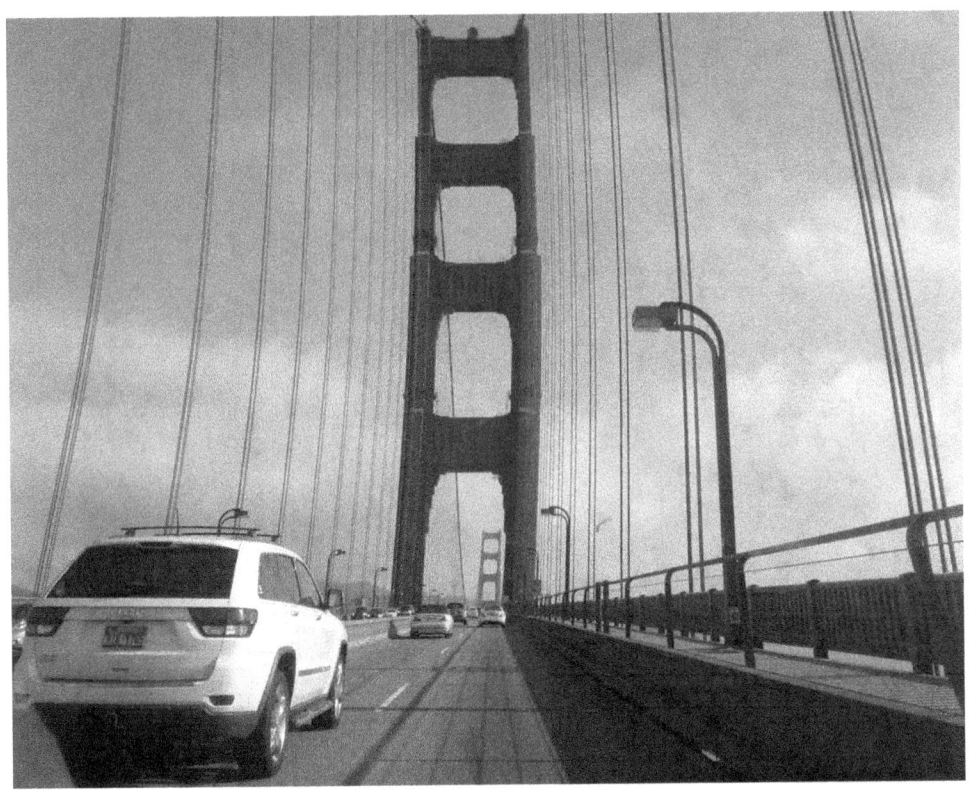

Sausalito seems neat! Smaller and very touristy but cute.

By this time of the morning I needed gas and really had to pee. I stopped at a little gas station in Sausalito. I was going to use the facilities then get a pop and pump gas. I didn't get to use this restroom though. The clerk came out and hollered at me about it not being a public restroom. I must be looking homeless, maybe I should have gotten gas first. Instead, I went back across the bridge.

Pro-tip: The Golden Gate Bridge has a toll when you are coming from the Sausalito side. Stay in the right lane and pay that toll now. If you miss it, you'll end up getting a ticket in the mail for 5x's the toll amount. Ask me how I know.

I went back across the bridge to the park and marina below. After watching this guy install the new stop sign, I sat and painted for a bit.

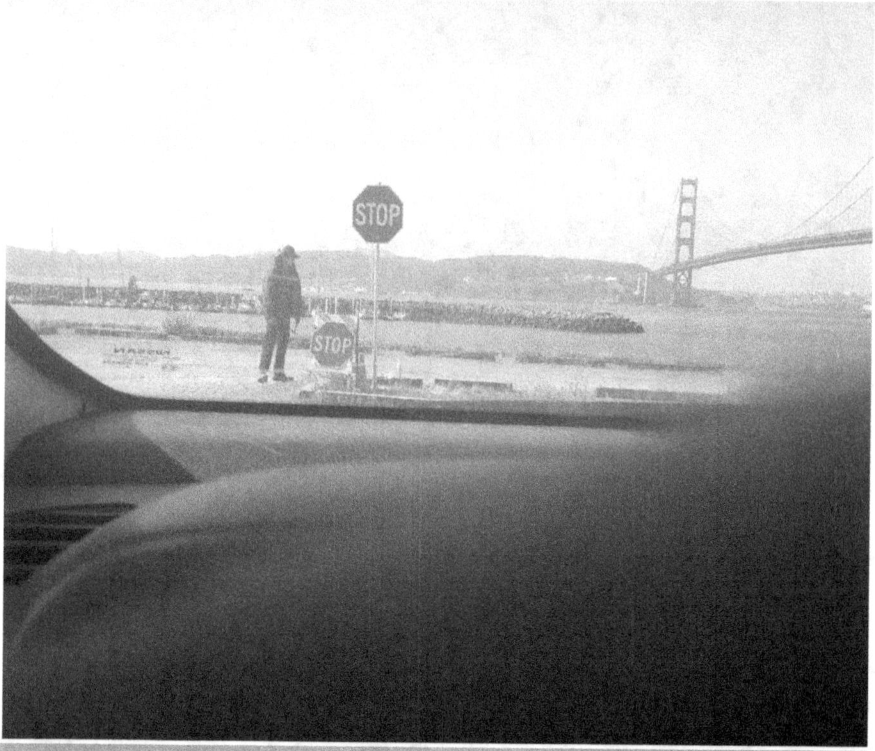

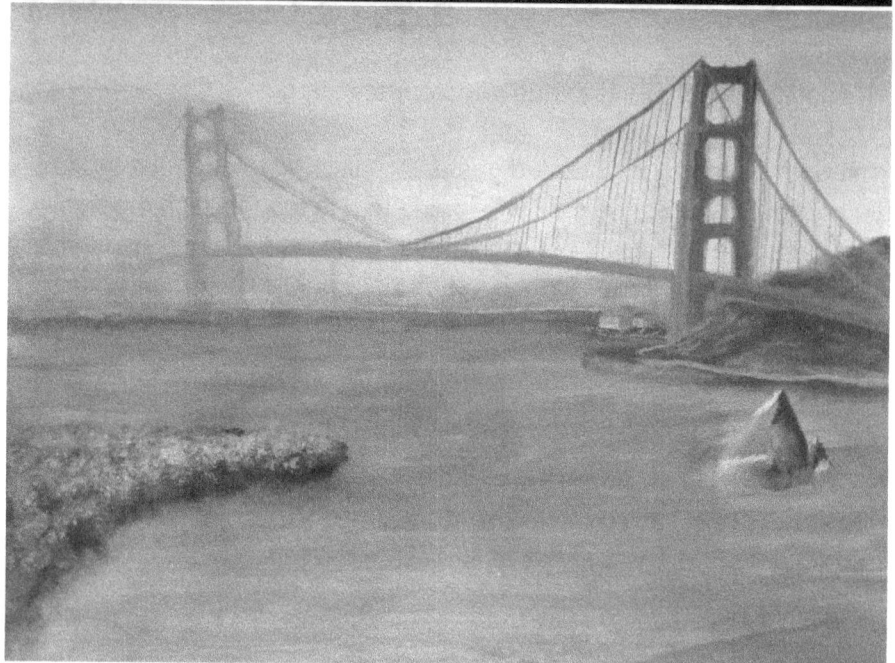

How do I even price these things!?

There are arguments on all sides as to how the best way is. Some say square inch. It's the easiest, simplest way. Others say Linear inch is better because it increases gradually rather than exponentially. Still others insist pricing should be done by first considering supplies, complexity, hourly wages, and overhead. Some simplify that by saying 2(time+materials)=price. These last two would have me back to punching a timeclock and then only accounting for time I actually have a brush in my hand. They would also have me having to measure out every ounce of paint and wouldn't account for all the other time that goes into running a full-time art business. It wouldn't account for the time I spend coming up with and planning ideas, nor the time spent in marketing and administration. It would mean every single price for every single painting would be individual. Dang. That's all way too complicated.

I'm leaning toward the first two, square inch vs linear inch.

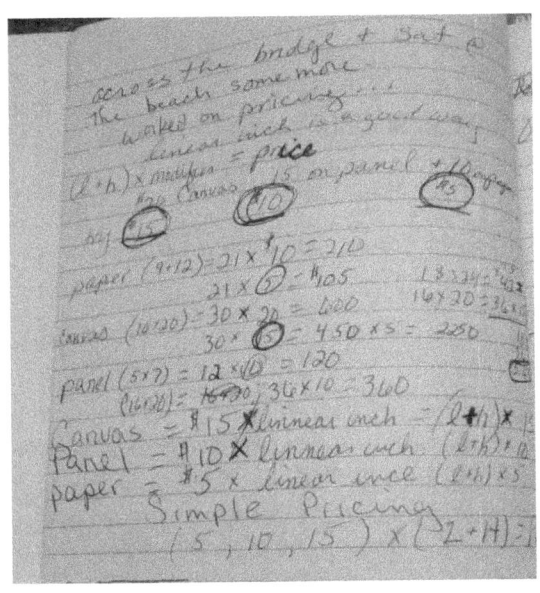

Square inch method = (Length x Width x Multiplier)=price modifier starts at $1or$2 for beginners and depends on skill and materials.

11x14=154x2=$308

10x20=300x2=$600

16x20=320x2=$640

20x24=480x2=$960

Man, for my canvases, for right now (2017), neither of those seem quite right... I feel like somewhere in the middle would be about perfect.

What about the Linear inch method = (L+W)xModifier=price; modifier = $15 for canvas, $10 for panel, and $5 for paper....

Let's see...

Paper: (9+12)x$5=21x5=$105 (seems about right)

Canvas: (10+20)x$15= 30x$15= $450 (hmmm, I'd really like a little more for Adam-Eve but this is pretty close, 30x$20=$600 that seems a little high at this point which they say means it's perfect?

Panel:(16+20)x$10=36x$10=$360 (for Waterbodies... not bad what's 36x$15? =$540... that's probably high for no frame at this point...)

Yeah, linear inch seems right. That's how I'll do it. They also say you should raise your prices every year by 10%-20%. So, what would that be for next year?
2018 panel: (16+20)x10=360x.10=36 so 360+36=396
2018 canvas: (11+14)x15=25x15=375x.10=37.50
         so 375+37.5=412.5 hmmmm... that still feels a bit high
2018 paper: (9+12)x5=21x5=105x.10=10.50 so 105+10.50=$115.50

Seems fair...
I think this is how I'll do it.

What about framed? Do I only add on the cost of the frame? Is it cost plus time? Is it arbitrary? They say cost times 2 for the frame.

I don't know. I guess really, it's whatever the market will bear? Who's my market?

Square one...

*** Present day note *** *Linear inch is the best method I've found for pricing studio works (works on canvas, paper, panel, etc.) It covers the time spent as well as materials and considers cost of overhead. Commissions require a $50-$100 non-refundable deposit which covers the additional design fee and allows for 2 adjustments to the design sketches and 1 adjustment to the actual painting. Murals are priced by the square foot and go up 10% every year. For 2017/2018 my mural price started at $10/square foot + $100 nonrefundable design fee (same rules) and it covers paint and time and design. Equipment such as a lift or scaffolding if needed and special requests like clear coat or glow finish are extra.*

Now, back to San Francisco in 2017...

When it was time, I headed toward my Airbnb. I wanted to get some groceries first. I passed several grocers (Chinese, Korean, Mexican, Greek, etc.) I went in to one that I thought was just going to be a corner grocery or maybe Mexican grocer (tacos are my go-to) it turned out to be Chinese. There was no salsa or sour cream, haha. I ended up getting some ground pork and some beans. I still had avocados from the fruit stand a day or two ago. It'll do, I suppose, haha.

———————

I'm feeling pretty awful today. Just low… Maybe it was sleeping next to the train tracks last night. Or no shower? I don't know… How does one always feel good? Do they?

———————

Maybe I just needed a shower; I feel a bit better now.

———————

I checked into my room. It's a nice house. There are several rooms with several roommates in each. My roommates are 3 guys. I haven't seen much of them though. I haven't seen much of anyone. I guess it's just as well. I have a lot of work to get done before my show in 5 days.

Tomorrow I must write my artist bio and statements for the pieces I'll be showing. Maybe I can get a few more local scenes done this week too.

5/16/17 Day 30

Spent the day working on my bio and statements while enjoying the view from my Airbnb kitchen window.

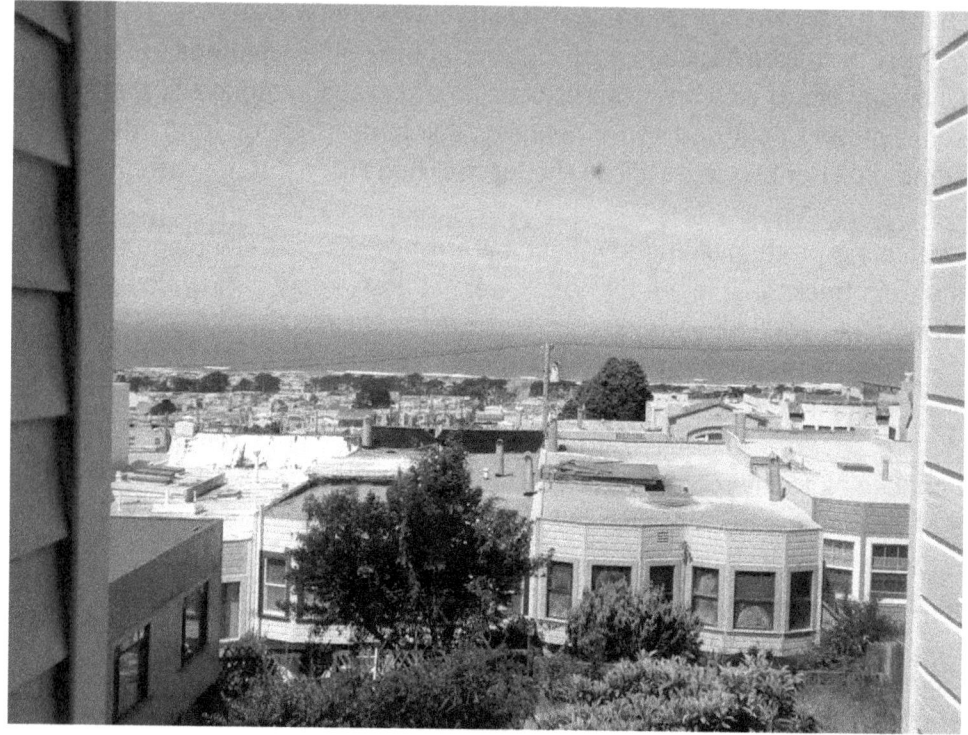

A bio is so weird. It's written in the third person as if someone else is saying it about you. What's important? What should
be included? What does one want to know about me? What would someone say about me? My work? Several drafts later, I settled on a presentable one. Below is one of the drafts…

Artist Bio

Lacey Finchum didn't always consider herself an artist, though she's always been a learner and creator. She went to college for outdoor recreation, leadership and management and psychology and business and environmental studies, dabbling in nearly everything including various creative pursuits.

She now combines her various educations, her passion for painting, her love of nature, and her observations of the world to create images that draw correlations between humans and nature.

Waterbodies

This series is a beginning of seeing humans as part of the landscape. I believe we are meant to live in harmony with nature rather than in opposition to it. These images are meant to show how beautiful it is when peace and harmony is the goal.

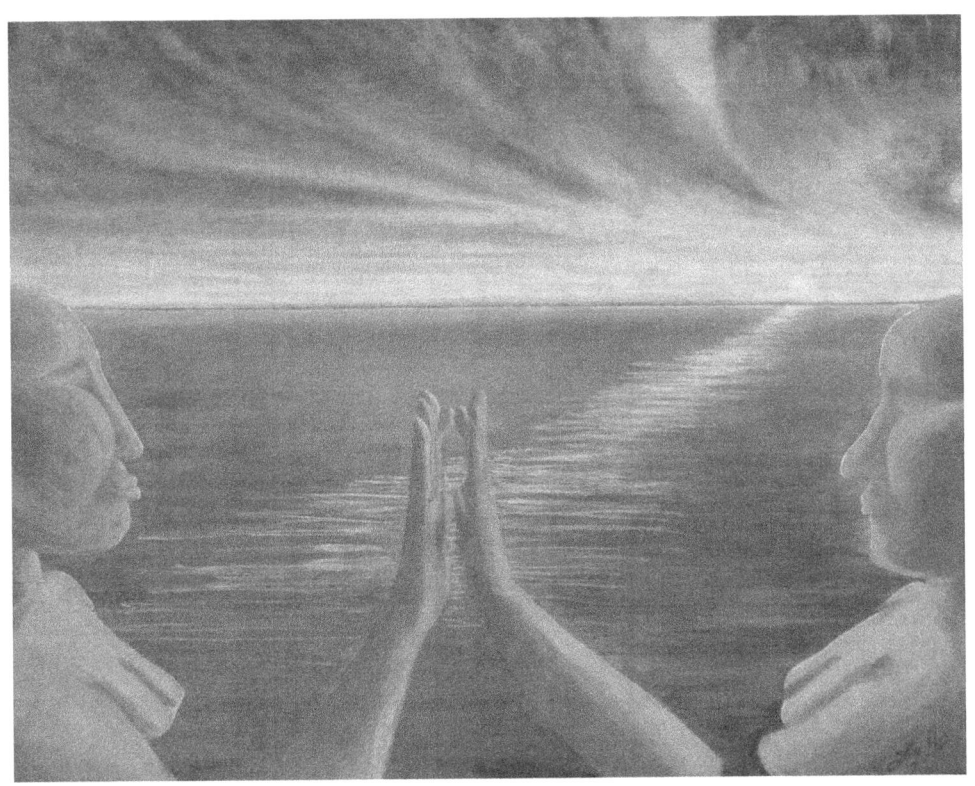

Adam-Eve

This series of paintings was given to me in a vision some years before I ever picked up a brush. I made some sketches of the images I saw and stuck them in one of my journals. After painting Waterbodies, I remembered these sketches and then saw the finished images in my head. These images are meant to show how males and females are less different than we think. I wanted them to show a progression from female to male (or vice versa)

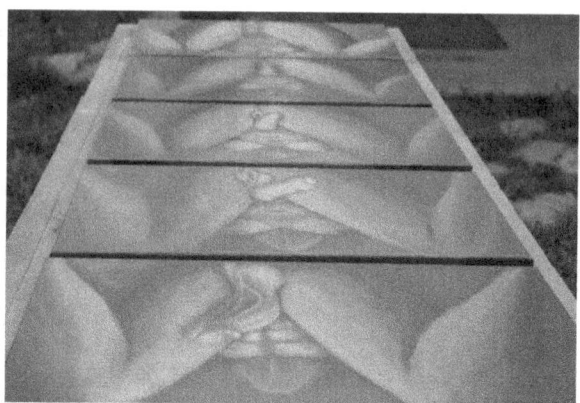

"Red, brown, yellow, black and white, they are precious in His sight, Jesus loves the little children of the world." - from Jesus Loves the Little Children by Krieger and Root

5/17/17 Day 31

Whew! What a day! I ventured into downtown and went looking for the post office, Aaron Bros, Dick Blick and some sightseeing.

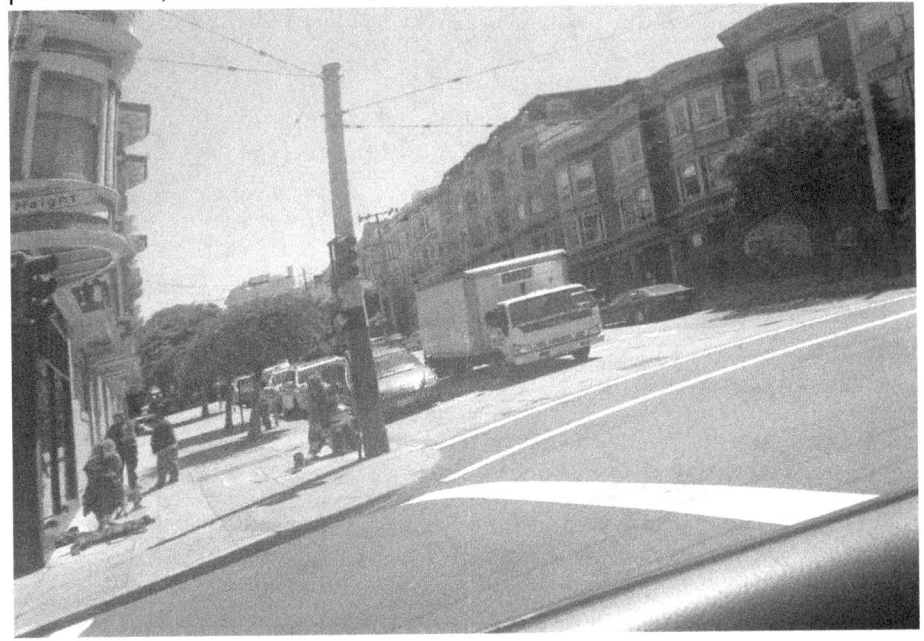

Haight-Ashbury was my favorite area. So much color! And fun and interesting shops. There were a lot more homeless in that area though.

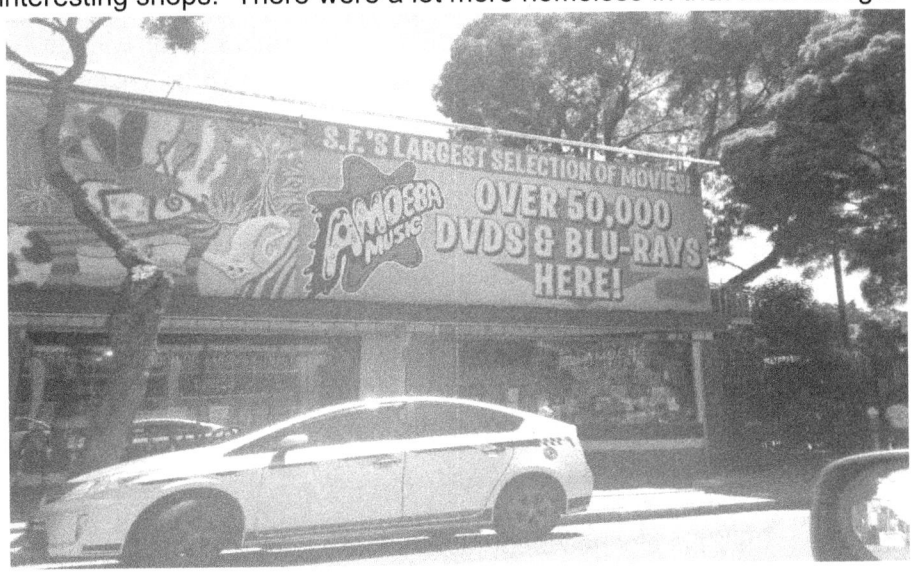

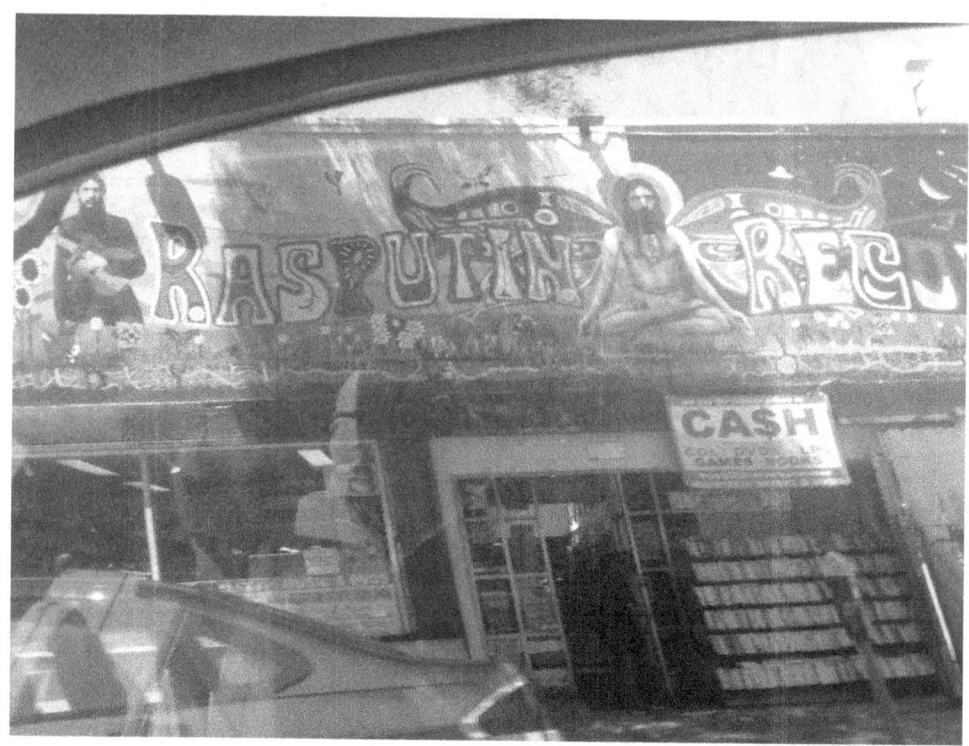

There was a lot of traffic in all downtown and it was hard to find parking spots. Also, it costs to park anywhere.

I like to visit cities for a minute, but I get overwhelmed fast. I'm definitely more of a country girl. I gotta find my country. Guess I'm a woman without a country lol… So far, Arkansas is the most beautiful. There isn't any place I've found that I'd rather go.

I ended up finding the Post Office and a couple supply stores. The only parking I could find was $2.25 an hour. I'm nearing broke. I had to pay in nickels. 45 nickels into the slot. I rushed to do my business and thought I was out of time. Turned out I had 20 more minutes. Doh…

I also found another market. This time, it was maybe Jewish? It was more expensive than the first, but they did have sour cream. I didn't recognize a lot of things….

It's really neat that this city has different ethnic districts. I mean, I guess most do, but this somehow felt different.

241

What's next is still very much on my mind. Where to go next, what to paint next, how to make an income from my art. If I sell Adam-Eve this weekend, I'll go straight to Eureka Springs. So far, it's the one I think I'd like the most. If I don't, I suppose I'll go back to mom and dad's in Indiana. I really wish I was going back to Bear Bottom (sans M). I'm tired and Bear Bottom is my rest. It's my home and my love and my sanctuary. Crap...

I am thinking of a future series though, maybe it's 2 series together. America the Beautiful and America's Trash. Human Footprint? It'll contain some of the beautiful scenery I've seen and then that scenery covered in trash. I'm not sure how to execute it yet though.

5/18/17 Day 32

I went to Dick Blicks early today and then went and found the brewery where the show will be. The brewery is much further away than I had guessed. It's in a neat industrial/arts district and there is a metalsmith across the way. There are also murals on many of the buildings. It seems like a fun area. I'm really excited about this show.

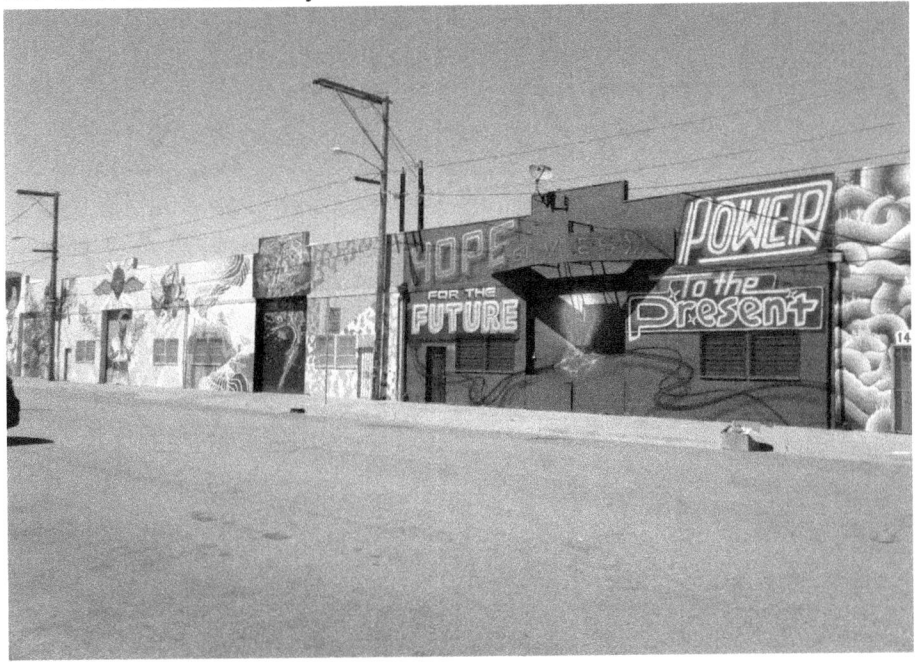

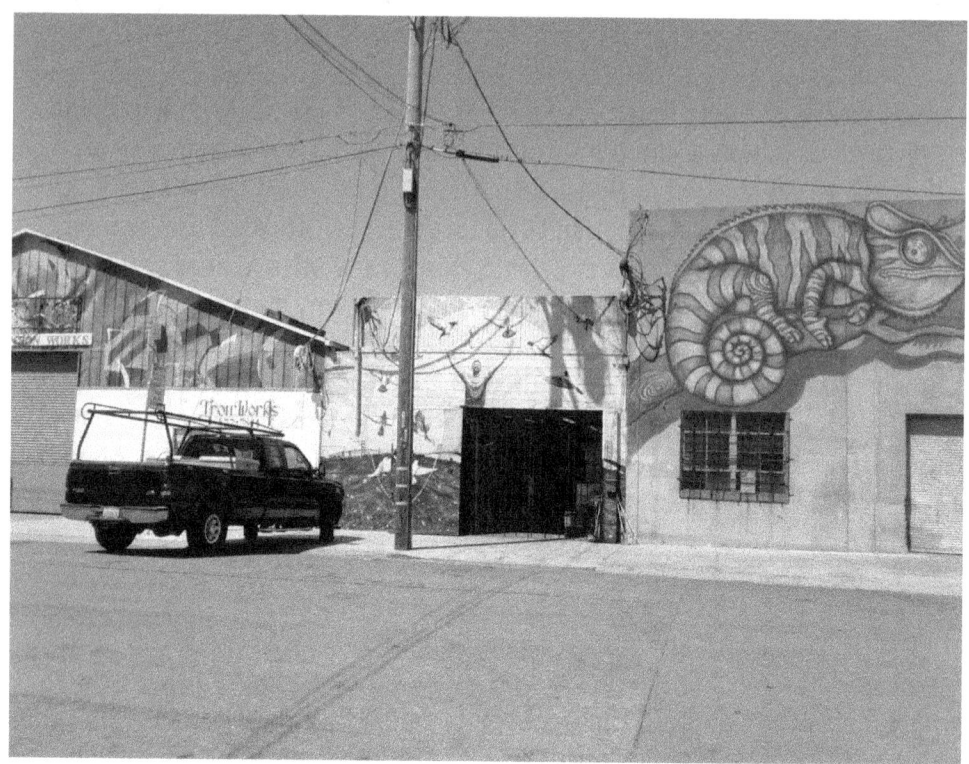

I definitely had a much better time today. Found my destinations and parking spots. I also found the supplies I needed.

I did a few paintings this week that were from my trip.

I used acrylic but the pieces are on paper and almost look like heavy watercolor, gouache(?). When I returned to my room, I finished up the last of those paintings, the view from my Airbnb. It's a view of the shoreline from a distant rooftop and looks over all the colorful roofs in between.

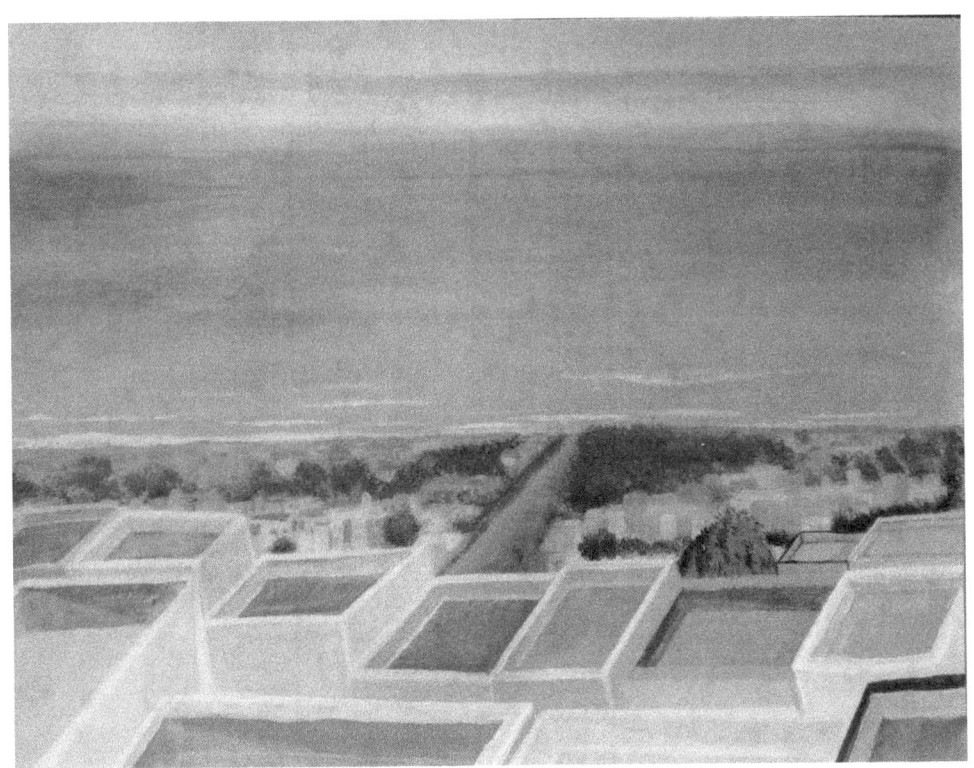

After finishing, I varnished all 5 pieces. I didn't have anywhere here to spray varnish, so I opted for a liquid paint on type. It's the first time I've used this type of varnish and I'm not really happy with how it turned out. The combo of the paper and liquid varnish left pools and puddles on the surface which will take much longer to dry. I wonder if they'll be noticeable when dried?

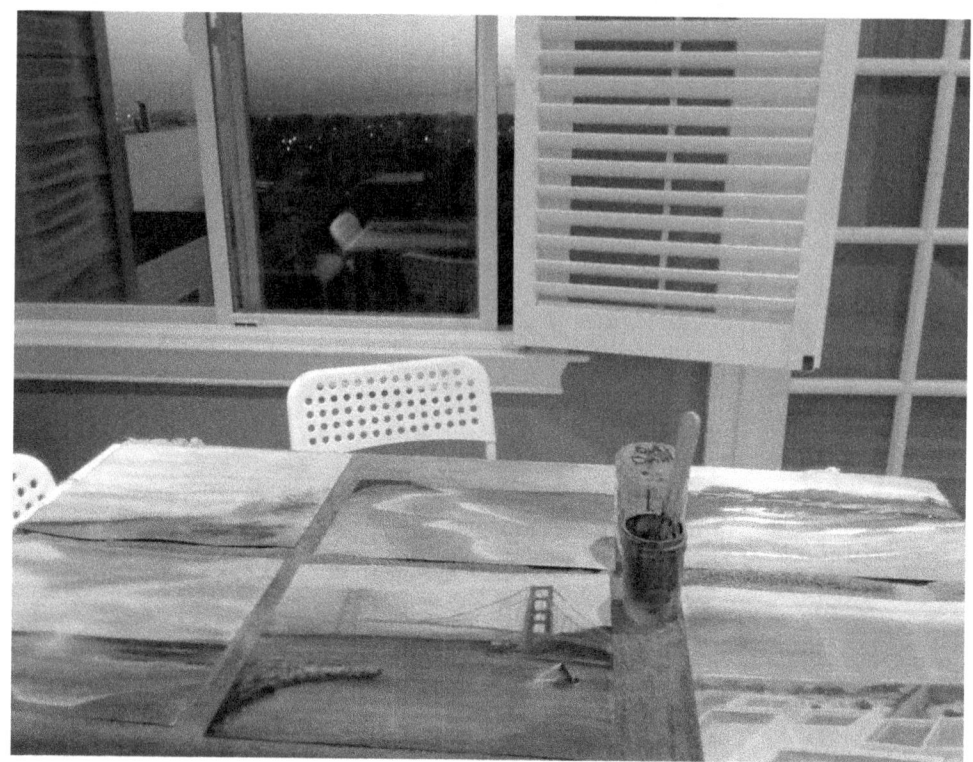

———

I went out for a walk while the paintings dried on the kitchen table. They were all laid out on a towel and obviously wet. I didn't think I needed to say don't touch. I didn't think anyone was here! Low and behold one of the guys sleeping in my room was evidently here or showed up while I was out. Dumb ass decided my paintings were placemats and sat his dinner right in the middle of them! There's now a bowl ring in the middle of The Golden Gate Bridge. I ripped him a new one and nearly threw his dinner across the room. Stupid fucker. I can't believe it! I should have put a sign on them.

Or maybe there is a bright side? Golden Gate is already the beginning of Human Footprint. Stupid fucker.

Unfortunately, the images still aren't dry yet. This time I slapped "wet paint" and "do not touch" notes all over the table and chairs.

Later, the kid saw me on the porch and apologized. Barely… He feels bad, I guess, but I suspect only because I verbally tore him apart over it when I found him sitting there with his bowl in the middle of my painting.

245

"You've seen me working on these things all week! Did you think I was just making placemats? And regardless, they're obviously still wet! How stupid and numb are you!? What do you do? Computer stuff? How about I let the cat pounce all over your keyboard just as you thought you were nearly finished with a week-long build!? Get it now dip shit!? I should make you pay for these!"

Deep Breathe…

Tomorrow I have my coaching call at 7am. I also have to finish my bio and statements, do some business cards, and finalize my price list. Busy day.

5/19/17 Day 33

I had a great chat with my coach today. We hashed out what it means to be an artist. Imposter syndrome has been kicking my ass! The truth? I am an artist! I don't need anyone's approval. Any reaction to my work means I did my job.

I am an artist! I do know what I'm doing and what I'm talking about! Thank God for her! Her pep talk set me up to be able to complete, confidently, all the remaining tasks on my plate.

I went to the library and printed my biz cards, signs, and statements. When I got home, I painted a tie-dye effect on the paper and then glued them to little mats I made from my heavy weight paper. Finally, I varnished each piece.   I finished it all just in the nick of time too.

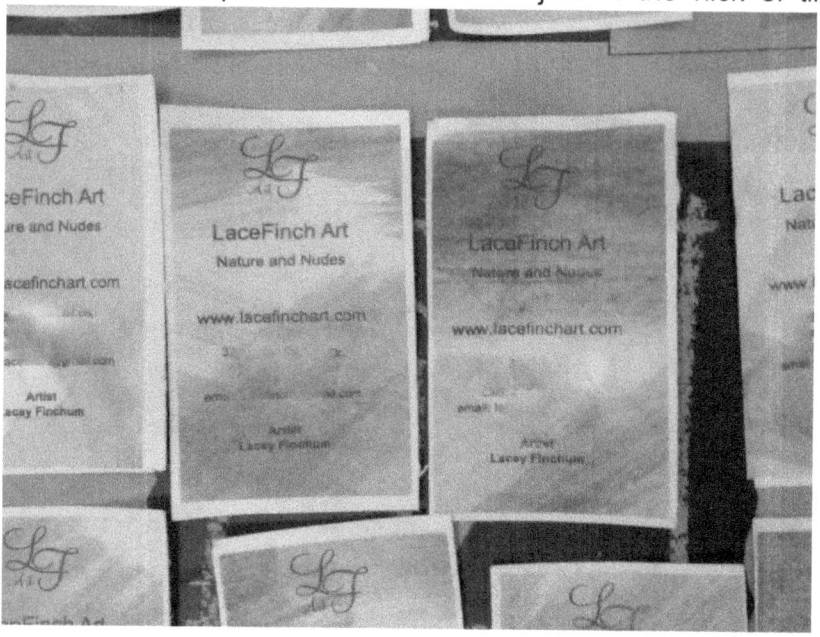

Artist Bio

"I always wanted to be an artist. I always wanted to be but only recently figured out that I always have been."

Lacey grew up painting with her grandmother but didn't pursue her talent seriously until she was in her mid 30's when she began painting on old saw blades. The more she painted, the more she realized that her grandma had already taught her many of the basic principles of color, composition, and perspective.

Her first few paintings were done by following tutorials or copying photos but she soon learned that she could create images by combining various photos with bits from her imagination. The results from these initial experiments soon turned into "Water Bodies" and "Adam- Eve"

As her style evolved, she realized that her artistic focus is predominantly centered around human relationships with the natural world. For example, her next project will consist of natural landscapes from across this country as well as images that show the impact that humans have had on those beautiful landscapes.

Tomorrow is my show! I'm so nervous! I hope I can sleep. I'm worthless when I don't get rest....

5/20/17 Day 34

EEEEEK! Show Day!!!

Thankfully, the cards and things look great this morning! The wet of the paint and varnish made the edges curl a bit though so I have everything being pressed in books while I get ready.

I'm so nervous... NO! I can change my mind.

I am excited!
I am an artist
I am a brilliant artist
I sell paintings
I am completely comfortable talking about my work
I ask smart questions
I am light
I am love
I am complete
I am the captain of my ship
I am in touch with my intuition
I love myself
I am an artist
I sell paintings

I am going to sell the Adam-Eve Series (5 paintings) today for $2250
I will sell several pieces today

I am here to be me. To upset the system.

~Emotions come from within~ I have the power to change my emotions.

————

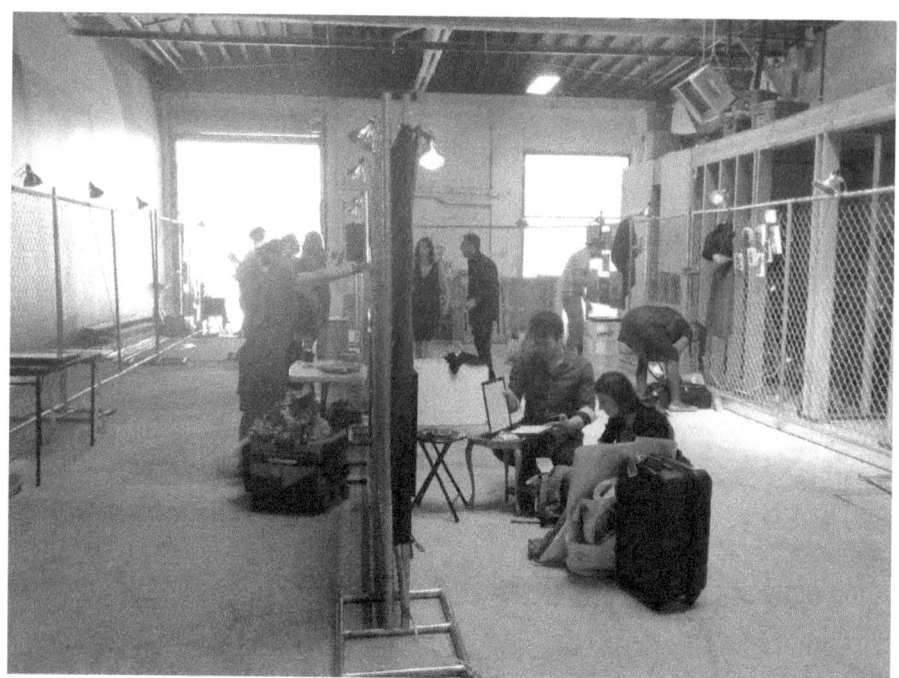

Set-up was super simple. Thankfully the person on the other side of the fence from me had a black sheet to put in between the fences. It really made the display so much nicer!

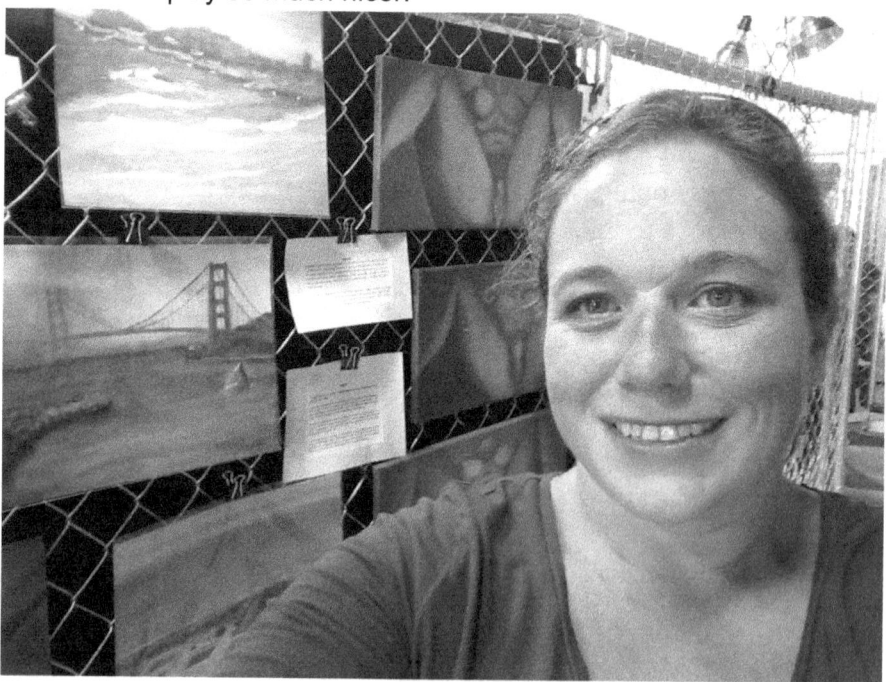

The show went well! No sales. As it turns out, this show wasn't quite what I thought. They market it as a "great show in the art world. Lots of collectors. Excellent for beginners. A great foot in the door..."

What it really is: this company makes money off the high fees they charge for tickets. The catch is, the artist must sell the tickets or buy them to participate. There were very few community members and maybe no actual art collectors. Most people are family and friends of the artists. Or maybe regulars at this brewery. They choose artists who have some talent and no experience to invite to the show and then charge us a huge fee to exhibit. We can offset that fee by selling tickets. The organizers don't fill the audience, the artists do. So, if you sold tickets, you have a room full of your supporters. If not...

I'm choosing to say the show went well though because there's no point in beating myself up over not knowing. Now I know. Also, I did talk to a bunch of people and got to show all my work. I passed out 35 biz cards and got some feedback. I LOVED seeing people's reactions to Adam-Eve. Next time I show it I'll have a camera set up to record reactions and I'll play those videos at future shows.

I also got to talk about future work with many people. One couple offered me an excellent idea for America's trash; Augmented Reality. So, I paint the America the Beautiful series and the trash series, and they can use their phone to see the trash over the beautiful. I'll have to figure out how to do that kind of thing, but the idea is amazing!

Ok, now what? Show's over and no sales which means I'm headed back to Indiana. I'm not even sure I have enough money left to make it back.

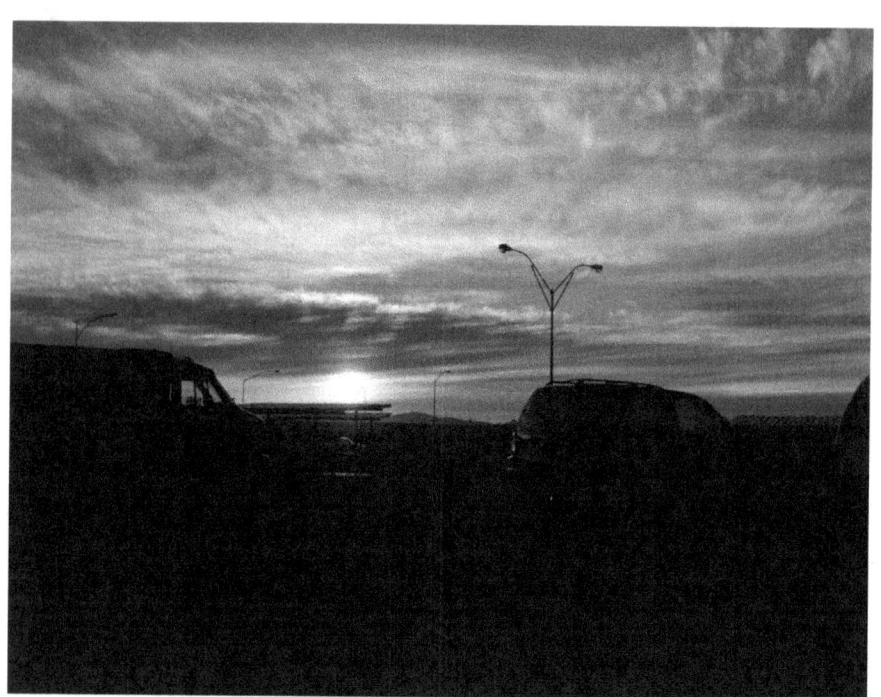

5/21/17 Day 35 - Headed Home

My mind was spinning a bit today. Scrambling for answers, for solutions. How can I stay out longer? How can I not have to go to Indiana? Is there a way to go to Eureka? Maybe I should just go to Indiana. I'm tired. I can rest there for a bit while I save up money and come up with a new plan.

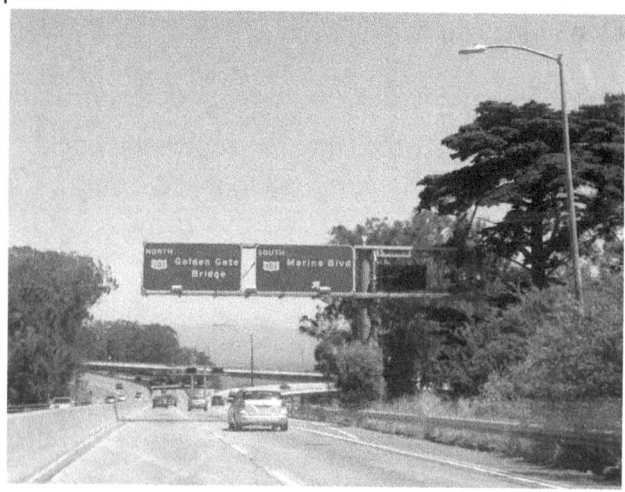

I left SF this morning. It took me 2 hours to get 6 miles across the city because of a fun run thing going on. At one point I was stuck in a right-hand lane and Ms. Google was hollering at me to turn left, but I couldn't. Eventually, I took a right.

I must have turned down one of the steepest roads in SF. There were several cars at the stop sign at the top of the hill. I managed to hold on through the first several cars. I sat feathering the clutch and the gas trying not to kill it and roll back and hit someone while also trying not to goose it forward and hit someone. I was able to hold it all the way until one more car when it died.
SHIT!

On a nearly vertical incline, manual transmission, traffic. This is terrible!

The jackass behind me is screaming and honking. I told him to go around, but he wouldn't. He just kept screaming and honking. I'm trying to remain calm. I know I've gotta move fast. That's an expensive car behind me. shit. ok. I got this.

Ready? No feathering this time. Just gotta go. Ok. Traffic is clear… 1. 2. GO!

I swear I had the car on two wheels! But I made it! Squealing tires and all!

OMG the adrenaline!!

———

Two hours later and I'm finally out of town and headed toward I-80. I drove back over the bridge on the way out. There was still fog. LOTS of it! It was pretty cool! I think I've got some really neat pictures of it too.

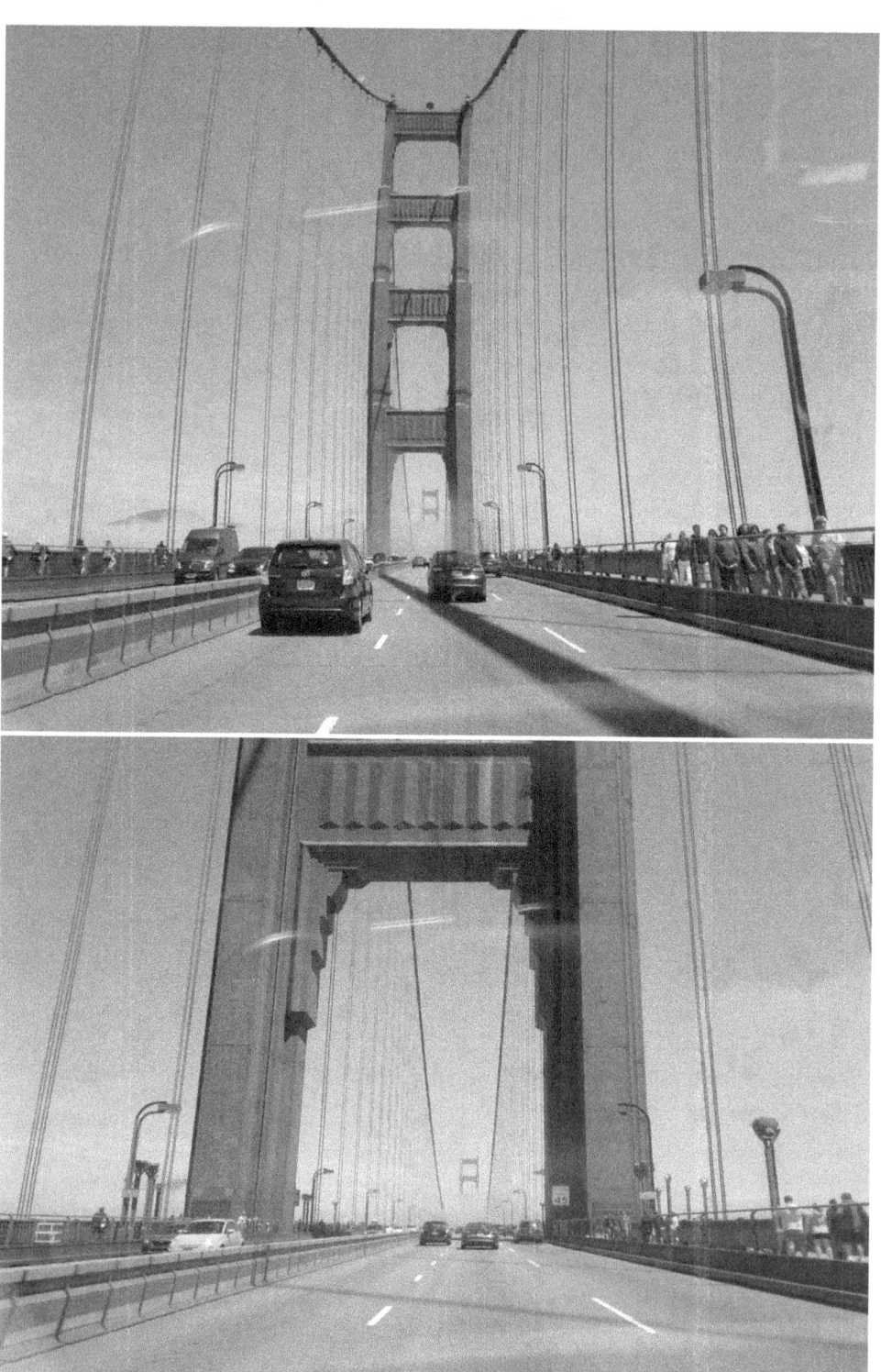

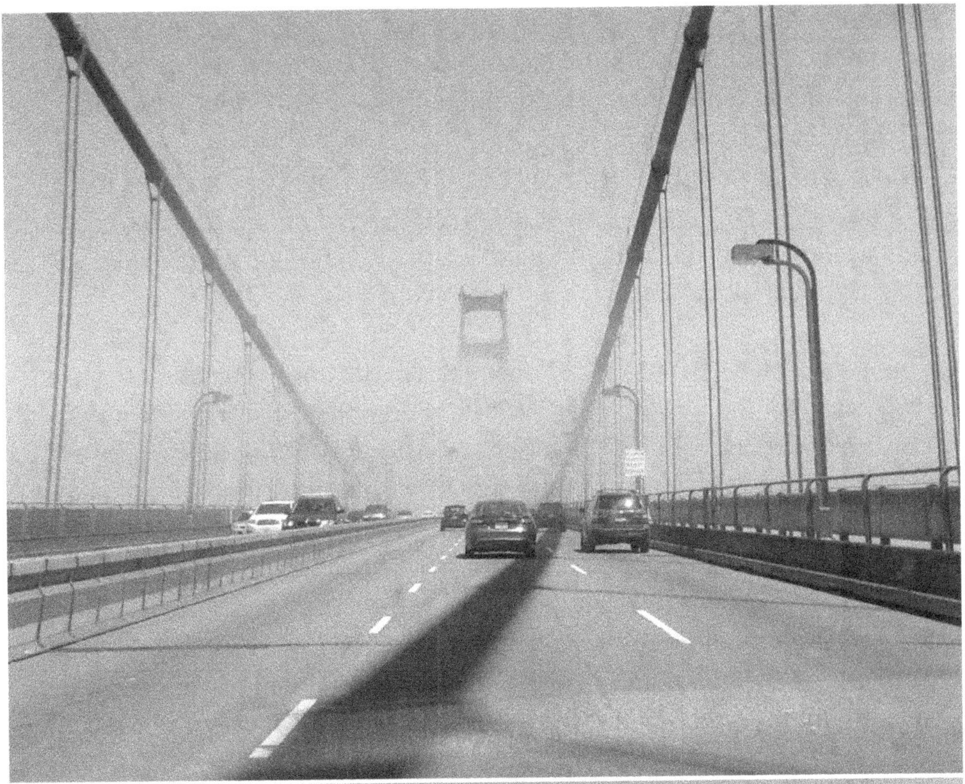

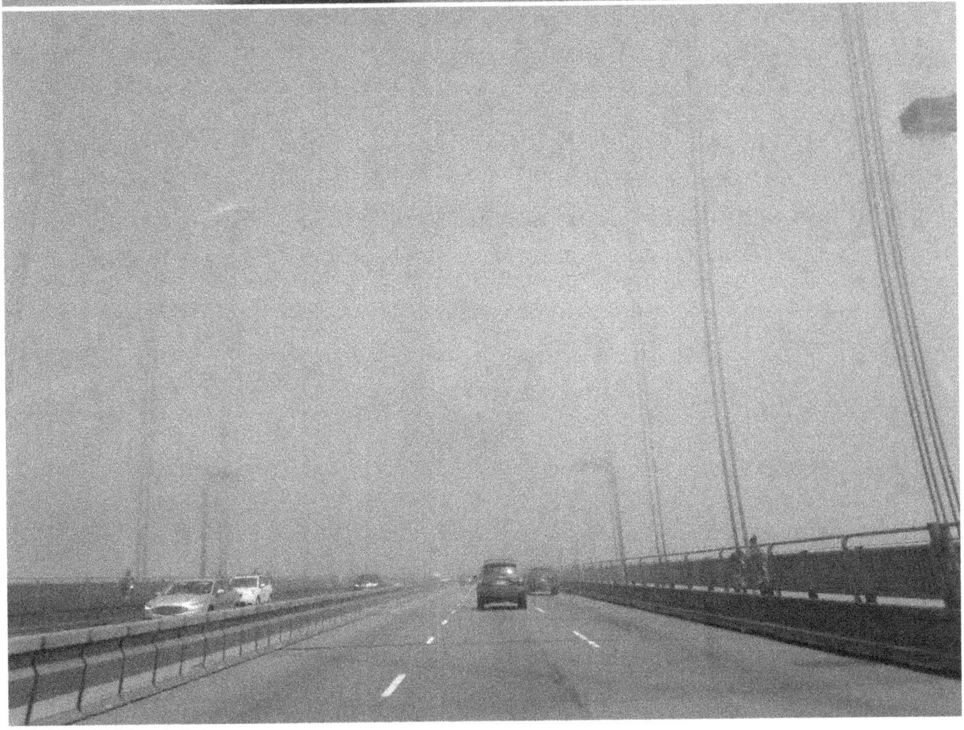

The road I took to get to I-80 went thru a watershed preserve that was pretty cool. There was a surprising amount of traffic on this road. But some Wycleff Jean and neat birds made the ride enjoyable.

"...Bring your ass. Pump the positivity... Ladies and gentlemen! Right about now if you're driving and stuck in traffic, turn up the radio! We are not stopping for no red lights tonight! Blow your horns!" (from Wyclef Jean's Carnival album intro)

On the ride I decided, my trip isn't over yet. I'm out here. I better see what I can, what's on the way at least! What If I go home and don't? What if I never make it back this way again!? "Yeah, I was about 50 miles from Yellowstone but didn't make it a point to stop...:" Screw that!

I want to stop at Yellowstone and Jackson and the Grand Tetons.

It's really kinda on the way. I-80 is at the south end and I-90 at the north end. Both go directly home. Before that though, I want to stop at Lake Tahoe, i.e. nature, art, and wealthy tourists.

I called dad. I'm so grateful for my parents and family. I know they are always there for me.

He wasn't happy about it, but he seemed to understand and agree because he agreed to send $200. I can pick it up in Salt Lake City. Between that and what I have, I should be able to do it. Just. I know I'll be rolling in on fumes, but it doesn't matter. I'll get to see a few more places.

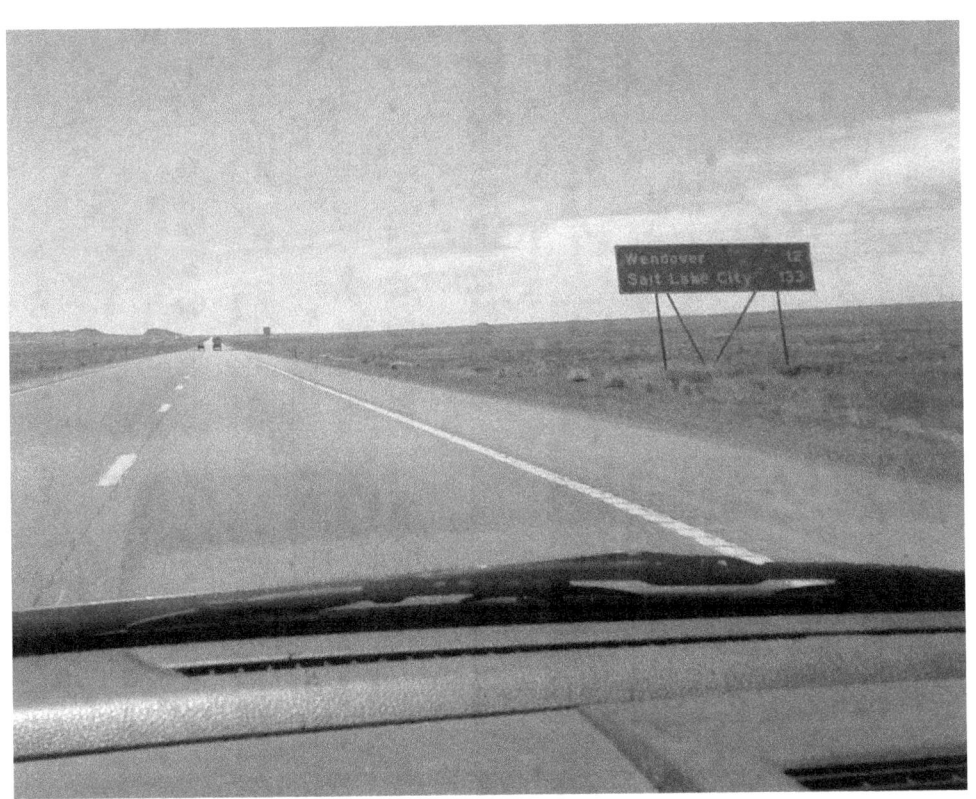

I broke off I-80 and drove around Lake Tahoe. It's not quite what I thought. I expected to see a town, a downtown, even if small. Did I miss it? Lake Tahoe is pretty but it's also kinda cold still here. So, expensive, cold, remote, and no downtown. Nope, that's not it.

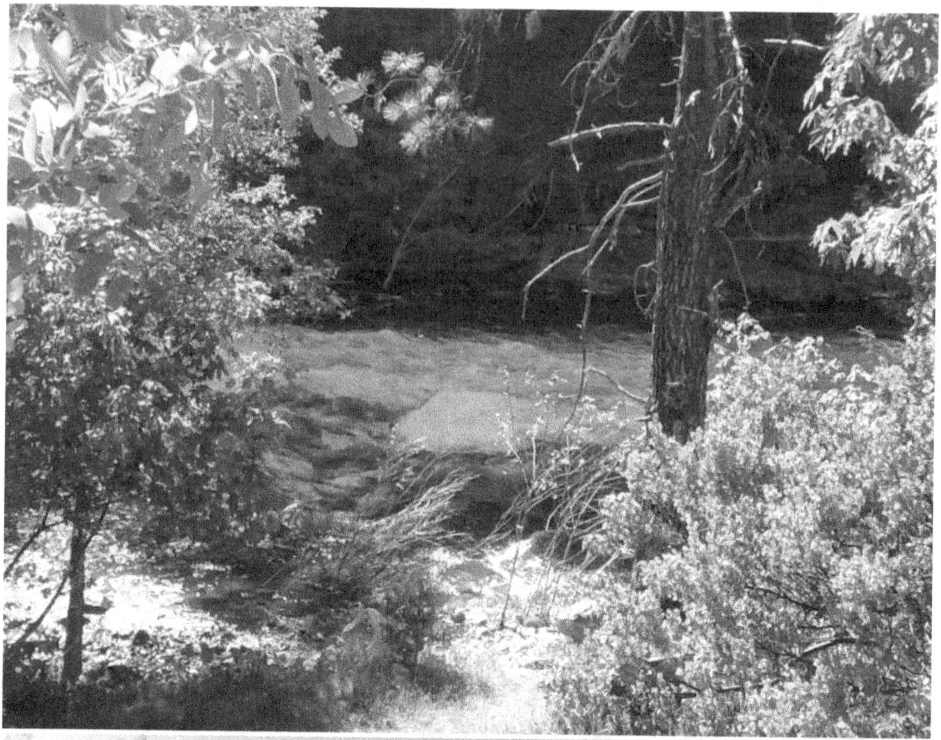

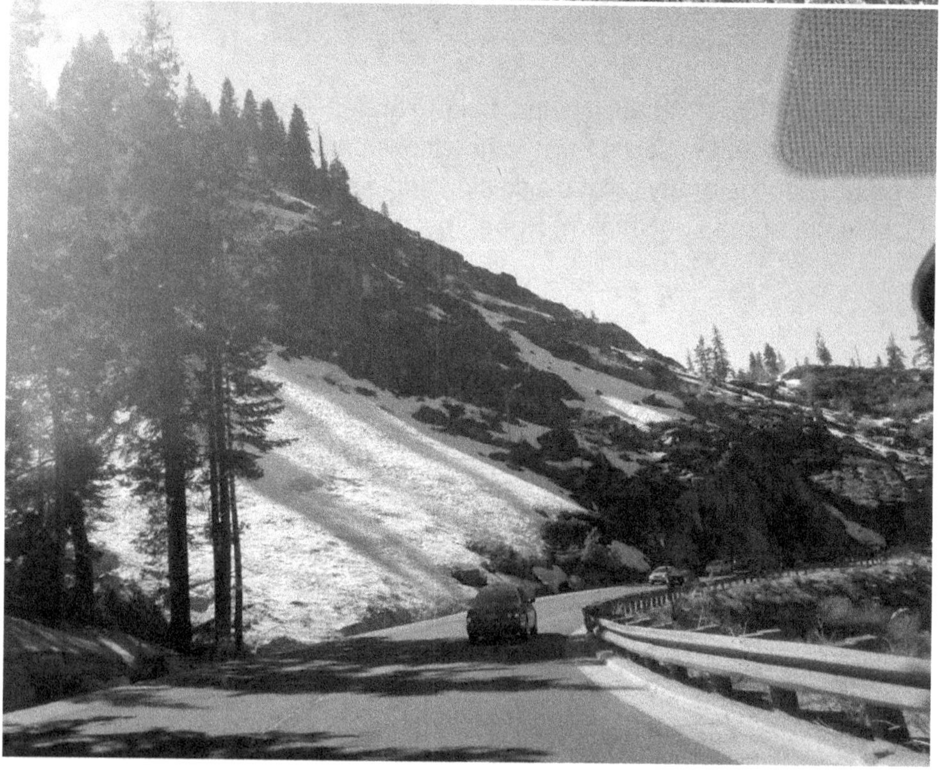

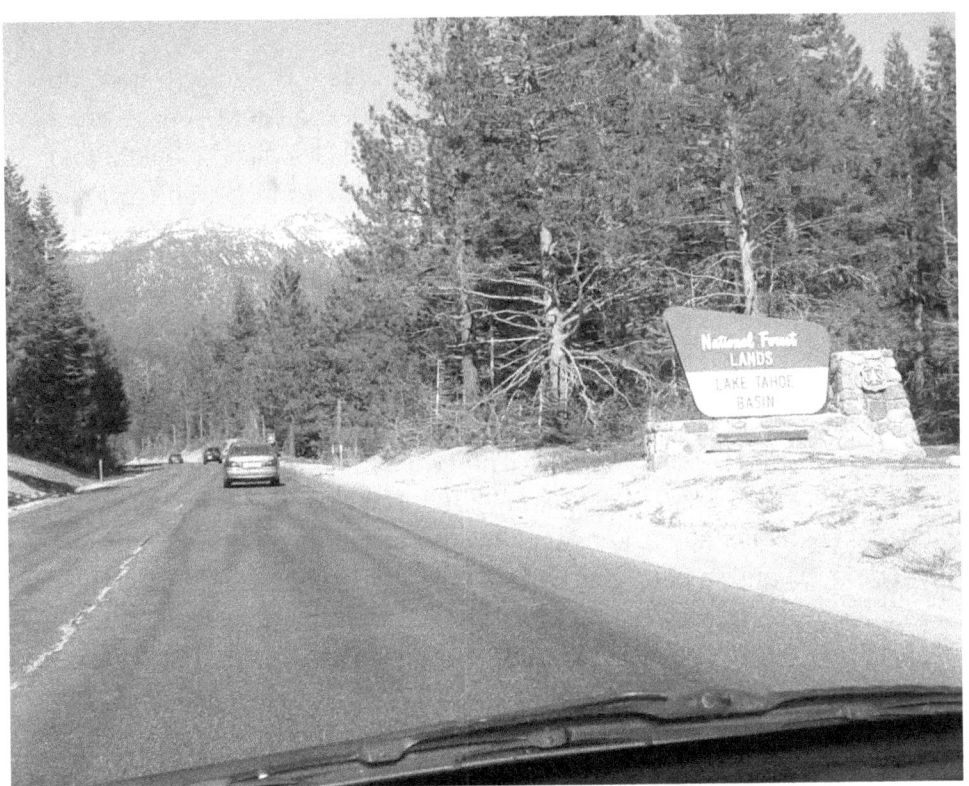

From there I headed toward Reno. Past Reno is Winnemucca. I was dying to hear the song and couldn't hear it anywhere haha. Do you know it? Sung by Johnny Cash?

"I was totin' my pack along the dusty Winnemucca road
When along came a semi with a high an' canvas covered load
"If you're goin' to Winnemucca, Mack, with me you can ride"
And so I climbed into the cab and then I settled down inside
He asked me if I'd seen a road with so much dust and sand
And I said, "Listen, I've traveled every road in this here land"
I've been everywhere, man
I've been everywhere, man
Crossed the desert's bare, man
I've breathed the mountain air, man
Of travel I've had my share, man
I've been everywhere..." ("I've been everywhere" - Johnny Cash)

Nearly. I can say I've been nearly everywhere lol

———

Tonight, I'm sleeping at a rest area along I-80/95. There isn't anything else around and I can't hold out any longer. I'm exhausted! There are a couple truckers here but that's it. There's a nice sidewalk in the light and some little picnic shelters off the side. There's not much traffic on this stretch of road and no signal. It's nice to sit here in the quiet. Albeit it's a tiny bit spooky…

———

Ooh, there's other people here! They came up from behind me, knocked on my window and scared the shit out of me! It's dark and spooky! And strangers knocking on my window! They want to know if there are rooms nearby. How the heck should I know? I'm traveling the same direction as them. My plates say Arkansas. How the hell should I know if there is anything at all ahead of us before Salt Lake City tomorrow? Easy Lace, calm down…

5/22/17 Day 36

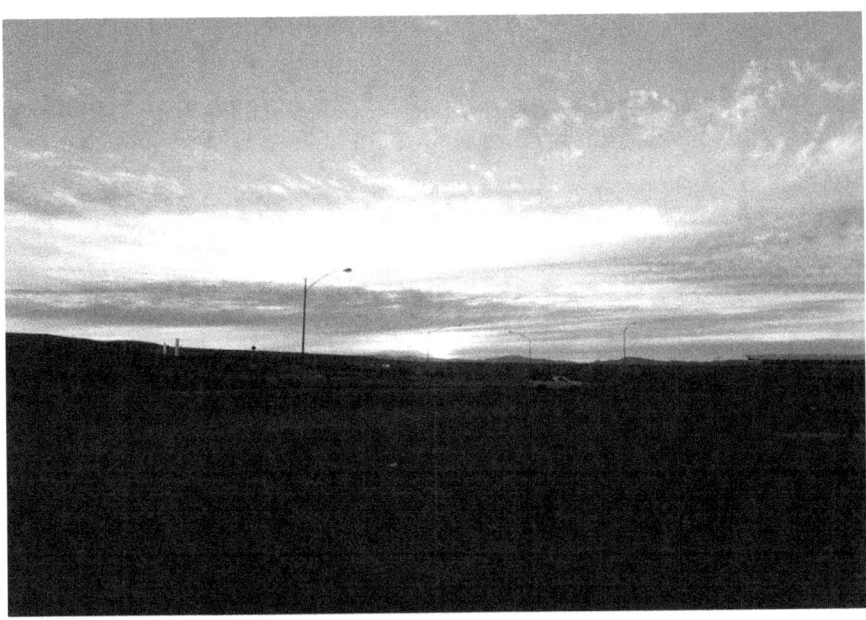

Well, I survived the night. No serial killers found me alone in the dessert. Haha.

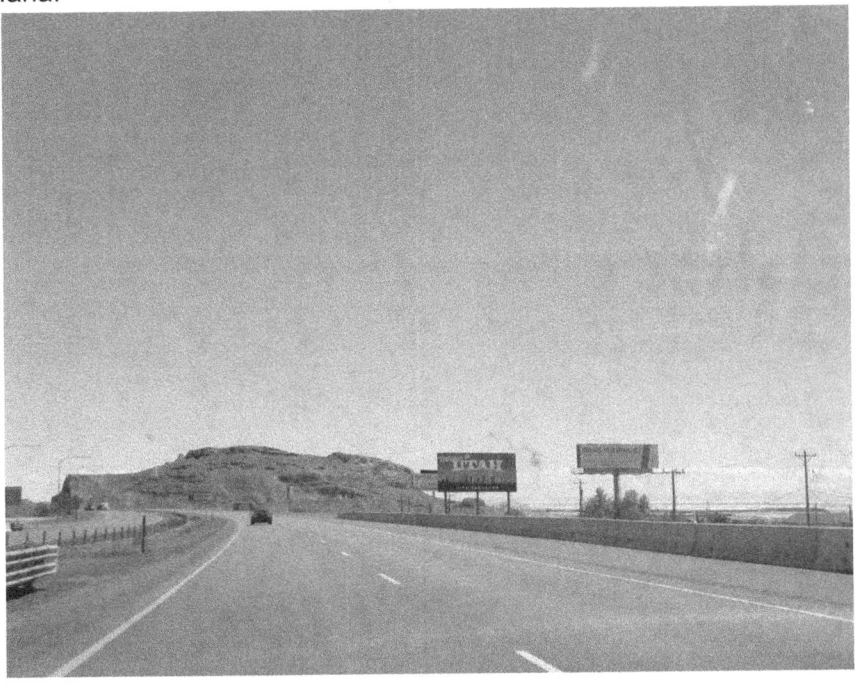

I drove to Salt Lake City and picked up the wire from dad then turned toward Yellowstone.

Salt Lake City is kinda neat. It's a big looking downtown but it's not busy at all. It's almost a little eerie. There are people and cars but it's not jam packed like other cities. The red mountains are really pretty and so is the Salt Lake. The salt flats are interesting but, he reflections on the Salt Lake are amazing!

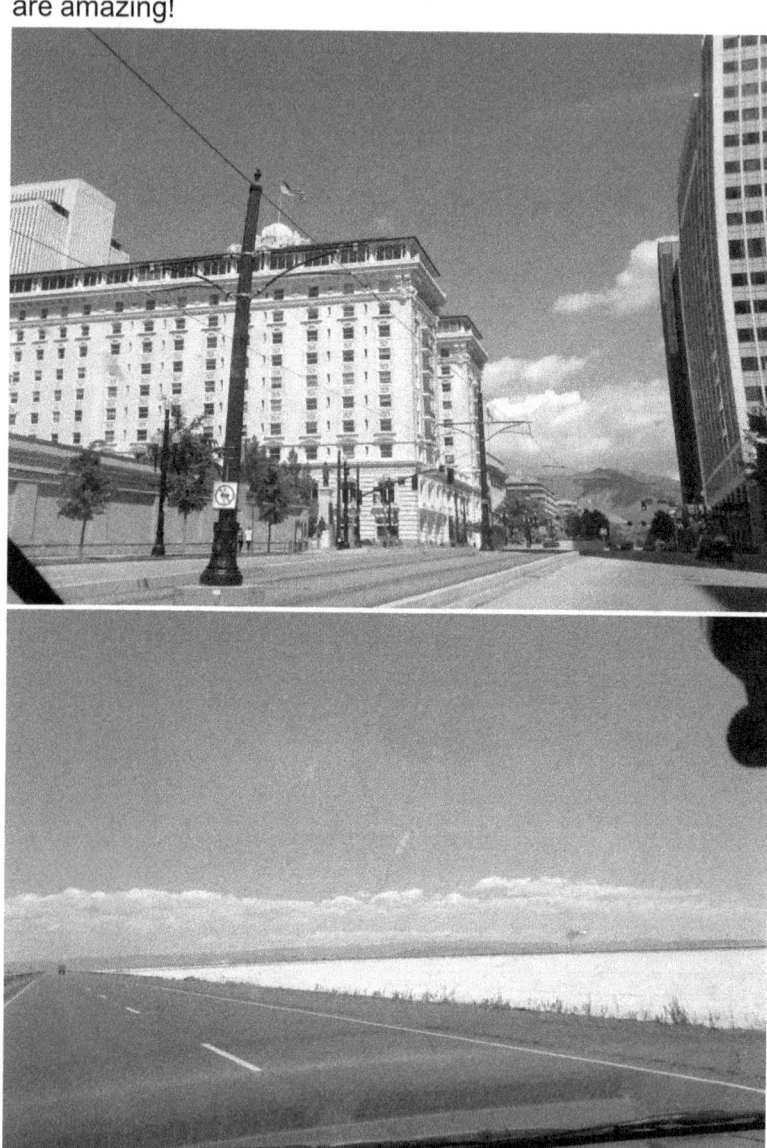

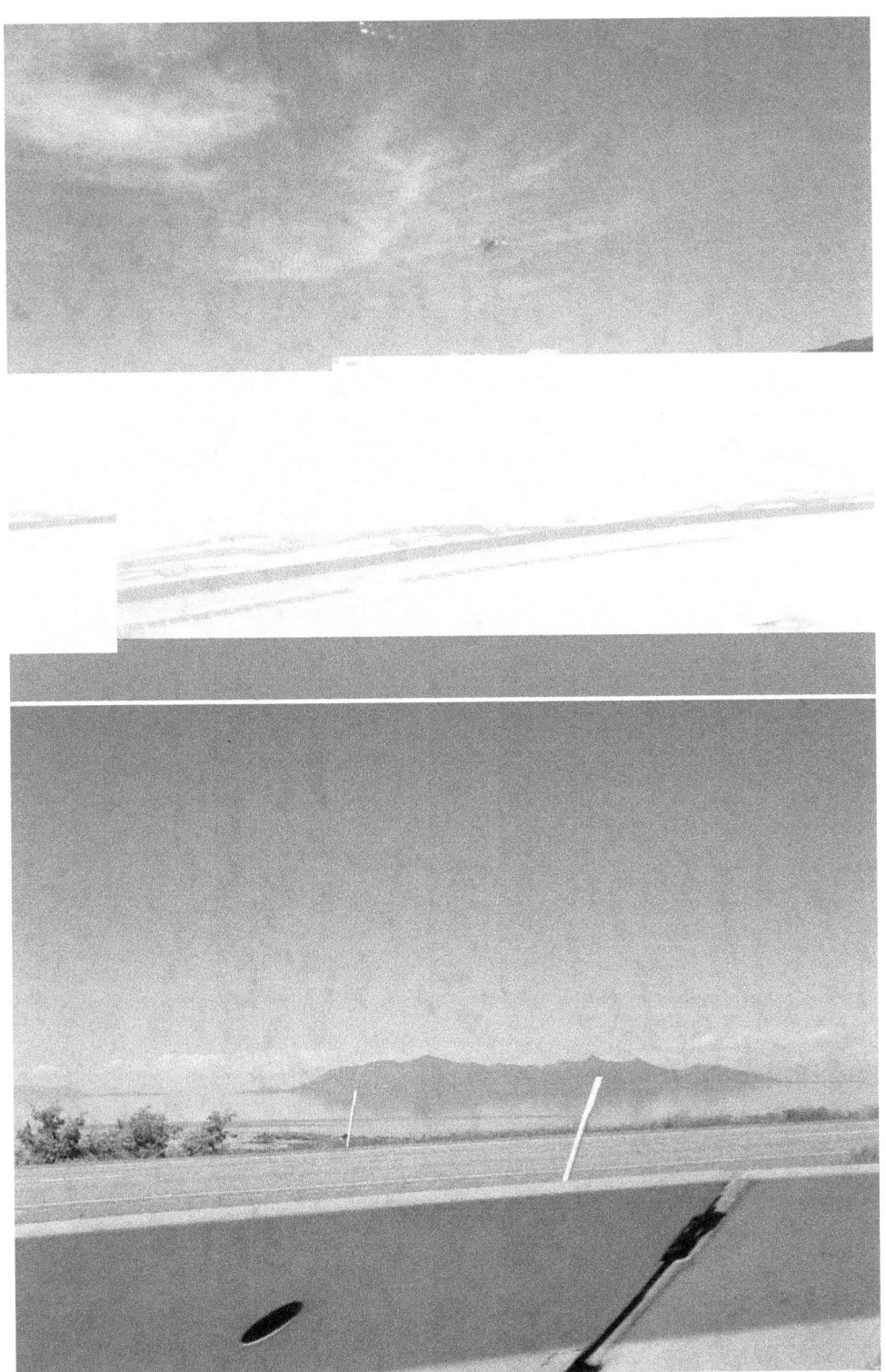

Tonight, is even better though. Tonight, I'm sleeping at the top of a mountain in Wyoming. Salt River Pass, Grey's River Rd. Elevation: 7630 feet.

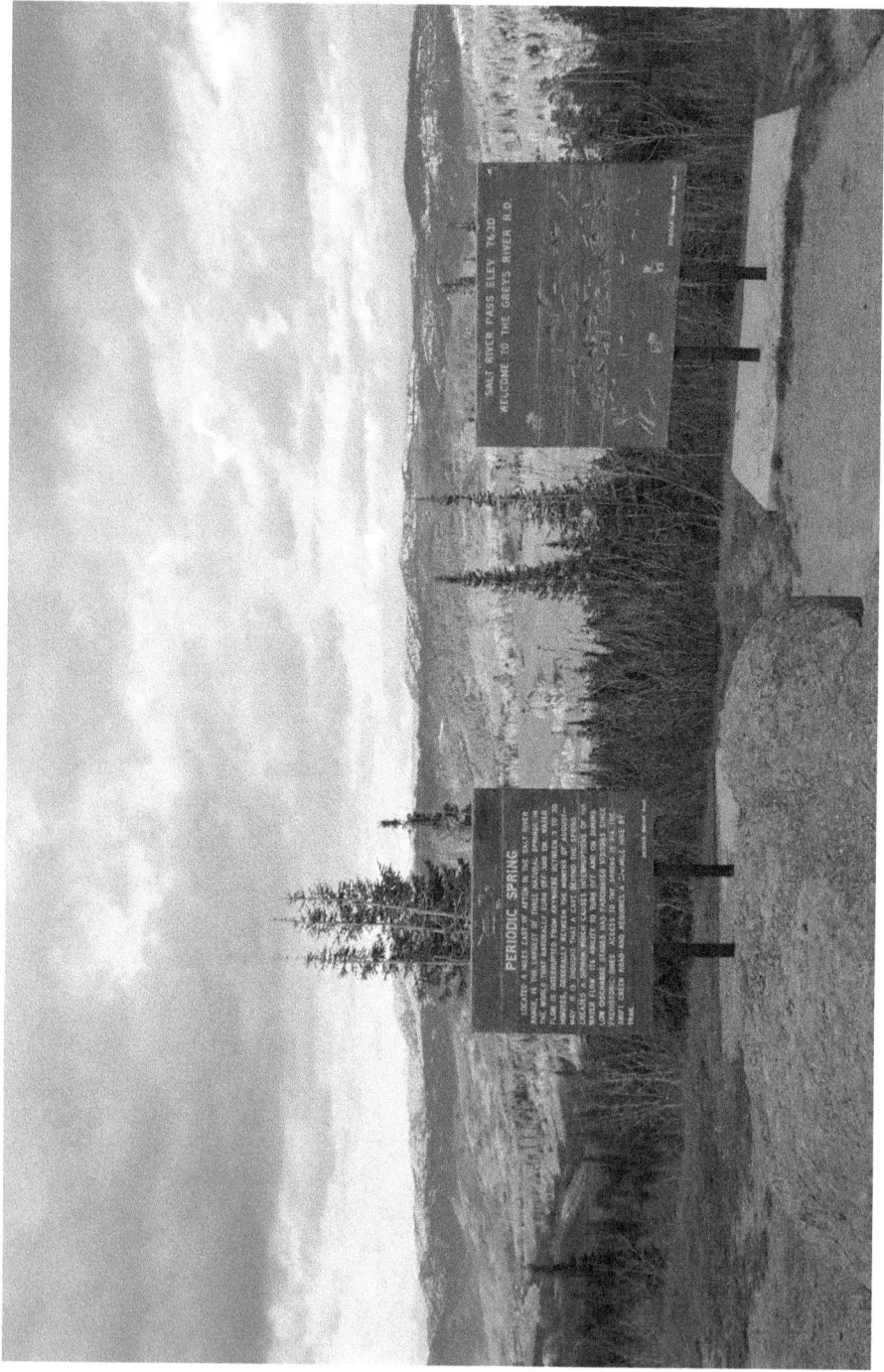

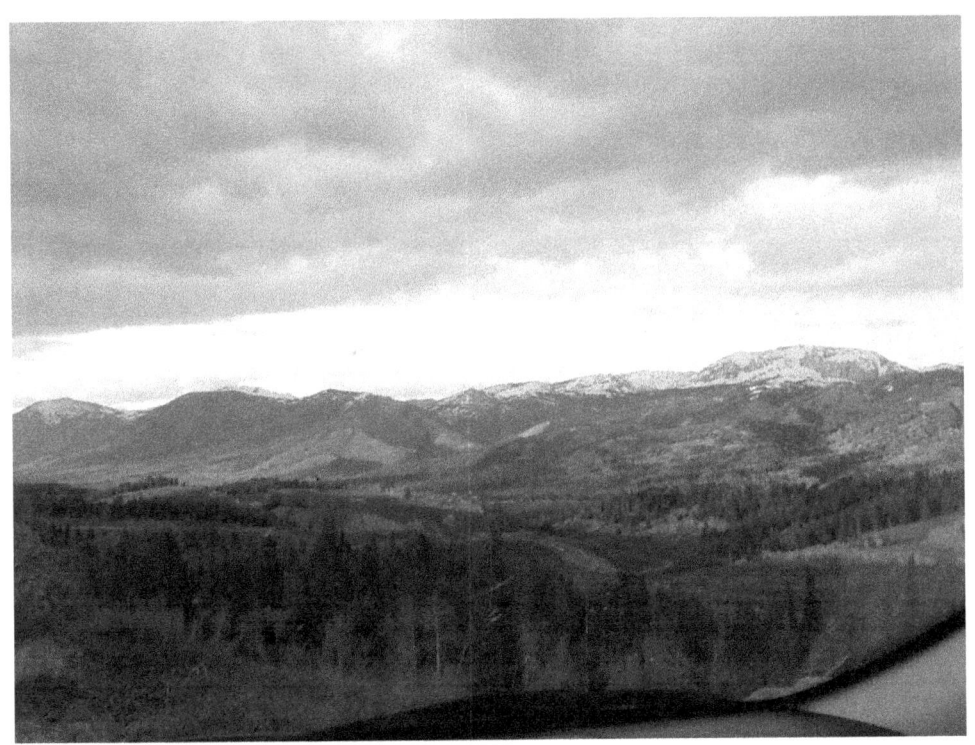

This view is gorgeous!

I stopped here because I had to go to the bathroom. Turns out the outhouse I saw is closed. crap... Oh well, this experience is so worth not having a bathroom.

I see snow on the next ridge and some little piles nearby. Wyoming is gorgeous and remote and quiet. It's just turning spring here. I bet the winter is cold. Cold, cold, with lots of snow. Also, wood heat would be hard. The mountains are woods, but the valleys are green pastures. Miles of it. Also, could I even keep up with wood heat on my own? That's hard work and would take away from painting and business time.

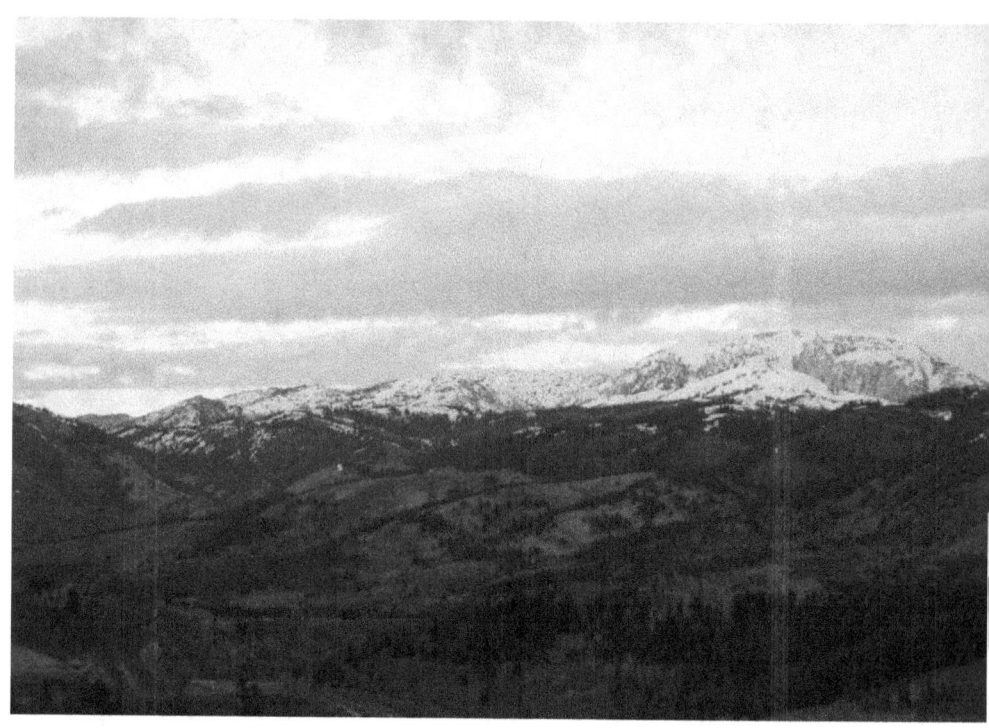

Maybe Jackson will be my speed/style? I'll look around while I'm there. Also, I wanna be sure to see Borbay and Ringholz. They're both here. Very different styles but I like them both. I like this area. The quietness. It's cold here. I don't know how to ski.

———

OMG! Moose!

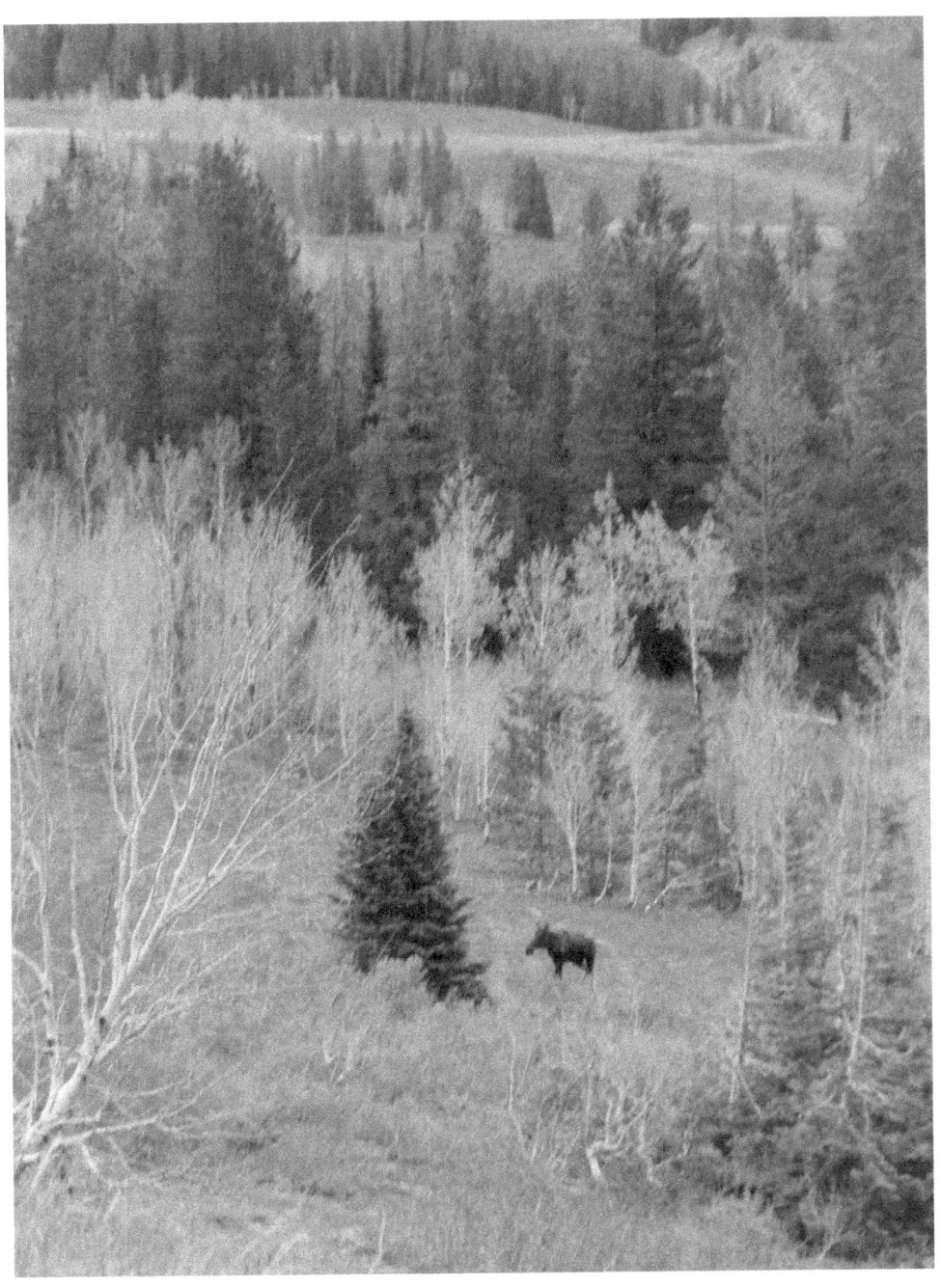

I'm sitting here watching the sunset and taking pictures and then there's a moose! All my years in the Upper Peninsula of Michigan and I saw none! 20 mins here and I see one!

I'm watching the first and ease back a bit to see if he'll come nearer when I see another behind me. I turn back around just in time to see a third go behind a tree between me and the creek. I don't seem to be spooking them. Holy Cow! Here's the 4th walking up from below! When I turn around again, I see three deer too! Holy Cow!!! Amazing!

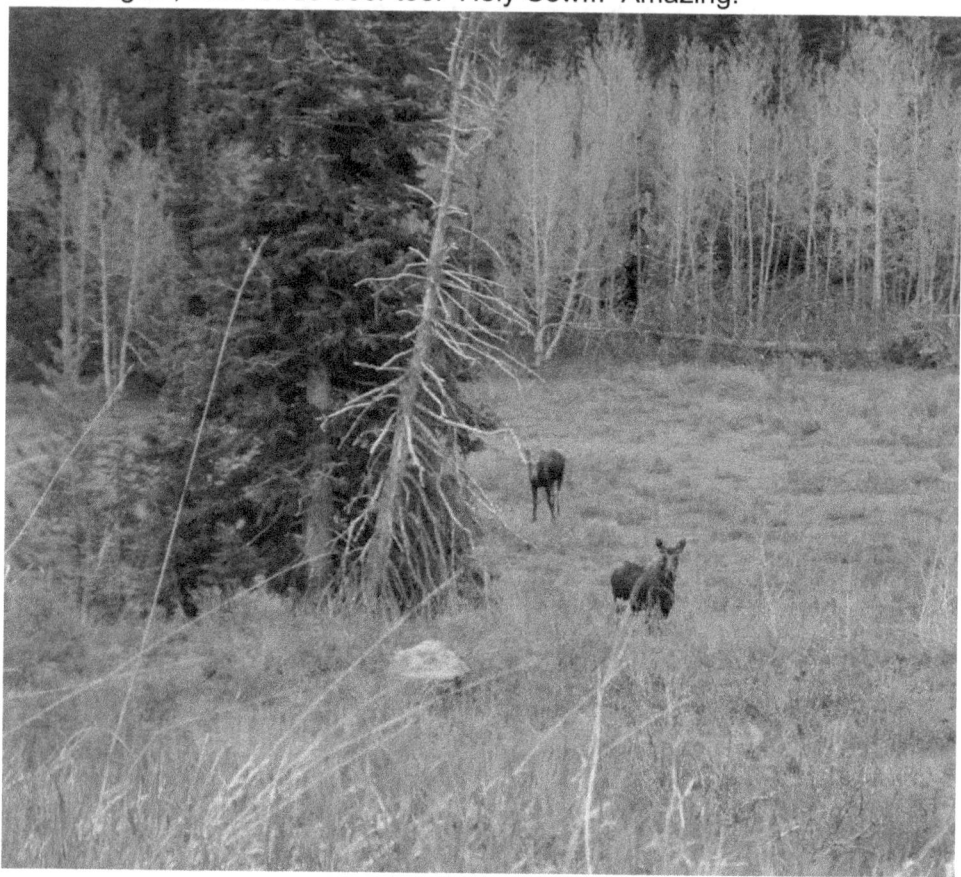

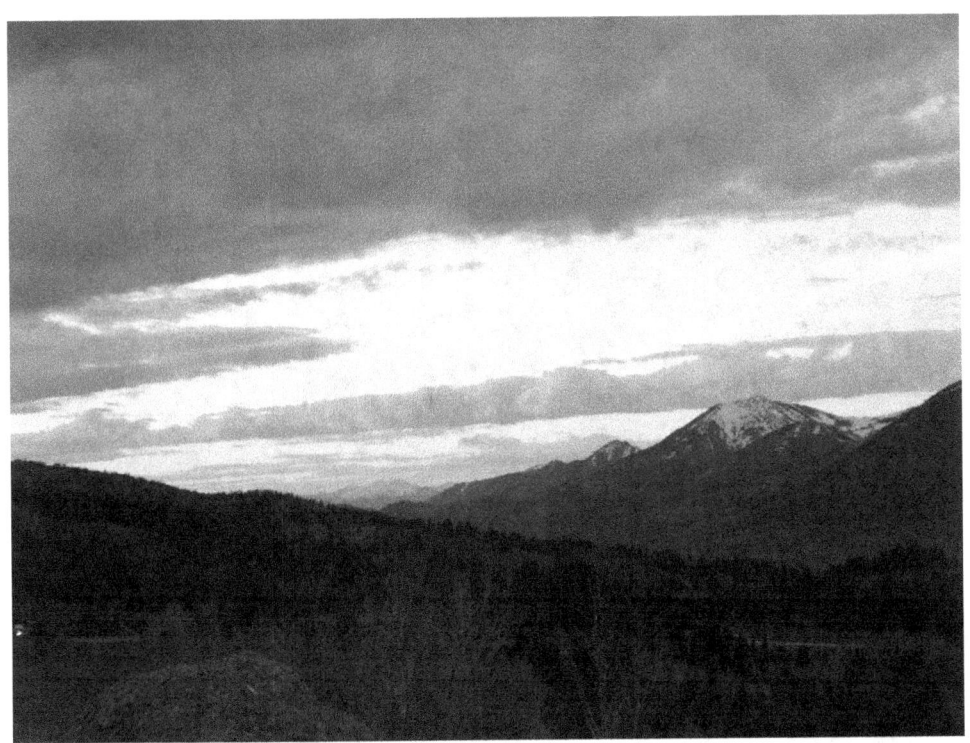

I love this! I love nature! I've loved seeing the National Parks. I love that they exist! But, visiting makes me hate people. The disrespect. The disregard. The traffic! The stupidity. The trash!

Or is it me? am I the one with the issue? Do I look to be irritated? Do I look to find the problem? In truth, I suppose, both... The traffic, disrespect, stupidity, and trash are there. I could choose to only see the beauty.

But really, if we all chose to only see beauty, we'd never change anything. The ugly, uncomfortable, and ungood are what spur us into action to create change. I suppose we must have both. The dark and the light. The yin and the yang.

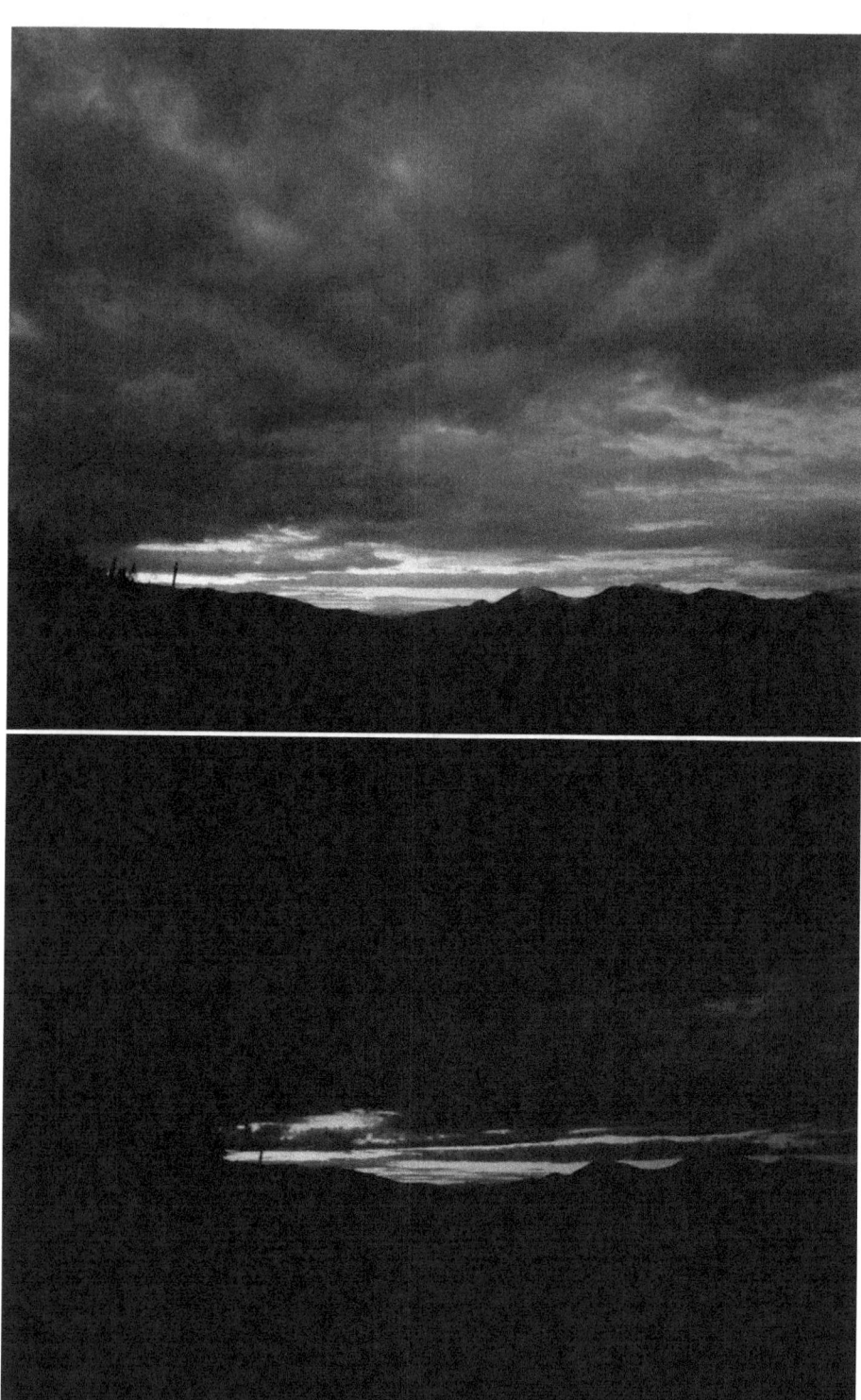

5/23/17 Day 37 - Jackson, Grand Tetons, and Yellowstone

Present day note: I didn't write anything in my journal over the next couple days. I remember I was feeling very contemplative; doing my best to see and experience all the amazing sites while my mind kept returning to my dilemma and sadness of my trip being over and not really having a good, happy plan.

My mind kept searching for some other reasonable solution. I don't remember now if I really did Yellowstone and The Badlands on separate days. It may have been the same day. I know I did a lot of driving and thinking.

I also know that I got to Jackson quite early. The galleries weren't open yet but that's ok, I wasn't really feeling sociable anyway. And I guess I didn't really feel like writing anything tonight either. What do I even say? I'm bummed. I don't want to go to Indiana. But I'm tired and I'll appreciate the rest. Jackson is cool. I loved Yellowstone. The Badlands were definitely a favorite stop. I took hundreds, if not a thousand, pictures on these two days alone.

Enjoy the pictures.

270

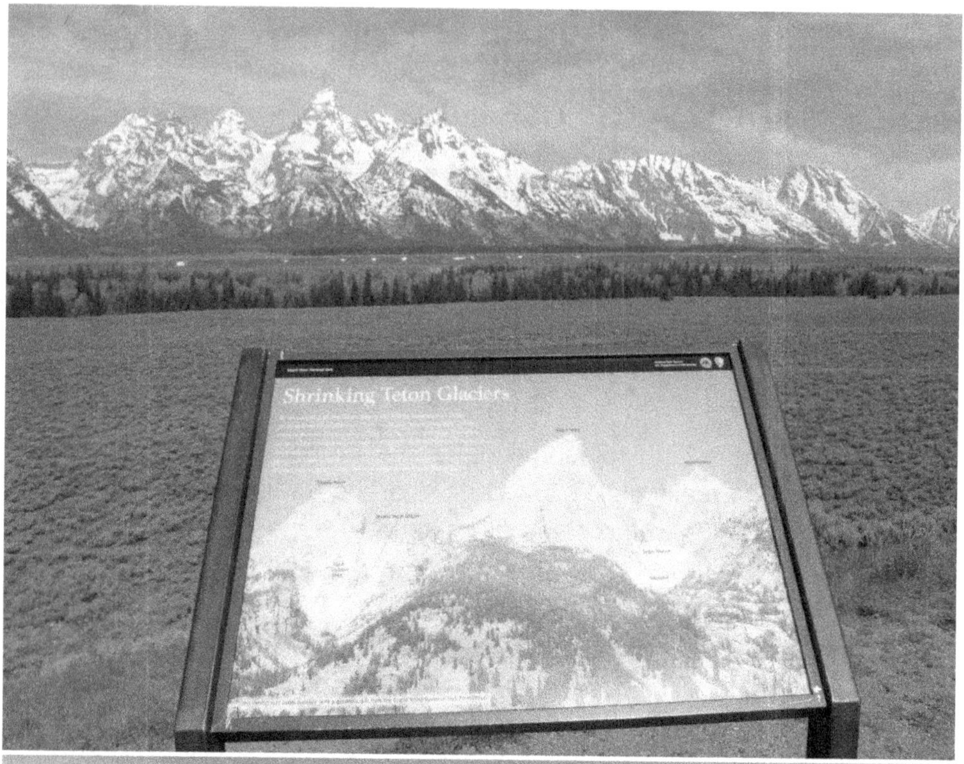

271

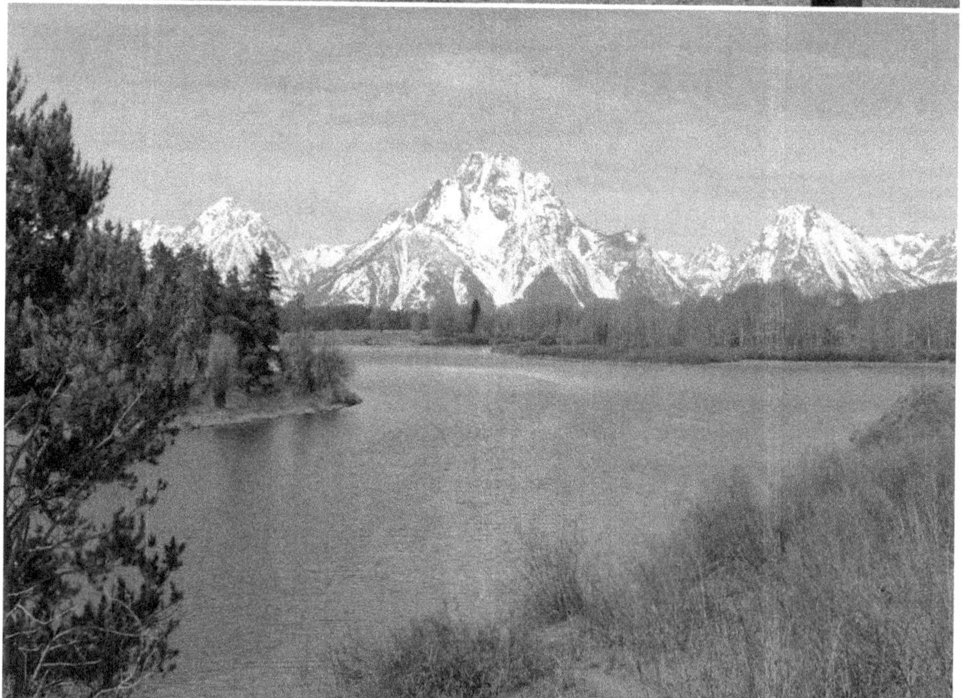

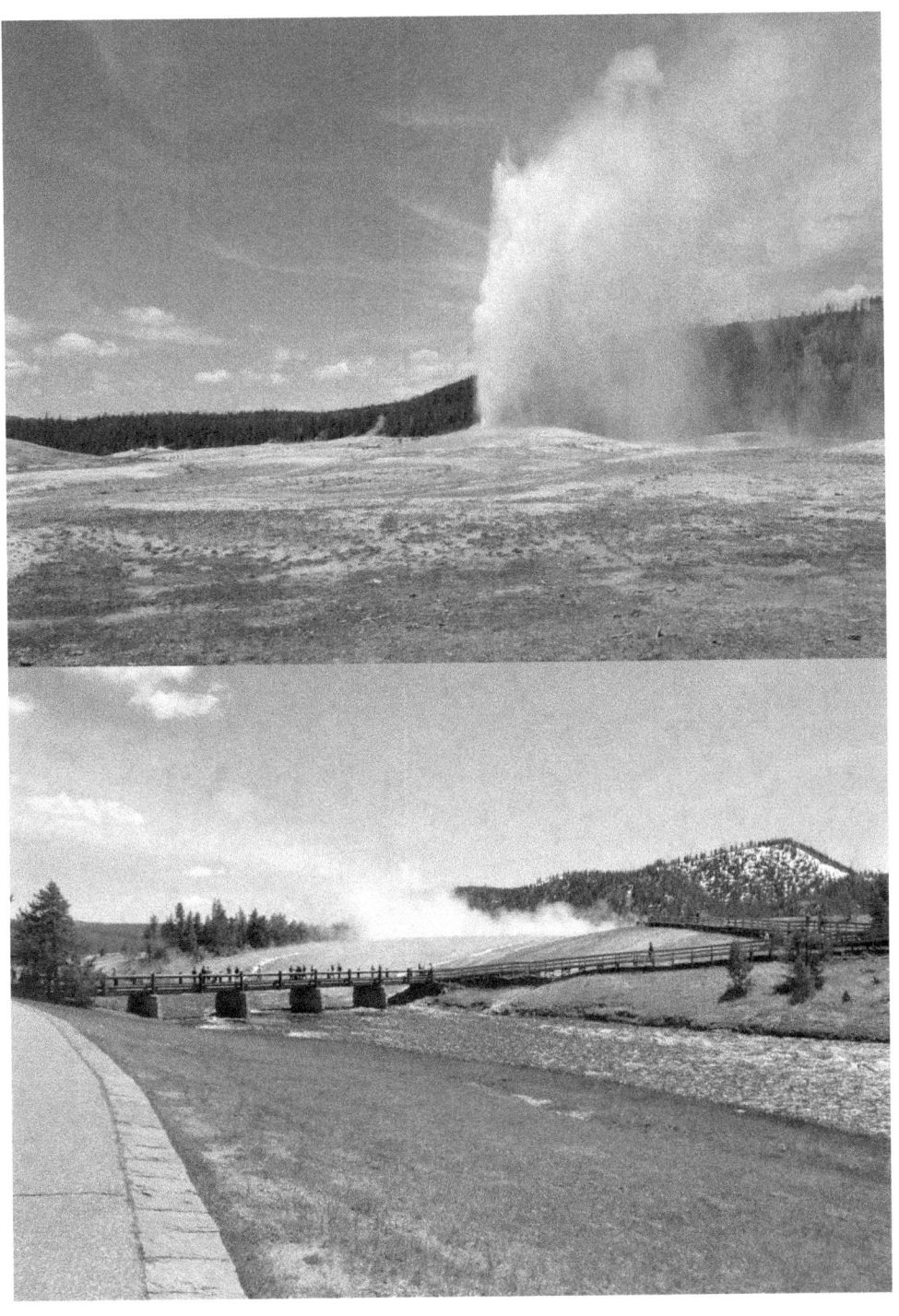

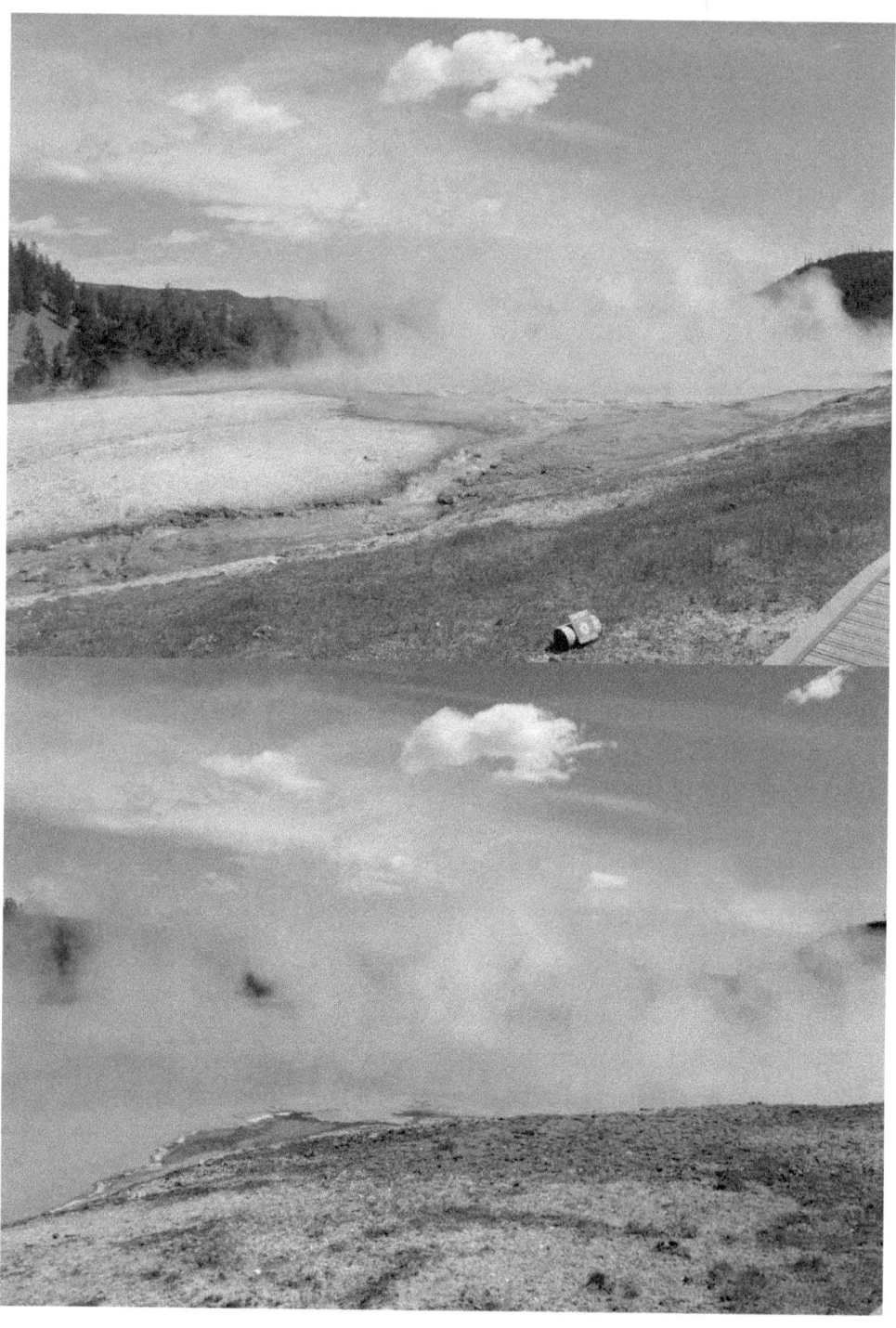

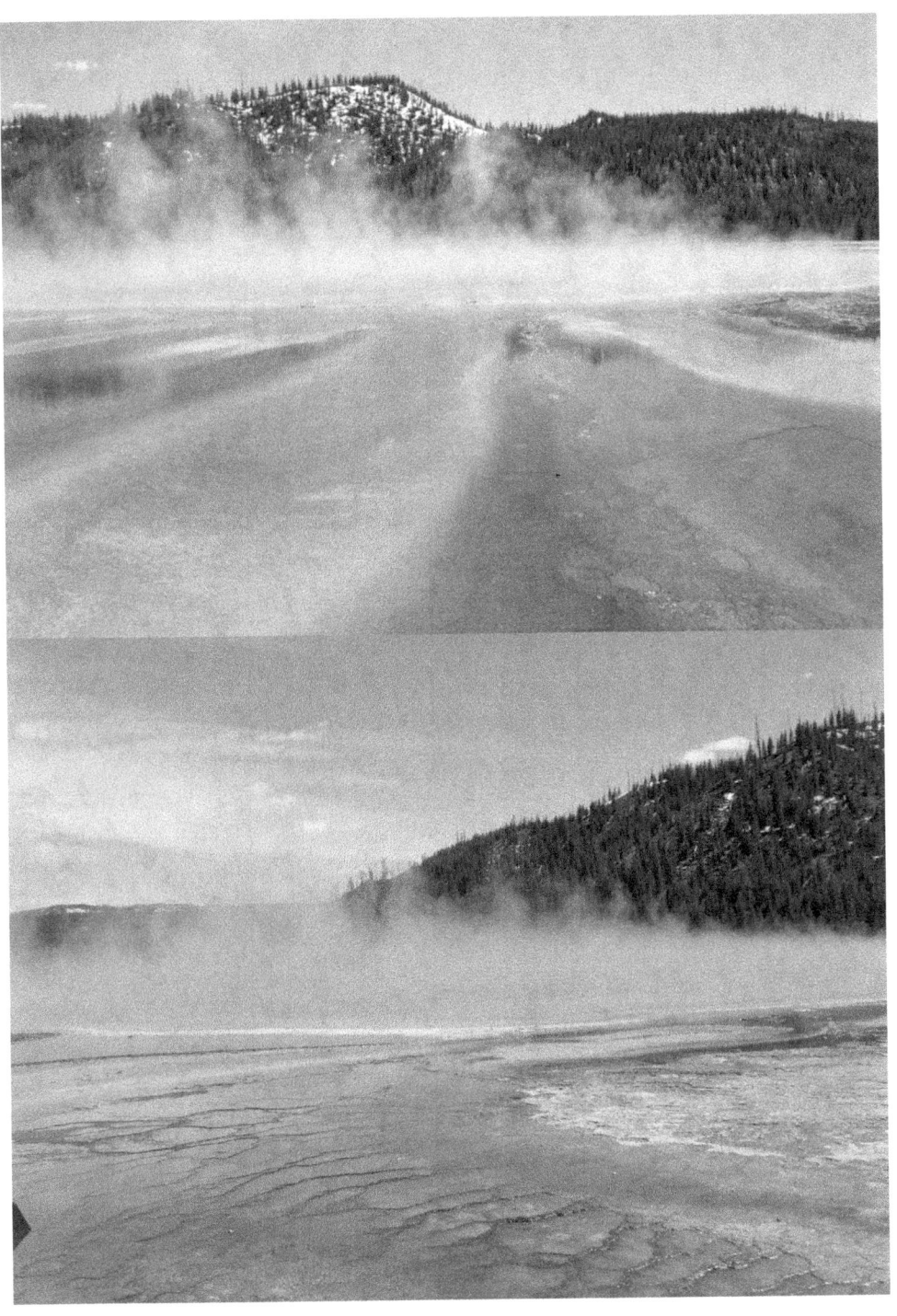

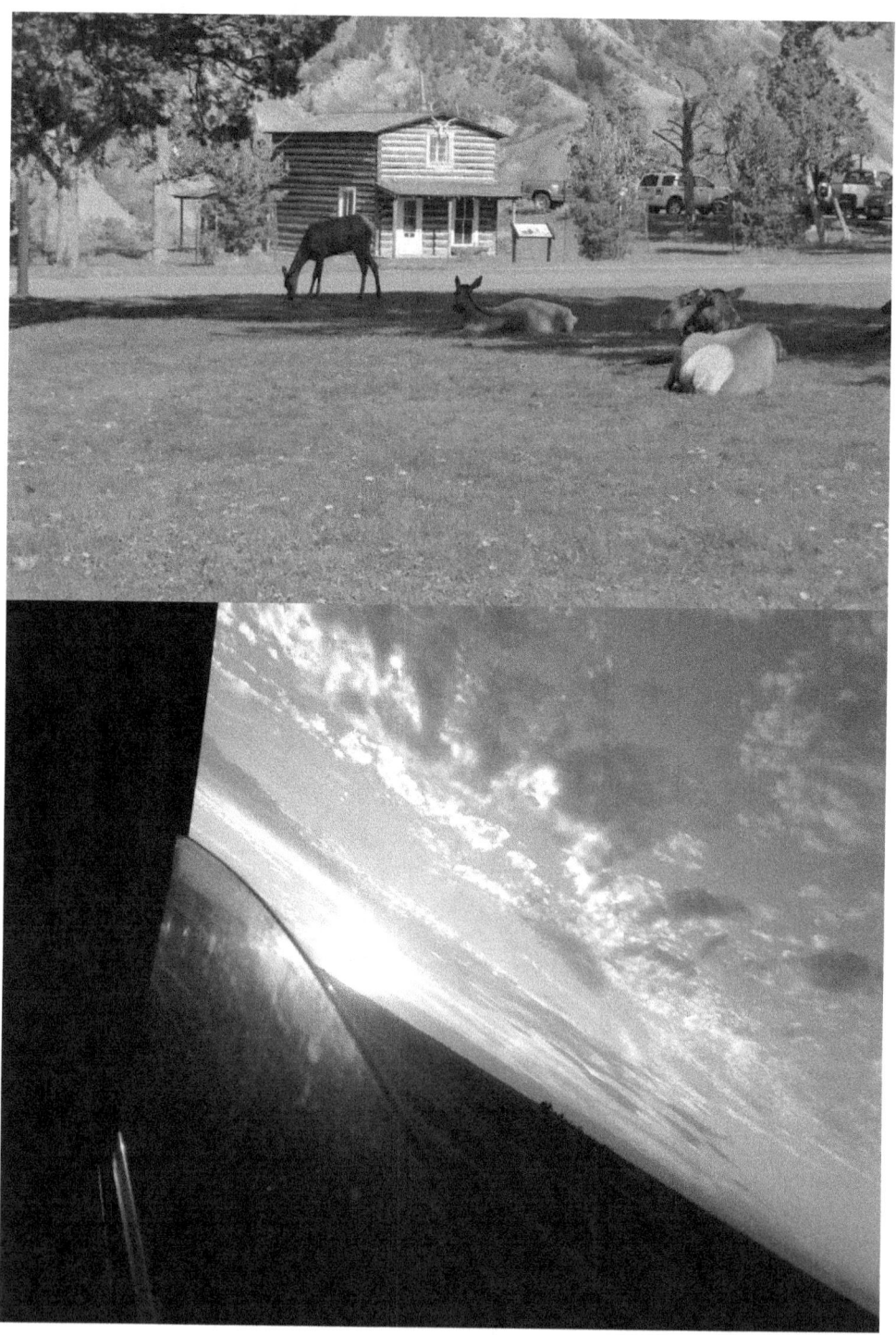

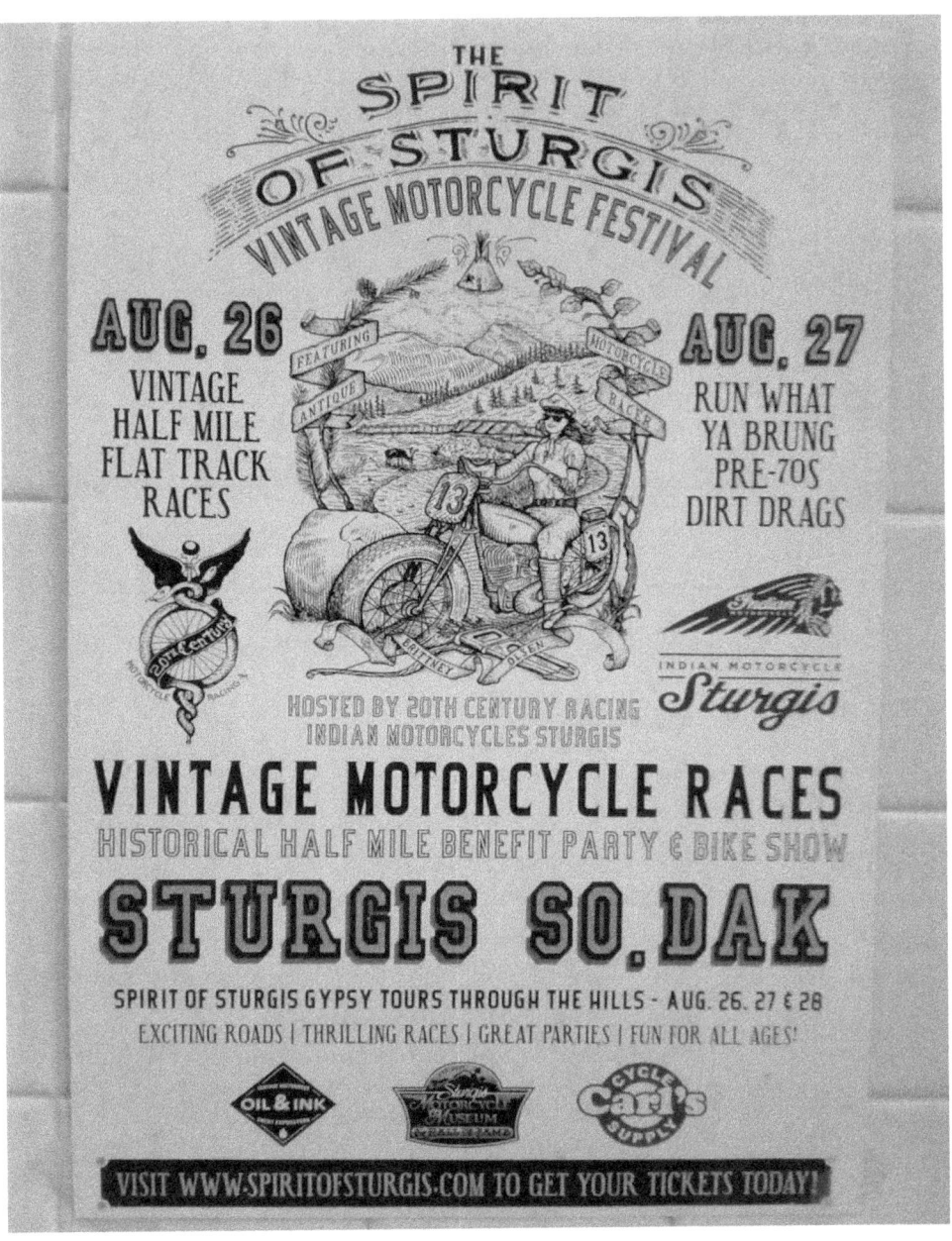

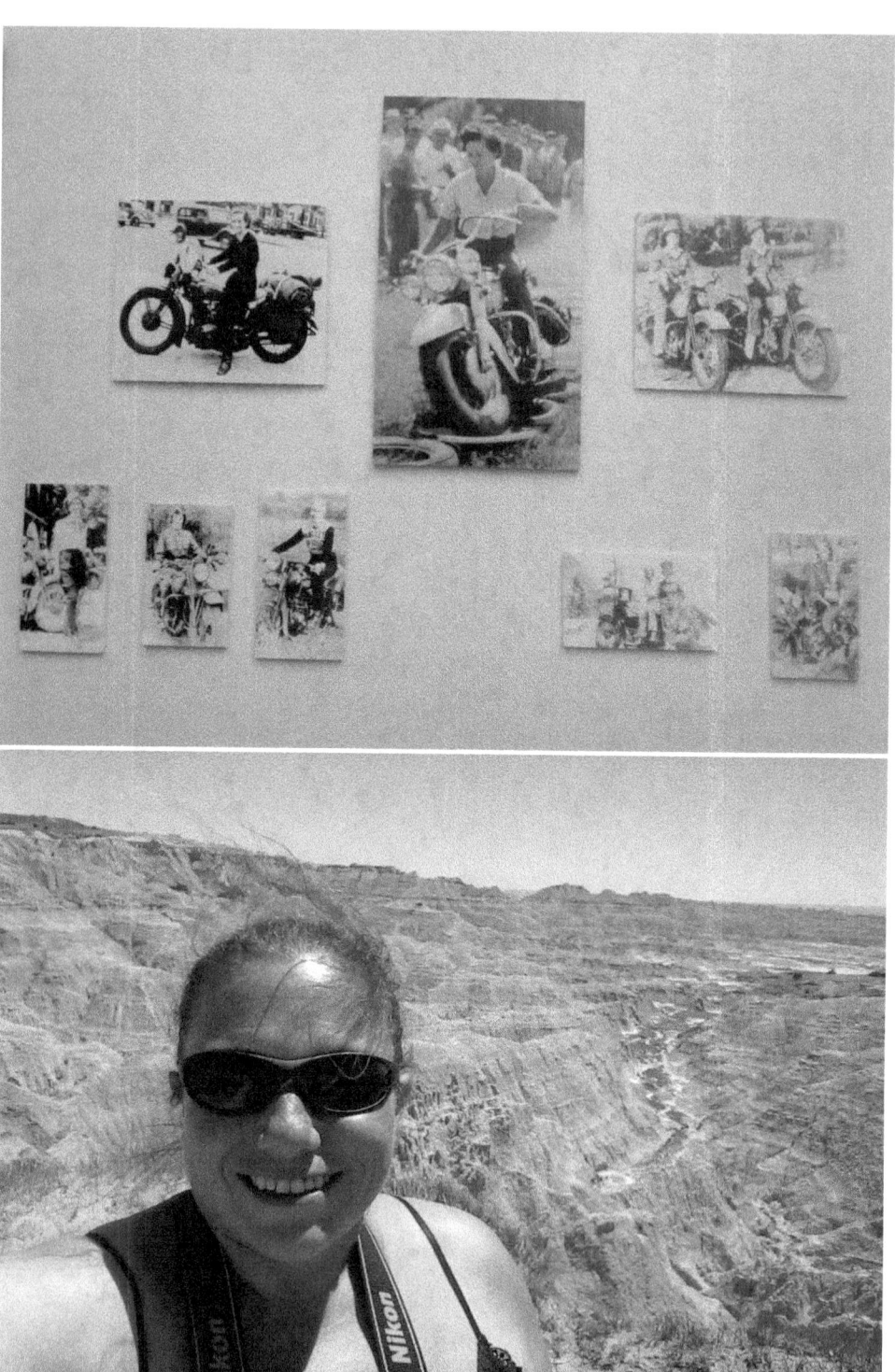

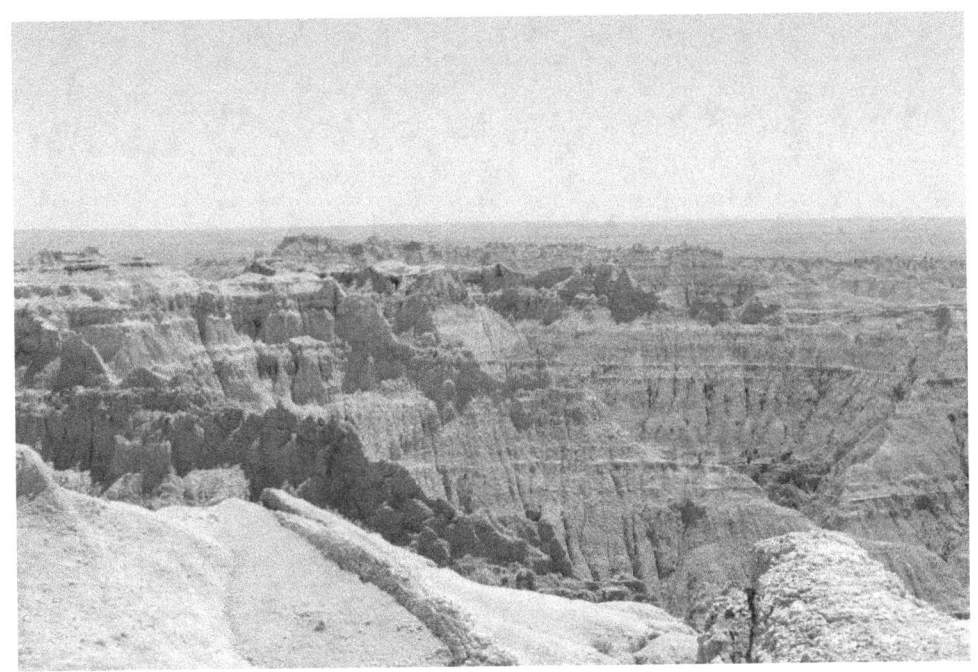

I particularly liked the Badlands. The colors weren't quite as fabulous as the Petrified Forest, but it was one of my favorites because I got to see mountain goats and prairie dogs.

At one point, I stopped at this pull off to take a picture of some mountain goats. There were several of us who stopped here. All of us taking pictures.

I'm standing near this guy and we're both in awe of this moment being so close to these goats. There were several goats to the right of us and then we see this one over to our left. She's coming towards us kinda fast. After a second I realize she's coming at us.

No, she's coming thru us!

I move back but the guy just keeps standing there. He doesn't move and doesn't even seem phased until I tell him to move. Seconds later, she charges thru the space we were standing.

He very nearly got himself trampled by a goat and knocked off the side of a bluff.

278

See the look she's giving me? "Bitch. I said move…" LOL

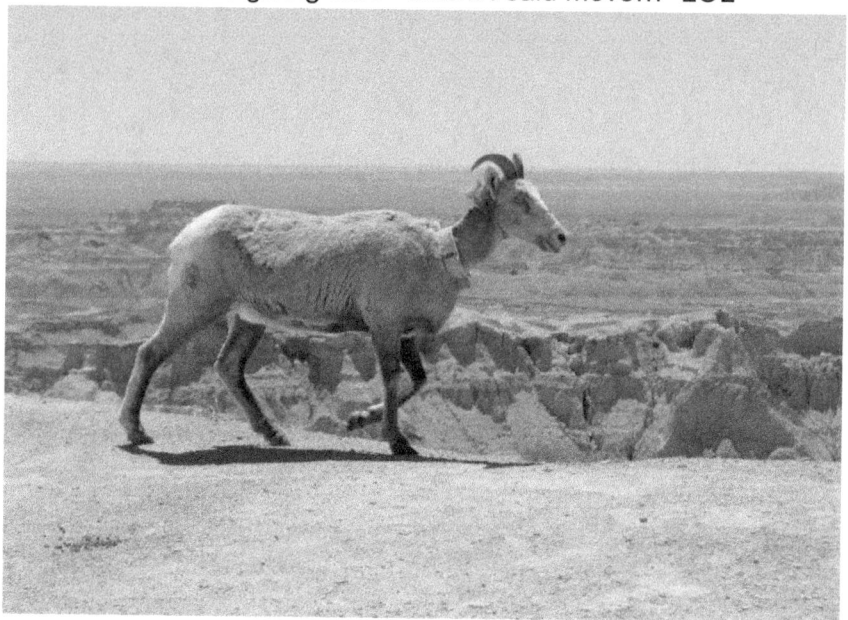

A few moments later I realize exactly why she was on such a mission.

This is momma and baby is with the group of goats on our right.

Don't stand in a momma's way of her kid.

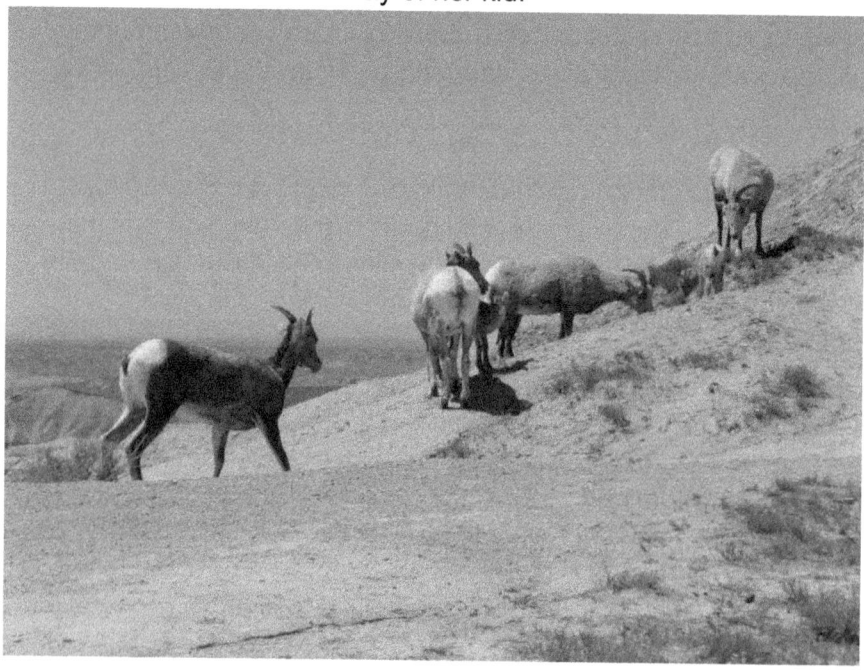

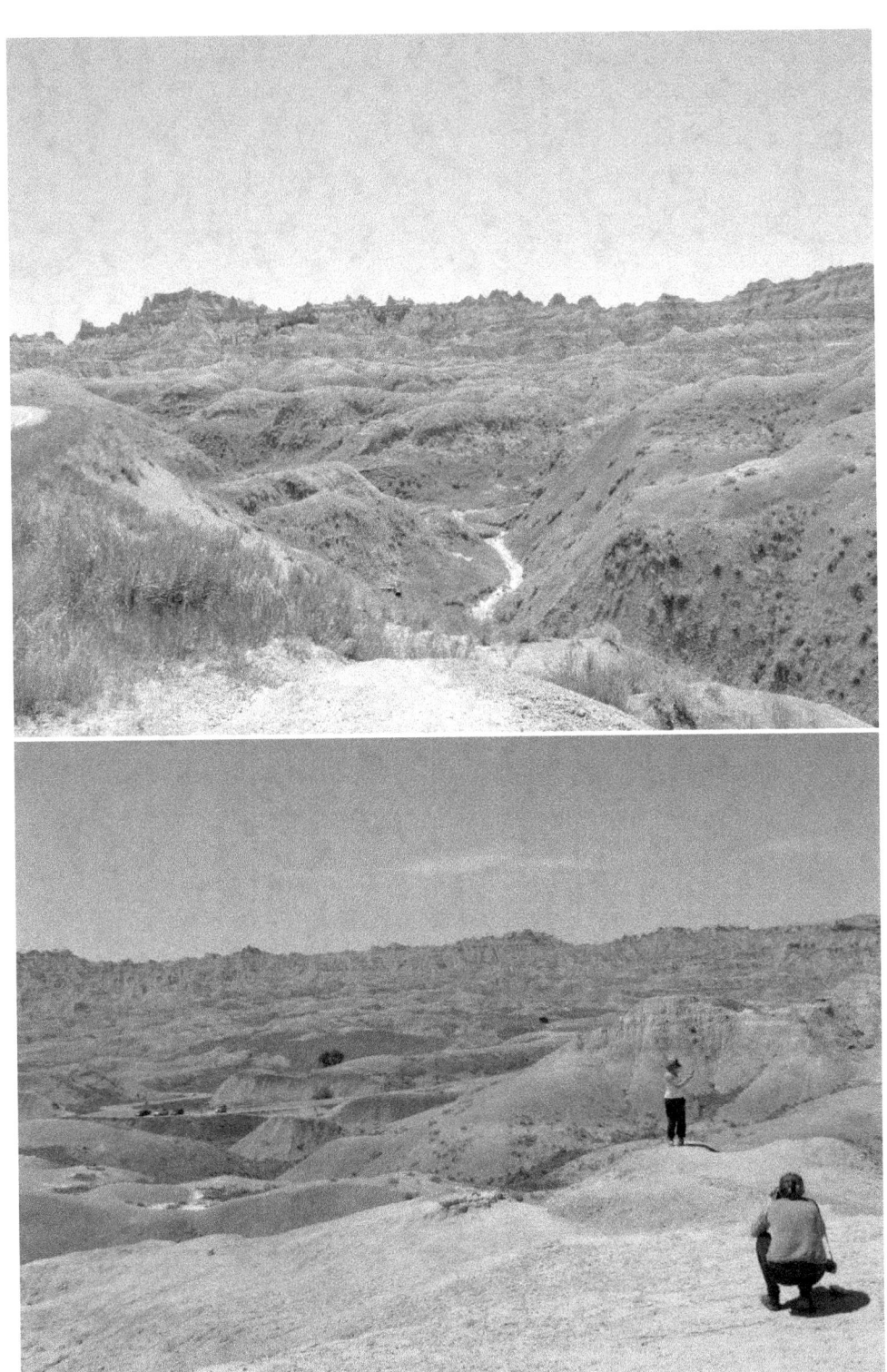

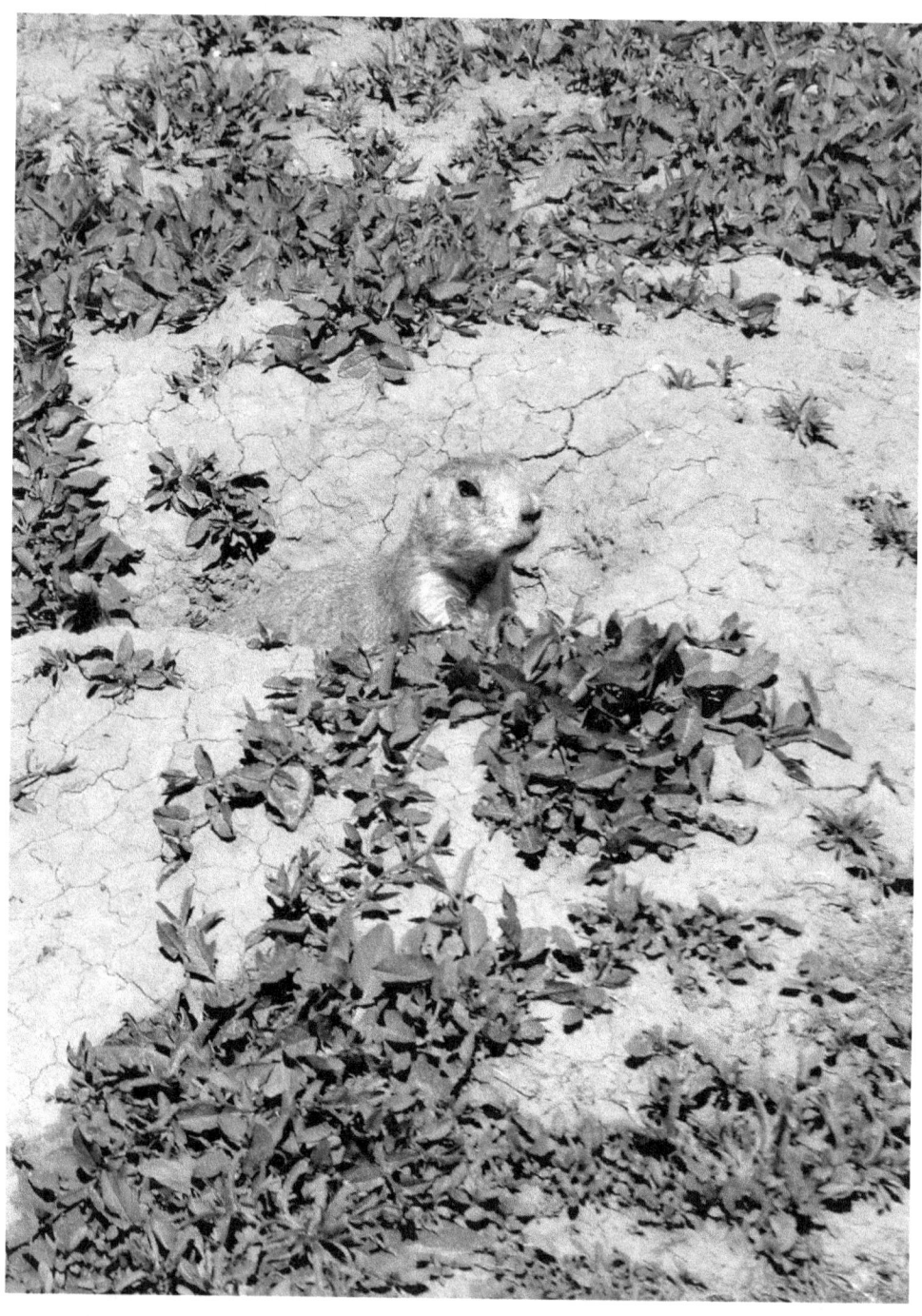

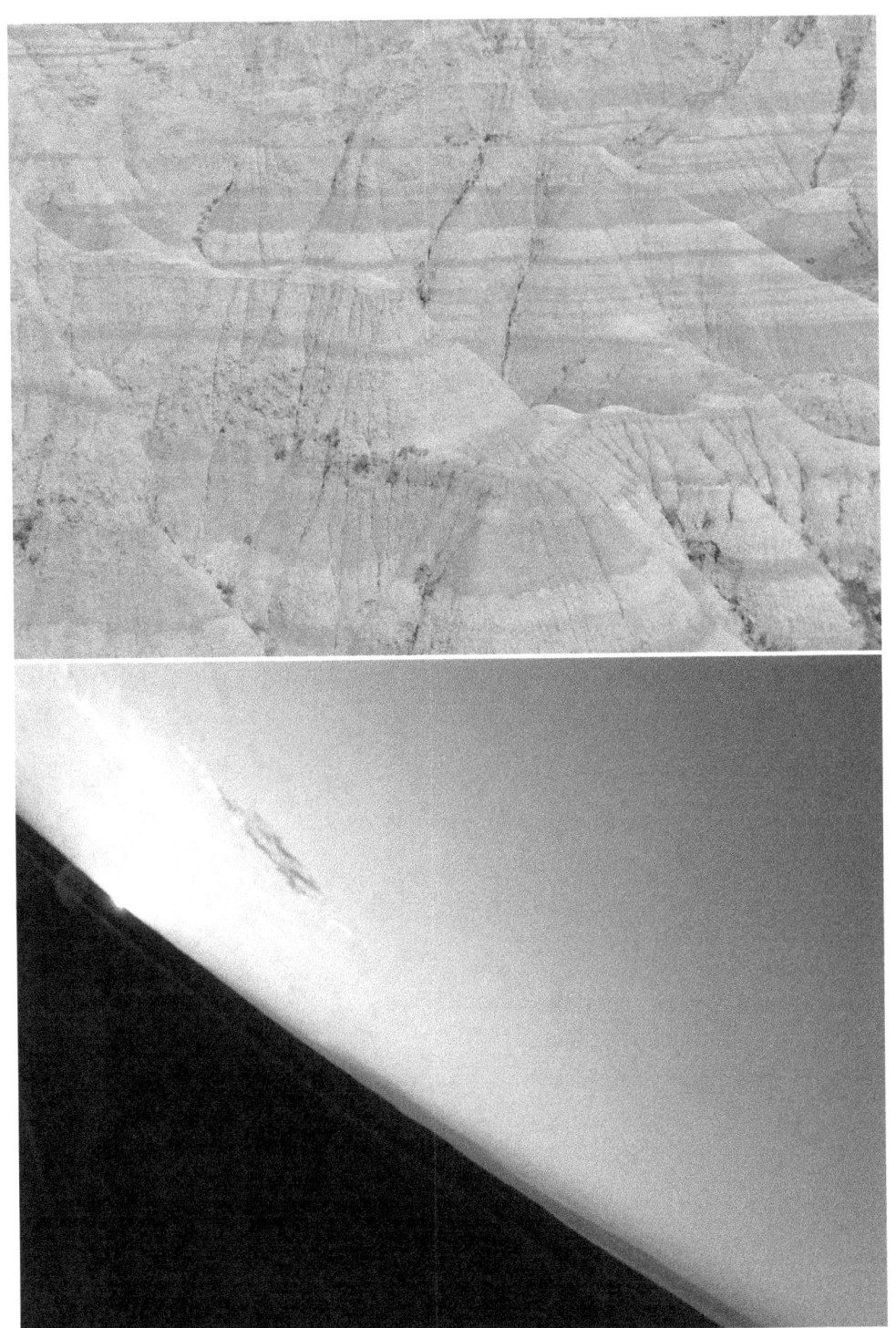

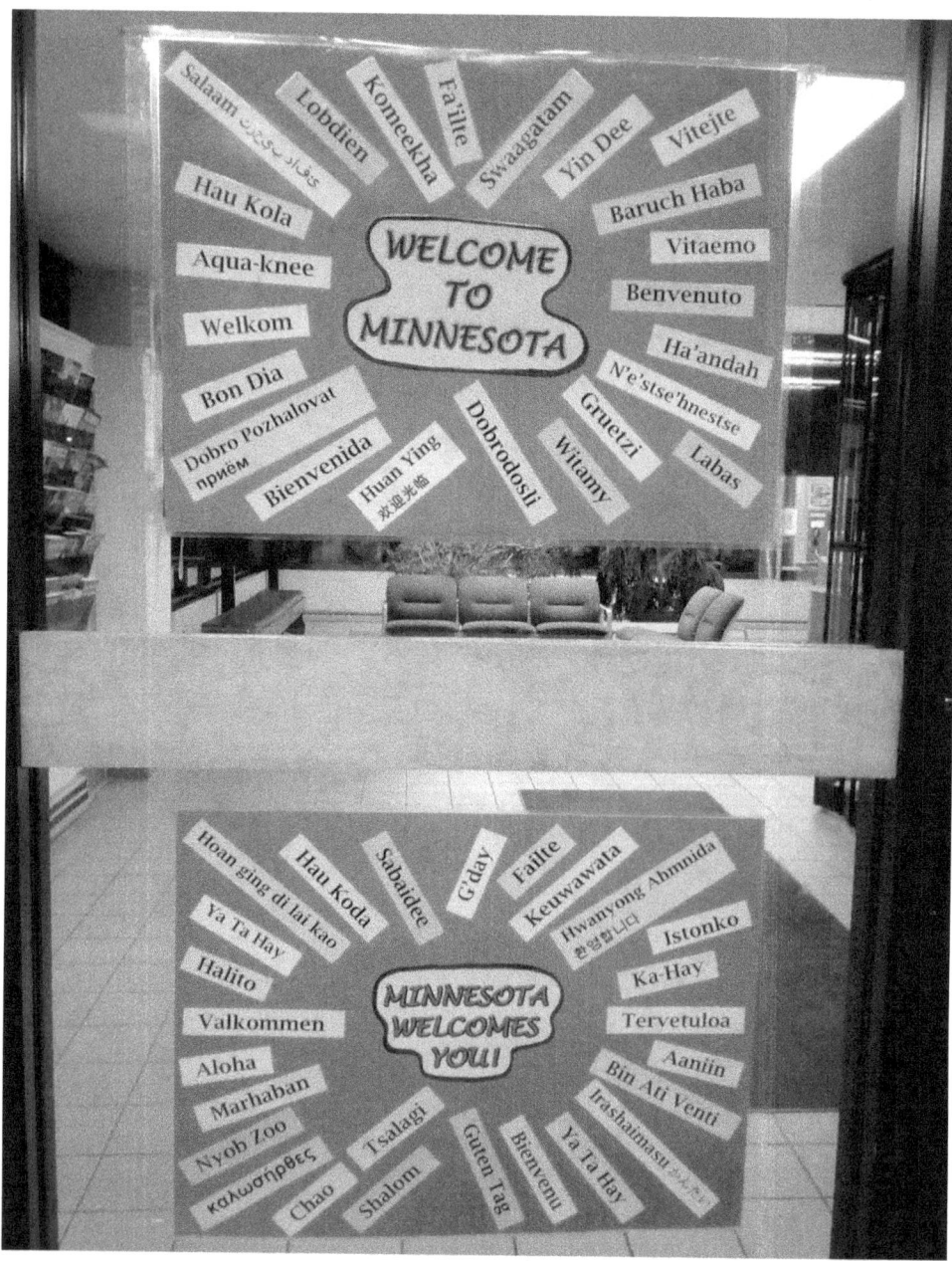

Slept last night in a Minnesota rest area. I've been pedal to the metal since leaving The Badlands. That was the last part of the trip and now I just want to get home, wherever that is.

I didn't stop until long after dark. When I pulled into a rest area, I was the only car. A semi pulled up a few minutes later and a guy got out and went into the rest area. I could see him in there hollering and pacing and generally acting nutso. I'm kinda freaking out. Then I realize he's on his phone. doh.

This morning I'll turn south off I-90 on I-35, drive thru Iowa to I-80, and take I-80 into Indiana. This is officially the home stretch.

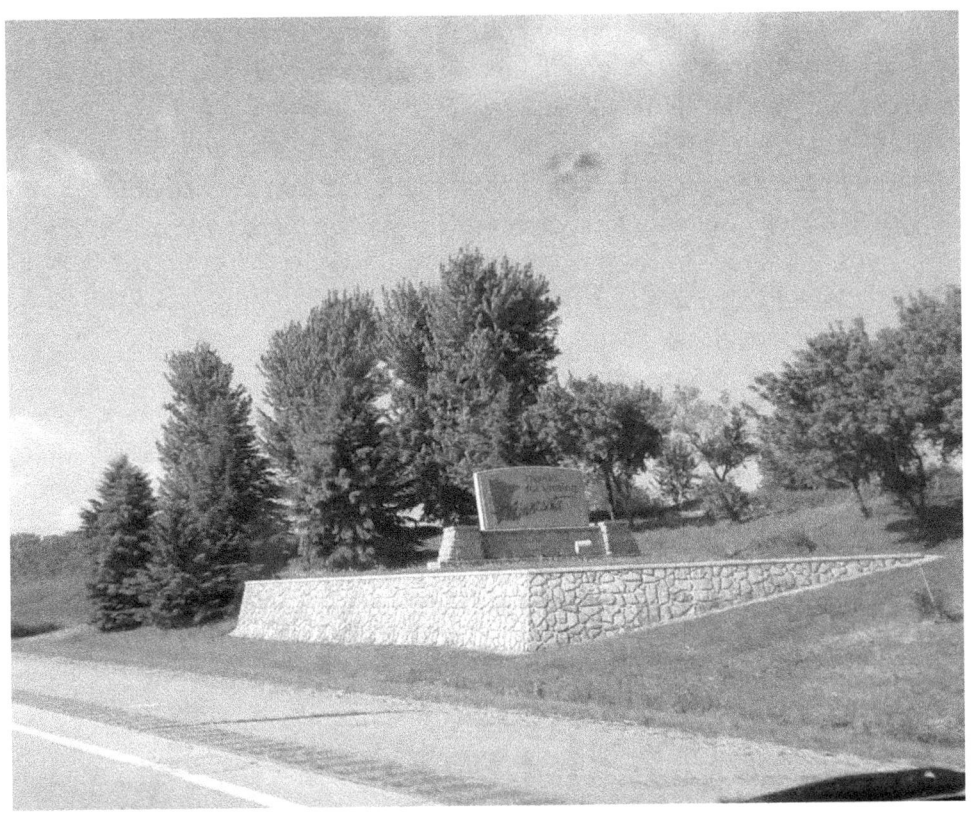

I'm dreading going back to Indiana. I'm dreading not having my own space nor my computer, but such is the position I'm in. I'm better off going where I have food, shelter, and income rather than wandering off into the unknown and unsecure (or am I?). where would I wing it anyway? Especially now that I'm this far and broke.

I could of wung it in Jackson. There were help wanted signs and places for rent. It might have been a little time but I could have figured it out. But, winter... It's so cold. I know I'm over the cold, cold.

I couldn't have made it to Arkansas. And what happens when I'm out of money? It'd take time to find some work. I probably would have run out of money in Oklahoma somewhere instead, haha.

No, I know this is the right choice. It's safe, anyway. Does that mean it's right? Mom's happy. Dad's not happy I had to borrow more money. Me? I don't know. I'm kinda bummed to be done. Kinda bummed to be headed back to Indiana and that I didn't figure out somewhere else to go. Maybe the rest and regroup time will do me good. This has been a wild and crazy ride. I'm sure I need some decompression time. I've already asked for my job back at the bar. I can use this time to build up my body of work and learn to sell. Save up a bit of money to make my next move.

"I could move to a small town
And become a waitress
Say my name was Stacy
And I was figuring things out
See, my baby, he left me
And I don't feel like staying here tonight
I remember sleepless nights
I remember Chicago
I remember the music
From the down stair's bar
Girls, they just want to have fun
And the rest of us hardly know who we are
It's a dark, twisted road we are on
And we all have to walk it alone

I could join the circus
When they come to town
Me and the freaks, the tamers
And that old sad clown
I'd walk across that tight rope
Head held high
So close to death

I'd never fell nor lie
'Cause you know, it's a dark, twisted road we are on
And we all have to walk it alone
I could drive out to the ocean
And just stare in awe
I could walk across the beaches
And   sleep   under   the   stars..."
Lyrics from Waitress Song by First Aid Kit

———

I'm rolling into Indiana on fumes. I put my last $10 of mostly change into my tank in Joliet, Illinois.

Wouldn't it suck to run out of gas on the Indiana state line? 13 miles from mom and dads?

Guess 13 is better than 1300.

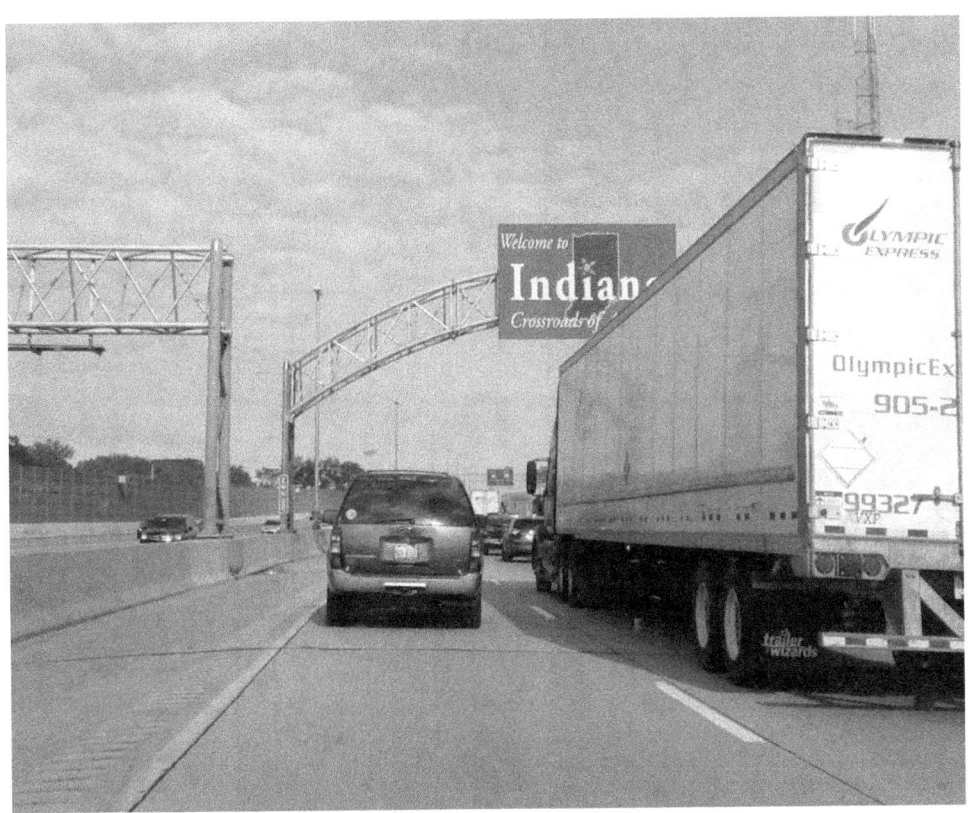

Breathe Lace. It'll be ok. Trust the process. Everything happens for a reason.

7500 miles. 39 days. 7 national parks, 2 Airbnb's, 1 motel, 5 campgrounds, and numerous parking lots, rest areas, and pull offs later, I'm home, I guess.

I wonder how this will play out.

I wonder what's in store for me next.

Over the next several months I stayed at mom and dads, cooked at my aunt's bar, and painted.

It was a good building time.

I had several dog portrait commissions, painted my biggest painting ever (3ft sq.), then was asked to paint a mural.

The mural started as just the ceiling but amazingly, my friend let me paint the whole room. And now, I'd rather paint murals than anything else. Big murals, whole room murals, Trompe l'oeil views thru painted windows murals, full sides of huge buildings murals.
Murals...

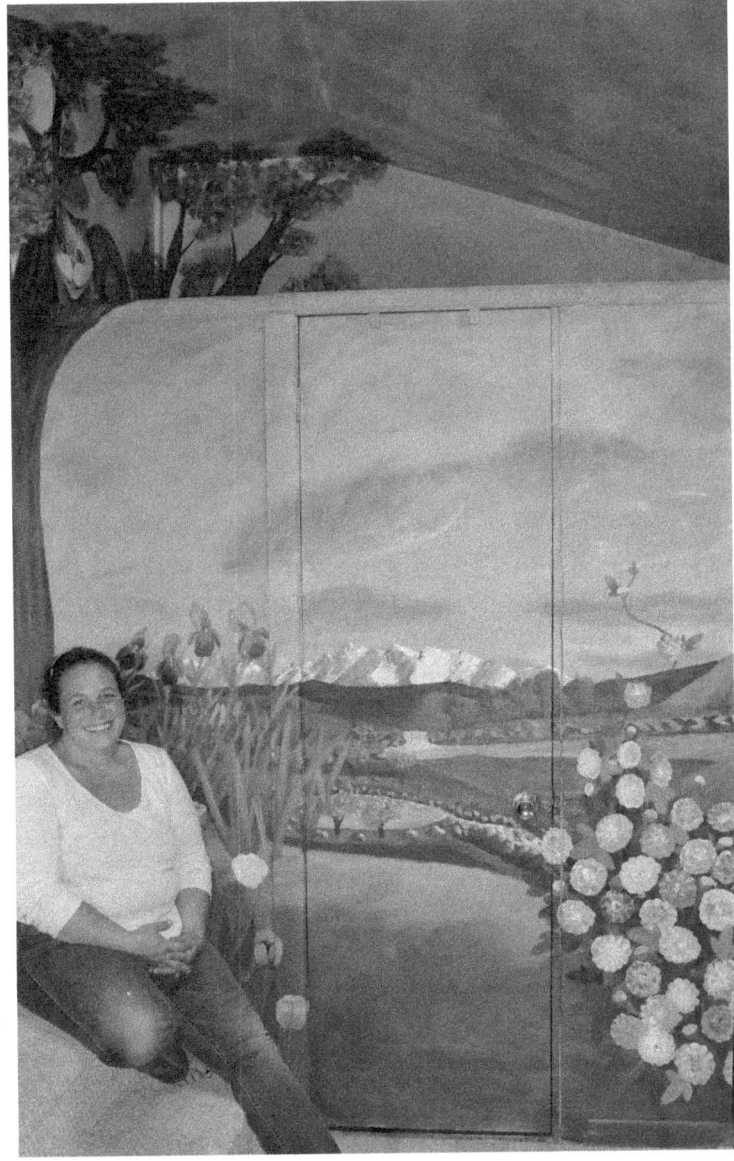

It was the most amazing feeling to walk into her new room and be in a space that was in my head a few months earlier. This one took me a long time but, I'll get faster.

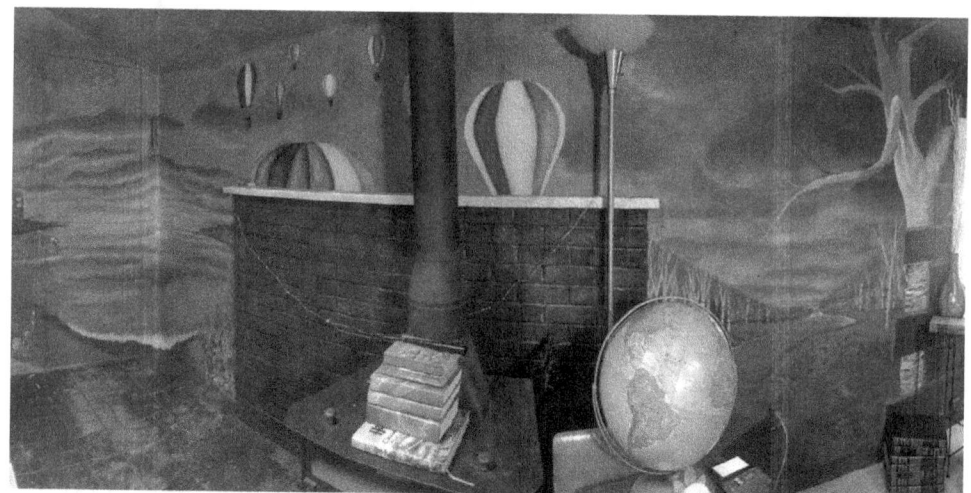

I also spent a lot of time at the beach. I felt lucky growing up in NWI because of the lakeshore and I've always enjoyed spending time there. It's changing though. There is way less shore these days. At one of my favorite spots, there is almost no beach left. The water is up to the rocks supporting the welcome center. It didn't used to be that way.

**** Present day note**** Last week in 2019 a different beach nearly washed away. In the video I saw, the waves had breached a small dune and were beating away at the dune that was left to hold up the building.

Summer wound into fall and fall into winter.

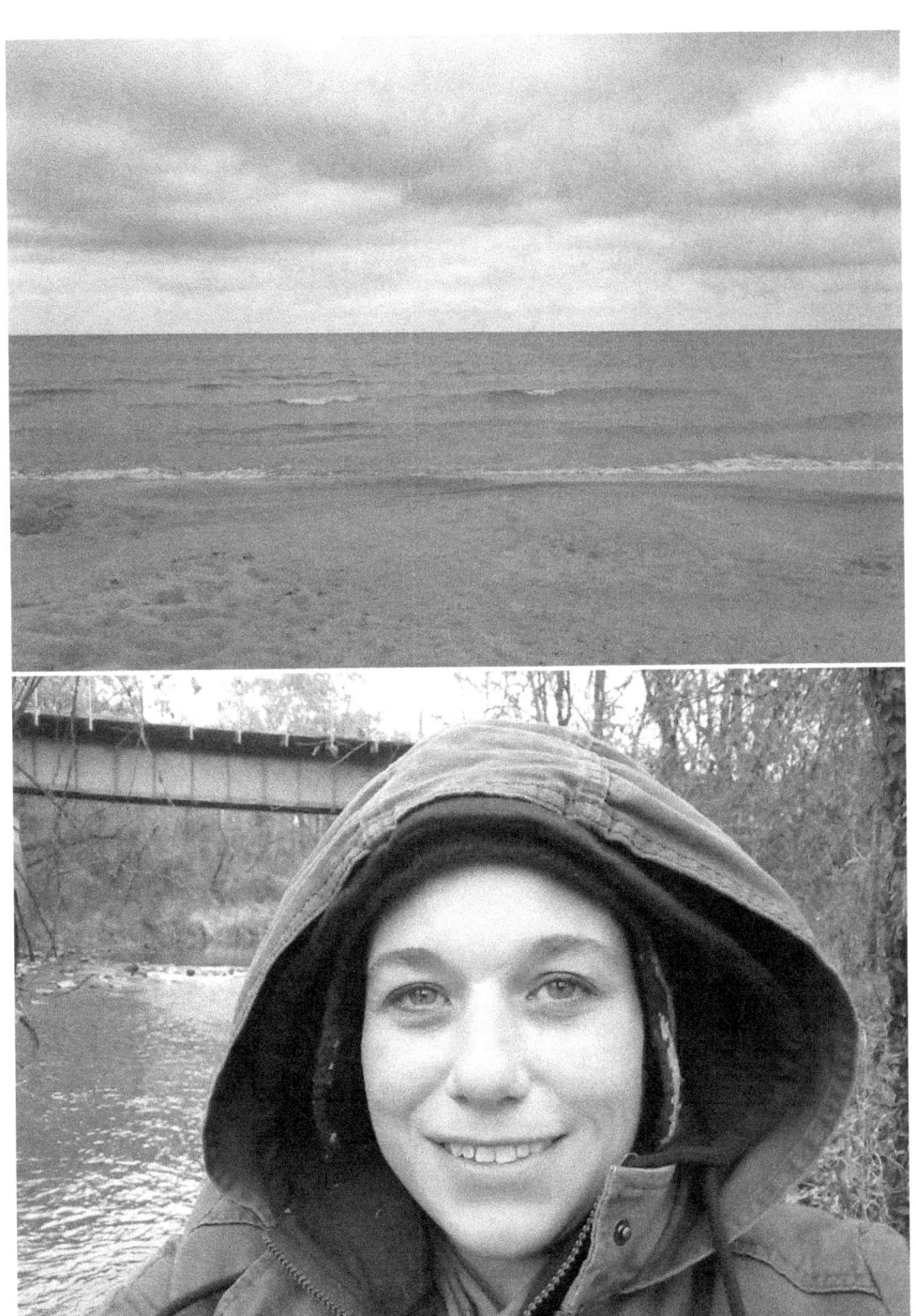

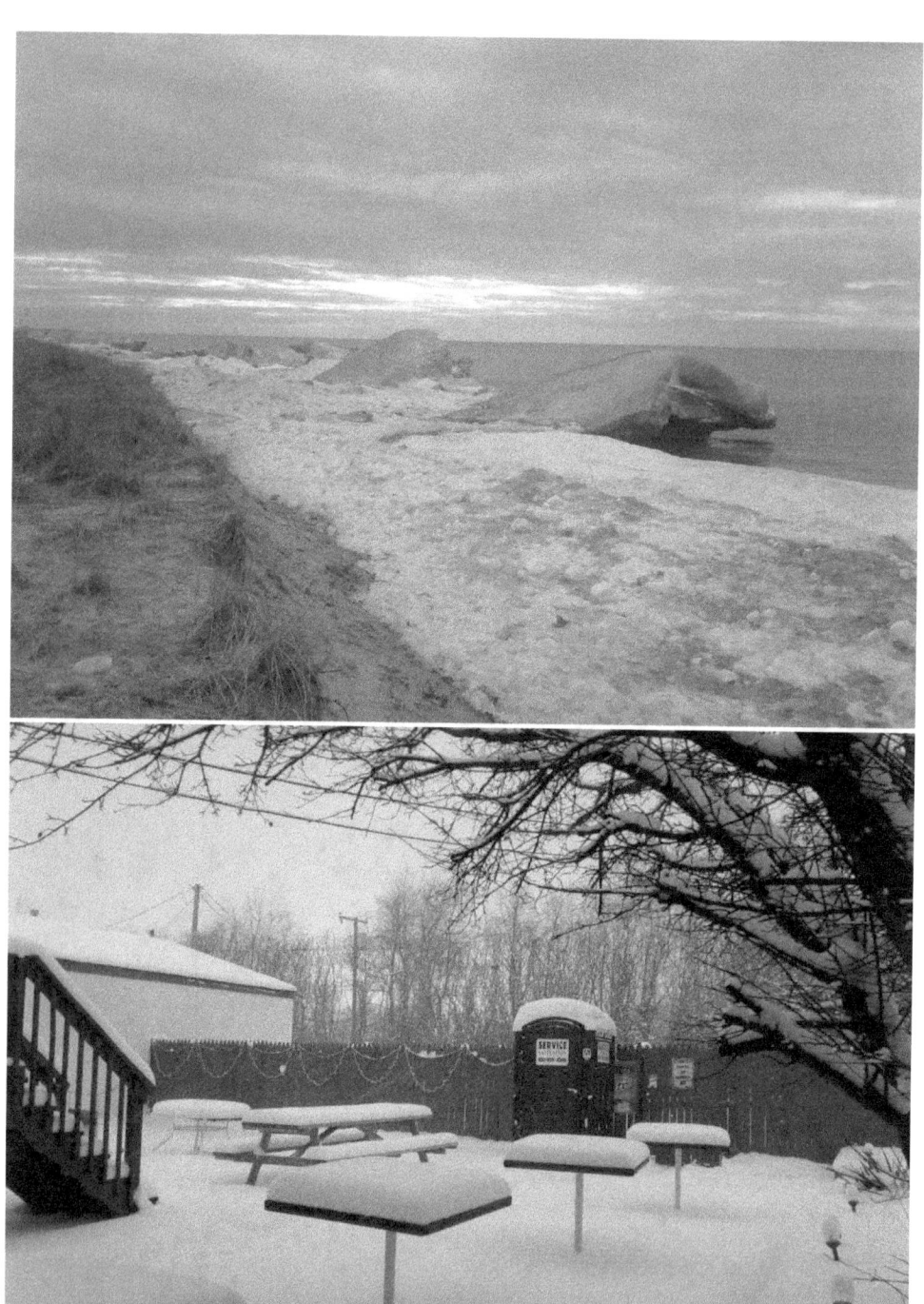

I was starting to feel like I was settling in a little. I'd made some new friends and had several commissions. I'd begun looking for an apartment and/or a studio. I still really missed Arkansas...

291

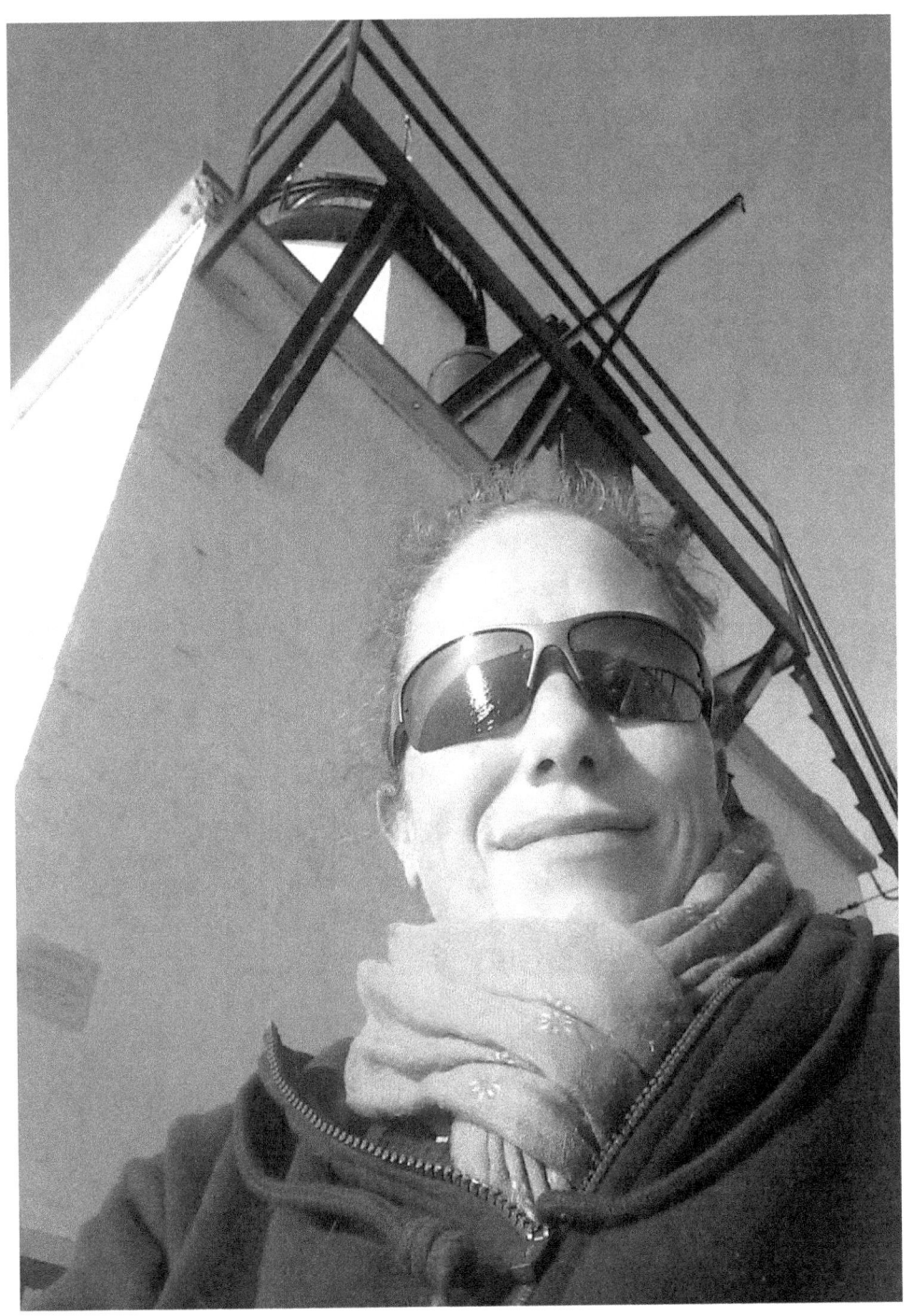

2/?/18 M calls…

M called me freaking out. I'm a little worried about him. I suppose it's a good time to make a decision. I'll head down and check on him then visit Eureka. I'll get my stuff this time, regardless.

Eureka Springs, AR or Lake Station, IN…

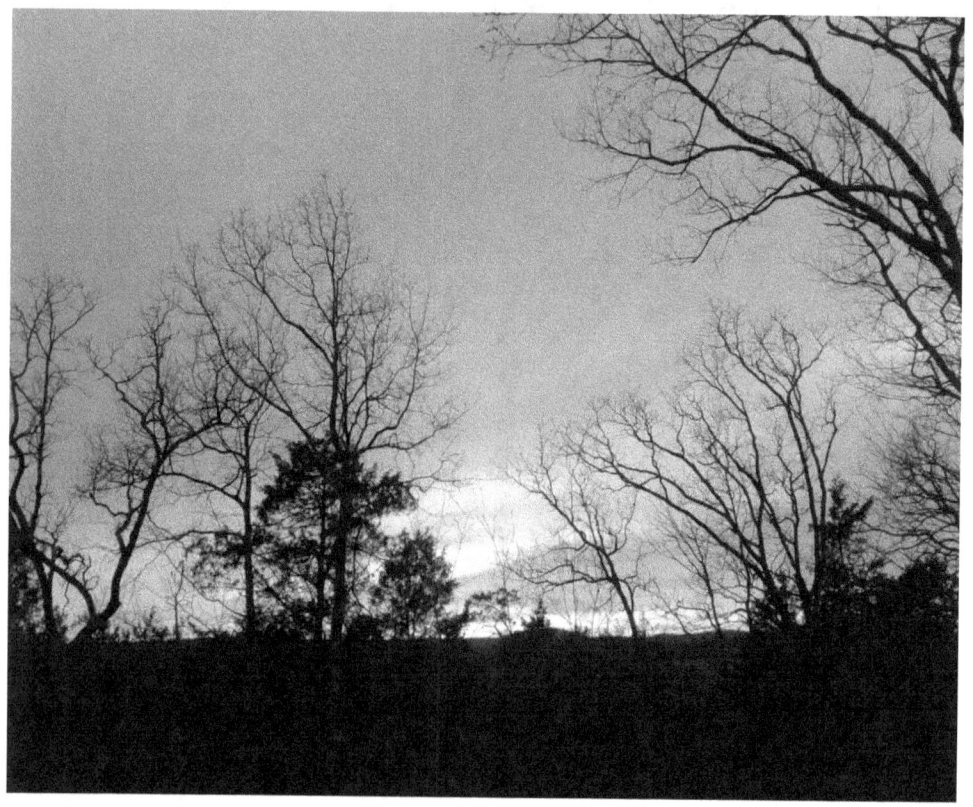

_____

I chose Indiana, again. What's wrong with me!?

Nothing is wrong… In Fact, I've been feeling pretty good lately and feeling like I'm growing as a person and an artist. I've gotten several dog portrait commissions, a moose, and a huge mural. I feel good and like I'm making progress toward my bigger goals and dreams.

Not quite enough progress to go to Eureka yet though. If I moved there right now, I'd go back to being no one and poor, to boot.

Push my comfort zone or safety. I've still been pushing my comfort zone in Indiana. Why make it harder on myself? Am I rationalizing my decision? I don't know.

Indiana just feels like the right move right now, Eureka doesn't.

Trust the process. This or something better.

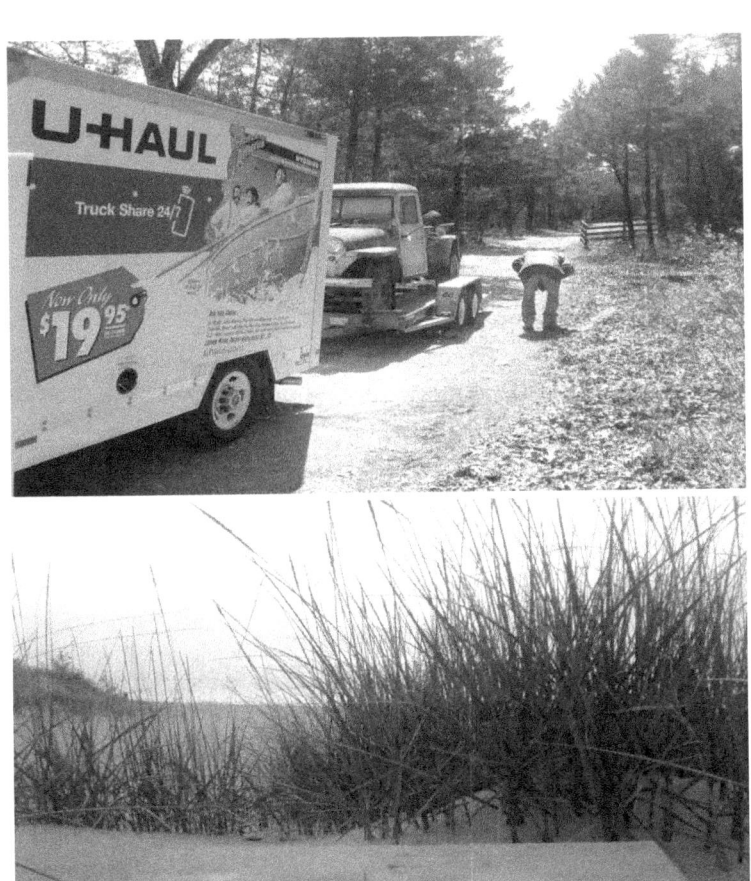

7/3/18 M calls again…

This time though, he's offering me Bear Bottom.

WHAT!? REALLY?!

He says he's serious and he's done. He's signing it over to me and leaving.

I hope he's leaving. That's my one condition. I'll be there in a week, but he must sign it over asap and leave by OCT 1.

That's my condition.

What if he doesn't leave? What if I go back and he never leaves!? What if he leaves but keeps coming back!?

It doesn't matter. I'll deal with it if it comes up. I've got to go see. I'd never forgive myself if I didn't go see; if I didn't take this chance.
If I didn't seize this opportunity.

———

I finished up the mural in a couple days and schedule an unveiling for the next weekend. I'll be leaving the day after.

I'm so proud of this mural project. It's my very first mural and it's a huge one and it all came out of my head! Have you ever walked into a real-life room that was once only an image in your head!? It's an amazing and magical feeling.

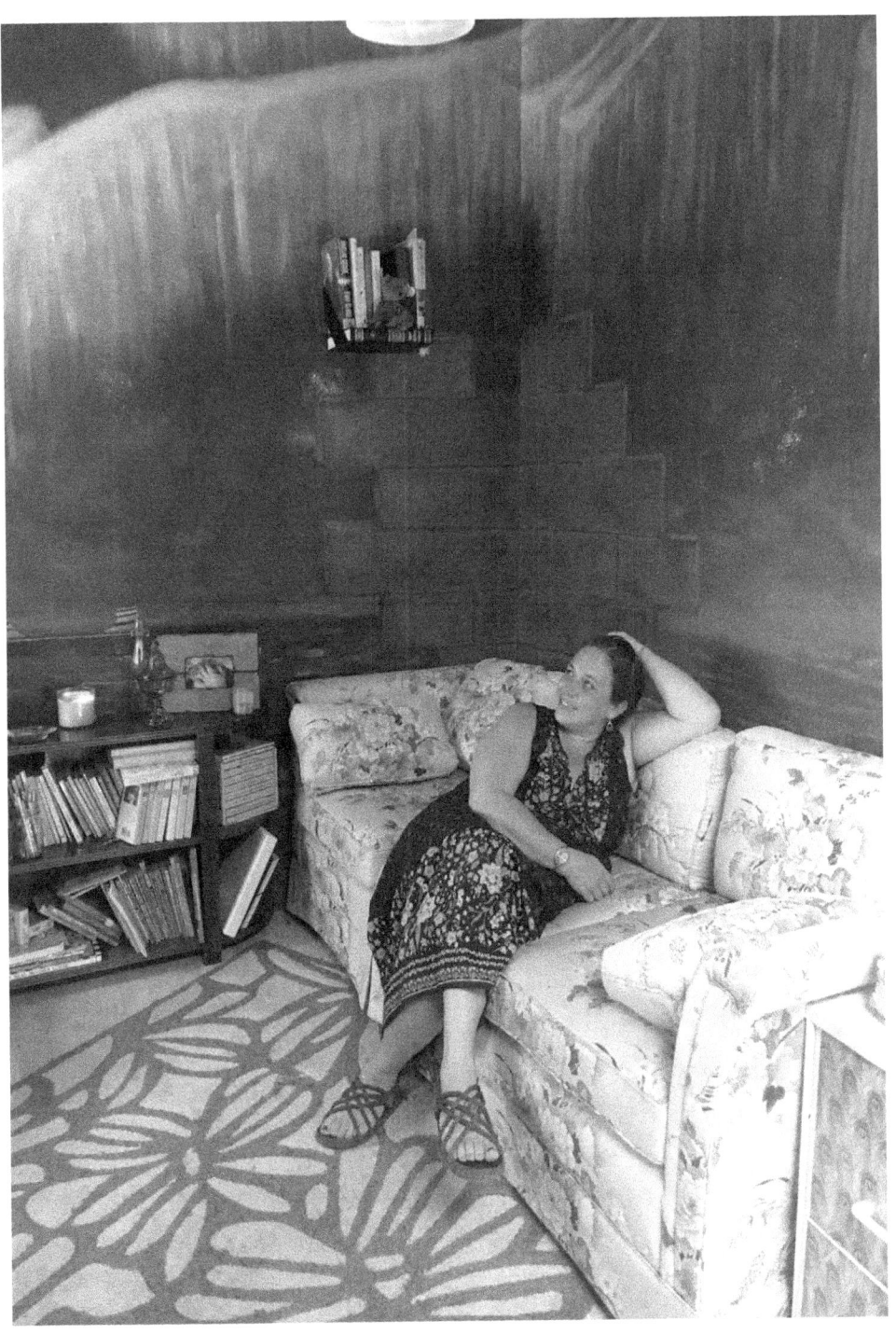

7/24/18 - It's really mine!

I can't believe it! He did it! He took his name off the property! I am now back at Bear Bottom and it's mine, free and clear!? Holy Wah!! I can hardly believe it! After all the last 2 years, how can this even be possible!?

I'm pretty sure I've never been more grateful for anything in my life.

My dreams coming true right before my eyes!

Trust the process! Everything happens for good! Magic is real!

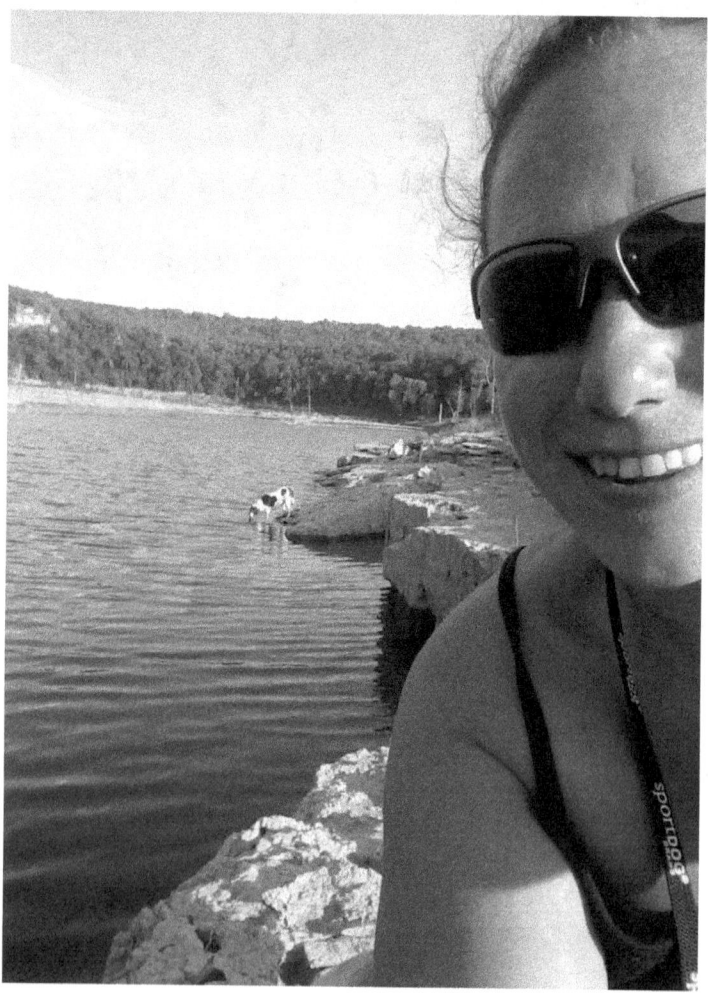

Epilogue

Now what? Well, now it's time to begin to carry out some of these ideas and plans I've been making. Bear Bottom is my home, my rest but eventually I'd like for it to be an arts and nature center.

Right now, Bear Bottom is a 20-acre parcel, surrounded by woods with access to public lands and water. There is a small cabin, 2 basic shop buildings, and a tiny barn.

As this dream plays out, my aim is that it will expand to some of the neighboring properties. There will be a few small cabins, studio and gallery space, workshop space, and an amphitheater.

I want to make the space available for retreats, workshops, and concerts and performances in order to help people experience and appreciate the healing qualities of creativity, art, and nature. I also want to promote and collaborate with emerging and established artists.

I have no idea how any of this will happen only that it will. It may not even happen at Bear Bottom, but this experience shows me that it will happen.

Already I've begun collaborating with other local artists and being more involved in the surrounding art communities. As I become more established and solvent, I'll begin building. In the meantime, I'll still be practicing art, meeting new people, showing my work, painting murals, and building my art business. These are my dreams.

Have you ever thought of investing in a dream?
Wanna know more?

Follow me on social media and share my work with your friends.
> Instagram: @lacefinch_art
> Facebook: @lacefinchart

Sign up for my newsletter on my website: www.lacefinchart.com

Purchase products from my store: www.lacefinchart.com/store

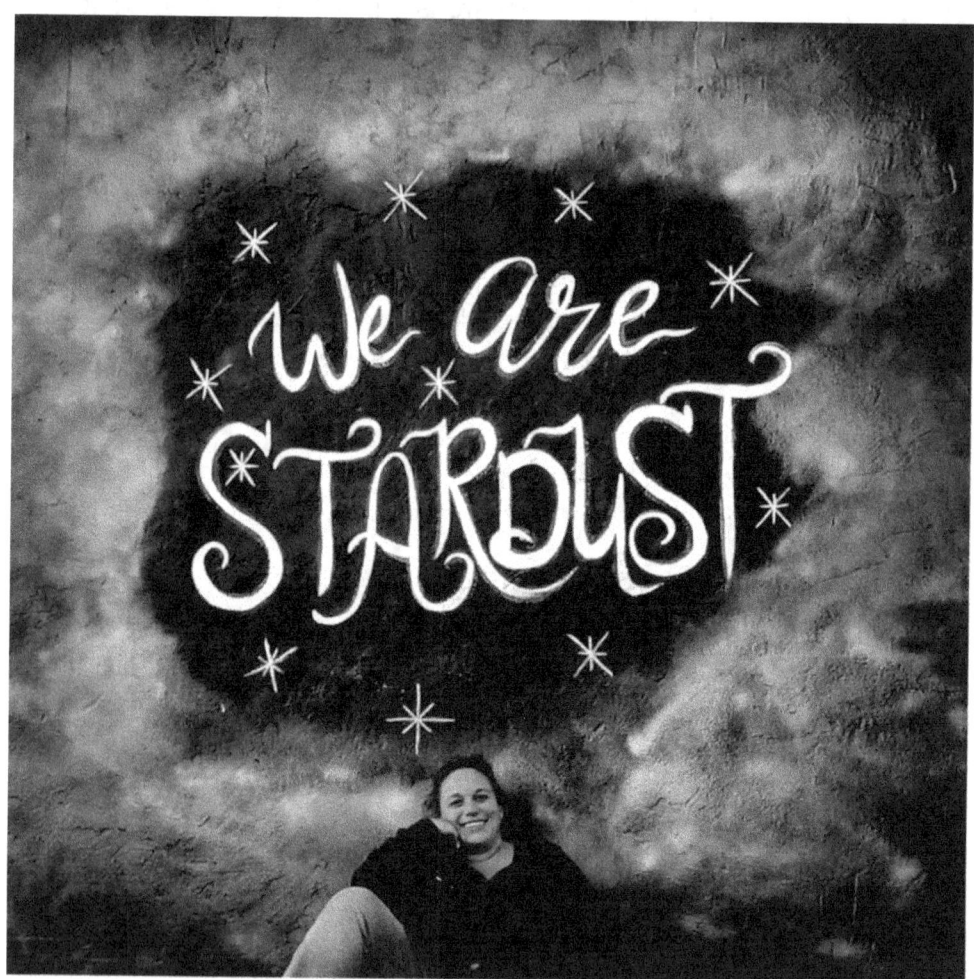

"Though we travel the world over to find the beautiful,
we must carry it with us or we find it not."
~ Ralph Waldo Emerson.

To be continued...

www.ingramcontent.com/pod-product-compliance
Lightning Source LLC
Chambersburg PA
CBHW070525220526
45467CB00003B/863